The Feminist Economics of Trade

The Feminist Economics of Trade is the first book to combine the tools of economic analysis and gender analysis to examine the interaction of international trade and gender relations. It shows that the relationship between gender inequality and trade is complex.

Gender inequality may both assist and hinder the development of international competitiveness and the distribution of gains from trade, within and between countries. At the same time, trade policies and flows have contradictory impacts on gender equality. The contributors argue that trade expansion and reduction of gender inequality can be combined, but only if an appropriate mix and sequence of trade and other economic policies is implemented.

The book demonstrates what feminist economics contributes to the analysis of international trade, through theoretical modelling, econometric analysis, and policy-oriented contributions. It includes evidence from industrialized, semi-industrialized and agrarian economies, using country case studies and cross-country analysis.

The book brings together fourteen contributions from a variety of economic perspectives, including structuralist, institutionalist, neoclassical, and Post-Keynesian. Authors include Lourdes Benería, William Darity, Jr, Marzia Fontana, and Mariama Williams. The book will benefit those studying international economics, gender and cultural studies, and politics and international relations, among other disciplines.

Irene van Staveren is Associate Professor of Feminist Development Economics at the Institute of Social Studies, The Hague, the Netherlands. She is also Professor of Economics and Christian Ethics at Radboud University, Nijmegen.

Diane Elson is Professor of Sociology at the University of Essex, UK, and Affiliated Professor in Feminist Development Economics at the Institute of Social Studies, The Hague, the Netherlands.

Caren Grown is a Senior Scholar in the Gender Equality and Economy Program at the Levy Economics Institute, Bard College, USA.

Nilüfer Çağatay is Associate Professor of Economics and a faculty member of the Middle East Studies and Women's Studies programs at the University of Utah, USA.

Routledge IAFFE Advances in Feminist Economics

IAFFE aims to increase the visibility and range of economic research on gender; facilitate communication among scholars, policy makers, and activists concerned with women's well-being and empowerment; promote discussions among policy makers about interventions which serve women's needs; educate economists, policy makers, and the general public about feminist perspectives on economic issues; foster feminist evalutions of economics as a discipline; expose the gender blindness characteristic of much social science and the ways in which this impoverishes all research, even research that does not explicitly concern women's issues; help expand opportunities for women, especially women from underrepresented groups, within economics; and encourage the inclusion of feminist perspectives in the teaching of economics. The IAFFE book series pursues the aims of the organization by providing a forum in which scholars have space to develop their ideas at length and in detail. The series exemplifies the value of feminist research and the high standard of IAFFE-sponsored scholarship.

The Feminist Economics of Trade

Edited by
Irene van Staveren
Diane Elson
Caren Grown and
Nilüfer Çağatay

Routledge
Taylor & Francis Group

LONDON AND NEW YORK

First published 2007
by Routledge
2 Park Square, Milton Park, Abingdon, Oxon OX14 4RN

Simultaneously published in the USA and Canada
by Routledge
711 Third Avenue, New York, NY 10017

*Routledge is an imprint of the Taylor & Francis Group,
an informa business*

© 2007 Editorial matter and selection, Irene van Staveren, Diane Elson,
Caren Grown and Nilüfer Çağatay; individual chapters,
the contributors

Typeset in Times New Roman by
Newgen Imaging Systems (P) Ltd, Chennai, India

British Library Cataloguing in Publication Data
A catalogue record for this book is available from the British Library

Library of Congress Cataloging in Publication Data
    The feminist economics of trade / edited by
Irene van Staveren . . . [et al.]. – 1st ed.
        p. cm. – (Routledge IAFFE advances in feminist economics)
    Includes bibliographical references and index.
        1. Feminist economics. 2. International trade. 3. Sex discrimination
against women – Economic aspects. I. Staveren, Irene van.

HQ1381.F464 2007
382.01–dc22   2006102815

ISBN13: 978–0–415–77059–0 (hbk)
ISBN13: 978–0–415–43637–3 (pbk)
ISBN13: 978–0–203–94607–7 (ebk)

Contents

Figures

Tables

Contributors

Stephanie Barrientos is a Research Fellow at the Institute of Development Studies, Sussex, UK. She has researched and published widely on gender and development in Africa and Latin America, globalization, informal work, corporate accountability, fair trade, ethical trade, and international labor standards. Her recent books include *Ethical Sourcing in the Global Food System*, edited with Catherine Dolan (Earthscan, 2006).

Lourdes Benería is Professor of City and Regional Planning and of Feminist, Gender and Sexuality Studies at Cornell University. Her books include *Gender, Development and Globalization: Economics As If All People Mattered* (Routledge, 2003), *Global Tensions: Opportunities and Challenges in the World Economy*, edited with Savitri Bisnath (Routledge, 2003), and *Labor Market Informalization, Precarious Jobs and Social Protection*, edited with Neema Kudva (Cornell e-publishing, 2006).

Günseli Berik is Associate Professor of Economics and Gender Studies at the University of Utah, Salt Lake City. She is guest co-editor of the Gender, China and the WTO Special Issue of *Feminist Economics*. Her recent research is on trade liberalization and labor standards in Asia.

Robert A. Blecker is Professor of Economics at American University, Washington, DC. His books include *Taming Global Finance* (Economic Policy Institute, 1999) and *Beyond the Twin Deficits* (Armonk, 1992). He received his PhD in Economics from Stanford University.

Nilüfer Çağatay is Associate Professor of Economics and a faculty member of the Middle East Studies and Women's Studies Programs at the University of Utah. In 1994, she founded, with Diane Elson and Caren Grown, the International Working Group on Gender, Macroeconomics and International Economics. Her areas of research include gender and development, international trade, and political economy and economic history of the Middle East.

William A. Darity, Jr is Professor of Economics at the University of North Carolina and Director of the Institute of African American Research. He also serves as Research Professor of Public Policy Studies, African and African American Studies and Economics at Duke University. His recent book is

Boundaries of Clan and Color: Transnational Comparisons of Inter-Group Disparity, edited with Ashwini Deshpande (Routledge, 2003).

Diane Elson is Professor at the University of Essex, UK; and Affiliated Professor in Feminist Development Economics at the Institute of Social Studies, The Hague. She has published widely on gender and development and co-edited two special issues of *World Development* (1995 and 2000).

Marzia Fontana is a Fellow at the Institute of Development Studies at Sussex, and a Research Associate at the Levy Economics Institute, Bard College. Marzia has worked extensively on issues related to gender inequalities, international trade, labor markets, and income distribution, mostly in South Asia.

Caren Grown is a Senior Scholar at the Levy Economics Institute, Bard College. She has written and edited several books, including *Trading Women's Health and Rights: Trade Liberalization and Reproductive Health in Developing Economies*, edited with Elissa Braunstein and Anju Malhotra (Zed Books, 2006), and *Taking Action: Achieving Gender Equality and Women's Empowerment*, edited with Geeta Rao Gupta (Earthscan, 2005). She is currently conducting research an gender and public finance.

Ebru Kongar is Assistant Professor of Economics at Dickinson College. Her research focuses on the links between gender inequalities, international trade, industrial restructuring, and technological change.

David Kucera is a Senior Research Economist with the International Labour Organisation. He does research on labor, development, and globalization, including the economics of labor standards as well as qualitative indicators of labor standards. His publications include the volumes *Gender, Growth and Trade: The Miracle Economies of the Postwar Years* (Routledge, 2001) and *Qualitative Indicators of Labour Standards: Comparative Methods and Applications* (Springer, 2007).

William Milberg is Associate Professor of Economics at the New School for Social Research and Program Coordinator of the New School's Schwartz Center for Economic Policy Analysis. His current research focuses on the effects of US off-shoring on income distribution, employment, and balance of payments adjustment.

Shaianne Osterreich is Assistant Professor at Ithaca College. Her areas of research include gender and international trade, development, and history of economic thought. She recently completed one year as a Fulbright Senior Scholar in Indonesia, where she taught and did research on women workers in the light-manufacturing export sector.

Şule Özler is Associate Professor of Economics at the University of California, Los Angeles. She is also a Research Associate at the Southern California Psychoanalytic Institute. Her research interests include inequalities in a globalizing world, productivity growth and international private capital markets, and psychoanalytic perspectives on the methodology and theory of the individual in economics.

Stephanie Seguino is Associate Dean and Associate Professor of Economics at the University of Vermont. Her research interests include macroeconomics, gender, and development; income distribution; effects of globalization on gender inequality; and determinants of well-being. She has collaborated with the American Federation of Labor – Congress of Industrial Organizations (AFL-CIO), United Nations, and United Nations Research Institute for Social Development (UNRISD) in this work.

Irene van Staveren is Associate Professor of Feminist Development Economics at the Institute of Social Studies in The Hague. In addition, she is Professor of Economics and Christian Ethics at Radboud University, Nijmegen, where she teaches and does research on the relationships between economics, ethics, and globalization. Her research interests include development, heterodox macro-economics, feminist economics, and ethics and economics.

Mariama Williams is an international economics consultant and Adjunct Associate at the Center of Concern, Washington, DC. She is also a Research Associate with the International Gender and Trade Network (IGTN) and Co-Research Coordinator of the Political Economy of Globalisation Program of Development Alternative with Women for a New Era. Williams is the author of *Gender Mainstreaming in the Multilateral Trading System* (Commonwealth Secretariat, 2003).

Acknowledgments

This book emerged from our desire to bring together the growing body of work by feminists and international economists on the relationship between gender equality and international trade. Over the past three years, several individuals, institutions, and networks have contributed to the production of this book.

First, we would like to acknowledge the International Association of Feminist Economics (IAFFE), which has provided us, several times, with a podium for presenting, discussing, and disseminating research on gender and trade. The early versions of several chapters in this book were presented at IAFFE's annual conferences – in Istanbul, Oslo, Los Angeles, and Ottawa. This volume is also part of the Feminist Economics book series edited by former IAFFE president Jane Humphries for Routledge.

Second, the International Working Group on Gender and Macroeconomics (IWG-GEM) (of which three of the editors are founding members) provided spiritual and material support for the development of much of the research in this volume. Several chapters were written under the auspices of IWG-GEM and published previously in two special issues of *World Development*. IWG-GEM sponsored several meetings at which various drafts of the chapters included here were discussed, including a workshop at the Levy Economics Institute in May 2002 and the summer conferences of the Engendering Macroeconomics Workshop at the University of Utah in 2002–5. Financial support for these meetings was provided by IWG-GEM and its funders, the International Development Research Centre (Ottawa) and the Ford Foundation (New York).

The regional branches of the International Gender and Trade Network offered intellectual stimulation during the development of the research as well as venues for discussing the ideas in several chapters.

We would like to express our appreciation for the support given by our respective institutions for our work on this book. We are grateful to the Institute of Social Studies (ISS) in The Hague, the University of Utah, the University of Essex, the International Center for Research on Women, and the Levy Economics Institute at Bard College, which generously allocated time for the editing of this book and writing parts of it. Tanya Kingdon at the ISS performed style editing and other work to complete organization of the book. Jessica Dixon and Maureen Deegan of the Levy Economics Institute provided editorial assistance on most of the chapters. We thank them for their conscientious and hard work.

Finally, we would like to acknowledge several institutions that kindly granted permission to reprint or use parts of earlier published texts:

- Blackwell Publishing, for a reprint (with revisions) of Robert Blecker and Stephanie Seguino, "Macroeconomic effects of reducing gender wage inequality in an export-oriented semi industrialised economy," *Review of Development Economics*, 6 (1), 2002, pp. 103–19.
- Taylor and Francis for reprints and use of material from Lourdes Benería, "Globalization, gender and the Davos Man," *Feminist Economics*, 5 (3), 1999, pp. 61–84; and Chapter 3 of Lourdes Benería, *Gender, Development and Globalization* (2003), London: Routledge, pp. 63–90; Günseli Berik, "Mature export-led growth and gender wage inequality in Taiwan," *Feminist Economics*, 6 (3), 2000, pp. 1–26; and Irene van Staveren, "Monitoring gender impacts of trade," *European Journal of Development Research*, 15 (1), 2003, pp. 126–45.
- Elsevier for reprints of William Darity, "The formal structure of a gender-segregated low-income economy," *World Development*, 23 (11), 1995, pp. 1963–68; and David Kucera and William Milberg, "Gender segregation and gender bias in manufacturing trade expansion: Revisiting the 'Wood Asymmetry,'" *World Development* 28 (7), 2000, pp. 1191–210.
- Wiley for a reprint (with revisions) of Stephanie Seguino and Caren Grown, "Gender equity and globalization: Macroeconomic policy for developing countries," *Journal of International Development*, 18 (8), 2006, pp. 1081–104.
- CEPII for a reprint (with revisions) of Marzia Fontana, "Modelling the effects of trade on women, at work and at home: Comparative perspectives," *Economie Internationale*, 99 (3), 2004, Paris, La Documentation Française.

This book is intended to be of service to academics, activists, and policy makers. As we look to the future, it is our hope that they will take up the ideas in the following chapters and help to make the formulation of gender-equitable trade and development policies a reality.

Irene van Staveren
Diane Elson
Caren Grown
Nilüfer Çağatay

1 Introduction

Why a feminist economics of trade?

Diane Elson, Caren Grown, and
Irene van Staveren

This book brings together 14 contributions that collectively represent the building blocks for a feminist economics of international trade. It shows how the tools of economic analysis, informed by gender analysis, can be used to examine the interaction of trade relations and gender relations. It is motivated by a concern to reduce gender inequality and increase the power and well-being of poor women in poor countries. It is concerned not only with the impact of trade on gender inequality, but also with the impact of gender inequality on trade.

Gender pay gaps and gender segregation in employment are a key focus, but gender analysis tells us that these labor market inequalities are underpinned by a deep structural inequality between the paid production of goods and services, and the unpaid social reproduction of the labor supply, households, and communities. Feminist economics argues that gender inequality stems from a system of gendered power relations that permeate the whole economy and underpin norms for male and female roles and responsibilities. Individuals themselves absorb these norms, which constrain their choices and structure the ways in which they define themselves. Not only are preferences endogenous, but also the sense of self (Ferber and Nelson 1993).

From the perspective of feminist economics, all economic policies are gendered, in the sense of being shaped by the system of gendered power in which they are formulated and implemented. In some cases this is explicit, with promotion of gender equality an objective (such as labor market policies designed to secure equal opportunities for women). But in many cases the content of gender relations is implicit. On the surface, a policy may appear to be gender neutral because it does not target either men or women. But the policy will be gender biased if it fails to take into account the gender differences that permeate economies (Elson 1995). For instance, trade policies that leave out consideration of the unpaid economy and only include the paid economy will tend to be biased against women, because women have a social obligation to ensure that families are cared for, in a way that men do not (though men do typically have a social obligation to bring money into the family).

This book situates gender inequality concerns within a broader concern for other types of inequality within and between countries. It aims to be of interest to trade and development economists as well as feminist economists. It is relevant to courses on international trade and development as well as to courses on the economics of gender. A feminist economics of trade is necessary because it prioritizes issues that are otherwise neglected and makes visible interactions that are otherwise invisible. It asks whether trade policies that are advocated to address inequalities between countries are sufficient to reduce gender inequality within countries. In doing so, it helps to identify which mix of trade and other policies is capable of addressing multiple inequalities simultaneously. It also inquires about the ways in which gender inequality may limit the gains from trade; for instance, through its impact on the terms of trade, or the process of innovation.

There is a large literature on trade and inequality, but most trade economists who discuss inequality do not engage with gender equality issues. For instance, none of the 13 contributors to John Toye's edited volume (2003) on trade, poverty, and inequality discuss gender inequality. Among the rare exceptions is Jagdish Bhagwati (2004), who devotes a chapter in his best selling book, *In Defense of Globalization*, to the question: "Women: Harmed or Helped?" His conclusion is that women in both developed and developing countries are helped by trade liberalization, which increases international competition, in turn weakening labor market discrimination against women and reducing the gender wage gap. However, the evidence he considers is very limited, and he does not cite many scholarly contributions on trade and gender from feminist economists. The study on which he relies for empirical evidence (Black and Brainerd 2004) is critiqued in Chapter 11, and the theory of discrimination and competition on which he relies is critiqued in Chapter 3.

Because feminist economics is concerned with economic power and adopts a critical approach to how economies function, it finds allies among other critical traditions in economics such as Marxist, post-Keynesian, structuralist, and institutional economics. Thus many of the contributions to this book explicitly draw upon heterodox economic theories. One exception is Chapter 7, which deliberately makes the choice to depart as little as possible from orthodox assumptions in modeling the effects of trade, in order to show that even with such assumptions, gender relations matter.

This book aims to give a higher profile to the research of feminist economists on trade and gender, bringing together some key contributions which have already been published in scholarly journals (Chapters 2, 5, 6, 7, 8, 10, and 15) and extending that literature by including some new or expanded studies (Chapters 3, 4, 9, 11, 12, 13, and 14). It incorporates discussion of gender and trade in industrialized (see especially Chapters 11 and 12), semi-industrialized (see especially Chapters 6, 8, and 9), and agrarian economies (see especially Chapter 5).

This book is methodologically pluralist. Trade and gender relations are explored through a number of research strategies: constructing analytical frames (Chapters 2 and 3); building formal models (Chapters 5, 6, and 7); conducting quantitative analysis (Chapters 4, 8, 9, 10, and 11); analyzing private and public systems of trade regulation (Chapters 12 and 14); identifying and using trade-related gender indicators (Chapter 13); and analyzing the macroeconomic policy aspects of trade and gender (Chapter 15). Some of the quantitative contributions focus on single countries (Chapters 7, 8, 9, and 11), while others are cross-country studies (Chapters 4, 10, and 13).

Organization of the volume

This book is organized as follows: Part I discusses how trade and gender issues should be framed; Part II examines the impact of gender inequality on trade; Part III investigates the impact of trade on gender inequality; and Part IV presents feminist approaches to trade policy.

The way in which trade and gender issues are framed structures what questions are asked and what factors are taken for granted, what is included in the analysis and what is left out. In Chapter 2, "Gender and the social construction of markets," by Lourdes Benería, the frame is provided by the institutional economics of Karl Polanyi whose 1944 book *The Great Transformation* traces the construction of "market society" in the nineteenth and early twentieth century. This frame directs attention to the way in which the expansion of trade changes the norms of human behavior. Unlike mainstream trade theory that takes the sense of self and the preferences of "rational economic man" as exogenous factors that shape commerce, Polanyi's institutional economics sees the growth of commerce as a process that helps to produce human beings that compete to maximize their individual gains. Benería agrees with this perspective, but points out that historically far fewer women than men competed in national and international markets, and that norms of female human behavior place more weight on altruism than individualist competition given women's primary responsibility for social reproduction. She discusses the implications for these norms of the increasing participation of women in national and international markets.

Gender and market competition is also a key theme of Chapter 3, "Mainstream, heterodox, and feminist trade theory" by Diane Elson, Caren Grown, and Nilüfer Çağatay. This chapter compares and contrasts orthodox and heterodox (Marxian and Post-Keynesian) theories of international trade, discussing how gender has been, or might be, incorporated into each type of theory. It concludes that heterodox theory, which argues that trade is governed by absolute rather than comparative advantage, is a better starting point for feminist trade theory. Heterodox trade theory does not assume full employment equilibrium, it emphasizes that there is no mechanism to ensure balanced trade, and it is more consistent with empirical evidence than mainstream theory. The chapter develops the notion of gendered competitive advantage and shows its relation to "low road" and "high road" development strategies.

Part II analyzes how gender inequality can have an impact on trade-related outcomes, such as the terms of trade and composition of output. All three chapters are explicitly located within heterodox economic theory. Chapter 4, "Gender, trade, and development: labor market discrimination and North–South terms of trade," by Shaianne Osterreich, takes as its starting point the Prebisch-Singer hypothesis that the net barter terms of trade between South and North tend to deteriorate (a hypothesis for which there is ample empirical support).

Prebisch (1950) and Singer (1950) argued that the underlying mechanism for this uneven distribution of gains from trade lies in differences in labor markets in the South and North, with workers in the South having less ability to bargain for rises in productivity to be matched by rises in wages. Osterreich hypothesizes that gender inequality is an important aspect of these labor market differences. Using data from a selection of Southern and Northern countries for the period 1975–95, she finds that a decline in the degree of labor market discrimination against women in the South relative to the degree of labor market discrimination against women in the North is associated with an improvement in the net barter terms of trade of Southern countries. She argues that policy makers should be interested in these results: if governments in the South take simultaneous action to reduce labor market discrimination against women, this will help to counteract the tendency of their terms of trade to fall, bringing a larger share of the gains from trade to the South.[1]

Chapter 5, "The formal structure of a gender-segregated low-income economy" by William Darity Jr, examines the ways in which unequal gender relations in agriculture interact with attempts to stimulate agricultural exports through devaluation of the currency. He develops a model of gender segregation of labor in smallholder export and subsistence (food) production, based on the empirical literature on sub-Saharan Africa. Both men and women participate in producing export crops, but only women produce subsistence goods. The model describes three different regimes of gendered power: coercion, in which men exercise power over the time women allocate to export crops, the sales of which are controlled by men; cooperation, in which women (guided by social norms of interfamilial behavior) willingly agree to allocate unpaid time to export crops; and compensation, in which women will not work on export crops without being compensated by their husbands. Darity models the effect of a currency devaluation, which raises the price that men get for export crops. Through coercion, cooperation, or compensation, women allocate more time to export crop production. The model illuminates how different regimes of gendered power affect the impact of export expansion. One inference is that if women resist coercion and are unwilling to work without pay, they will not switch into export crop production following devaluation, slowing export expansion (see also Warner and Campbell 2000).

Gender-segregation in production is also a theme of the model presented in Chapter 6, "Macroeconomic effects of reducing gender wage inequality in an export-oriented, semi-industrialized economy" by Robert A. Blecker and Stephanie Seguino. Their model is based on the stylized facts of semi-industrialized economies, in which women produce a good that is largely for export though some is consumed domestically, and men produce a good that is only for the domestic market. Women earn less than men. The model examines the effects on output of an exogenous rise in women's wages, holding male wages and the exchange rate constant. If export markets are price-elastic, and workers' consumption of the export good is low, the output of exports is likely to fall, while the effect on production of domestic goods is ambiguous. On the other hand, if export demand is price-inelastic and worker's consumption of the export good is high, export production will expand; again, the effect on production of domestic goods is ambiguous. But these conditions are less likely to be met. Given the assumptions of the model, reducing the gender-wage gap by raising women's wages is likely to depress exports and may also depress production of domestic goods. If nominal wages of both women and men are flexible, and there is a crawling peg exchange rate, the effects are more complex and an increase in women's wages may be combined with export expansion.

Part III, "Impacts of trade on gender inequality," contains five chapters. Chapter 7 examines the impact of changes in trade policy through the abolition of tariffs (e.g. the liberalization of international trade), while the other chapters focus instead on impacts of changes in the share, level, and growth of exports or imports (the expansion of international trade). This is consistent with the general literature on trade, which relies primarily on data on exports and imports rather than data on the general level of tariffs and subsidies. It is important not to draw conclusions about trade liberalization solely from the studies of the effects of trade expansion (Rodrik and Rodriguez 2000).[2]

Of all the chapters in this section, Chapter 7, "Modeling the effects of trade on women, at work and at home: comparative perspectives" by Marzia Fontana, uses the widest range of gender equality variables and captures both unpaid work and paid work. This chapter employs a sex-disaggregated computable general equilibrium model to simulate the impact of trade liberalization (through tariff reductions) in Bangladesh and Zambia, two very different low-income countries. The strength of gender norms is modeled by making substitution between male and female labor inelastic. Exchange rate depreciation is assumed to restore balanced trade following tariff reductions. Given these assumptions, the simulations suggest that trade liberalization will increase time spent on producing exports and reduce time spent in unpaid work and leisure. Women's paid employment and wages rise in both Bangladesh and Zambia, but in Bangladesh (where the biggest export is garments) the gender-wage gap narrows, while in Zambia (where the main export is copper) it widens. The model shows how trade liberalization has different gendered impacts in economies with different economic structures and how women's employment gains may come at the cost of time to care for families and enjoy leisure.

Two studies of semi-industrialized countries follow, both of which examine sex-disaggregated employment and earnings in export-oriented and domestic market-oriented production. Each produces results that are at odds with some of the conventional wisdom. Chapter 8, "Mature export-led growth and gender wage inequality in Taiwan" by Günseli Berik, uses industry level data to estimate the role of export-orientation in determining male and female wages, as Taiwan shifted to more skill and capital intensive manufacturing exports in the period 1984–93. Berik finds that, controlling for a range of other influences, working in a more export-oriented industry adversely affected wages of both women and men. The gender-wage gap was in fact lower in the more export-oriented industries than in the more domestic-oriented industries in part because the wage penalty on men in those industries was higher than on women. However, as expected, women workers' wages were adversely affected in both absolute and relative terms as the occupation mix shifted to include more technical skills.

Chapter 9, "Export-led industrialization and gender differences in job creation and destruction: micro evidence from the Turkish manufacturing sector" by Şule Özler, uses plant level data for the period 1986–96 to examine employment by sex and skill level in three types of production, non-tradable, import-competing, and export. As expected, net job creation rates were higher in the export sector than the other sectors for all groups of workers. Net job creation rates were higher for females than for males in all sectors, but the biggest gender gap was in the import-competing sector, which had the highest ratio of female to male job creation rates for production workers. Although women benefited from the gender gap in net job creation, women's employment was more volatile than men's, as measured by the female and male gross job reallocation rate (the sum of gross job creation and gross job destruction rates). While the growth of export production increased women's share of the labor force, economy-wide factors contributed to making women's work more precarious than that of men.

The focus switches to import-related job losses in OECD countries in Chapter 10, "Gender segregation and gender bias in manufacturing trade expansion: revisiting the 'Wood Asymmetry'" by David Kucera and William Milberg. They challenge the thesis put forward by Adrian Wood that the trade-related increase in the female share of employment in developing countries had no negative symmetric effect on the female share of employment in the export sector of industrialized countries. Applying factor content analysis to data on 22 manufacturing industries for 10 OECD countries for the period 1978–95, Kucera and Milberg find that in most of the countries in the sample employment declines disproportionately affected women. These employment losses across countries were due mainly to differences in trade performance in the textiles, apparel, leather, and leather goods industries, all female-intensive industries. In countries where these industries remained competitive (such as Italy), there was less gender bias in employment loss but in those where they did not (such as the USA) the gender bias was more pronounced. The overall conclusion of this chapter is that trade expansion cannot be assumed to be a win-win for women in the North and the South.

Chapter 11, "Importing equality or exporting jobs? Competition and gender wage and employment differentials in US manufacturing" by Ebru Kongar, challenges the optimistic conclusion of Black and Brainerd (2004) (referred to earlier in the chapter) that increased import competition has reduced discrimination against women and the gender-wage gap. Kongar investigates the wage and employment effects (disaggregated by sex and occupation) of increased import competition in the USA in the period 1976–93, distinguishing between concentrated and competitive manufacturing industries.[3] Wages are measured as "residual wages" net of the impact of the effects of personal characteristics of workers other than sex, such as education, experience, marital status, race, and location. The study shows that the decline in the residual manufacturing gender wage gap, in a context of declining overall employment, was driven by changes in the composition of the female labor force rather than by a reduction of discrimination against women. In the concentrated industries, female low-wage production workers suffered disproportionately from import-related job losses, raising the average wages of the remaining smaller, more highly skilled, female work force, thus reducing the gender wage gap. By contrast, in the competitive industries, the female share of low-wage production occupations increased and average female wages declined. These differences probably reflect different firm strategies in the two sectors, with those in the concentrated sector meeting import competition by adopting more skill-intensive production and those in the competitive sector increasing their use of cheap labor.

Part IV, "Feminist approaches to trade policy," contains four chapters that examine different aspects of trade policy. Chapters 12 and 14 explore how to regulate international trade, Chapter 13 proposes a method for monitoring the impact of trade agreements, and Chapter 15 considers the overall set of macroeconomic polices needed for trade to have positive effects on gender equality.

Chapter 12, "Gender, codes of conduct, and labor standards in global production systems" by Stephanie Barrientos, compares three strategies for improving the impact of trade expansion on women's rights: social clauses in trade agreements, corporate codes of conduct, and ILO's decent work approach. Barrientos situates international trade in the context of global production systems that entail complex chains of sub-contracting dominated by corporations based in the North. She argues that social clauses in trade agreements have limitations because they put the onus for workers' rights on governments of exporting countries rather than on the Northern companies that dominate the global production systems. Corporate codes of conduct put the onus to improve labor standards on these corporations. But voluntary codes are driven by a concern to limit risks to the reputation of the corporation and do not adequately address the ways in which pressure to keep their prices low makes it hard for sub-contractors to comply with the codes. Moreover, these codes do not succeed in reaching the women informal workers at the bottom of the sub-contracting chain. The ILO's decent work initiative encompasses both rights at work and rights to social protection; it aims to engage governments, corporations, and workers' representatives, but its only instruments are dialogue and persuasion. Barrientos concludes that elements of all three approaches are needed.

Policies to improve the impact of trade on gender equality need to be informed by regular monitoring. In Chapter 13, "Gender indicators for monitoring trade agreements," Irene van Staveren presents a set of indicators that may be used by policy makers, women's organizations, trade unions, and other stakeholders to monitor the impacts of trade agreements. The indicators are formulated as trade elasticities of gender equality, in which the denominator measures changes in trade and the numerator measures changes in gender equality. A sub-set of these indicators examines how gender equality has changed in Mercosur (Argentina, Brazil, Paraguay, and Uruguay) following the trade agreement with the EU. Trade expansion related to this agreement was not accompanied by any positive gender effects in Mercosur, and there are warning signs of possible negative effects through an increase in food prices, the lack of increases in the female share of employment in the export sector, and an increase in women's share of employment in the import-competing sector. Not surprisingly, the conclusion is that the trade agreement needs to be complemented by other measures if it is to contribute to reducing gender inequality.

The most comprehensive trade agreements are negotiated globally through the World Trade Organization (WTO). The gender dimensions of some key agreements are discussed in Chapter 14, "Gender issues in the multilateral trading system" by Mariama Williams. Particular attention is paid to the Agreement on Agriculture, the General Agreement on Trade in Services, and the Trade Related Intellectual Property Rights Agreement. Williams shows how these Agreements are implicated in undermining the livelihoods of women self-employed farmers in poor countries and have the potential to jeopardize poor women's health and their ability to ensure good health for their families. The chapter concludes with suggestions on how gender inequality can be addressed in some of the measures that are allowable under the WTO rules for mitigating adverse effects of trade liberalization. It also makes clear that a gender-equitable multilateral trading system requires a different set of core principles.

The final chapter, "Gender equity and globalization: macroeconomic policy for developing countries" by Stephanie Seguino and Caren Grown, sets trade liberalization in the context of liberalization of foreign direct investment and international finance. It shows how together these polices have led to slower growth and economies that operate at far less than full employment, a context not favorable for the goal of achieving gender equality while sustaining the well-being already achieved by men. Alternative policies are outlined which include a stronger role for the state in controlling flows of physical and financial capital and in stimulating improvements in productivity. WTO rules would need to change to permit developing countries flexibility to manage their economies.

Conclusion

The picture that emerges from this book is that the feminist economics of trade, which consists of a rich array of methodological approaches, produces multiple and complex findings on the relationship between trade expansion and liberalization and gender inequality. As a result, the message from feminist economics cannot be reduced to a simple calculus of whether trade liberalization and/or expansion is "good" or "bad" for women. Because trade practices and gender relations are diverse, there will always be contradictory impacts, both within and across countries. This applies both to the impact of trade on gender inequality and to the impact of gender inequality on trade. The type of trade policy change and nature of trade expansion will affect the employment and earnings of women and men in different ways, depending on their location, class, ethnicity, and nationality. Similarly, gender inequality will affect trade outcomes in different ways, depending on the type of inequality, the structure of the economy, its level of technological development, and the particular trade policy regime.

Nevertheless, insofar as trade liberalization is part of a set of policies that contribute to undermining the capacity of governments to invest in public infrastructure and services, and to take responsibility for guiding economic and social development, it is likely to perpetuate inequalities and limit the extent to which less powerful people, firms, and countries can gain from trade. For example, insofar as trade liberalization reduces public revenue and constrains public investment in services that reduce poor women's unpaid work, it will contribute to the perpetuation of the underlying structure of gender inequality. A market-driven society is unlikely to find an egalitarian resolution to the problem of how to ensure sufficient care as well as sufficient commodities (Folbre 1994). Improved outcomes for both trade and for gender relations can be achieved together, but only if an appropriate mix and sequence of public investment and regulation of markets is achieved.

As noted earlier, there is much further work to be done on the feminist economics of trade. For instance, the insights of the various chapters can be used to develop formal models, whether of the heterodox or CGE variety. Additional research is needed on the impact of trade policies (as opposed to trade expansion) on paid and unpaid work and earnings, as well as the ways that different types of gender inequalities (in social reproduction and markets) affect trade outcomes. More analysis to distinguish causes and effects (whereby gender inequality is sometimes the one, other times the other) would be especially useful.

In the next twenty years, we expect the feminist economics of trade to mature and flourish. We also hope the insights of feminist economics will help to change the decisions of international institutions, governments, and firms so as to increase the power and well-being of poor women in poor countries.

Notes

1 It is important that the action be taken simultaneously; if one country does this alone, it risks losing export markets – as is shown by the analysis in Chapter 6.
2 As Rodrik and Rodriguez (2000: 3) point out, while trade policies do affect the volume of trade, "there is no strong reason to expect their effect...to be quantitatively or even qualitatively similar to the consequences of changes in trade volumes that arise from reductions in transport costs or increases in world demand."
3 A competitive industry is defined as one where the biggest four firms hold less than 40 percent of the US market.

References

Bhagwati, J. (2004) *In Defense of Globalization*, Oxford: Oxford University Press.
Black, S. and Brainerd, B. (2004) "Improving equality? The impact of globalization on gender discrimination," *Industrial and Labor Relations Review*, 57 (4): 540–59.
Elson, D. (1995) "Male bias in macro-economics: the case of structural adjustment," in D. Elson (ed.), *Male Bias in the Development Process*, Manchester: Manchester University Press.
Ferber, M. and Nelson, J. (eds) (1993) *Beyond Economic Man: feminist theory and economics*, Chicago, IL: University of Chicago Press.

Folbre, N. (1994) *Who Pays for the Kids? Gender and the Structures of Constraint*, London and New York: Routledge.

Prebisch, R. (1950) *The Economic Development of Latin America and its Principle Problems*, New York: United Nations.

Rodrik, D. and Rodriguez, F. (2000) "Trade policy and economic growth: a skeptic's guide to the cross-national evidence," in B. Bernanke and K. Rogoff (eds), *National Bureau for Economic Research Macroeconomics Annual 2000*, Cambridge, MA: MIT Press.

Singer, H.W. (1950) "The distribution of gains between investing and borrowing countries," *American Economic Review*, 40 (2): 473–85.

Toye, J. (2003) *Trade and Development. Directions for the 21st Century*, Cheltenham: Edward Elgar.

Warner, J. and Campbell, D. (2000) "Supply response in an agrarian economy with non-symmetric gender relations," *World Development*, 28 (7): 1327–40.

Part I

Trade and gender: framing the issues

2 Gender and the social construction of markets

Lourdes Benería

Introduction[1]

This chapter includes two quite distinct but inter-related parts. The first part focuses on the construction of global markets during the late twentieth century, beginning with Karl Polanyi's book *The Great Transformation. The political and economic origins of our time* (1944). It discusses his analysis of the self-regulated market and the profound changes in human behavior associated with its functioning. It goes on to examine the extent to which Polanyi's notion of "market society" and his analysis of the growth of the market as a social construction during the nineteenth and early twentieth centuries in Europe can be applied to the more recent formation of global markets in late twentieth century. The second part deals with the significance of gender for the analysis of markets and asks the question whether globalization has implications for the construction of feminist models of economic analysis and social change; it aims to "engender" Polanyi's work by arguing that the construction and growth of markets has gender dimensions, and by pointing out that there is a tension between the assumptions of economic rationality associated with market behavior and the real life experiences and desires of men and women. It goes on to discuss questions of gender and global markets and summarizes some of the themes that have emerged from the abundant body of literature that has appeared on this subject since the 1970s. It further discusses the extent to which women's values and choices are likely to be influenced by their increasing participation in market society and encouraging them to follow the norms of behavior associated with "economic man." Finally, it argues that the predominant assumptions in orthodox neoclassical models need to be expanded or replaced by alternative "transformative models" of human behavior which include feminist visions.

The social construction of global markets

Many parallels can be traced between the social construction of national markets analyzed by Polanyi for nineteenth-century Europe and the expansion and deepening of both national and transnational markets across the globe during the past quarter century. Polanyi's analysis centered on the profound change in human behavior represented by market-oriented choices and decisions in which gain replaced subsistence as the center of economic activity. Gain and profit, Polanyi argues, had never before played such an important role in human activity. Critical of Adam Smith's suggestion that the social division of labor depended upon the existence of markets and "upon man's propensity to barter, truck and exchange one thing for another" (Polanyi 1957: 43), Polanyi argued instead that the division of labor in earlier societies had depended on "differences inherent in the facts of sex, geography, and individual endowment" (p. 44). Production and distribution in many earlier societies, Polanyi explains, were ensured through reciprocity and redistribution, two principles not currently associated with economics. These principles were part of an economic system that was "a mere function of social organization," that is, at the service of social life. Instead, capitalism evolved in the opposite direction, leading to a situation in which it is the economic system that determines social organization, its goals, and outcomes. Commenting on Smith, Polanyi argues that "no misreading of the past ever proved to be more prophetic of the future" (p. 43) in the sense that, one hundred years after Adam Smith wrote about man's propensity to barter, truck, and exchange, this propensity became the norm – theoretically and practically – of industrial capitalist/market society. Although Polanyi is not always persuasive in terms of whether the pursuit of economic gain is a result of market society, its fundamental role in a market economy, and in the theoretical models that sustain it, is clearly central.

For Polanyi, a crucial point in this gradual transformation toward the predominance of "the economic" was the step "which makes isolated markets into a [self-regulated] market economy." One of his central points is that, contrary to conventional wisdom; this change was not "the natural outcome of the spreading of markets" (p. 57). On the contrary, Polanyi argues, the market economy was socially constructed and accompanied by a profound change in the organization of society itself. Thus, the construction of a laissez-faire market economy required "an enormous increase in continuous, centrally organized and controlled interventionism." For example, Polanyi mentions the enormous increase in the administrative functions of the state newly endowed with a central bureaucracy, the strengthening of private property, and the enforcement of contracts in market exchange and other transactions. He also raises the seemingly contradictory notion of laissez-faire liberalism as "the product of deliberate state action," including "a conscious and often violent intervention on the part of the government" (p. 250).

The profound change represented by the gradual construction of a market society had a strong influence on human behavior, leading toward the prevalence of rational economic man, the selfish individual in pursuit of his own desires through the market. Polanyi emphasizes that "a market economy can only exist in a market society," that is, it can only exist if it is accompanied with the appropriate changes in norms and behavior that enable the market to function. Economic rationality is based on the expectation that human beings behave in such a way as to pursue maximum gains; as emphasized in any course in introductory economics, while the entrepreneur seeks to maximize profit, the employee seeks to attain the highest earnings possible, and the consumer the maximization of his/her utility. At the theoretical level, Adam Smith linked the selfish pursuit of individual gain to the maximization of the wealth of nations through the invisible hand of the market and, in so doing, he saw no contradiction between the two. The orthodox tradition in economics has continued to rely on this basic link without questioning the consequences of its corresponding institutions and norms on human behavior.

The intensification of global market transactions during the past 30 years has been unprecedented. The financial sector has led in the degree to which its markets have transcended national boundaries. Likewise, trade liberalization and the internationalization of production have accelerated the global integration of markets in goods and services. At the social and cultural level, the melting pot of cultures has affected everyday life across the globe, resulting in the intensification of multicultural currents but also in tensions across cultures. Thus, despite the strong forces leading toward convergence of market societies, we have witnessed deep misgivings about the significance and consequences of such trends.

At the national level, these processes have been facilitated by numerous efforts on the part of governments that have played an active role in the globalization of domestic economies and of their social, political, and cultural life. In late twentieth century, however, the construction of global markets took place in particular under the umbrella of interventions on the part of international forces beyond national boundaries. This is the case with the regional formation of free trade areas and common markets and the growth and increasing power of multinational corporations. To these we must add the role of international organizations such as the World Bank and the International Monetary Fund and the interventions of dominant foreign governments and other international actors in determining policy. The following paragraphs provide examples of such dynamics from an economic perspective.

First, the role of the nation state in enacting deregulation schemes in financial, goods, and labor markets has been instrumental in the gradual erosion of economic borders across countries. Although the degree of deregulation varies by economic sector, markets, and countries, the tendency to "free" the market from intervention became an integral part of economic policy throughout. During the final decades of the twentieth century, these policies created tensions and opposition on the part of social groups that lost relative power and previously won benefits, as in the case of trade unions and labor in general in many countries. For this and other reasons, interventions to deal with this opposition required a strong hand – à la Polanyi – on the part of the state. The deep cuts in the social services provided by the welfare state in high income countries and the dismantling of many of these services in former centrally planned economies provided many examples of how state actions along these lines have eroded a variety of historically won rights and privileges for large sectors of the population (Moghadam 1993; Tilly *et al.* 1995; Standing 1999). During the 1980s and 1990s, examples of opposition and challenges to these trends were numerous, both in low- and high-income countries.[2] The so-called anti-globalization movement represents a more recent and repeated expression of discontent with global proportions. Despite this strong opposition at many levels, and subject to the ups and downs linked to changes in national governments, states have pursued a neoliberal agenda leading toward a higher degree of globalization.

Second, the formation of transnational entities and regional trade areas such as the European Union, ASEAN, NAFTA, and Mercosur have been instrumental in promoting the globalization of markets, responding to the initiatives and interests of social actors likely to benefit from such projects.[3] To be sure, globalization has been channeled through the action of individual governments as the main agents in international negotiation. For example, the Uruguay Round of trade negotiations that led to the replacement of GATT (General Agreement on Tariffs and Trade) by WTO (World Trade Organization) in 1995 resulted in the most global of existing international bodies. Under the leadership of the United States and the G-7, and despite opposition from developing countries, the creation of the WTO represented a substantial acceleration in trade liberalization across the globe and the integration of new sectors into liberalization schemes – such as intellectual property rights and services not previously included in GATT. Unlike its predecessor, the WTO has independent jurisdiction beyond national legislation and its rules on trade, patents, and intellectual property rights are binding on all members. The continuing tensions that emerged particularly visible in the WTO Seattle meeting in 1999 have reflected many questions on the extent to which the organization is serving the interests of developing countries (Kohr 2000). Despite these tensions and the maintenance of protectionist measures in the United States and other high-income countries, the march toward further trade liberalization has been led particularly by the United States, not only through WTO channels but also through other emerging international organizations such as the Free Trade of the Americas Association (FTAA).

Third, policies designed at the national level and leading to a higher degree of globalization of domestic economies have often been inspired, and at times dictated, from the outside. The structural adjustment policies adopted by a large number of countries since the early 1980s provided a typical example. While affecting, in particular, countries dealing with debt repayment problems, Structural Adjustment Programs (SAPs) represented a profound shift with respect to the expansion and deepening of the market in the countries affected. Their Washington Consensus-inspired measures of deep economic restructuring and belt tightening followed agreements between national governments, creditor countries, commercial banks, and international organizations such as the International Monetary Fund and the World Bank who imposed, and continue to do so, harsh conditionalities for negotiating new loans and terms of payment. Conditions included the well-known efforts to set up the right environment for the expansion of markets, including government budget cuts, privatization programs, deregulation of markets, trade liberalization, the easing of controls on foreign investment, and shifts from import substitution to export promotion development models. Many of these measures resulted in a much higher degree of integration of these countries into the global economy. They also fostered the liberalization of the financial sector, the opening of doors to foreign investment, and the enforcement of rules and regulations for the smooth functioning of the market à la Polanyi – such as the strengthening of property rights, enterprise reform, and decentralization policies aimed at "liberating" the private sector from government intervention in the economy.[4]

To be sure, these policies increased the economic freedom of many actors involved in the functioning of markets. However, they also resulted from the use of a strong hand on the part of national governments and international institutions to build the neoliberal model of late twentieth century. This responded to the interests of national and global elites, rather than to the wishes of most citizens, and the policies became instruments to lock in the rules associated with (globalized) markets and the "new economy" of late capitalism. To invoke Polanyi, they were the product of deliberate state intervention – often carried out in the name of market freedoms – imposed from the top-down and without a truly democratic process of discussion and decision-making among all affected parties. As the *Wall Street Journal* put it for the case of Argentina, "[T]he reforms were largely accomplished by the political will of a presidential strongman who invoked executive decrees over 1,000 times" (O'Grady 1997). In Latin America, the only country that consulted its citizens about privatization was Uruguay, and the vote was negative. Many of the measures were also applied in most of the countries of the former Soviet Union. In this case, the shock therapy of structural adjustment has taken place simultaneously with the profound changes in economic/social relations and institutions represented by the transition from central planning to market economies.

During the 1980s and 1990s, the expansion of markets, associated also with the intensification of processes of "modernization" across the globe, was accompanied with triumphalist (re)statements and affirmations of hegemonic discourses emphasizing the norms and behavior associated with economic rationality and with the assumption that the invisible hand of the market is a better form of organizing the economy and society than any form of state intervention. This discourse can easily be seen as part of the process of constructing markets à la Polanyi. We have witnessed this process in different forms, ranging from the strong emphasis on productivity, efficiency, and financial rewards to shifts in values and attitudes – typified by the yuppies in the 1980s and by the investment bankers of the 1990s. The result was a new emphasis on individualism and competitive behavior, together with an apparent tolerance and even acceptance of social inequalities and greed.[5] The neoliberal weekly *The Economist* associated this set of factors with the emergence of the "Davos Man" who, according to a 1997 editorial, replaced the "Chatham House Man" in its influence in the global marketplace.[6] The Davos Man, the editorial pointed out, included businessmen, bankers, officials, and intellectuals who "hold university degrees, work with words and numbers, speak some English and share beliefs in individualism, market economics and democracy. They control many of the world's governments, and the bulk of its economic and military capabilities." The Davos Man does not "butter up the politicians; it is the other way around . . . finding it boring to shake the hand of an obscure prime minister." Instead, the editorial pointed out, he prefers to meet the Bill Gates of the world.

Written as a critique of Samuel Huntington's thesis in his book *The Clash of Civilizations and the Remaking of the World Order*, the praise of Davos Man by

The Economist was also an ode to the global and more contemporary version of economic man:

> Some people find Davos Man hard to take: there is something uncultured about all the money-grubbing and managerialism. But it is part of the beauty of Davos Man that, by and large, he does not give a fig for culture as the Huntingtons of the world define it. He will attend a piano recital, but does not mind whether an idea, a technique or a market is (in Mr. Huntington's complex scheme) Sinic, Hindu, Islamic or Orthodox.
>
> (*The Economist*, February 1, 1997: 18)

Thus, at least in 1997, *The Economist* expected that the Davos Man, through the magic powers of the market and its homogenizing tendencies, was more likely to bring people and cultures together than force them apart. In the United States at least, the assumption that "everybody was eating MacDonald's, wearing Nike sneakers, buying in Walt Mart and being very happy learning the English language" seemed to be part of conventional wisdom.[7]

In many ways, the Davos Man represented the rational economic man in its incarnation through contemporary global elites, and the triumphalism of the period could not predict the global tensions that emerged in the early part of the twenty-first century symbolized by the 9/11/01 events. In recent years, global protests at international gatherings – from Seattle to Quebec to Genoa – have toned down this triumphalist discourse. What *The Economist* did not originally recognize is that the commercialization of everyday life and of all sectors of the economy generates social dynamics that many individuals and cultures across the globe might find repulsive. In many ways we have witnessed, in Polanyi's terms, the tendency for society to become "an accessory to the economic system" rather than the other way around. A Colombian friend expressed her version of this phenomenon with complaints about her perception of market society: "now we are living to work, work and produce, not to enjoy life." An integral part of this discourse is the survival of the fittest, hence the view that bankruptcy is a necessary punishment for those who do not perform efficiently and according to the dictates of the market as the following quote indicates in reference to the Asian Financial crisis: "corporations are 'failing' in record numbers, but many keep on going anyway. As a result, the feeble are not eliminated, the fat is not trimmed, and the region's long-term prospects suffer" (WuDunn 1998).

The hegemonic assumption in orthodox economics that the feeble must be eliminated rather than "transformed" or helped in order, for example, to prevent massive layoffs and human suffering is thus not questioned – thereby reflecting the centrality given under capitalism to efficiency rather than to people and human development. Likewise, the possibility that the Asian way may be a model for diminishing the social costs of the crisis while searching for long-term solutions is not considered by the hegemonic discourses feeding market fundamentalism.

The significance of gender

Gender and markets

Polanyi's analysis of the social construction of markets has important gender-related implications that he did not take into consideration. My central argument in this section is that the links to the market have been historically different for men and women, with consequences for their preferences, choices, and behavior. Although Polanyi pointed out that in a market society all production is for sale, he failed to discuss the fact that, parallel to the deepening of market relations, a large proportion of the population engages in unpaid production that is only indirectly linked to the market. Women are disproportionately concentrated in this type of work, which includes agricultural family labor – particularly but not solely in subsistence economies – domestic work, and volunteer work. In contemporary societies, women perform by far the largest proportion of unpaid activities. According to UNDP's "rough estimates" at the global level, if unpaid activities were valued at prevailing wages, they would amount to $16 trillion or about 70 percent of total world output ($23 trillion). Of this $16 trillion, $11 trillion, or almost 69 percent represent women's work (UNDP 1995).

Thus, to a large extent, men and women have been positioned differently with respect to market transformations. The literature has discussed extensively that while the market has been associated with public life and "maleness," women have been viewed as closer to nature and reproduction – generally in essentialist ways – instead of as a result of historical constructions. This view in turn has had an impact on the meanings of gender, a subject analyzed extensively in the feminist literature dealing with the construction of femininity and masculinity (Gilligan 1982; Butler 1993; McCloskey 1993; Guttman 1996; Andrade and Herrera 2001). Similarly, it has affected our notions of the market itself (Strassmann 1993). In this sense, Polanyi's analysis needs to be expanded to incorporate gender dimensions.

The norms and behavior associated with the market do not apply to the sphere of unpaid work that produces goods and services for use rather than for exchange. To the extent that unpaid work is not equally subject to the competitive pressures of the market, it can respond to motivations other than gain, such as nurturing, love, and altruism, or to other norms of behavior such as duty and religious beliefs/practices. Without falling into essentialist arguments about men's and women's motivations and keeping in mind the multiple differences across countries and cultures, we can conclude from the literature that there are gender-related variations in norms, values, and behavior (England 1993; Nelson 1993; Seguino *et al.* 1996). Likewise, the literature has discussed extensively women's concentration in caring/nurturing work, either unpaid or paid (Folbre 1995). Women have also concentrated in the service sector in large numbers, including paid and unpaid activities, but changes are taking place globally in the nature and extent to their involvement in this sector (see later).

Although the above UNDP data show that the current predominance of women in unpaid work and that of men in paid activities is beyond dispute, engagement in nongainful activities is not the exclusive domain of women, nor is market work exclusive to men. In earlier societies, the principles of reciprocity and distribution described by Polanyi did not necessarily function according to the rules of market rationality. Instead, tradition, religion, kin, community, and social status played an important role in setting up norms and affecting collective and individual values; many of these factors do not respond to market economic rationality. But non-maximizing behavior can also be found in contemporary societies. In subsistence economies, production is not geared to the market and family labor is motivated primarily by needs rather than gain. Likewise, in market economies, behavior following norms of solidarity and work/leisure choices not necessarily pursuing gain or following the dictates of efficiency, competition, and productivity associated with economic rationality has so far not disappeared. This is illustrated by the high levels of volunteer work found in empirical studies and by the numbers of people engaged by choice in creative and/or in poorly remunerated work (AARP 1997; Lind 1997). Volunteer work, such as that carried out at the community level, might be motivated by a sense of collective well-being, empathy for others, or political commitment; and artistic work is often associated with the pursuit of beauty and creativity, irrespective of its market value.

Feminist economists have emphasized the need to develop alternative models based on assumptions of human cooperation, empathy, and collective well-being (Ferber and Nelson 1993; Folbre 1994; Strober 1994). In so doing, they join other scholars who have also questioned neoclassical assumptions, pointing out that they are predicated upon the Hobbesian view of self-interested individuals. These authors argue that the numerous exceptions to this rule suggest that human behavior responds to a complex set of often contradictory tendencies (Marwell and Ames 1981; Frank *et al.* 1993). Thus, neoclassical assumptions seem to contradict "real-life experiences in which collective action and empathetic, connected economic decision-making are observed" (Seguino *et al.* 1996: 4). A variety of studies have shown that this type of behavior is often found among women (Guyer 1980; Gilligan 1982; Benería and Roldán 1987; Folbre 2000).

In a study comparing the behavior of economists and noneconomists, Seguino *et al.* (1996) suggest that "social structures that shape our preferences may differ along gender lines, with women more likely to exhibit constitutive desires and empathetic or connected behavior in contributing to public goods than do males" (p. 15). And recent experiments with individual preferences have shown that many alternatives exist to the traditional self-interested model, with motivations responding, for example, to notions of altruism, fairness, and reciprocity (Croson 1999). In addition, other authors have emphasized the extent to which social codes and identities are constructed "at the deepest cognitive levels through social interaction" – therefore questioning the validity of static assumptions about tastes and preferences in conventional economic models which take them as given (Cornwall 1997). As product developers and advertising agencies know well, this implies that social codes and individual preferences are subject to social constructions and to exogenous interferences that result in dynamic and continuous change.

The claim on the part of feminist economists that models of free individual choice are not adequate to analyze issues of dependence/interdependence, tradition, and power (Ferber and Nelson 1993) is of particular relevance for cultures in which individualistic, market-oriented behavior is more the exception than the norm. Feminists have also pointed out that neoclassical analysis is based on a "separate self-model" in which utility is viewed as subjective and unrelated to that of other people. As Paula England has argued, this is linked to the assumption that individual behavior is selfish since "emotional connection often creates empathy, altruism, and a subjective sense of social solidarity" (England 1993). Thus, to the extent that women tend to be more emotionally connected than men, particularly as a result of their role in child rearing and family care and as part of the prevalent gender ideology, the separate self-model has an androcentric bias. Similarly, to the extent that this model typifies Western individualism, it also has a Western bias and is foreign to societies with more collective forms of action and decisionmaking. Orthodox economic analysis has had little to say about these alternative modes of behavior and their significance for different forms of social organization and for policy and action under alternative institutions.

A different question is whether women's behavior is changing as they enter national and international markets in increasing numbers. Before examining this question, the following section focuses on the observed trends linking gender with the dynamics of global markets.

Gender and globalization

Since the late 1970s, studies began to analyze the effects of the relocation of production to low-wage countries and began to note a preference for women workers, particularly in export-oriented, labor-intensive industries relying on low-cost production for global markets. Globalization has intensified these tendencies. In its initial steps, the body of research that documented these trends tended to focus on the jobs created by transnational corporations in low-wage industrializing areas such as South East Asia. The emphasis was placed on the exploitation of women by multinational capital and its ability to take advantage of female stereotypes associated with women workers: docility, nimble fingers, young age, often of rural origins and from developing countries, low wages and poor working conditions. This analysis reflected a "women as victims approach" that gradually was seen as simplistic and unable to deal with the complexities involved (Lim 1983; Pyle 1983; Elson and Pearson 1989). Lim, for example, noted that women's employment in multinational corporations did result in improvements in their lives. Various authors began to point out the ways in which women were not passive victims of exploitative conditions and illustrated the multiplicity of factors that affected their work (Ong 1987).

As a result, this initial period was gradually replaced by analyses of female employment that captured the complexities and the often contradictory effects involved (Elson and Pearson 1989). Studies since then have also focused on forms of female employment other than that provided by multinational capital – including subcontracting and informal employment (Benería and Roldán 1987; Kabeer 2000). In contrast to the women-as-victims approach, the emphasis in many studies has been on illustrating the negative and positive effects of women's participation in production for global markets, including the gains resulting from women's increased autonomy and bargaining power as a result of employment. In Naila Kabeer's words, women's paid work has been associated with an increase in the "power to choose," even if within the many still existing constraints facing those she calls "weak winners" (Kabeer 2000). Likewise, it has been associated with women's ability to act and defend their interests and those of their family and community in the face of most adverse circumstances.

A significant proportion of studies of women's employment have continued to focus on low-wage production for export where female labor tends to concentrate. Such is the case with export processing zones and informal employment in low-wage, labor-intensive manufacturing; the latter includes, for example, lower-tier subcontracting chains, microenterprises, and self-employment. Both rely on systems of flexible production that find in women's labor the most flexible supply, such as in the use of temporary contracts, part-time work, and unstable working conditions; they are at the heart of low-cost production for global markets and tied to the volatility of global capital's mobility in search of the lowest cost location. Women's high level of employment in export processing zones (EPZs) is illustrated in Table 2.1, which provides figures for selected countries. Based on data for 2000–3, it shows that the proportion of female labor in the EPZs tended to be well above 50 percent – reaching 90 percent in the case in Nicaragua. However, as can be seen for the Republic of Korea, Sri Lanka, and Malaysia, these percentages are generally lower than in earlier periods for a variety of reasons having to do with the changing nature of production in the EPZs, technological change, and the effects of male unemployment, on the increasing tendency to employ men in some of these global production processes.

Table 2.1 Share of female employment in export processing zones (EPZs): selected countries, 2000–3

Country	Total employment	No. of EPZs	Female share of employment (%)
Kenya	27,148	6	60
Mauritius	83,609	Whole island	56
South Korea	39,000	2	70
			(77 in 1980)
Sri Lanka	111,033 (EPZs)	12	77.72
	350,000 (ind. parks)	4 (ind. parks)	(88 in 1980)
Malaysia	200,000 (EPZs)	14	54
	122,000 (ind. parks)	200 (ind. parks)	(75 in 1980)
Philippines	820,960	34	74
			(74 in 1980)
Guatemala	69,200	20	70
Honduras	106,457	28	67
Nicaragua	40,000	1	90

Source: J.-P. S. Boyenge (2003) *Database on Export Processing Zones*, Geneva: ILO.

Expanding services associated with global markets tend to employ low-skill women in pink-collar offices; for example, for data entry and data processing in mail order business, airlines and rail systems, credit card providers and other financial services like banking and insurance. These activities can be highly concentrated geographically such as in the Caribbean and in some Asian countries such as China, India, Malaysia, and the Philippines. Referring to the case of Barbados, Carla Freeman (2000) has written about this offshore clerical work in the Caribbean as resulting in "a convergence between realms of tradition and modernity, gender and class – where transnational capital and production, the Barbadian state, and young Afro-Caribbean women together fashion a new 'classification' of woman worker who, gendered producer and consumer, is fully enmeshed in global and local, economic and cultural processes" (p. 22). Women's employment has also expanded in the tourist sector across countries. Some estimates indicate that women's share of employment in these services is as high as in the export sector and almost completely female in the case of the Caribbean (United Nations 1999). Needless to say, employment in this sector tends to be seasonal and unstable, depending also on the ups and downs of international demand, and with a variety of effects on global migration (Ehrenreich and Hochschild 2002).

The feminization of export manufacturing, and of the labor force in general, has taken place even in countries where women's participation in paid work was traditionally low and socially not acceptable. The speed at which this phenomenon has taken place has raised interesting questions about the processes through which traditions and gender construction can be dismantled or adapted to economic change. This has produced an interesting body of literature that analyzes the tensions and contradictions involved in the process (Pyle 1983; Ong 1987; Feldman 1992, 2001; Kabeer 2000; Ehrenreich and Hochschild 2002).[8] In this respect, sociological, and cultural studies have made a rich contribution – incorporating levels of analysis that combine the more strictly economic aspects of globalization and women's employment with a focus on changes in gender relations, social constructions about the division of labor, women's agency, and household–market connections.

What generalizations can be made with regards to the gender effects of globalization? First, the literature has emphasized the notion that export expansion and the feminization of the labor force have been parallel to the processes of labor market deregulation and flexibilization registered across countries during the past three decades, as a result of neoliberal policies. It has affected both men and women even though not necessarily in the same ways. Feminization has been linked to the deterioration of working conditions and as part of the race to the bottom resulting from global competition (Standing 1989 and 1999). Although some have criticized this view for blaming this deterioration on women's new roles in production, a different interpretation emphasizes the role of economic restructuring in dealing with the market pressures of international competition, and the use of women's labor supply to deal with the pressures of global markets. In addition, although a large proportion of women's jobs are located at the lower echelons of the labor hierarchy, the increasing economic polarization among women and North–South differences imply that some women at least have a relatively advantageous position in the global economy.

Second, generalizations about the effects of globalization on women must be approached with great caution, since effects vary according to historical, socioeconomic, and other conditions across countries. To illustrate, export-oriented manufacturing in South East Asia since the 1970s has in the long run resulted in improvements, even if far from spectacular, in women's earnings (Lim 1983; Dollar and Gatti 1999; Seguino 2000). Yet, the Asian experience cannot be generalized. For instance, the maquiladora sector in the US–Mexican border represents a model of export-oriented production that over the years has not resulted in significant gains for the large majority of women employed (Cravey 1998; Fussell 2000). Fussell's study for the case of Tijuana, Mexico, found that, in their drive to keep production costs low, multinational manufacturers have tapped into women's low-wage labor, "thereby taking advantage of women's labor market disadvantages and making a labor force willing to accept more 'flexible' terms of employment" (p. 59). Thus, differences between these outcomes are due to factors having to do with labor availability (relatively limited in the case of the Asian countries and practically unlimited in the Mexican case), degrees of wage inequality, and the dynamics of the labor market with respect to male/female employment.[9]

As a result, a debate has been generated on the relationship between export-oriented growth, women's wages and working conditions, and gender equality. The debate has taken place between: those who hold a more optimistic view of the connections between the two and have argued that gender inequality has been reduced in terms of wage differentials, access to jobs, and educational achievement (Dollar and Gatti 1999) and those who take a less optimistic view and argue that, for example, in the case of the Asian growth, it was correlated to gender wage gaps. Taking the second position, Seguino (2000) has shown that the Asian economies that grew most rapidly had the widest wage gaps. Similarly, Hsiung (1995) illustrates how Taiwan's high level of flexibility and market adaptability has been solidly based on low wages and poor working conditions of women as home-based workers.

A different issue is what we might call the globalization of social reproduction, a phenomenon observed particularly since the 1990s. I am referring to the increasing migration of women from Southern countries for care and domestic work in Northern countries, either in the sphere of the household or elsewhere. This is the result of several processes. On the one hand, in the North, the increase in women's labor force participation, very low birth rates (especially in western Europe), and the crisis of care has resulted in a growing demand for paid labor provision in the sphere of social reproduction, namely, domestic work and the care of the children and the elderly. On the supply side, the persistence of poverty and economic crises in the South and in Eastern Europe, together with growing inequalities between countries, has fed the large supply of labor ready to emigrate to the North; this is the case even in countries with positive economic growth such as Mexico. Women find care work easy to find and, even if they are married and with children, tend to emigrate first, sometimes with the expectation that their families will follow. Many countries have been affected by this trend, often creating a national debate about its possible effects; the cases of the Philippines, Mexico, and the Andean and Caribbean countries are well-known (Salazar Parrenas 2002; Camacho and Hernandez 2005; Herrera 2005). The remittances of migrants have become an important source of foreign exchange for many countries; in the case of Mexico and Ecuador they represent the second source after oil.

These processes have resulted in profound changes in the ways families survive and organize their activities. We have witnessed the formation of transnational families in which traditional gender roles have been both maintained and reversed. Migrant women continue to perform traditional female care work, but migration implies their shift from unpaid care work in their homes to paid care work in the immigrant country. Their role as mothers is transformed; transnational motherhood weakens the contact with their families and strengthens their role as family providers, particularly through their remittances. Normally, other family members, including some fathers but mostly other women, take up the tasks of the mother. This implies a transformation of the division of labor in the emigrant countries and might result in an intensification of work for those, especially older women, who take up the new responsibilities.

The ambiguities of market effects

The extension and deepening of markets at the global level raises many questions about their impact on individual behavior. More specifically, how are women affected as the relative weight of their paid labor time increases and that of unpaid work diminishes? Does it imply that women are increasingly adopting the norms of economic rationality à la "economic man?" Are women becoming more individualistic, selfish, and less nurturing? Is market behavior undermining "women's ways of seeing and doing?" Are gender identities being reconstituted? The answer to these questions is far from being clear-cut. A nonessentialist view of gender differences implies that economic social change is likely to influence gender (re)constructions and gender roles. As women become direct participants in national and international markets, their motives and aspirations will be shaped by the ways in which they respond to this processes, probably adopting patterns of behavior traditionally observed more frequently among men. From casual observation, many of us think that this is already happening. However, there are areas of ambiguity, tensions, and contradictions in the answer to these questions.

To begin with, the market can have positive effects for women and men, such as the breaking up of patriarchal traditions like arranged marriages that limit individual autonomy; and the liberation from divisions of labor associated with disproportionate burdens for women. In this sense, it can accelerate the diffusion of "liberating" practices. But it can also introduce or intensify sexist or gender-based discriminatory and exploitative practices and it can introduce tensions regarding individual freedom and collective security.[10] Differences between countries can also be important as a result of historical circumstances and cultural factors.

To illustrate, this is clearly reflected in the following quote from a World Bank report referring to societies of the former Soviet Union:

> Transition affects women much differently in some ways that it does men. In considering whether transition has increased welfare for women, the real test is whether it has left them freer than before, or more constrained. So far, at least, the answer in many transition countries appears to be the latter.
>
> (World Bank 1996: 72)

Several authors have pointed out how gender ideology is changing in these countries, emphasizing that the transition has exacerbated "latent and manifest patriarchal attitudes," increasing women's vulnerability both culturally and economically (Moghadam 1993). Bridger *et al.* (1996) have written that "[T]he initial rounds of democratic elections in Russia have virtually wiped women off the political map and their re-emergence is now painfully slow and fraught with difficulty" (p. 2). In some of the Central Asian republics, new restrictions on women's lives were imposed during the post-1989 transition, such as the prohibition of appearing in public without a male or an elder woman, wearing trousers and driving cars (Tohidi 1996). However, a key question is the extent to which market forces transform these norms and how the modernity spread through the market might break patriarchal forms.

Current tensions in global capitalism have brought a turning point in the triumphalism of Davos Man, and an increasing number of people have been decrying his excesses. More than 50 years after Polanyi wrote *The Great Transformation*, his call for subordinating the market to the priorities set by democratic societies resonates as an urgent need, even though the ways to achieve this goal have to accommodate to the realities of our times. This has been reflected in the many activities and groups associated with the World Social Forum, the worldwide network set up as a response to the World Economic Forum that meets annually in Davos.

This poses challenging questions for feminism, which, in its varied forms, could in fact be viewed as one of Polanyi's counter-movements in late twentieth century.[11] Linked to the search for gender equality but also to wider social issues, some key questions deriving from feminism are whether women can make a contribution to the quest for new directions towards human development. Can the alternative models discussed by feminists be used as guidelines for how to construct alternative societies? Can women provide different voices as they become more integrated in the market and public life? Can "difference," at least to the extent that it might be maintained, be a source of inspiration for progressive social change?

This means, for example, questioning rational economic man's objectives as the desired norm. For Polanyi, moving beyond economic man does not necessarily imply a rejection of markets as a way to organize production and distribution of goods and services. As he stated, "the end of market society means in no way the absence of markets" (p. 252). However, his view calls for subordinating markets to the objectives of truly democratic communities and countries. The goal is to place economic activity at the service of human or people-centered development and not the other way around, or to reach an era in which productivity/efficiency is achieved not for its own sake but as a way to increase collective well-being sustainability of our planet.

All of this implies placing issues of distribution, inequality, ethics, the environment and other social goals, and the nature of individual happiness, collective well-being, and social change at the center of our agendas. It follows that an urgent task for economists and social scientists is to translate these more general objectives into relevant theoretical, empirical, and practical work. For economists, the task of building a socially relevant economic theory should be a priority. What if, for example, production models assumed that the firm does not have to maximize profits and, instead, viewed profits as a left over after key social objectives are met? For example, among the various objectives of the Zapatista movement in Mexico, one of the most emphasized is the need to provide individual and collective dignity – and more specifically for indigenous groups. The dictionary defines dignity as "bearing conduct or speech indicative of self-respect," "worthiness," and "degree of excellence," definitions that take us back to the notion of human development: the "intuitive idea of a life that is worthy of the dignity of the human being...for each and every person." To be sure, the concept of dignity might seem ambiguous but the same can be said for utility around which a good part of economic theory is built. The notion of dignity for everyone suggests well-being associated with social equality, self-esteem, and respect/recognition across social groups. It brings up questions about who contributes and to what extent to social welfare as well as questions of distribution, clearly topics worthy of scrutiny by economists. Many interesting questions surface along these lines. What if, instead of maximizing utility, economic models toyed with the notion of maximizing dignity? In what sense might this objective have different implications for men and women? What implications does it have for distributive justice between capital and labor and for wage distribution and individual income?

People-centered development calls for transforming knowledge so as to rethink conventional approaches to theory and decision-making. As Elizabeth Minnich has put it:

> Behind any particular body of accepted knowledge are the definitions, the boundaries, established by those who have held power. To disagree with those boundaries and definitions, it has been necessary to recognize them; to refuse them is to be shut out even from debate; to transgress them is to mark oneself as mad, heretical, dangerous.
>
> (Minnich 1990: 151)

Definitions, boundaries, and power have a historical specificity. Polanyi dared to say that "[T]he passing of market-economy can become the beginning of an era of unprecedented freedom...generated by the leisure and security that industrial society offers to all" (p. 256). Written in the 1940s, at a time when it was difficult to predict the problems that state interventions would create, reality did not live up to his optimism. Written at the beginning of the twentieth century, it is likely to be read as hopelessly utopian, even naïve. Yet, since the break in the Washington Consensus, the notion that "there is no alternative" to the neoliberal model seems increasingly less acceptable. At the same time, questions of global governance that would introduce checks and balances to uncontrolled markets have been subject to debates. The present danger is that proposals for global governance might be introduced in a top-down fashion and without worldwide negotiations based on democratic debates. The growing concentration of power in the hands of large global corporations and in the hands of G-9 country governments should be a source of concern to all those looking for alternatives. Feminism has been very important in the struggle for solutions at the decentralized, local, and institutional level; it has fought discrimination and inequalities at many levels; it has changed institutions and decision-making processes; it has incorporated new agendas in the politics of daily life; it has affected national policies; it has made an impact on international agendas; and it has been influential in bringing human welfare first to the center of debates on economic and social policy. It now has to meet the challenges posed by the unprecedented reach of global markets.

Notes

1 This chapter draws upon my article "Globalization, gender and the Davos Man," *Feminist Economics* (1999) 5 (3): pp. 61–84; and Chapter 3 of my book *Gender, Development and Globalization* (2003) London: Routledge.

2 The opposition to structural adjustment policies, which, as argued below, were instrumental in introducing market deregulation programs in many developing countries, was very loud in many cases. In Latin America, for example, protests around economic and social conditions that followed these policies have been numerous throughout the past two decades, and in some countries have continued up to the present. This included women's organizations that were instrumental in voicing their protests during the 1980s and early 1990s (Montecinos 2001). In Argentina, the continuous financial crises experienced for more than a decade and culminating in a practical default in late 2001 have brought thousands of people to the streets, contributing to political crisis and government changes. In high-income countries, the fiscal pressures, unemployment, and the weakening of the welfare state associated with neoliberal policies and globalization also generated strong contestations. For example, the political debates during the 1997 French election provided a clear illustration of how the public perceived the objectives of the European Union's Maastricht Treaty as contrary to the interests of a large proportion of the population. Similar protests emerged in the Asian countries affected by the 1997 economic crisis.

3 To be sure, economic interests are not the only driving forces behind such schemes. In the case of the European Community, for example, the political objectives of European unification were important, from its early stages, as a way to overcome historical tensions and divisions in the continent. However, trade liberalization and economic integration schemes have largely been promoted by financial and industrial capital including transnational corporations, and specific economic sectors expecting to profit from expanding and less regulated trade and foreign investment. For some specific examples, see Epstein *et al.* (1990).

4 For a more detailed analysis of these policies, see World Bank (1996).

5 Despite continuous debates and even resistance to these changes, the evidence supporting this shift has been overwhelming. As an article in *The New York Times* put it, "[W]ith the growth of free markets generally accepted around the world, debates focus less on whether greed is good or bad than on specific checks on excess: on when or which super-payments may be deserved" (Hacker 1997: 3). For a typical view of the preeminence of productivity as a social objective, see "The future of the state. A survey of the world economy," *The Economist* (September 20, 1997).

6 The reference is to the annual meeting in Davos, Switzerland, of "people who run the world." The Chatham House refers to the "elegant London home" of the Royal Institute of International Affairs where "diplomats have mulled the strange ways of abroad" for "nearly 80 years" ("In praise of the Davos man," *The Economist*, February 1, 1997).

7 This could be observed even in academic circles. At a meeting to discuss development studies I attended in the mid-1990s, a representative of a business school announced proudly that in his school it was assumed that there was no need to teach foreign languages since the international business world could function perfectly in English. This was a few years before the US government realized that, as a result of the 9/11/01 events, it didn't have enough people that could understand Arabic.

8 Some exceptions to these trends can be found in the economies of the former Soviet Union where the post-1989 period created contradictory tendencies. Women in these countries had registered very high labor force participation rates during the Soviet era, but they have suffered disproportionately from the social costs of the transition, including unemployment, gender discrimination, and reinforcement of patriarchal forms. In many cases, the transition to more privatized market economies reduced women's employment opportunities and relegated women to temporary and low-pay jobs (Moghadam 1993; Bridger *et al.* 1996; The World Bank 2000). At the same time, the new market forces have generated jobs for women as a source of cheap labor, particularly in labor-intensive production for global markets. Hence, contradictory tendencies have been observed.

9 In the Mexican case, the proportion of women in the maquiladora labor force, which originally reached levels above 60 percent, began to decrease since the mid-1980. This was due to several reasons, including technological shifts in production toward more flexible production systems requiring new skills and increasing employment and availability of male labor (due to unemployment and migration, particularly of young males willing to work for low wages).

10 These tensions are especially relevant for indigenous women (and perhaps also for indigenous men) who might feel torn between the freedom that the logic of the market might provide for them and the logic of collectivity within which their identity and security has been shaped (Agarwal 1994; Deere and León 2001).

11 "The Great Transformation" referred to by Polanyi included a great variety of social groups, including left-leaning political parties, that organized their activities to counteract the negative effects of the market in late-nineteenth- and early-twentieth-century Europe.

References

AARP (1997) *The AARP Survey of Civic Involvement*, Washington, DC: American Association of Retired Persons.

Agarwal, B. (1994) *A Field of One's Own: gender and land rights in South Asia*, Cambridge: Cambridge University Press.

Andrade, X. and Herrera, G. (eds) (2001) *Masculinidades en Ecuador*, Quito: FLACSO.

Benería, L. (1999) "Globalization, gender, and the Davos Man," *Feminist Economics*, 5 (3): 61–84.

Benería, L. and Roldán, M. (1987) *The Crossroads of Class & Gender: industrial homework, subcontracting, and household dynamics in Mexico City*, Chicago, IL: University of Chicago Press.

Bridger, S., Kay, R., and Pinnick, K. (1996) *No More Heroines? Russia, women and the market*, London: Routledge.

Butler, J. (1993) *Bodies that Matter: on the discursive limits of "Sex,"* London: Routledge.

Camacho, G. and Hernandez, K. (2005) *Cambió mi Vida. Migración femenina percepciones e impactos*, Quito: UNIFEM CEPLAES.

Cornwall, R. (1997) "Deconstructing silence: the queer political economy of the social articulation of desire," *Review of Radical Political Economies*, 29 (1): 1–130.

Cravey, A. (1998) *Women and Work in Mexico's Maquiladoras*, Lanham, MD: Rowan and Littlefield Publishers.

Croson, S. (1999) "Using experiments in the classroom," *CWEP Newsletter*, Winter.

Deere, C.D. and León, M. (2001) *Empowering Women. Land and property rights in Latin America*, Pittsburg: University of Pittsburg Press.

Dollar, D. and Gatti, R. (1999) "Gender inequality, income, and growth: are good times good for women?" Working Paper Series, No. 1, The World Bank: Policy Research Group on Gender and Development.

Ehrenreich, B. and Hochschild, A.R. (eds) (2002) *Global Women: nannies, maids, and sex workers in the new economy*, New York: Metropolitan Books.

Elson, D. and Pearson, R. (1989) *Women's Employment and Multinationals in Europe*, London: MacMillan.

England, P. (1993) "The separative self: androcentric bias in neoclassical assumptions," in M. Ferber and J. Nelson (eds), *Beyond Economic Man. Feminist theory and economics*, Chicago, IL: University of Chicago Press.

Epstein, G., Graham, J., and Nembhard, J. (eds) (1990) *Creating a New World Economy*, Philadelphia, PA: Temple University Press.

Feldman, S. (1992) "Crisis, Islam and gender in Bangladesh: the social construction of a female labor force," in L. Beneria and S. Feldman (eds), *Unequal Burden: Economic crises, persistent poverty, and women's work*, Boulder, CO: Westview Press.

—— (2001) "Exploring theories of patriarchy: a perspective from contemporary Bangladesh," *Signs Journal of Women, Culture and Society*, 26 (4): 1097–127.

Ferber, M. and Nelson, J. (eds) (1993) *Beyond Economic Man*, Chicago, IL: University of Chicago Press.

Folbre, N. (1994) *Who Pays for the Kids? Gender and the Structures of Constraint*, New York: Routledge.

—— (1995) "Holding hands at midnight: the paradox of caring labor," *Feminist Economics*, 1 (1): 73–92.

—— (2000) *The Invisible Heart, Economics and Family Values*, New York: The New Press.

Frank, R., Golovich, T., and Regan, D. (1993) "Does studying economics inhibit cooperation?" *Journal of Economic Perspectives*, 7 (2): 159–71.

Freeman, R.B. (1996) *The New Inequality*, Boston, MA: Boston Review, December/January 1996/1997.

Fussell, M.E. (2000) "Making labor flexible: the recomposition of Tijuana's maquiladora female labor force," *Feminist Economics*, 6 (3): 59–80.

Gilligan, C. (1982) *In a Different Voice*, Cambridge, MA: Harvard University Press.

Guttmann, M. (1996) *The Meanings of Macho: being a man in Mexico city*, Berkeley and London: University of California Press.

Guyer, J. (1980) "Households, budgets and women's incomes," Africana Studies Center, Working Paper, No. 28, Boston, MA: Boston University.

Hacker, A. (1997) "Good or bad, greed is often beside the point," *The New York Times*, June 8, 1997.

Herrera, G. (2005) "Work and social reproduction in the lives of Ecuadorian domestic workers in Madrid," paper prepared for the International Conference on Migration and Domestic Work in Global Perspective, The Netherlands Institute for Advanced Studies, Wassenaar, May 26–29, 2005.

Hsiung, P.-C. (1995) *Living Rooms as Factories: class, gender, and the satellite factory system in Taiwan*, Philadelphia, PA: Temple University Press.

Kabeer, N. (2000) *The Power to Choose: Bangladesh women and labor market decisions in London and Dhaka*, London: Verso.

Kohr, M. (2000) "North–south tensions at the WTO: the need to rethink liberalization and reform the WTO," paper presented at the Global Tensions Conference, Cornell University, March 2000.

Lim, L. (1983) "Capitalism, imperialism, and patriarchy: the dilemma of third world women workers in multinational factories," in J. Nash and M. Fernandez-Kelly (eds), *Women, Men, and the International Division of Labor*, Albany, NY: State University of New York Press.

Lind, A. (1997) "Gender, development, and urban social change: women's community action in global cities," *World Development*, 25 (8): 1205–23.

McCloskey, D. (1993) "Some consequences of a conjective economics," in B. Nelson and M. Ferber (eds), *Beyond Economic Man*, Chicago, IL: University of Chicago Press.

Marwell, G. and Ames, R. (1981) "Economists free ride, does anyone else? (Experiments in the Provision of Public Goods)," *Journal of Public Economics*, 15 (3): 295–310.

Minnich, E. (1990) *Transforming Knowledge*, Philadelphia, PA: Temple University Press.

Moghadam, V. (1993) *Democratic Reform and the Position of Women in Transitional Economies*, Oxford: Clarendon Press.

Montecinos, V. (2001) "Feminists and technocrats in the democratization of Latin America: a prolegomenon," *International Journal of Politics, Culture and Society*, 15 (1): 175–99.

Nelson, J. (1993) "Some consequences of conjective economics," in M. Ferber and J. Nelson (eds), *Beyond Economic Man: Feminist theory and economics*, Chicago, IL: University of Chicago Press.

O'Grady, M. (1997) "Don't blame the market for Argentina's woes," *Wall Street Journal*, May 30, 1997.

Ong, A. (1987) *Spirits of Resistance and Capitalist Discipline: women factory workers in Malaysia*, Albany, NY: SUNY Press.

Polanyi, K. (1957) [1944] *The Great Transformation*, Boston, MA: Beacon Press.

Pyle, J. (1983) "Export-led development and the underemployment of women: the impact of discriminatory employment policy in the Republic of Ireland," in J. Nash and M.P. Fernandez-Kelly (eds), *Women, Men and the International Division of Labor*, Albany, NY: SUNY Press, 85–112.

Salazar Parrenas, R. (2002) "The care crisis in the Philippines: children and transnational families in the new global economy," in B. Ehrenreich and A.R. Hochschild (eds), *Global Woman: nannies, maids and sex workers in the new economy*, New York: Henry Holt and Company, LLC.

Seguino, S. (2000) "Accounting for gender in Asian economic growth: adding gender to the equation," *Feminist Economics*, 6 (3): 27–58.

Seguino, S., Stevens, T., and Lutz, M. (1996) "Gender and cooperative behavior: economic man rides alone," *Feminist Economics*, 2 (1): 1–21.

Standing, G. (1989) "Global feminization through flexible labor," *World Development*, 17 (7): 1077–95.

——(1999) *Global Labour Flexibility: seeking distributive justice*, New York: St. Martin's Press.

Strassmann, D. (1993) "Not a free market: the rhetoric of disciplinary authority in economics," in M. Ferber and J. Nelson (eds), *Beyond Economic Man*, Chicago, IL: University of Chicago Press.

Strober, M. (1994) "Rethinking economics through a feminist lens," *American Economic Review*, 84 (2): 143–7.

Tilly, C., Wallerstein, I., Zolberg, A., Hobsbawm, E.J., and Beneria, L. (1995) "Scholarly controversy: global flows of labor and capital," *International Labor and Working-Class History*, 47 (Spring): 1–55.

Tohidi, N. (1996) "Guardians of the nation: women, Islam and Soviet modernization in Azerbaijan," paper presented at the conference on Women's Identities and Roles in the Course of Change, Ankara, Turkey, October 23–25, 1996.

UNDP (1995) *Human Development Report*, New York: Oxford University Press.

United Nations (1999) *Women Survey on the Role of Women in Development: globalization, gender and work*, New York: United Nations.

World Bank (1996) *From Plan to Market* (World Development Report), New York: Oxford University Press.

——(2000) *Making the Transition Work for Women and Central Asia*, Washington, DC: World Bank.

WuDunn, S. (1998) "Bankruptcy the Asian way," *The New York Times*, September 8, 1998.

3   Mainstream, heterodox, and feminist trade theory

Diane Elson, Caren Grown,
and Nilüfer Çağatay

Introduction

The system of rules and agreements that currently governs international trade is based on the view that expanding global trade is beneficial to all countries and their citizens. Trade liberalization, as part of a larger set of liberalization policies that increase the role of markets and reduce the role of states, is regarded as the key to such an expansion. These views derive from mainstream trade theory, which holds that specialization in production according to each nation's comparative advantage typically leads to a more efficient allocation of resources in the world economy, and consequently to higher levels of output and economic growth in all countries. It is recognized that trade liberalization creates both winners and losers within each country, but net gains are assumed overall, allowing losers to be compensated by government polices such as trade adjustment assistance.

Alternative (or heterodox) trade theories reject the idea that trade liberalization will lead to economic growth and improved allocation of national resources from inefficient import substitutes to more efficient exportable goods. Rather, alternative theories postulate that relative prices of international goods and hence a nation's terms of trade are regulated through a process of competition whereby the strongest actors use strategy to dominate the weaker actors. In this process, high-cost producers lose out to low-cost ones and high-cost countries tend to suffer trade deficits, which have to be covered by corresponding capital inflows or borrowing (Shaikh 2007). No magic mechanisms exist that will automatically result in balanced trade. Indeed, persistent trade imbalances covered by foreign capital flows are the norm of international trade between unequally competitive trade partners. International trade is seen as the "conduit of uneven development" (Çağatay 1994: 241). Powerful firms in countries that are already industrialized are able to influence the provisions of international trade agreements in their favor and to preserve their technological advantage through restrictive laws on patents.

Feminist theories of trade go beyond both mainstream and heterodox theories and explore the role that gender inequalities play in international competitiveness as well as the role that international competition plays in reshaping and reconstituting gender inequalities. For feminist economists, the question is not whether "free trade" is better than "some trade" or "no trade." Like heterodox theorists, feminist economists ask whose interests do specific trade practices serve

(Çağatay 1994: 243)? But they go beyond heterodox economists in considering outcome indicators that take into account differences in economic, social, and political power, between and within countries and along sex and other dimensions.

Feminist economists seek to assess the gendered impacts of trade reform and trade performance in terms of changing patterns and conditions of work, including paid and unpaid work; changes in gender gaps in wages, earnings, patterns of ownership, and control over assets; technical change, changes in consumption patterns, and use of technology by men and women; changes in public provisioning of services (through impacts on taxes and expenditures) and their gendered impacts, as well as the gender-differentiated empowerment implications of trade flows.

This chapter compares and contrasts mainstream and heterodox theories of international trade. It considers how gender analysis has been or might be incorporated into each type of trade theory, and which provides a better starting point for feminist trade theory. It is organized as follows. The first section considers mainstream trade theory, which is based on the theories of comparative advantage and perfect competition. It discusses whether the predictions of this theory are supported by empirical evidence and considers the so-called New Trade Theory that emphasizes departures from perfect competition but nevertheless considers comparative advantage to be a good basis for policy formulation. It also discusses two attempts to bring gender issues into mainstream trade theory. The second section examines heterodox theories of international trade based on post-Keynesian and Marxian concepts, which emphasize the difference between barter economies and monetary economies. These theories argue that trade is based on absolute advantage rather than comparative advantage and that competition should not be understood in terms of norms of perfect competition but in terms of a proactive search for competitive advantage. This section discusses empirical support for heterodox theory and argues that while heterodox theorists have not incorporated gender into their analysis, the heterodox approach provides a better basis for incorporating gender issues into trade theory. The third section of the chapter contributes to the development of a feminist-heterodox theory of trade by outlining the concept of "gendered competitive advantage" and discussing its relevance to trade liberalization in developing countries. A short conclusion summarizes the key points.

Mainstream theories: comparative advantage, trade, and gender

Mainstream assessments of trade liberalization are based on the belief that international trade works best if it is governed by the principle of comparative advantage. This principle implies that a country would always stand to gain from trade if it were to export the goods it could produce comparatively more cheaply at home, in exchange for those it could get comparatively more cheaply by importing from abroad. Thus even if one country can produce everything more cheaply than another country, both countries would benefit from trade, if there are differences in their comparative costs. As Krugman (1993) points out, this rests on the belief that the market will ensure that exports are exchanged for an equivalent amount of imports so that trade will be balanced. For the latter to hold, the terms of trade (or real exchange rate) of a country must fall whenever a country has a trade deficit, and the trade deficit must diminish in response. In addition, any loss of employment in the import-competing sector must be purely transitional, so that full employment is maintained in the longer run.

Explanations of differences in comparative costs are typically based on differences in relative factor endowments (the Hecksher–Ohlin–Samuelson theorem, hereafter referred to as H–O–S). This implies that a country with a relative abundance of labor will export labor-intensive goods and import capital-intensive goods. Two theorems associated with H–O–S – the Stolper–Samuelson Theorem (SS) and the Factor Price Equalization Theorem (FPE) – predict the distributive implications of trade liberalization within and across nations for owners of different "factors of production," such as labor and capital, or for skilled versus unskilled labor. At the most simplified level, if the two factors of production are capital and labor, trade liberalization should reduce the return on capital while increasing it on labor in developing countries. The opposite should occur in industrialized countries. SS thus predicts that trade liberalization should decrease income inequality in developing countries and increase it in developed countries. If the two factors of production are unskilled and skilled labor, trade liberalization should reduce the wage differentials between them in developing countries (whose comparative advantage is assumed to be in goods that make intensive use of unskilled labor), while in developed countries (whose comparative advantage is assumed to be in goods that make intensive use of skilled labor) the gaps should widen.[1] FPE also predicts that the real wage in developed and developing countries will, under certain conditions, converge at some intermediate point as wages of workers in developed countries fall and wages of workers in developing countries rise.

The versions of mainstream trade theory described here draw no direct relationship between trade flows and gender. Yet, they imply the following: since trade liberalization in developing countries should increase the return to unskilled labor, it should be particularly beneficial to women, since their main asset is unskilled labor, and they are more concentrated than men in unskilled jobs. Thus, mainstream trade theory would lead us to expect trade liberalization to contribute to reducing gender inequality in developing countries.

In spite of its preeminence, H–O–S has been widely criticized on both theoretical and empirical grounds. A review of the extensive theoretical arguments is beyond the scope of this chapter; for penetrating critiques, see Steedman (1979) and Subasat (2003). Suffice to note for the purposes of this chapter two issues. First, the assumptions of full employment and balanced trade are contrary to the workings of a capitalist economy (Çağatay 1991), where un- and under-employment are chronic features and trade imbalances can be sustained over long periods of time. Second, the assumption of perfect competition does not reflect the power struggle for market share between firms in a capitalist economy (Shaikh 1980 and 2007).

H–O–S and the related distributive theorems have also been challenged on empirical grounds for failing to predict trade patterns on a correct and consistent basis (Trefler 1995). H–O–S predicts that relatively capital (labor) abundant countries will export capital (labor) intensive commodities, so most trade should be between labor-abundant developing countries and capital-abundant developed countries. Yet, since the 1960s, both developed and developing countries have increased trade among rather than between themselves (Borkakoti 1998). As Trefler (1995: 1029) notes, "the theory correctly predicts the direction of... trade about 50 percent of the time, a success rate that is matched by a coin toss." Second, H–O–S predicts that, with trade liberalization, factor prices will equalize internally and internationally. However, there is no evidence of factor-price equalization (Leamer 1984; Bliss 1989; Wood 1994). Finally, time series evidence from Latin America in the 1980s and 1990s shows that trade is associated with an increase, not a decrease, in the relative demand for skilled labor and hence rising wage inequality within several countries in the region (Robbins 1996; Freeman 2005).[2]

Two collections of case studies that focus on the impact of liberalization on economic performance, inequality, and poverty in different countries find a diversity of outcomes (Ganuza *et al.* 2000; Taylor 2001).[3] In the introduction to the collection he edited, Taylor concludes that "diversity of outcomes is a result in itself." He adds that

> the evidence certainly shows that in the post-liberalization era few if any of the countries considered seem to have found a sustainable growth path. Employment growth has generally been slow to dismal and rising primary income disparity (in some cases over and above the already high levels of income inequality) has been the rule.
>
> (Taylor 2001: 9)

To be fair, mainstream theory does recognize that trade liberalization produces "losers" alongside "winners" and the redistributive effects can be large in relation to the size of overall gains. For everyone in a country to gain from trade liberalization, the state must redistribute benefits from winners to losers.[4] However, there is no consideration of the fact that trade liberalization itself reduces the fiscal capacity of the state by reducing the revenue from trade taxes. For instance, in the studies cited earlier, Taylor (2001) and Ganuza *et al.* (2000) show that in most instances the state lacked the administrative or fiscal capacity to counter the adverse social consequences of liberalization. Khattry and Rao (2002) have also found that trade liberalization in poor countries has undermined capacity to collect tax revenue.

Gender and recent mainstream analyses

Until recently, mainstream trade theory has been gender-blind. In light of evidence that the impact of trade liberalization varies, both across countries and across different segments of the population, a few mainstream economists now take some account of these differences. For example, Winters (2000) proposes a method of analyzing the effects of trade and trade policy on poverty in developing countries, starting with a stylized "farm household" as the economic unit that makes consumption, production, and labor supply decisions. He analyzes the effects of trade reform through their impact on the price of goods or services the household sells or consumes. Whether trade reforms are anti-poor or pro-poor depends on the relative effects of these prices. Although Winters acknowledges other aspects of poverty, he adopts an absolute consumption approach as the simplest way to consider the impact of trade. He also breaks new ground by paying some attention to gender-based inequalities within households.

Winters proposes a number of questions that policy makers ought to investigate, such as whether reform is likely to create or destroy effective markets, whether its spillovers are concentrated on areas/activities of relevance to people living in poverty, whether success depends on people's ability to take risks, and how the reform might affect government revenues. He provides a checklist that contains the following questions, among others, to guide policy makers:

- Will the effects of changes in border prices be passed through to the rest of the economy?
- Is reform likely to destroy effective markets or create them and allow poor consumers to obtain new goods?
- Is it likely to affect different household members differently?
- Will its spillovers be concentrated on areas/activities of relevance to the poor?
- What factors are used most intensively in the most affected sectors? What will be the mix of wage and employment effects? Will wages exceed poverty levels?
- Will it lead to discontinuous switches in activities? If so, will the new activities be riskier than the old ones?
- Does the reform depend upon, or affect, the ability of the poor to take risks?
- If the reform is broad and systemic, will any growth it stimulates be particularly disequalizing?
- Will the reform imply major shocks for particular localities?

Even though Winters recognizes that the impact of trade on poverty differs across countries, making policy prescriptions for one country unsuitable for others, he argues that trade liberalization is "a strongly positive contributor to poverty alleviation – it allows people to exploit their productive potential, assists economic growth, curtails arbitrary policy interventions and helps insulate against shocks." He adds, "most reforms will create some losers (some even in the long run) and that some reforms could exacerbate poverty temporarily" but argues, "in these circumstances policy should seek to alleviate the hardships caused rather than abandon reform altogether" (Winters 2000: 43).

Although Winters recognizes intra-household gender inequalities, his analysis leaves out several questions that are crucial for assessing the links between trade, poverty, and gender. For example, he notes that trade reform may increase women's overall work burden, but he does not include this as a specific question in his checklist for policy makers. And while he asks whether the success of reforms depends on the ability of poor people to take risks, he does not ask whether men and women have differential capacities for, or attitudes toward, risk-taking because of gender-based differences in control over resources and responsibilities in provisioning.[5]

Similarly, Winters' analysis does not sufficiently address the significance of other policies that mediate the influence of trade reform. Although he considers the possibility that trade reforms may lead to reduced government revenues and includes this question in his checklist, he does not address the consequences of reduced fiscal capacity (noted earlier) and the introduction of regressive revenue measures, such as user fees and sales taxes, with adverse consequences for poor people, especially women. The checklist does not address whether women or the poor have institutional mechanisms for voicing their interests. In practice, trade liberalization is accompanied by other policies, such as capital account liberalization and labor market deregulation, that may make it more difficult for poor people or for women to organize effectively to articulate their interests (Elson and Çağatay 2000). Finally, it does not address whether trade reform and the incentives it creates lead to changes in production relations such as reduction of workers' rights within the workplace or to increased appropriation of women's unpaid labor within households to produce export crops for which men receive the payment.

Other mainstream theorists have also recently begun to pay attention to gender differences in trade outcomes. Beyond arguing that women stand to gain more than do men from trade liberalization on the basis of H–O–S and its distributive theorems, Jagdish Bhagwati (2004) argues that trade liberalization also benefits women by reducing pro-male labor market discrimination. He relies upon the theory of discrimination put forward by Becker (1971) who argues that discrimination by employers is a market imperfection that is rooted in prejudiced preferences, such as a "taste" for employing men and for paying them more than women, even though men are not more productive. However, such prejudice has costs since it implies that the male wage is higher than the competitive wage (which is defined as equal to the value of marginal productivity of labor). This implies that discriminating firms have higher labor costs than nondiscriminating firms. Becker argues that with sufficient time and strong enough competition, nondiscriminating firms will out-compete discriminating firms and discrimination will wither away.

Bhagwati (2004) extends Becker's theory in the context of international trade. He postulates a closed national economy in which all domestic firms share a prejudice against women to the same extent. In this case, discrimination will not disadvantage any particular firm. If not all foreign firms share this prejudice, when the economy is opened to trade, nondiscriminating foreign firms will be able to supply the market more cheaply than discriminating domestic firms, putting pressure on the latter to change their behavior and reduce the wage premium paid to men. He therefore concludes that "The gender wage gap will narrow in the industries that must compete with imports produced by unprejudiced firms elsewhere" (Bhagwati 2004: 75). Even if foreign firms are no less prejudiced than domestic firms, but they have other cost advantages, opening the economy to trade will still put pressure on domestic firms to abandon their prejudices against women, since, by assumption, this prejudice raises their costs.

Bhagwati finds confirmation of his argument in the empirical findings of Black and Brainerd (2004) on the decline of the gender wage gap in the USA between 1976–93, but as Kongar (this volume) shows, their argument is flawed, and the decline can be explained by other factors. Specifically, the fall in gender wage inequality is most likely the effect of the disproportionate loss of employment for low-wage women, which increased the average wages of women who remained employed and thus narrowed the gender wage gap.

Bhagwati might also have appealed to the reduction in the gender employment gap to support his argument. Becker's theory implies that women's share of employment will be less than it would be in the absence of employer's prejudice in favor of men. As documented in this volume and elsewhere, women's share of paid employment has risen in most developing countries in the last two decades, corresponding to a period of trade liberalization. In a pioneering article, Elson and Pearson (1981) drew attention to women's increased employment in "world market factories" and the role gender played in the constitution of a perceived "docile" and low-paid labor force in export-oriented production. Since then, many studies have confirmed the association between export-oriented manufacturing and women's employment, both within and across countries, especially in the early stages of export-oriented growth (e.g. Standing 1989, 1999; Wood 1991; Çağatay and Özler 1995; Joekes 1995, 1999). Reviewing evidence from a variety of sources, Joekes (1995) concludes: "In the contemporary era no strong export performance in manufactures by any developing country has ever been secured without reliance on female labor" (1995: 3).

However, these studies do not necessarily substantiate the claim that trade liberalization has reduced discrimination against women. Labor market discrimination against women is not best understood as a preference for hiring men that reduces competition and profitability through paying men a wage higher than male marginal productivity. Rather, feminist economists argue that competition and labor markets do not work in the way that mainstream theory suggests (Figart 1999). Labor markets are segmented rather than unified, and competition does not tend to produce wages that are equal to marginal products. Gendered social norms and bargaining power help to determine the pattern of labor use and wages in developed and developing economies (Elson 1999).

One important way in which discrimination works is through crowding women into a narrow range of occupations. This occurs both through demand-side factors, with firms considering women best suited to these occupations and men better suited for all the other occupations, and through supply-side factors, with women's experience of discrimination outside the labor market, women's social responsibility for unpaid domestic work, and the pressure of social norms predisposing them to seek jobs in this narrow range of occupations. As Bergmann (1974) argues, this labor market crowding drives down women's wages below what they would otherwise be in the absence of occupational segregation. Thus, labor market discrimination against women may enhance, rather than weaken, the competitive position of firms by reducing their money costs. Firms may reinforce occupational segregation with low pay for "women's work" and through the rules and procedures they adopt for job evaluation, hiring and firing, and promotion.

Such discrimination has implications for trade. As Seguino (2000: 1214) points out:

> job segregation that crowds women into export industries where price elasticities of demand are relatively high may artificially lower women's wages, due to their restricted bargaining power. The resulting gender wage differentials (taking the male wage as a benchmark) may be a stimulus to export expansion.

Seguino's econometric cross-country study of semi-industrialized economies in the period 1975–95 confirmed that this was the case (Seguino 2000), and her detailed case study of South Korea found that discriminatory practices were part of the competitive strategies of Korean firms in Korea's export-led growth (Seguino 1997). In a more recent study, the gender wage gap has been found to be positively and significantly associated with the share of labor-intensive manufactures in exports in a sample of 38 developed as well as developing countries in the period 1975–2000 (Busse and Spielman 2005).

An adequate theoretical framework for examining trade and gender would be built on a different view of competition, one that takes account of the issues raised by Bergmann and Seguino. Indeed, the mismatch between the predictions of mainstream trade theory and the results of empirical investigations has led to increasing attempts to incorporate departures from "perfect competition" in mainstream trade theory. One example is the development of New Trade Theory (NTT), which incorporates assumptions such as imperfect competition and increasing returns to scale and emphasizes technical change, technological gaps, technology transfer, innovation, product cycles, and the like (see, for example, Krugman 1990).

Yet, even with these new features, NTT still relies on assumptions of full employment and balanced trade. Although there may be a role for government policy to enhance competitiveness of certain industries, presumably affecting the composition of trade, "there are strong equilibrating forces that normally ensure that any country remains able to sell a range of goods in world markets, and to balance its trade on average over the long run, even if its productivity, technology and product quality are inferior to those of other nations" (Krugman 1991: 811). In the end, even among NTT theories, H–O–S still maintains its supremacy in underpinning policy formulation.

For example, Paul Krugman, one of NTT's principal architects, justifies the mental space that H–O–S occupies among policy makers and in academia. In an article titled "Is Free Trade Passé?" (Krugman 1987) he answers this question with a definite no, on the grounds that it provides a simple rule of thumb for policy that is more often right than wrong. Thus, NTT simply adds additional factors to explain the empirical trade patterns that differ from theoretical predictions, but does not abandon the idea, based on comparative advantage, that free trade is optimal (Çağatay 1994: 244).

In our view, the NTT has no particular features that make it a more useful framework than mainstream trade theory – even with Winters' innovations – for feminist concerns. In the field of international trade, a more adequate formulation of competition and discrimination is provided by Marxian and post-Keynesian theories that explain trade through a theory of absolute advantage, rather than comparative advantage, and focus on the acquisition of competitive advantage rather than on perfect competition. We turn to these next.

Heterodox trade theories: absolute advantage and capital accumulation

There are a number of heterodox approaches to international trade, including theories of uneven development and unequal exchange (e.g. Singer 1950) and theories of balance of payments constrained growth (McCombie and Thirlwall 1994). Here we focus on the Marxian and post-Keynesian challenge to comparative advantage, in both its positive form (i.e. the theory's ability to predict patterns of international trade) and in its normative form (i.e. the theory's ability to provide a good guide for policy). This challenge rejects the underlying assumptions of full employment, perfect competition, and an automatic price adjustment mechanism that brings about balanced trade in each period. As Milberg (1994: 227) points out, both Marxian and post-Keynesian theories posit that the effect of an initial trade imbalance will be on interest rates and incomes, not on relative prices. This reflects the view in both traditions that production in a capitalist economy is an inherently monetary process and that unemployment and excess capacity are inherent features of the economy, not merely transitional features.[6]

We focus specifically on two recent contributions to this literature by William Milberg and Anwar Shaikh.[7] Milberg (1994) and Shaikh (2007) start from the fact that the empirical evidence does not support the orthodox claim that trade liberalization leads to balanced trade between countries. Balance of payment imbalances have persisted for long periods, especially in the period since 1980.[8] They critique the theory of comparative advantage using insights from Marx and Keynes. Milberg's approach might be considered more "Post-Keynesian" in that he emphasizes deficient aggregate demand and technology gaps between countries, while Shaikh's approach might be considered more "Marxian" in that he emphasizes the specific characteristics of capitalist competition and technology gaps between firms.

Milberg (1994: 227) argues that even if wages are infinitely elastic, trade imbalances will not necessarily be eliminated because there is no guarantee that countries with trade surpluses will spend the currency they accumulate on goods and services produced by trade deficit countries. Milberg proposes a model of trade based on the principle of absolute advantage in production, in which trade is based on absolute differences in money costs.[9] These differences are governed by technology gaps, wage gaps, and demand gaps. Demand has an impact on money costs through its impact on dynamic economies of scale at the sectoral level. Milberg describes his model as "an input-output, vent-for-surplus model in which scarcity of demand – not resources – is the key component" (Milberg 1994: 231). He concludes that there is no guarantee that a country's industries will be competitive in international markets, if trade is liberalized. So, while the comparative advantage approach assumes that all countries will have a comparative advantage in production of some good, the absolute advantage approach recognizes that some countries may not have an absolute advantage in any good. If governments do not introduce policies to reduce technology gaps, then they are left with low wages as their only competitive strategy. Such policies should be firmly in place before trade is liberalized.

Shaikh (2007) does not focus so much on demand as on conditions of competitive production. He argues that it is not the real world that is "imperfect" in the way it lives up to trade theory, but rather that the theory itself is inadequate. He emphasizes that the Classical tradition in economics has a different understanding of competition, as a process of proactive struggle rather than as a state of optimal adjustment to given circumstances. "Firms utilize strategy and tactics to gain and hold market share, and price cutting and cost reductions are major features in this constant struggle" (Shaikh 2007: 57). He proposes an alternative trade theory, one that is based on the principle of "competitive (absolute) advantage." From this perspective, trade within and between countries is driven by absolute costs: firms with lower unit costs of production out-compete firms with higher unit costs of production.

Shaikh claims there is no mechanism that equalizes competitive power between the firms in different national economies. For that to happen the terms of trade would have to be free to adjust automatically to eliminate trade imbalances; that, in turn, requires that the underlying costs of production in each country be free to adjust. He argues that this is not the case, because the costs of production "depend on real wages and productivity, and while international trade affects these, they also have many other social and historical determinants" (Shaikh 2007: 57). Technological differences are particularly important. The outcome is that trade between unequal partners will be "normally" accompanied by persistent trade imbalances covered by foreign capital flows. Shaikh (2007: 57) concludes that international trade "exposes the weak to the competition of the strong. And in most such cases, the latter devour the former." He suggests that trade liberalization will principally benefit developed country firms since they are the most advanced technologically, and concludes that trade liberalization is promoted to achieve precisely that result. He advocates that governments should first put in place policies to make individual industries sufficiently competitive in world markets before considering trade liberalization.

Empirical evidence supports some of the key features of the absolute advantage approach. For instance, a large empirical literature on technology gaps and export performance finds that technology gap variables are significant in most industries, though price variables are often not significant (Fagerberg 1996). In addition, large firms with headquarters in developed countries are responsible for a growing share of world trade (OECD 2002: 159). Cross-border trade between transnational corporations (TNCs) and their affiliates accounts for around one-third of exports of goods from Japan and USA (OECD 2002: 163). The shares of affiliates of foreign-owned TNCs are high in trade between developed countries and middle-income industrializing countries. For instance, in 2000, two-thirds of US imports from Mexico were from affiliates of US firms (OECD 2002: 164).

Neither Milberg (1994) nor Shaikh (2007) considers the implications of trade for inequalities within countries. Both papers judge the impact of trade policy in terms of market criteria, such as the ability of lower-income countries to "catch up" with higher-income ones. However, Milberg and Houston (2005) subsequently carried out research on the relation between international competitiveness and "social gaps," as indicated by national differences in social protection and labor relations. They found no clear negative relation between unit labor costs and international competitiveness among OECD countries in the period 1973–95. More generous social spending and more cooperative labor relations (in which bargaining between employees and employers was more centralized and institutionalized) were not always linked to low competitiveness (as indicated, for example, by growth in share of export markets). Countries achieved international competitiveness in a variety of ways. Higher public spending and higher wages, if combined with innovation and rapid productivity growth, could be consistent with a strong trade performance.

The Marxist and neo-Keynesian theoretical frameworks utilized by both Shaikh (2007) and Milberg (1994) provide openings for the incorporation of gender inequality. First, they both recognize the specificity of particular kinds of social relation of production and distribution: capitalist economies do not function like barter economies. This provides an entry point for the feminist account of the particularities of specific gender regimes, and economies as gendered institutions in which labor markets are segmented by sex and women have less bargaining power than men (Elson 1999). Second, as implied by Shaikh, the underlying theory of wage determination recognizes that labor is not like any other commodity. It is sold in the market but it is not produced for the market. Rather, it is produced by a nonmarket process, subject to social and historical determinants. This provides an opening for the feminist account of the production of labor whereby most unpaid work caring for families and communities is allocated to women and girls, which enables firms to avoid paying the full costs of the reproduction of labor (Picchio 1992; Folbre 2001). Third, as Shaikh and Milberg emphasize, costs are not determined by "given" endowments of factors of production and knowledge, but by active, socially and historically shaped processes of technology and knowledge creation, and acquisition of rights and bargaining power. This provides an opening for the feminist account of the social and historical shaping of gender differences in knowledge, rights, and command over resources (Agarwal 1994; Goetz and Gupta 1996; Huyer 2004; Deere and Doss 2006). Fourth, as Milberg notes, capitalist economic processes are contradictory. They produce more income in total, but in conditions that necessarily exclude some people from sharing in it, owing to systematic unemployment. This provides an opening for the feminist account of the multidimensionality of economic change, which cannot be reduced to simple trade-offs or cost-benefit ratios (Kabeer 1994; Elson 2007), and of the contradictory relation between capitalist economic growth and the process of social reproduction (Humphries and Rubery 1984; Walters 1995).

Much more work could be done to produce a feminist-heterodox economics of international trade that takes absolute, not comparative, advantage as its point of departure. The next section contributes by sketching a way to analyze competitive advantage as a gendered process.

Feminist-heterodox theories of trade: gendered competitive advantage and trade liberalization in developing countries

The acquisition of competitive advantage is a gendered process. In examining it, we need to distinguish between the ways in which gender inequality shapes the roles of women as achievers of competitive advantage and as sources of competitive advantage. The former refers to women as owners of businesses, employing other people, and as own-account, self-employed producers; the second refers to women as unpaid family workers and wageworkers contributing to businesses run by others, largely men.

To achieve competitive advantage, a business-owner or own-account producer needs access to land, technology, knowledge, finance, a labor supply, social networks, freedom from other demands on their time, markets, and a favorable policy environment, including tax breaks/subsidies and regulations. Social inequalities structure this access and the use that can be made of these resources. The relation between the acquisition of competitive advantage and social inequalities is cumulative and self-reinforcing. In a society marked by gender inequality, it is harder for women to gain access to all these resources and often deep cultural barriers prevent women from using them to compete against men in the market place. The gender gaps, which permeate the acquisition of competitive advantage, are related to the socially constructed division of labor in the unpaid care economy. When women business-owners or own-account producers achieve a competitive advantage, it is often in a niche market, at the local level, where competition is limited.

Women predominate as owners of microenterprises and as own-account workers in food production in many poor countries, especially in sub-Saharan Africa and Southeast Asia. They produce for their own families and also sell surpluses in local markets. Feminist-heterodox trade theory would predict that cutting tariffs and other barriers to food imports in poor countries is likely to expose women small-scale food producers to competition from foreign agribusinesses, and that the latter would be likely to have the competitive advantage. Studies have found that trade liberalization in smallholder agricultural economies does lead to rises in imports of food and loss of markets for women farmers producing food crops (Fontana *et al.* 1998; UNCTAD 2004: chapter 3). If new opportunities emerge with trade liberalization, women farmers find it hard to take advantage of them, as they often lack access to credit, new technologies, knowledge on marketing, and it is harder for them to take on new risks. Reviewing a range of studies, Joekes (1999) finds that trade liberalization in economies where women are mainly engaged in small-scale business-ownership and own-account production has more adverse consequences for women's livelihoods than it does in economies where there are more opportunities for wage labor. This supports the view that gender inequality positions women more as sources of competitive advantage for male-owned businesses than as achievers of competitive advantage themselves.

Women are a source of competitive advantage for producers using labor-intensive production methods because of gender gaps in power in households and labor markets. In smallholder production of traditional agricultural cash crops for export (such as tea, coffee, and cocoa), women tend to work as unpaid family labor under the direction of their male relatives, to whom the cash is paid; they also produce food on their own account. If trade liberalization increases market access for traditional cash crop exports, and production is expanded, the household may get more income, but the effects for women are contradictory (UNCTAD 2004: chapter 3). The extent to which they share in the increased income depends on their intra-household bargaining power. Insofar as food imports deprive women of markets for their surplus production, they may be willing to become unpaid family labor on export crops. But they will be exposed to new risks, as their ability to feed their families depends both on the relative prices of food imports and exports of cash crops and on their ability to secure income transfers from their husbands (see Darity this volume).

The production of non-traditional agricultural exports (NTAEs) such as fruit, vegetables, and flowers is growing in many developing countries. Rural women are sources of competitive advantage for the large-scale domestic farmers and foreign agribusinesses that produce and trade NTAEs. UNCTAD (2004) documents how trade liberalization has created jobs for women in NTAEs but notes that women are much more likely than men to be employed in low-wage insecure seasonal jobs, with no social protection, all of which reduce firms' costs (UNCTAD 2004: 112). NTAEs are typically not traded between arms-length buyers and sellers, but as part of global production systems dominated by large agribusinesses or developed country retailers (see Barrientos this volume). Competitive advantage for the system lies with combining modern technology in transport and marketing with cheap, disposable labor in agricultural production.

Similar factors are at work in the manufacturing sector in semi-industrialized developing countries, where large-scale producers or retailers, whose headquarters are in developed countries, produce labor-intensive exports in developing countries or subcontract such production to locally owned firms. Again, competitive advantage of such systems in the world market lies in the combination of modern technology in transport and marketing with use of cheap labor; and it accrues to transnational firms (see Barrientos this volume). Women workers are incorporated into the global production systems as factory workers (Razavi 1999) and also as subcontracted outworkers who produce in small workshops or their own homes (Carr *et al.* 2000; Balakrishnan 2002). As is well known, in labor intensive manufacturing the labor force is mainly female (Joekes 1995). Although export expansion in semi-industrialized countries seems to advantage women in terms of availability of wage employment, the competitive advantage of the local subcontracted firms that employ them depends greatly on women's lower pay and poorer conditions, compared to men.

Wage employment for women in NTAES and in export-oriented manufacturing is contradictory for women (Elson and Pearson 1981). Old structures of gender inequality tend to be undermined, as women work outside the home and earn an income of their own. But new structures of gender inequality are constructed, in which women are crowded into a few occupations on disadvantageous terms. Moreover, women who make gains on some criteria, such as employment, may be losing in other dimensions, such as time for leisure and sleep.

Underpinning gender inequalities in the labor market is the pursuit of competitive advantage through avoidance of paying the full costs of the reproduction of the labor force (Folbre 2001: chapter 8). Firms may actively seek competitive advantage by choosing a labor force that is minimally responsible for caring for children (i.e. men and childless women) or by penalizing employees who have care responsibilities by paying them less and not providing social protection (i.e. sequestering women employees in temporary, part-time, and precarious jobs). Firms may also seek jurisdictions where they do not pay taxes that support public health, education, and care services. The prevalence of such strategies makes it impossible for women to enter the labor market on an equal footing with men, irrespective of the personal prejudices (or lack of them) of employers. Such strategies are also contradictory in the longer run for business as a whole, undermining the conditions for reproducing a well-educated, healthy labor force and a stable and secure society in which people respect one another.

Policy issues

Resolving these contradictions requires collective action and multidimensional public policy. Measures are needed to promote sharing the responsibility for unpaid care work equally between women and men in households, to ensure that employers recognize and accommodate workers' domestic responsibilities, and to provide quality care and other services through state agencies, businesses, or community organizations. This will require providing a structure of incentives and penalties that guide businesses away from short-term competitive advantage, toward strategies that are more compatible with sustainable people-centered societies (UNDP 1999: chapter 3; Folbre 2001). An environment of free trade cannot provide this guidance. Trade policy needs to be sequenced with other policies that will reduce gender gaps, including the care gap. The prioritizing and sequencing of the policy mix will be country-specific and is likely to be different for agrarian, semi-industrialized, and industrialized countries.

Governments may change policy if they realize that reliance on the cheap labor of women as the main source of competitive advantage in the lower tiers of global production systems has disadvantages for the national economy. Reliance on cheap labor and little social protection is a strategy that can trap local firms and national economies on a "low-road" development path. This strategy can hinder the transition to a "high-road" development path, which involves improving productivity through technical innovation and skill development. "Low-road" firms and economies find it difficult to compete when other lower-cost producers enter the market. Bangladesh, for instance, is being undercut by China in textile and garment exports since it lost the trade preferences conferred by the Multi-Fibre Arrangement, which came to an end in January 2005.

However, it is possible that women's employment may be jeopardized in firms and countries that decide to switch to the "high road" to improve productivity and quality of output. This has occurred in the later stages of export-led growth in some developing countries (notably Mexico and Taiwan) where the mix of export products changed and occupational segregation prevented women from entering the higher-skilled, more capital-intensive jobs. The challenge is to ensure that women workers participate equally in the "high road."

Conclusions

This chapter has argued that although gender concerns can be incorporated into mainstream trade theory, this does not provide a satisfactory foundation for a feminist theory of trade that is concerned with the question, "Whose interests do specific trade practices serve?" A better starting point is heterodox trade theory, which allows for systematic imbalances in economic power and does not assume that economies tend toward a state of full employment equilibrium with balanced trade.

Combining a feminist and a heterodox perspective on trade enables us to go beyond mapping which men and women lose and which gain in terms of employment and incomes. It enables us to identify the social relations through which production and distribution take place and are transformed as firms seek competitive advantage in the world market. Women's lack of economic power as business owners and own-account producers is likely to put them at a competitive disadvantage in the process of trade liberalization and to propel them into becoming a source of competitive advantage as cheap labor for others. But the same lack of economic power gives firms who hire them a competitive advantage. Many women may enjoy higher incomes as employees than as owners of small businesses and as own-account producers, but they also lose much of the freedom to organize their own time.

More work is needed to develop formal feminist-heterodox models and quantitative analysis of trade that investigate the role of gender inequality in determining patterns of trade and international competitiveness. Next steps might include incorporating gender in technology and demand gaps model of determination of exports, such as those used by Milberg (1994), or to develop specific gender gap indicators that can be included as a social gap in cross-country regression analysis, again building upon Milberg and Houston (2005).

Policies to support the reduction of gender inequality in earnings by raising women's pay could be complementary to the trade policies called for by heterodox economists like Milberg and Shaikh. By restricting the availability of competitive strategies focused on cutting labor costs, they could create pressure for innovations to improve productivity and reduce technological gaps. They could also help reduce demand gaps through supporting the development of mass markets by increasing women's purchasing power. However, such policies could backfire for women if they lead to the defeminization of the labor force, and increases in women's unemployment rates, already higher than those of men in most regions of the world (ILO 2004). If the technology-focused trade polices recommended by heterodox economists are to be equally beneficial to women as to men, they must be accompanied by measures to reduce occupational segregation by sex, increase women's access to technical skills, and expand decent jobs for women in the non-tradable sector.

Notes

1 The predictions of SS become more complicated as factors and countries are added to the model.
2 Marquez and Pages (1998) estimate labor demand models with panel data for eighteen Latin American countries and find that trade reforms had a negative effect on employment growth.
3 In practice, it is difficult to separate out the impact of trade liberalization, since it is often accompanied by capital account liberalization as well as macroeconomic stabilization policies.
4 Mainstream trade theory is based on several unrealistic assumptions, for example, constant returns to scale, full employment, perfect mobility of labor and capital, perfect competition in all markets, given technology, and smooth substitution between factors of production. If these are violated, predictions about trade flow determinants will not hold. In particular, cases arise where both factors of production can lose or gain together. While more complex theories yield indeterminate results with regard to distributive effects, most policy discourses ignore these complications (see Ocampo *et al.* 1998).
5 Floro and Seguino (2002) have noted gender differences in risk-seeking behavior.
6 For a discussion of the trade theory of Keynes and Marx, see Milberg (2002).
7 Heterodox theories recognize labor market segmentation and asymmetric bargaining power of different groups in the workforce, which play important roles in the determination of competitiveness. The articles we discuss here, however, do not focus on these issues.
8 A study of 22 developing countries that have adopted trade liberalization policies since the mid-1970s found that liberalization stimulated export growth, but raised import growth by more, leading to a worsening balance of payments (Santos-Paulino and Thirlwall 2004).
9 Authors outside the Marxian and Post-Keynesian tradition have also defended the principle of absolute advantage; see Macdonald and Markusen (1985) and Jones (1980).

References

Agarwal, B. (1994) *A Field of One's Own: gender and land rights in South Asia*, Cambridge: Cambridge University Press.

Balakrishnan, R. (ed.) (2002) *The Hidden Assembly Line: gender dimensions of sub-contracted work in the global economy*, Bloomfield: Kumarian Press.

Barrientos, S. (2007) "Gender, codes of conduct, and labor standards in global production systems," in I. van Staveren, D. Elson, C. Grown, and N. Çağatay (eds), *Feminist Economics of Trade*, London: Routledge.

Becker, G.S. (1971) *The Economics of Discrimination*, Chicago and London: University of Chicago Press.

Bergmann, B.R. (1974) "Occupational segregation, wages and profits when employers discriminate by race or sex," *Eastern Economic Journal*, 1 (2/3): 103–10.

Bhagwati, J. (2004) *In Defense of Globalization*, New York and Oxford: Oxford University Press.

Black, S. and Brainerd, B. (2004) "Improving equality? The impact of globalization on gender discrimination," *Industrial and Labor Relations Review*, 57 (4): 540–59.

Bliss, C. (1989) "Trade and development," in H. Chenery and T.N. Srinivasan (eds.), *Handbook of Development Economics*, vol. 2, Amsterdam: North-Holland.

Borkakoti, J. (1998) *International Trade: causes and consequences*. London: Macmillan.

Busse, M. and Spielmann, C. (2005) "Gender inequality and trade," HWWA Discussion Paper 308, Hamburg: Hamburg Institute of International Economics.

Çağatay, N. (1991) "Ricardo's Theory of International Trade Distribution and Accumulation Revisited," unpublished ms, University of Utah, Department of Economics.

—— (1994) "Themes in Marxian and Post-Keynesian theories of international trade: a consideration with respect to New Trade Theory," in M. Glick (ed.), *Competition, Technology and Money, Classical and Post-Keynesian Perspectives*, Cheltenham: Edward Elgar.

Çağatay, N. and Özler, S. (1995) "Feminization of the labor force: the effects of long-term economic development and structural adjustment," *World Development*, 23 (8): 1183–94.

Carr, M., Chen, M., and Tate, J. (2000) "Globalization and home-based workers," *Feminist Economics*, 6 (3): 123–42.

Darity, Jr, W. (2007) "The formal structure of a gender-segregated low-income economy," in I. van Staveren, D. Elson, C. Grown, and N. Çağatay (eds), *Feminist Economics of Trade*, London: Routledge.

Deere, C.D. and Doss, C. (2006) "The gender asset gap: what do we know and why does it matter?" *Feminist Economics*, 12 (1–2): 1–50.

Elson, D. (1996) "Appraising recent developments in the world market for nimble fingers: accumulation, regulation, organization," in A. Chaacchi and R. Pittin (eds), *Confronting State, Capital and Patriarchy: women organizing in the process of industrialization*, Basingstoke: Macmillan/Institute for Social Studies.

—— (1999) "Labour markets as gendered institutions: equality, efficiency and empowerment," *World Development*, 27 (3): 611–27.

—— (2007) "The changing economic and political participation of women: hybridization, reversals and contradictions in the context of globalization," in I. Lenz, C. Ullrich, and B. Fersch (eds), *Gender Orders Unbound*, Leverkusen Opladen: Barbara Budrich Publishers.

Elson, D. and Çağatay, N. (2000) "The social content of macroeconomic policies," *World Development*, 28 (7): 1347–64.

Elson, D. and Pearson, R. (1981) "Nimble fingers make cheap workers," *Feminist Review*, 7: 87–107.

Fagerberg, J. (1996) "Technology and competitiveness," *Oxford Review of Economic Policy*, 12 (3): 39–51.

Figart, D.M. (1999) "Discrimination, Theories of," in J. Peterson and M. Lewis (eds), *The Elgar Companion to Feminist Economics*, Cheltenham and Massachusetts: Edward Elgar.

Floro, M. and Seguino, S. (2002) "Gender effects on aggregate savings: a theoretical and empirical analysis," *Policy Research Paper on Gender and Development*, 23, Washington, DC: World Bank.

Folbre, N. (2001) *The Invisible Heart, Economics and Family Values*, New York: The New Press.

Fontana, M., Joekes, S., and Masika, R. (1998) "Global trade expansion and liberalization: gender issues and impacts," *Bridge Report No. 42*, Brighton: Institute of Development Studies.

Freeman, R. (2005) "What really ails Europe (and America): the doubling of the global workforce," *The Globalist* (3 June 2005).

Ganuza, E., Taylor, L., and Vos, R. (eds) (2000) *External Liberalization and Economic Performance in Latin America and the Caribbean*, New York: Oxford University Press.

Goetz, A. and Gupta, R. (1996) "Who takes the credit? Gender power and control over loan use in rural credit programs in Bangladesh," *World Development*, 24 (1): 45–63.

Humphries, J. and Rubery, J. (1984) "The reconstitution of the supply side of the labour market: the relative autonomy of social reproduction," *Cambridge Journal of Economics*, 8: 331–46.

Huyer, S. (2004) *Gender, Science and Technology from an International Perspective*, Washington, DC: Office of Science and Technology of the Organisation of American States.

International Labour Organization (ILO) (2004) *Global Employment Trends for Women*, Geneva: ILO.

Joekes, S. (1995) "Trade-related employment for women in industry and services in developing countries," Occasional Paper 5, Geneva: UNRISD.

—— (1999) "A gender-analytical perspective on trade and sustainable development," in UNCTAD, *Trade, Sustainable Development and Gender*, New York and Geneva: UNCTAD.

Jones, R. (1980) "Comparative and absolute advantage," *Swiss Journal of Economics and Statistics*, 3: 235–60.

Kabeer, N. (1994) *Reversed Realities: gender hierarchies in development*, London: Verso.

Khattry, B. (2003) "Trade liberalisation and the fiscal squeeze: implications for public investment," *Development and Change*, 34 (3): 401–24.

Khattry, B. and Rao, J.M. (2002) "Fiscal faux pas: an analysis of the revenue implications of trade liberalization," *World Development*, 30 (8): 1431–44.

Kongar, E. (2007) "Importing equality or exporting jobs? Competition and gender wage and employment differentials in U.S. manufacturing," in I. van Staveren, D. Elson, C. Grown, and N. Çağatay (eds), *Feminist Economics of Trade*, London: Routledge.

Krugman, P.R. (1987) "Is free trade passé?" *Journal of Economic Perspectives*, 1 (2): 131–44.

—— (1990) *Rethinking International Trade*, Cambridge, MA: MIT Press.

—— (1991) "Myths and realities of US competitiveness," *Science*, V: 254.

—— (1993) "What do undergrads need to know about trade?" *The American Economic Review*, Papers and Proceedings of the Hundred and Fifth Annual Meeting, 83 (2): 23–6.

Leamer, E.E. (1984) *Sources of International Comparative Advantage: theory and evidence*, Cambridge, MA: MIT Press.

McCombie, J. and Thirlwall, A. (1994) *Economic Growth and the Balance-of-Payments Constraint*, London: Palgrave Macmillan.

Macdonald, G. and Markusen, J. (1985) "A rehabilitation of absolute advantage," *Journal of Political Economy*, 93: 277–97.

Marquez, G. and Pages, C. (1998) "Trade and employment: evidence from Latin America and Caribbean," Working Paper No. 366, Washington, DC: Inter-American Development Bank Research Department.

Milberg, W. (1994) "Is absolute advantage *passé*? Towards a Post-Keynesian/Marxian theory of international trade," in M. Glick (ed.), *Competition, Technology and Money, Classical and Post-Keynesian Perspectives*, Cheltenham: Edward Elgar.

—— (2002) "Say's law in the open economy: Keynes's rejection of the Theory of Comparative Advantage," in S. Dow and J. Hillard (eds), *Keynes, Uncertainty and the Global Economy: beyond Keynes*, vol. 2, Northampton: Edward Elgar.

Milberg, W. and Houston, E. (2005) "The high road and the low road to international competitiveness: extending the neo-Schumpeterian trade model beyond technology," *International Review of Applied Economics*, 19 (2): 139–64.

Ocampo, J., Taylor, A., and Taylor, L. (1998) "Trade liberalization in developing economies: modest benefits but problems with productivity growth, macro prices, and income distribution," *Economic Journal*, 108 (450): 1523–46.

OECD (2002) *Economic Outlook*, No. 71, Paris: OECD.

Picchio, A. (1992) *Social Reproduction: the political economy of the labour market*, Cambridge: Cambridge University Press.

Razavi, S. (1999) "Export-oriented employment, poverty and gender: contested accounts," *Development and Change*, 30: 653–83.

Robbins, D.J. and Gindling, T.H. (1999) "Trade liberalization and the relative wages for more-skilled workers in Costa Rica," *Review of Development Economics*, 3: 140–54.

Santos-Paulino, A. and Thirlwall, A.P. (2004) "The impact of trade liberalization on exports, imports and the balance of payments of developing countries," *Economic Journal*, 114: 50–72.

Seguino, S. (1997) "Gender wage inequality and export-led growth in S. Korea," *Journal of Development Studies*, 34 (2): 102–32.

—— (2000) "Gender inequality and economic growth: a cross-country analysis," *World Development*, 28 (7): 1211–30.

Shaikh, A. (1980) "The law of international exchange," in E. Nell (ed.), *Growth, Profits and Property*, Cambridge: Cambridge University Press.

—— (2007) "Globalization and the myth of free trade," in A. Shaikh (ed.), *Globalization and the Myths of Free Trade*, London: Routledge.

Singer, H.W. (1950) "The distribution of gains between investing and borrowing countries," *American Economic Review*, 40 (2): 473–85.

Standing, G. (1989) "Global feminization through flexible labor," *World Development*, 17 (7): 1077–95.

—— (1999) "Global feminization through flexible labor: a theme revisited," *World Development*, 27 (3): 583–602.

Steedman, I. (1979) *Trade among Growing Economies*, Cambridge: Cambridge University Press.

Subasat, T. (2003) "What does the Heckscher–Ohlin model contribute to international trade theory? A critical assessment," *Review of Radical Political Economics*, 35 (2): 148–65.

Taylor, L. (ed.) (2001) *External Liberalization, Economic Performance and Social Policy*, New York: Oxford University Press.

Trefler, D. (1995) "The case of the missing trade and other mysteries," *American Economic Review*, 85 (5): 1029–46.

United Nations Conference on Trade and Development (UNCTAD) (2002) *World Investment Report 2002*, Geneva: UNCTAD.

——(2004) *Trade and Gender: challenges and opportunities*, Geneva: UNCTAD.

——(2005) *TNCs and the Removal of Textiles and Clothing Quotas*, UNCTAD/ITE/ITA/2005/1, Geneva: UNCTAD.

United Nations Development Programme (UNDP) (1995, 1996, 1997, 1999) *Human Development Report*, New York: Oxford University Press.

Walters, B. (1995) "Engendering macroeconomics: a reconstruction of growth theory," *World Development*, 23 (11): 1953–61.

Winters, A.L. (2000) "Trade and poverty, is there a connection?" in World Trade Organization Special Studies No. 5, *Trade, Income Disparity and Poverty*, Geneva: WTO: 43–69.

Wood, A. (1994) *North–South Trade, Employment and Inequality: changing fortunes in a skill-driven world*, Oxford: Clarendon Press.

Part II

Impacts of gender inequality on trade

4 Gender, trade, and development

Labor market discrimination and North–South terms of trade

Shaianne Osterreich

Introduction

This chapter investigates the links between gender inequalities in labor markets and the outcomes of North–South trade in manufacturing. Many semi-industrialized Southern countries are integrating into world markets via their manufacturing sectors, and some have achieved significant GDP growth. However, this is accompanied by occupational sex segregation in both the North and the South in which women tend to be crowded into manufacturing sectors that use low-skilled, low-wage, labor-intensive processes of production. Men tend to specialize in occupations and sectors that use more skilled labor and more advanced technologies. Northern exports of manufactures are more male-intensive than Southern exports.

This chapter hypothesizes that trade patterns, and gains from trade, are affected by gendered labor markets. In both North and South, women's wages in manufacturing tend to be less than those of men, even taking into account gender differences in education. This gap is an indication of discrimination against women in labor markets and in wider society. The degree of discrimination against women in manufacturing labor markets in the semi-industrialized South has shown some tendency to rise, in relation to the degree of discrimination against women in the manufacturing labor markets of the North. The empirical findings reported here provide support for the hypothesis that this is associated with a decline in the manufacture–manufacture terms of trade of semi-industrialized Southern countries vis-à-vis industrialized countries of the North.

Development and trade

One side of the globalization debate argues that expanding the global flow of goods and financial capital is beneficial to all trading countries (Dollar and Collier 2002) because they will be better-off than they were in autarky. Opening up domestic markets to global competition is expected to lead to higher levels of output and growth as countries specialize according to their comparative advantage (Dollar 1992; Sachs and Warner 1995; Dollar and Kraay 2001). This will improve standards of living and reduce poverty, defining poverty as a state of income deprivation. It is admitted that the gains from trade may be unequally distributed between and within countries, but it is assumed that output could be redistributed with suitable tax and expenditure policies.

Critics of this argument suggest that trade liberalization does not necessarily lead to growth. Moreover, growth alone is not a sufficient condition for development, especially if the income is poorly distributed across and within households. There is no guarantee that redistribution will in fact take place. The expansion of trade may perpetuate and intensify inequalities. Trade policies should be evaluated in terms of their impact on human development (UN 1999; Rodrik 2001).

There is a long-standing concern that North–South trade in manufacturing goods serves to perpetuate inequalities between North and South. In 1950 it was argued by Prebisch and Singer (Prebisch 1950; Singer 1950) that the relative prices of exports of primary goods vis-à-vis imports of manufactured goods (known as the Net Barter Terms of Trade) had a tendency to deteriorate. Given that countries in the South were exporting primary goods and countries in the North were exporting manufactured goods, this implied that the Net Barter Terms of Trade of the South tended to deteriorate, and thus any gains from trade would not be equally shared. Prebisch and Singer argued that the reason for this lay in the differential functioning of product and labor markets in the North and South. In the North, firms tended to compete via product quality and product differentiation, not price. The labor force was unionized and able to bargain for wage rises to secure a share of increased productivity. As a result, improvements in productivity did not tend to lead to falls in price. In the South, product and labor markets were more competitive, and productivity increases manifested themselves in lower prices, while wages remained constant. This was reinforced by the fact that the Southern economies are labor surplus economies, as described by Lewis (1954). These conditions served to keep wages and prices low, relative to wages and prices in the North. The outcome was a deterioration of the NBTT of the South vis-à-vis the North.

Sapsford's (1990) survey of theoretical and empirical work on the terms of trade between primary commodities and manufactures provides an extensive discussion of the Prebisch–Singer hypothesis. Sapsford points out that Viner (1955) criticized Prebisch and Singer for not taking account of declines in transport costs as well as improvements in the quality of manufactures; however, he also notes that Spraos (1980), after correcting for shipping costs and quality improvements, concluded that the empirical basis for the Prebisch–Singer hypothesis still stands. In addition, Spraos (1983) defined an alternative terms of trade measure, an employment corrected factoral terms of trade, which he argued was an even better measure of distribution of the gains from trade. Using this measure, he found a significant deterioration for the South through the postwar period. Finally, Sapsford (1986) demonstrated that between 1900 and 1980, when a structural break for the two World Wars is taken into account, there was a strong tendency for the Southern NBTT to deteriorate.[1]

Since the 1970s many countries in the South have achieved significant industrialization. The composition of their exports has diversified to include manufactured goods (Sarkar and Singer 1991, 1993; Rodrik 2001). From 1970 to 1984 manufactured exports from the South to the North rose at an annual rate of 25 percent. Valued in US dollars, manufactured exports from the South to the North rose from $6 billion in 1970 to $273 billion in 1991. For low- and middle-income countries, the share of manufactures as a percentage of exports rose from 15 percent in 1964 to 66 percent in 1999 (World Bank 2001). However, this diversification of exports does not appear to have prevented the decline in the terms of trade for newly industrializing countries (Sarkar and Singer 1991; Maizel *et al*. 1998; Maizel 2000). This evidence has given rise to a second version of the Prebisch–Singer thesis, which argues that the underlying economic processes that lead to a deterioration of the terms of trade of primary products from the South relative to manufactures from the North still persist and result in deterioration of the terms of trade of manufactures exported by the South relative to manufactures exported by the North.

Vernon's theory of the International Product Cycle (Vernon 1966) is relevant for understanding the underlying economic processes. The kinds of manufactured goods exported by the newly industrializing countries of the South tend to be highly standardized and are produced by relatively low-skilled labor and compete primarily on the basis of price. This creates pressure to keep wages low to maintain a competitive advantage vis-à-vis other newly industrializing countries. This is in contrast to the manufactured goods produced and exported by the North, which embody advanced technology and highly skilled labor. For these types of manufactures, non-price forms of competition, such as product differentiation and advertising, are more important than price competition.

The persistent deterioration in the NBTT of the South, despite the diversification of Southern exports to include manufactured goods, does not mean that absolute decreases in income have accompanied this trend. At the same time as the NBTT have continued their decline, some countries have experienced an improvement in their Income Terms of Trade (ITT), a measure of the purchasing power of a country's exports in terms of their imports (Sarkar and Singer 1991; Maizel 2000). Due to the price and income elasticity of demand for the manufacturing exports of the newly industrializing South, export revenues have in some cases increased and have contributed to increases in GDP. However, the implications for uneven development depend on the underlying causes of the trends in NBTT or ITT (Wilson *et al*. 1969). If the trends are predicated on the perpetuation of unjustified inequalities, then economic growth does not fully translate into human development.

Gender, trade, and development

The following sections investigate the gender dimensions of differences in the operation of labor markets in the North and South, which underlie the trends in the NBTT and ITT. Explanations for the differences in the labor markets have, for the most part, relied on the predominance of competitive labor markets in the South and on the predominance of unionization in the labor markets of the North. However, labor markets in both North and South are gendered institutions (Elson 1999).

The production of Southern manufacturing exports is significantly more female-intensive than that of Northern manufacturing exports. This reflects the patterns of occupational sex segregation in the North and the South, in which women tend to be crowded into manufacturing sectors that use low-skilled, labor-intensive processes of production, whereas men tend to specialize in sectors that use relatively highly skilled labor and more advanced technologies. Another gendered feature of labor markets is the presence of pervasive gender-based wage gaps, which cannot be fully explained in terms of education gaps between men and women, and which reflect discrimination against women.

A number of studies have demonstrated that export-oriented manufacturing is associated with female-intensive employment, both within and across Southern countries (Elson and Pearson 1984; Standing 1989, 1999; Wood 1991; Çağatay and Özler 1995; Joekes 1999). This association has motivated much discussion concerning the ways in which gender relations affect and reflect the industrialization process that drives the integration of Southern countries into global markets (Çağatay 2002). Çağatay and Özler (1995) conclude there is a positive relationship between openness to international trade and the feminization of the labor force. Feminization in this sense implies a secular change in the gender composition of the labor force. Joekes (1995: 3) argues that, "in the contemporary era no strong export performance of manufactures by any developing country has ever been secured without reliance on female labor."

The share of women in manufacturing has increased in countries as diverse as Egypt, Thailand, Tunisia, and Honduras (Standing 1989, 1999; Joekes and Weston 1994; Wood 1994). The growth of exports with concurrent feminization of the industrial labor force is impervious to previous patterns of women's employment and women's education levels (Joekes 1995). Often, the pay in these jobs is superior to the alternatives, especially those in agricultural or in domestic work. However, many employees are still subject to exposure to carcinogens, eyestrain, long hours, and other risks to health and safety (Joekes 1993).

It might be expected that over time, export-led growth would lead to a decline in gender-based wage gaps. However, Seguino (2000a) concluded that such wage gaps widened for Taiwan, and showed only a marginal reduction in South Korea. This persistence in the wage gaps for Taiwan and South Korea is confirmed by Berik (2000), who found that increased international competitiveness is associated with larger residual wage gaps, that is, gaps not related to differences in education, between men and women in these countries. Seguino (2000b) investigated the relation between gender wage gaps and GDP growth. For a sample of semi-industrializing middle-income Southern countries, gender wage gaps, adjusted for differences in education, were found to be positively correlated with GDP growth. Relatively low wages for women, compared to men, led to increases in export earnings, making it possible to import more and better technologies, and thus achieve higher growth.

The connection between wage discrimination against women in the South and trade outcomes is clearly articulated by Joekes:

> The relevance of gender discrimination is plain. . . . Basic manufactures . . . are the most female-intensive in terms of the gender composition of the workforce.

In these sectors, the low wages paid to women workers have allowed the final product prices to be lower than they would otherwise have been (without compromising the profit share). For countries concerned, this has minimized the national value added generated in international markets over what would have been possible if women's relative wages were not so low.

(Joekes 1999: 55)

This study extends Joekes' analysis by comparing the degree of wage discrimination against women in Southern labor markets with that against women in Northern labor markets. Similar to the Southern countries described above, discriminatory gender wage gaps also persist in Northern labor markets (UN 1999: 14–15). This study highlights labor market discrimination against women as an explanation for why the NBTT of the South has a tendency to decline. The empirical findings provide support for Joekes' (1999) thesis by demonstrating that a tendency for discriminatory gender wage gaps in selected semi-industrializing Southern countries to rise relative to the discriminatory wage gaps in their Northern trading partners is associated with a decline in their manufacture–manufacture terms of trade vis-à-vis these Northern economies.

Model specification

The empirical specification of this model is derived from a standard classical version of price determination where relative international prices (NBTT), as is the case with all prices, are a function of wages, productivity, and profit rates.[2] There are two countries and two commodities (in this case both are manufactures), and capital and labor are the only inputs. There is complete specialization, where country A (North) produces only commodity 1, and country B (South) produces only commodity 2. The price equations, which express the prices of production in the classical sense, can be explained in the following way:

$$P_1 = w^A l_1^A + \left(1 + r^A\right)\left(P_1 a_{11}^A + P_2 a_{21}^A\right)$$
$$P_2 = w^B l_2^B + \left(1 + r^B\right)\left(P_1 a_{12}^B + P_2 a_{22}^B\right)$$

(4.1)

In this model P_1 and P_2 represent the prices of goods 1 and 2 that correspond to countries A and B. Further, w represents wages, r is profit, a is the capital requirement, and l the labor requirement in the production of goods 1 and 2. The model has two equations and six unknowns: P_1, P_2, w^A, w^B, r^A, r^B. With the classical assumption of internationally mobile capital it is assumed that there is a long-run tendency for profit rates to equalize, such that $r^A = r^B = r$.[3] Further, if we assume that P_1 is the numeraire, then this system is reduced to two equations with four unknowns; that is r, $P = P_2/P_1$, and w^{*A} and w^{*B}, where w^* is equal to the real wages in country A or B, in terms of commodity 1.

Since we are investigating the impact of wage determination on the NBTT, we take wages to be exogenous, so that w^{*A} and w^{*B} are fixed. If the price equations are solved for $R = r + 1$ and expressed in terms of P, with $[A]$ representing the vector of capital requirements, then a price-wage relation can be expressed as follows:

$$P = P_1/P_2 = f(w^A, w^B, [A], l^A, l^B) \tag{4.2}$$

This model relates the NBTT to the level of wages in each country. Since our purpose is to investigate the relation between the degree of wage discrimination against women and the NBTT, we use education-adjusted gender wage ratios in the South as a percentage of education-adjusted gender wage ratios in the North instead of wage levels in the two countries. The objective is to capture the linkage between the degree of discrimination against women and the country level distribution of the gains from trade. As a result of this, the following substitutions are made:

$$w^A = \left(\frac{w^f}{w^m}\right)^A \quad \text{and} \quad w^B = \left(\frac{w^f}{w^m}\right)^B \tag{4.3}$$

where w^f and w^m represent female and male wages respectively (adjusted for the differences in male and female education). When these are substituted into equation (4.2), P can be expressed in the following general form:

$$P = f\left(\left(\frac{w^f}{w^m}\right)^A, \left(\frac{w^f}{w^m}\right)^B, l^A, l^B, \phi\right) \tag{4.4}$$

The adjusted gender wage ratios are taken to reflect labor market discrimination against women in both North and South. Differences in the labor market position of men in the South, relative to men in the North, are captured by l^A and l^B, which represent the degree to which changes in men's wages are linked to productivity changes. Finally, ϕ represents other factors that affect the international NBTT, such as capital requirements, government policy and supply shocks, and the elements of excess capacity and market power that are not fully captured by their impact on wages.

Two different data sets and specifications were used. Model I includes 10 Southern countries with data for four five-year average time periods from 1975 to 1995 and was estimated using an Error Components Random Effects method. Model II includes a sub-sample of seven Southern countries with data for each year in the 10-year period from 1980 to 1990 and was estimated using a Fixed Effects Dummy Variable method. Model II has fewer countries, and the time span is shorter but includes data for each of the 10 years. This allows for an increased number of observations. The choice of years is limited by the availability of data. For reasons to be explained later a hybrid model was also constructed which used the Error Components Random Effects method and the data for seven countries for each year in the 10-year period from 1980 to 1990.

The Error Components Random Effects method uses a generalized least-squares estimation method to find the best linear unbiased estimate for the coefficients. This method is preferred for with small sample sizes and particularly for pooled data where the number of cross sections is greater than the number of time periods (Greene 2002). The general form of this equation is:

$$Y_{it} = j_t\beta_1 + X_{it}\beta_2 + u_i j_t + \varepsilon_{it} \quad \text{for } i = i,...N; \ t = 1,...T \tag{4.5}$$

The βs can be estimated using a generalized least-squares procedure. The estimation works by transforming the observations and then applying ordinary least squares to the transformations. The variables are transformed into a measure that represents each observation's deviation from the mean.

The Fixed Effects Dummy Variable method uses pooled cross-sectional and time series panel data. The general form of the regression equation is:

$$Y_{it} = X_{it}\beta + u_i j_t + \varepsilon_{it} \quad \text{for } i = i,...N; \ t = 1,...T \tag{4.6}$$

where β is K $\times$ 1 vector of unknown parameters, j are country dummies, ε_{it} is the error term, and therefore μ_i represents a fixed parameter to be estimated to represent the country i effect. This method assumes that the $u_i j_T$ term will capture country specific variances in the form of the constant term, and the regression is estimated using the least-squares dummy variable estimator.

Selection of countries

The Southern countries were selected from those countries listed in the 1999 World Development Indicators (WDI) as low and high middle-income countries. Hong Kong, Singapore, and Cyprus were added as they have only recently entered the WDI high-income category, and the trade strategy which got them there falls within the parameters of this study. Next a Semi-industrialized Export Index was created by (a) averaging each country's exports as a percentage of GDP, (b) averaging each country's annual export growth, and (c) averaging manufactures as a percentage of exports, all over the period 1975–95.

The threshold value for the index was determined by the value that would be obtained with approximately 25 percent of GDP coming from exports, 10 percent annual average growth in exports, and manufactures as 10 percent of exports. These parameters ensured the sample would include high growth semi-industrializing relatively open economies. The countries that fell within the index parameters were then checked against those countries that have gender disaggregated wage data for the manufacturing sector. This severely limited the sample size, although it covers many of the "newly industrializing economies." Because of time series limitations on the gender disaggregated wage data, two sets of Southern countries were investigated. These two different data sets are summarized in Table 4.1, which also identifies the model specification used with each data set.

Tables 4.2–4.5 provide descriptive data for the Southern sample countries. All of the data in these tables were retrieved from the World Bank's *World Development Indicators* CD-ROM 2000. Table 4.2 shows exports as a percentage of GDP. All of the Southern countries in the sample rely significantly on exports and for most that reliance has grown since the mid-1970s. As shown in Table 4.3 all the countries have seen manufacturing as a share of exports grow, and since exports represent a large and growing share of GDP, production conditions in the manufacturing sector are fundamental to their economic growth.

The Northern countries were selected according to their significance as trading partners for the sample of Southern countries. It was found that the United States, United Kingdom, Germany, Japan, and France were the countries most likely to be listed in the top 10 importers of manufactures from the sample Southern countries.

Table 4.1 Structure of sample: country and years

Model I *Southern sample* *countries (1975–95)*	*Model II* *Southern sample* *countries (1980–90)*	*Northern sample*
Cyprus	Cyprus	United States
Egypt	Egypt	United Kingdom
El Salvador	El Salvador	Japan
South Korea	South Korea	Germany
Hong Kong	Hong Kong	France
Malaysia	Sri Lanka	
Singapore	Turkey	
Sri Lanka		
Thailand		
Turkey		

Table 4.2 Exports as a percentage of GDP

	1975–80	*1980–5*	*1985–90*	*1990–5*
Cyprus	44.0	50.3	48.7	48.5
Egypt, Arab Rep.	23.3	27.8	16.7	26.1
El Salvador	34.8	26.0	18.3	18.9
Hong Kong, China	87.3	94.9	126.8	142.2
Korea, Rep.	29.6	35.1	35.7	29.9
Malaysia	49.3	53.2	67.5	85.3
Singapore	169.7	194.8	189.2	184.3
Sri Lanka	31.8	29.0	26.5	32.7
Thailand	20.2	22.6	31.3	38.3
Turkey	3.9	10.7	15.4	16.6

Source: World Development Indicators CDROM; World Bank 2001.

Note
The figures for Hong Kong, China, and Singapore reflect the large scale re-export of imports.

Table 4.3 Manufacturing as a percentage of exports

	1975–80	1980–5	1985–90	1990–5
Cyprus	42.7	54.4	58.2	55.9
El Salvador	26.0	34.1	25.4	43.5
Hong Kong, China	77.0	81.3	75.8	79.7
Korea, Rep.	86.1	90.6	92.3	93.1
Malaysia	16.7	22.5	39.1	68.6
Singapore	43.6	48.5	63.7	78.8
Sri Lanka	7.1	24.3	44.5	69.0
Thailand	18.5	28.2	48.8	69.8
Turkey	24.2	41.5	63.0	71.2
Egypt, Arab Rep.	26.6	10.7	27.7	35.7

Source: World Development Indicators CDROM; World Bank 2001.

Table 4.4 Trends in the manufacturing–manufacturing NBTT and ITT of Southern sample relative to Northern sample, 1975–95[a]

Country	Estimates of annual average rate of NBTT change	R^2	Durbin–Watson statistic	Estimates of annual average rate of ITT change	R^2	Durbin–Watson statistic
Cyprus	−9.8*	0.21	1.7	−4.49*	0.13	1.19
Egypt	−14.2*	0.73	1.75	24.67*	0.73	0.73
El Salvador	−17.7	0.73	1.75	0.02	0.10	0.97
South Korea	−6.9*	0.12	2.17	0.69	0.52	2.12
Hong Kong	−0.72	0.04	1.03	−0.99	0.19	1.65
Malaysia	12.4	0.07	2.41	0.06	0.41	1.07
Singapore	−15.3*	0.17	2.47	−0.04	0.13	0.56
Sri Lanka	−4.7	0.10	1.18	0.18	0.77	0.62
Thailand	−14.8*	0.50	1.74	0.10	0.07	0.95
Turkey	−14.9*	0.68	1.83	0.21	0.85	0.75

Source: Author's calculations based on data extracted from United Nations' COMTRADE.

Notes
a Estimates are obtained by fitting an exponential trend equation.
* Significant at less than 5% level (t-test findings).

Table 4.5 Export-weighted gender wage ratios (GWR) in manufacturing for Southern sample

	Cyprus	Egypt	El Salvador	South Korea	Hong Kong	Malaysia	Singapore	Sri Lanka	Thailand	Turkey
1975–80	55	71	78	52	78	50	61	75	74	98
1980–5	61	84	80	53	78	52	63	74	76	96
1985–90	66	84	76	58	71	54	59	75	78	83
1990–5	71	86	93	58	64	58	62	85	80	97

Source: Author's calculations based on ILO (various years) *Yearbook of Labour Statistics*, UN *International Yearbook of Trade Statistics* (various years).

These Northern countries imported approximately 50 percent of the exports of the selected countries. In contrast, it should be noted that the sample selection of Southern countries only imported an average of 10 percent of exports from the selected Northern countries (UN, various years).

Data construction

The manufacture–manufacture NBTT of the Southern sample countries relative to the Northern sample was calculated using data extracted from the Commodity Trade Statistics (COMTRADE) database of the United Nations.[4] This database provides export and import values and quantities, for all reporting countries by year, by trading partner, and by commodity at the five-digit SITC level. For the sample of Southern and Northern economies defined earlier, data was extracted on values and quantities of all manufactured commodities, as defined by the most common and acceptable determination, that of Standard International Trade Classification (SITC) 5–8, minus 68, plus 931. This excludes nonferrous metals and includes "other manufactured goods." The NBTT for each Southern country was calculated as a weighted average of the ratio of average unit values of manufactured exports (to each of the sample Northern countries) to average unit values of manufactured imports (from each of the sample Northern countries). The weights were the share of exports from the Southern country to each of the Northern countries as a share of total manufactured exports from the Southern country to the sample Northern countries as a group. (The formula for the calculation is given in Appendix 4.A.)

The methodology developed to calculate the NBTT was created in response to the various data sets and competing methodologies used in testing the hypothesis of declining terms of trade between manufactures exported by developing countries and those exported by developed countries (cf. Sarkar and Singer 1991, 1993; Athukorala 1993, 1998; Maizel et al. 1998; Maizel 2000). Some of these studies made problematic data choices. For example, replication of part of the Sarkar–Singer (1991) study is difficult because they employed unpublished United Nations data to provide unit values of manufacturing exports for specific countries. Further, another test in Sarkar–Singer (1991) and Athukorala (1998) used published data from the United Nation's *Monthly Bulletin* that aggregates manufacturing export unit values for "Developing Countries," and "Developed Countries." Unfortunately, these are aggregate categories for all countries that have data, and the individual country unit values are not available. Both of these approaches have the problem of including all countries considered as "developing." They lump together countries that are successful exporters of manufactures with those whose exports are mainly primary products. Admittedly, Athukorala (1998) includes country level studies of India, South Korea, and Taiwan, but the data include all their manufacturing exports and imports, and not only exports to and imports from the North.

This study avoids these problems because the NBTT are calculated with respect to Southern exports of manufactured commodities to the North and

Southern imports of manufactures from the North. Intraregional trade within the South and North is excluded. Calculated in this fashion, the trends in the NBTT of each of the Southern sample countries are shown in Table 4.4 with annual percentage change estimates based on fitting an exponential trend equation.[5] Table 4.4 also shows trends in the manufacturing–manufacturing Income Terms of Trade (ITT), calculated by multiplying the NBTT by export quantities. There is clear evidence of deterioration in the NBTT for the majority of the countries. However, there is no discernable trend in the ITT for manufacturing exports.

Table 4.4 shows two outliers. Malaysia has a large improvement in its NBTT, while Egypt has a large positive improvement in its ITT. Both of these countries maintained significant import tariffs in the sample period (Economic Research Forum in Arab Countries 2000; Rasiah 2002).

Gender gaps in wages were measured as the ratio of female to male wages. The gender wage ratios were calculated primarily from data in the International Labor Organization (ILO) *Yearbook of Labour Statistics*. The ILO publishes wages in manufacturing, often disaggregated by International Standard of Industrial Classification (ISIC) system at the three-digit level, and disaggregated by sex. Therefore, where available, the raw gender wage ratios (GWR) were calculated based on a weighted average of female to male wages. The weights were determined by the share of each three-digit ISIC industry in total manufactured exports for each country. Where possible, these wage ratios are corrected for hours worked. (See Appendix 4.A for details.)

Following Seguino (2000b) these wage ratios were adjusted for educational attainment in the following ways. The average number of years of secondary educational attainment by men and women 15 and over, respectively, was used to adjust the wage ratios to accommodate for education differences between men and women. As a measure of discrimination, this approach has some limitations. For example, it does not adjust for other factors that might influence gender wage differences, such as labor market attachment (real or perceived), differential unionization, differential productivity, and so on. But data are not available on these other factors.

The education data were taken from Barro and Lee (1996). If educational attainment ratios are larger than the wage ratios, the wage ratio is adjusted downward to indicate that the labor market discrimination is worse than is revealed by the raw wage ratio alone. Alternatively, if the wage ratio is greater than the educational attainment ratio, the wage ratio is adjusted upwards. (See Appendix 4.A for details.) In this way we constructed EGWR, the education-adjusted gender wage ratio. The higher this ratio, the lower is the degree of wage discrimination against women.

Table 4.5 shows the export-weighted gender wage ratios in the manufacturing sectors in the sample Southern countries, while Table 4.6 shows the export-weighted gender wage ratios in manufacturing in the Northern sample, together with a simple average of these wage ratios. As can be seen most countries have experienced some improvement in their gender wage ratios over the 20 years covered by the study, though the ratio has fallen in Hong Kong and stayed approximately the same in Singapore and Turkey; and deteriorated slightly in Japan and the United Kingdom.

Table 4.6 Export-weighted gender wage ratios (GWR) in manufacturing for Northern sample

	France	Germany	Japan	UK	US	North
1975–9	77	72	46	69	66	65
1980–4	79	73	43	69	66	66
1985–9	82	73	42	68	69	65
1990–5	82	74	43	68	71	69

Source: Author's calculations based on ILO (various years) *Yearbook of Labour Statistics*, UN *International Yearbook of Trade Statistics* (various years).

Table 4.7 Women's secondary educational attainment relative to men's

	North	Cyprus	Egypt	El Salvador	South Korea	Hong Kong	Malaysia	Singapore	Sri Lanka	Thai-land	Turkey
1975–80	94	65	39	62	57	68	54	74	80	69	44
1980–5	92	71	47	88	66	79	60	80	81	72	47
1985–90	92	79	49	90	76	81	70	83	85	78	49
1990–5	96	82	57	93	78	88	78	92	87	87	49

Source: Author's calculations based on Barro, R. and Lee, J.W. (1996) "International measures of schooling years and schooling quality," *American Economic Review*, 86 (2): 218–23.

It is noteworthy that the ratio for Japan is much lower than for any other country in the sample. This depresses the average ratio for the North below that of several countries in the South, most notably Egypt, El Salvador, Sri Lanka, Thailand, and Turkey. However, the ratios in these countries are likely to be inflated by incomplete coverage of the manufacturing sector in the wage data reported to ILO. For instance, for Turkey, the data are taken from social insurance records which only cover permanent workers at larger firms, while lower-paid women workers are more likely to be employed on temporary contracts and in small firms.

Table 4.7 shows the ratio of female to male secondary educational attainment, as a simple average for the North and individually for the Southern countries. This has risen in all the sample countries. Table 4.8 shows the education-adjusted gender wage ratios (EGWR) as a simple average for the North and individually for the Southern countries. Again the record of Japan keeps the Northern average below that of several of the Southern countries. These have improved in four of the Southern countries and in the North, but have deteriorated in South Korea, Hong Kong, Malaysia, Singapore, Thailand, and Turkey.

The ratio of each Southern country's EGWR relative to the average of the Northern sample EGWRs was used as the main independent variable in the econometric specification. This variable, SNEGWR, represents a measure of the degree of labor market discrimination against women in the South relative to discrimination against women in the North. The annual change in this indicator (GSNEGWR) is shown in Table 4.9. Clearly, the degree of relative discrimination has increased for most of the sample.

Table 4.8 Education-adjusted gender wage ratios (EGWR)

	North	Cyprus	Egypt	El Salvador	South Korea	Hong Kong	Malaysia	Singapore	Sri Lanka	Thai- land	Turkey
1975–80	46	50	95	91	50	85	49	54	72	77	149
1980–5	49	55	115	74	47	78	48	53	69	78	143
1985–90	48	58	114	66	47	64	45	45	67	77	111
1990–5	50	64	111	93	46	48	47	44	83	74	142

Source: Author's calculations based on ILO (various years) *Yearbook of Labour Statistics*, UN *International Yearbook of Trade Statistics* (various years), and Barro, R. and Lee, J.W. (1996) "International measures of schooling years and schooling quality," *American Economic Review*, 86 (2): 218–23.

Table 4.9 Change (%) in degree of discrimination against women in the South relative to degree of discrimination against women in the North, 1975–95[a]

Cyprus	Egypt	El Salvador	South Korea	Hong Kong	Malaysia	Singapore	Sri Lanka	Thailand	Turkey
19	9	−5	−13	−47	−11	−24	7	−11	−12

Source: Author's calculations based on ILO (various years) *Yearbook of Labour Statistics*, UN *International Yearbook of Trade Statistics* (various years), and Barro, R. and Lee, J.W. (1996) "International measures of schooling years and schooling quality," *American Economic Review*, 86 (2): 218–23.

Note
a Measured as change in ratio of education-adjusted gender wage ratio in Southern country to average education-adjusted gender wage ratio in the North (GSNEGWR) (see Appendix 4.A).

The wage data are the weakest link in the data analysis as they are not always available for each country for all the years of the study. As a result of this limitation, two sets of the sample countries were used. In the first set, used in Model I, all 10 countries were analyzed using five-year period averages. When only one data point was available over several years, that data point was approximated to represent the five-year average in which it fell. Operating under the assumption that gender wage ratios change relatively slowly, this is not expected to alter the results, while allowing for increased numbers of observations for the whole country sample. A second set, used in Model II, includes the seven countries for which data on gender wage ratios were available every year from 1980 to 1995. When the sample is limited to this subset of countries the number of observations is much larger because more time periods can be taken into account. In addition, the degree of gender wage inequality is likely to be underestimated due to biases in the sample selection when the wage data was collected at country level. These official reports of wage data are often derived only from firms that pay social insurance or are of a certain size. They leave out informal manufacturing employment, where wages are lower than in the formal sector, and which is disproportionately female. This source of underestimation is likely to be more significant in the countries in the South than in the North.

Labor productivity was calculated by using data from the World Bank's Growth and Development Database, which was provided by Easterly and Levine (1999),

Table 4.10 Ratio of Southern to Northern output per worker (RELPROD) (1975–90)

	Cyprus	Egypt	El Salvador	South Korea	Hong Kong	Malaysia	Singapore	Sri Lanka	Thailand	Turkey
1975–9	0.40	0.22	0.28	0.31	0.49	0.35	0.59	0.16	0.06	0.29
1980–4	0.49	0.26	0.22	0.36	0.61	0.43	0.68	0.20	0.02	0.27
1985–9	0.55	0.25	0.20	0.45	0.71	0.38	0.73	0.20	0.05	0.28
1990	0.62	0.24	0.19	0.55	0.78	0.43	0.83	0.20	0.10	0.29

Source: Author's calculations based on Easterly, W. and Ross Levine (1999) "It's not factor accumulation: stylized facts and growth models," mimeo, World Bank and University of Minnesota, September; extracted from Growth and Development Database; World Bank.

which includes output per worker, over time per country and was available annually for the period 1975–90. Although this measures labor productivity across the whole economy, given the large share of manufactured exports in the GDP of the sample countries, it operates as a close approximation to labor productivity in manufacturing. The ratio of output per worker for each country in the South vis-à-vis the average ratio for the North was used to proxy the relative productivities in manufacturing (RELPROD). This variable is shown in Table 4.10.

Although this productivity measure has limitations, the ratio clearly illuminates the tendencies in relative technologies and productive capabilities. The annual average rate of change in the ratio of Southern to Northern productivity was also constructed (GRELPROD). (For details see Appendix 4.A.)

This chapter tests two hypotheses. First, when labor market discrimination against women in the South is reduced relative to discrimination against women in the North, the NBTT of the South will improve. This suggests that the coefficient on SNEGWR and GSNEGWR will be positive. Second, as the productivity gap for the South vis-à-vis the North shrinks, the NBTT of the South will deteriorate (the general Prebisch–Singer relationship). The coefficients on RELPROD and GRELPROD are therefore expected to be negative.

Results

Table 4.11 reports the results of the regressions, based on the following estimated equations:

$$\text{NBTT}_{it} = j_{it}\overline{\beta} + \text{RELPROD}_{it}\beta_1 + \text{SNWEGWR}_{it}\beta_2 + u_i j_t + \varepsilon_{it} \qquad (4.7)$$

$$\text{NBTT}_{it} = \text{RELPROD}_{it}\beta_1 + \text{SNWEGWR}_{it}\beta_2 + u_i j_t + \varepsilon_{it} \qquad (4.8)$$

$$\text{GNBTT}_{it} = \text{GRELPROD}_{it}\beta_1 + \text{GSNWEGWR}_{it}\beta_2 + u_i j_t + \varepsilon_{it} \qquad (4.9)$$

In these equations *it* represents country *i* in time *t*. Equation (4.7) is estimated with the Error Component method, using two different data sets: data for four five-year time period averages and 10 countries (Model I) and data for four five-year time period averages and seven countries (Hybrid Model). Equations (4.8)

Table 4.11 Estimation results

Variables	(1) Eq (4.7) Model I	(2) Eq (4.7) Hybrid Model	(3) Eq (4.8) Model II	(4) Eq (4.9) Model II
Dependant variable	NBTT	NBTT	NBTT	GNBTT
Independent variables				
RELPROD	0.000474	−2.3525	−14.968	
	(12.19)****	(−1.282)*	(−3.801)****	
SNEGWR	1.2863	1.1423	0.83477	
	(3.510)****	(2.305)***	(1.323)*	
GRELPROD				−31.568
				(−10.18)**
GSNEGWR				2.9384
				(3.629)****
	4–5 year time periods	4–5 year time periods	1980–90	1980–90
	10 countries	7 countries	7 countries	7 countries
	$R^2 = 0.7903$	$R^2 = 0.2723$	$R^2 = 0.6771$	$R^2 = 0.8329$
	N = 40	N = 28	N = 77	N = 66

Notes
Model I – Error Components Model.
Model II – Fixed Effects Dummy Variable Model.
Numbers in parenthesis are t-statistics; * = significant at 90% level; ** = significant at 95% level;
*** = significant at 97.5%; **** = significant at 99.5% level.

and (4.9) both used Model II, a Fixed Effects Dummy Variable method, with 10 years and 7 countries. The difference between equations (4.8) and (4.9) is that equation (4.9) captures the lagged effects of relative discrimination and productivity on the growth rate of NBTT.

The results for equation (4.7), Model I are reported in Table 4.11, column 1. The estimated equation, with 40 observations, resulted in a correlation coefficient of 0.79, the largest correlation coefficient of all estimations. The sign on the parameter for SNEGWR is positive, as expected, and significant at the 99.5 percent level. As SNEGWR increases, the education-adjusted gender wage ratios in the South are improving relative to those in the North. This can be interpreted as the degree of discrimination against women in the South declining relative to the degree of discrimination against women in the North. Thus, as SNEGWR increases, the reduced relative discrimination against women in the South would be reflected in rises in women's wages, which exerts upward pressure on the export prices and hence causes the NBTT to increase. More specifically, the results suggest if SNEGWR increases by one percentage point, that is, if women's wages in the North are 100 percent of men's wages, and women's wages in the South increase from 80 to 81 percent of men's, this will increase the Southern NBTT by 0.013.

The second hypothesis predicted that the sign on the coefficient of RELPROD would be negative. As RELPROD increases, the Southern country's productivity relative to the North increases, and the technological divide shrinks. The

Prebisch–Singer hypothesis argues that the productivity gains are transferred to the North in the form of reduced prices, and so would cause the NBTT to deteriorate; one would expect there to be a negative relationship between RELPROD and NBTT. Yet, contrary to prediction, the coefficient is positive and significant at the 95 percent level (column 1, Table 4.11). This means that as RELPROD increases by one percentage point (i.e. Southern productivity increases from 80 percent of the North's to 81 percent), this will motivate an increase in the NBTT by 0.000474. Even though this is contrary to the hypothesis, the effect (as measured by the size of the coefficient) is small. Column 2 of Table 4.11 presents the results from the Hybrid Model, which attempts to explain the unexpected positive sign on the RELPROD coefficient. The specification in column 2 is estimated with the smaller sample of countries (as in Model II), but with the four five-year period averages and the Error Components method (as in Model I). The objective was to determine if the countries left out of this smaller sample were the cause of the positive sign. In this specification, the sign on the RELPROD coefficient is now negative and significant at the 90 percent level, while the coefficient on SNEGWR is still positive and significant at the 97.5 percent level. This implies that the three countries – Malaysia, Singapore, and Thailand – that were left out of the specification in column 1 influence the productivity–NBTT relationship. However, the first hypothesis is confirmed with or without these three countries.

Equations (4.8) and (4.9) employ the Dummy Variable Fixed Effects specification with the smaller Southern country sample. In this sample, the number of cross sections is less than the number of time periods and therefore the Fixed Effects specification is preferred. Equation (4.8) uses exactly the same variables used in equation (4.7), namely, RELPROD and SNEGWR. Again, the two hypotheses predict that the parameter estimate for SNEGWR will be positive and the parameter estimate for RELPROD will be negative. The results, shown in columns 3 and 4 of Table 4.11, confirm our hypotheses: the parameter estimate for SNEGWR is positive and significant at the 90 percent level, implying that a one percent increase in SNEGWR improves NBTT by 0.084. RELPROD is negative and significant at the 99.5 percent level, suggesting that a one percent improvement in RELPROD decreases NBTT by 0.15.

Equation (4.9), based on 66 observations, uses lagged values of the changes in the variables. The dependant variable is measured as the annual rate of change of the NBTT (i.e. GNBTT), and the independent variables were one-period lagged values of the annual rates of change of the relative education-adjusted gender wage ratios (GSNEGWR) and the productivity ratio (GRELPROD). This specification, reported in column 4 of Table 4.11, tests the hypothesis that a higher rate of change in the relative gender wage ratios of the South vis-à-vis the North will cause the South's rate of change in NBTT to be positive. That is, a positive relationship is expected between the GNBTT and the GSNEGWR, with a one-period lag. Similarly, if the rate of change of the productivity ratio is positive, the rate of change in the NBTT will be negative, and there will be a negative relationship between the GNBTT and GREL-PROD. The results of equation (4.9) demonstrate strong support for this hypothesis. The coefficient for GSNEGWR is positive and significant at the 99.5 percent level, indicating that a one percent increase in the rate of improvement of the education-adjusted gender wage ratio in the South, relative to that in the North, leads to an increase in the rate of improvement of the NBTT by 0.029. The parameter for GRELPROD is negative and significant at the 99.5 percent level, and indicates that when the rate of Southern productivity increases by one percent relative to the North, the rate of change of the NBTT will decrease by 0.316.

The results of these various specifications provide overall support to the first hypothesis that if education-adjusted gender wage ratios in the South rise relative to those in the North, the South's NBTT will improve. In some cases the size of the estimated coefficients are quite small. However, that they are robustly positive suggests that: (a) there is a discernable trend in a diverse set of countries across time, and (b) country- and time-specific analysis would likely reveal larger impacts for some countries. Given the Prebisch–Singer thesis, and the sample Southern countries' tendencies for the manufacture–manufacture NBTT to dete-riorate, the results imply that if the education-adjusted gender wage ratios in the South decrease relative to those in the North, the South's NBTT will deteriorate.

The results for the second hypothesis are mixed. The positive coefficient on RELPROD in equation (4.7) (column 1, Table 4.11) possibly reflects the impact of the three countries that are omitted in equations (4.8) and (4.9). The results of the Hybrid Model specification in column 2, Table 4.11 further support this possibility. However, the results of equations (4.8) and (4.9), with the smaller sample, do confirm the second hypothesis. Further, because the late 1970s and early 1990s were included in equations (4.8) and (4.9), and not in equation (4.7), it is possible that a time-specific effect was not taken into account.

The results of the study support the hypothesis that the degree of gender-based discrimination in labor markets, which in turn affects international wage ratios, helps explain changes in NBTT. Further, declines in discrimination against Southern women relative to discrimination against Northern women tend to improve NBTT. Given the trends in the sample countries' NBTT, this would imply that the feminization of the labor force and the persistence of labor market dis-crimination in the successful manufacturing-based exporting countries are two additional factors explaining the Prebisch–Singer hypothesis. In addition, when productivity of the Southern countries increases relative to that of the Northern countries, the NBTT of the South deteriorates. This latter result is consistent with the narrative developed by Prebisch and Singer to explain productivity growth in the South given the nature of competition between the North and South.

Conclusions and policy recommendations

This chapter has sought to illuminate connections between international trade, gendered labor markets, and economic development via manufactured exports. The latest version of the Prebisch–Singer thesis posits deterioration in the manufacture–manufacture Net Barter Terms of Trade of Southern countries relative to their Northern trading partners. The empirical results confirm that this is related to deterioration in the education-adjusted gender wage ratios of the South relative to those of the North. It suggests that barriers in the ability of women in the South to translate their rising education and labor market participation into a more rapid rise in their relative wages lead to a loss of potential gains from trade for the economies of the South.

Trade policy makers should acknowledge the connections between gender and international trade policy outcomes. Not only do men and women experience the impacts of trade policy differently, gender relations also affect the outcomes of trade policies, in terms of the distribution of benefits between countries. Obviously, improving the wages and working opportunities for women is a valuable goal in itself; however, this research demonstrates that there are also benefits to working men, and countries as a whole, when labor market discrimination against women is reduced. The UN Millennium Project Task Force Report on achieving Millennium Development Goal 3 (Promote Gender Equality and Women's Empowerment) highlights some areas where attention can be directed to reduce gender-based labor market discrimination (Grown *et al.* 2005: 96). As occupational segregation is clearly characteristic of the economies discussed in this chapter, legislation requiring that women and men doing the same job be paid the same wage, although necessary, is not sufficient. Legislation requiring equal pay for jobs of comparable worth is also required. In addition, other equal opportunity and anti-discrimination policies are needed, such as entitlement to leave for family responsibilities and measures to prevent sexual harassment in the work place. Nor will passing new laws be sufficient. Resources need to be directed at enforcing legislation and supporting women to claim their rights. It is also crucial to engage in capacity building on questions of gender and gender equality, as they relate to economic policy.

In order to diminish occupational segregation in manufacturing export production, women need access to a wider range of educational and training opportunities, and specific encouragement to take up training for occupations in which they are very much in a minority. Moreover, women's bargaining position in the manufacturing export sector needs to be strengthened through access to alternative sources of better incomes. Microfinance programs and public employment programs would both help, especially if coupled with investment in infrastructure to reduce the time that women have to spend in unpaid domestic work providing services for their families. Improved social protection and safety net programs would also strengthen women's bargaining power.

Governments in the South need to act together to reduce labor market discrimination against women, so as to avoid the loss of market share to countries in which discrimination continues, and which might hope to see an increase in their Income Terms of Trade, even though their Net Barter Terms of Trade deteriorated. Regional trade and development bodies, such as ASEAN, MENA, CARICOM, and MERCOSUR, are appropriate institutions for coordinating policy.

This chapter has provided evidence that increasing gender wage ratios in the South, relative to gender wage ratios in the North, would likely be associated with an improvement in the NBTT of the South, and a bigger share of the gains of trade would accrue to the South, capable of benefiting all its citizens. Overall, the results from this research demonstrate that there is strong connection between gender inequality and international trade outcomes. To improve the link between trade openness and human development, policies must address this connection.

Appendix 4.A Variable construction

Variable	Description	Construction
NBTT	Manufacture–manufacture NBTT of Southern country relative to sample Northern countries	1. $EUV_{i,j}^t = \dfrac{\text{commodity value exported}_{i,j}^{c,t}}{\text{commodity quantity exported}_{i,j}^{c,t}}$ = unit value of commodity c exported by country i to country j in year t
t = year		2. $IUV_{i,j}^t = \dfrac{\text{commodity value imported}_{i,j}^{c,t}}{\text{commodity quantity imported}_{i,j}^{c,t}}$ = unit value of commodity c imported by country i from country j in year t
i = Southern country		3. $RWEUV_{i,j}^t = \sum\limits_c EUV_{i,j}^t * \dfrac{100}{PPI_{US}^t} * \dfrac{\text{commodity value}_{i,j}^{c,t}}{\text{total value of exports from country } i \text{ to country } j^t}$ = Real weighted average of unit values of all manufactured commodities exported by country i to country j in year t (weighted by commodity c's share of manufactured exports from i to j in year t)
j = Northern country		4. $RWIUV_{i,j}^t = \sum\limits_c IUV_{i,j}^t * \dfrac{100}{PPI_{US}^t} * \dfrac{\text{commodity value}_{i,j}^{c,t}}{\text{total value of imports by country } i \text{ from country } j^t}$ = Real weighted average of unit values of all manufactured commodities imported by country i from country j in year t (weighted by commodity c's share of manufactured imports by i from j in year t)
PPI = US producer price index (base year = 1982)		5. $NBTT_i^t = \sum \dfrac{RWEUV_{i,j}^t}{RWIUV_{i,j}^t} * \dfrac{\text{total value of exports from country } i \text{ to country } j^t}{i\text{'s total exports to sample Northern countries}^t}$
GNBTT	Change in NBTT	$(NBTT_i^t - NBTT_i^{t-1})/NBTT_i^{t-1}$

(*Appendix 4.A continued*)

Appendix 4.A Continued

Variable	Description	Construction
GWR	Gender wage ratio	1. $GWR_n^t = \sum_k \left(\dfrac{w^f}{w^m}\right)_{n,k}^t * \dfrac{\text{total value of exports of manufacturing sector } k}{\text{total manufacturing exports}_n^t}$
$n = i$ or j		
k = International Standard Industrial Classification, 2–3 digit code		2. $GWR_n^t = \left(1 + \left(\dfrac{w^f}{w^m}\right)_n^t - \left(\dfrac{\text{SYRF}}{\text{SYRM}}\right)_n\right) * \left(\dfrac{w^f}{w^m}\right)_n^t$
		w^f = average female worker earnings in sector k in year t in country n (corrected for hours worked where possible)
		w^m = average male worker earnings in sector k in year t in country n (corrected for hours worked where possible)
		SYRF = average years of secondary educational attainment by females
		SYRM = average years of secondary educational attainment by males (method derived from Seguino 2000b)
EGWR	Education-adjusted gender wage ratio	$(\text{EGWR}_i^t) / (\text{EGWR}_{\text{north}}^t)$
SNEGWR	South–North ratio of education-adjusted gender wage ratios	ratio of country i's education-adjusted gender wage ratio relative to the average of sample Northern countries' education-adjusted gender wage ratios
GSNEGWR	Annual change in ratio of South–North education-adjusted gender wage ratios	$(\text{SNEGWR}_i^t - \text{SNEGWR}_i^{t-1})/\text{SNEGWR}_i^{t-1}$
PROD	Labor productivity	Output per worker in country n in time t
RELPROD	South–North productivity ratio	$\text{PROD}_i^t / \text{PROD}_{\text{north}}^t$ Ratio of output per worker in each Southern country relative to simple average of output per worker in Northern Sample
GRELPROD	Annual change of South–North productivity ratio	$(\text{RELPROD}_i^t - \text{RELPROD}_i^{t-1})/\text{RELPROD}_i^{t-1}$

Notes

1 For more recent evidence see Sarkar (1986), Grilli and Yang (1981), and Cuddington and Urzua (1989).
2 Evans (1984) reviews various theories of unequal exchange, and the model used here is derived from the analytical framework he uses to formalize these theories.
3 This chapter uses a classical price specification. It would be interesting to see Post-Keynesian models that incorporate a more specific mark-up rate in future research.
4 Full details of the variable construction are available from the author by request.
5 Sarkar and Singer (1991) argued for a deteriorating trend for a sample of Southern countries vis-á-vis the United States for the period 1965–85 based on a similar exponential trend equation, but used a different methodology for calculating the terms of trade.

References

Athukorala, P. (1993) "Manufactured exports from developing countries and their terms of trade: a reexamination of the Sarkar-Singer results," *World Development*, 21 (10): 1607–13.
—— (1998) *Trade Policy Issues in Asian Development*, London: Routledge.
Barro, R. and Lee, J.W. (1996) "International measures of schooling years and schooling quality," *American Economic Review*, 86 (2): 218–23.
Berik, G. (2000) "Mature export-led growth and gender wage inequality in Taiwan," *Feminist Economics*, 6 (3): 1–26.
Çağatay, N. (2002) *Trade, Gender, and Poverty*, New York: Social Development and Poverty Elimination Division, United Nations Development Programme.
Çağatay, N. and Özler, S. (1995) "Feminization of the labor force: the effects of long term development and structural adjustment," *World Development*, 23 (11): 1883–94.
Cuddington, J. and Urzua, C. (1989) "Trends and cycles in the net barter terms of trade: a new approach," *Economic Journal*, 99: 426–42.
Dollar, D. (1992) "Outward-oriented economies really do grow more rapidly: evidence from 95 LDCs, 1975–85," *Economic Development and Cultural Change*, 40 (3): 523–44.
Dollar, D. and Collier, P. (2002) *Globalization, Growth, and Poverty: building an inclusive world economy*, New York: World Bank.
Dollar, D. and Kraay, A. (2001) *Growth is Good for the Poor*, Washington, DC: World Bank, Development Research Group.
Easterly, W. and Levine, R. (1999) "It's not factor accumulation: stylized facts and growth models," Mimeo: World Bank and University of Minnesota, September.
Economic Research Forum for the Arab Countries (ERF) (2000) *Economic Trends in the MENA Region, 2000*, Cairo: Economic Research Forum for the Arab Countries, Iran and Turkey.
Elson, D. (1999) "Labor markets as gendered institutions: equality, efficiency and empowerment issues," *World Development*, 27 (3): 611–27.
Elson, D. and Pearson, R. (1984) "The subordination of women and the internationalization of factory production," in K. Young, C. Wolkowitz, and R. McCullugh (eds), *Of Marriage and the Market: women's subordination in international perspective*, 2nd edn, London: Routledge.
Evans, D. (1984) "A critical assessment of some neo-Marxian trade theories," *Journal of Development Studies*, 20 (2): 202–26.
Greene, W.H. (2002) *Econometric Analysis*, 5th edn, Upper Saddle River, NJ: Prentice Hall.

Grilli, E. and Yang, M. (1981) *Real and Monetary Determinants of Non-oil Primary Commodity Price Movements*, Washington, DC: World Bank.

Grown, C., Rao Gupta, G., and Kes, A. (2005) *Taking Action: achieving gender equality and empowering women*, UN Millennium Project Task Force on Education and Gender Equality, London: Earthscan.

Joekes, S. (1993) *The Influence of Trade Expansion on Women's Work*, Geneva: Interdepartmental Project on Equality for Women in Employment, International Labor Office.

—— (1995) *Trade Related Employment for Women in Industry and Services in Developing Countries*, Occasional Paper 5, Geneva: UNRISD.

—— (1999) "A gender-analytical perspective on trade and sustainable development," in UNCTAD, *Trade, Sustainable Development and Gender*, New York and Geneva: UNCTAD.

Joekes, S. and Moayedi, R. (1987) *Women and Export Manufacturing: a review of the issues and AID policy*, Washington, DC: International Center for Research on Women.

Joekes, S. and Weston, A. (1994) *Women and the New Trade Agenda*, New York: UNIFEM.

Lewis, A. (1954) "Economic development with unlimited supplies of labour," *Manchester School of Economic and Social Studies*, 22: 139–91.

Maizel, A. (2000) "The manufacturing terms of trade of developing countries with the United States, 1981–97," Working Paper 36, Queen Elizabeth House, Oxford University. Online available http://www.qeh.ox.ac.uk/pdf/qehwp/qehwps36.pdf (accessed October 19, 2006).

Maizel, A., Palaskas, T., and Crowe, T. (1998) "The Prebisch–Singer hypothesis revisited," in D. Sapsford and J.-R. Chen (eds), *Development Economics and Policy: the conference volume to celebrate the 85th birthday of Sir Hans Singer*, New York: St. Martin's Press.

Prebisch, R. (1950) *The Economic Development of Latin America and its Principle Problems*, New York: United Nations.

Rasiah, R. (2002) "Manufactured exports, employment, skills, and wages in Malaysia," Employment Paper Series 2002/35, Geneva: ILO.

Rodrik, D. (2001) *Global Governance of Trade as if Development Really Mattered*, New York: Social Development and Poverty Elimination Division, UNDP.

Sachs, J. and Warner, A. (1995) "Economic reform and the process of global integration," Brookings Papers on Economic Activity no. 1: 1–118.

Sapsford, D. (1986) "The statistical debate on the Net Barter Terms of Trade between primary commodities and manufactures: a comment and some additional evidence," *Economic Journal*, 9 (379): 781–8.

—— (1990) "Primary commodity prices and the terms of trade," *Economic Record*, 66: 342–56.

Sarkar, P. (1986) "The Singer–Prebisch hypothesis: a statistical evaluation," *Cambridge Journal of Economics*, 10 (4): 355–71.

Sarkar, P. and Singer, H.W. (1991) "Manufactured exports of developing countries and their terms of trade since 1965," *World Development*, 19 (4): 333–40.

—— (1993) "Manufacture–manufacture terms of trade deterioration: a reply," *World Development*, 21 (10): 1617–20.

Seguino, S. (2000a) "The effects of structural change and economic liberalization on gender wage differentials in South Korea and Taiwan," *Cambridge Journal of Economics*, 24 (4): 437–59.

—— (2000b) "Gender inequality and economic growth: a cross-country analysis," *World Development*, 28 (7): 1211–30.

Singer, H.W. (1950) "The distribution of gains between investing and borrowing countries," *American Economic Review*, 40 (2): 473–85.

Spraos, J. (1980) "The statistical debate on the net barter terms of trade between primary products and manufactures," *Economic Journal*, 90 (357): 107–28.

—— (1982) "Deteriorating terms of trade and beyond," *Trade and Development: United Nations Conference on Trade and Development Review*, 4: 97–118.

—— (1983) *Inequalising Trade*, London: Oxford University Press.

Standing, G. (1989) "Global feminization through flexible labor," *World Development*, 17 (7): 1077–95.

—— (1999) "Global feminization through flexible labor: a theme revisited," *World Development*, 27 (3): 583–602.

UN (1999) *World Survey on the Role of Women in Development: Globalization, Gender, and Work*, New York: United Nations.

United Nations (Various years) *Commodity Trade Statistics Database* (COMTRADE).

—— (Various years) *Yearbook of International Trade Statistics*, New York: United Nations.

Vernon, R. (1966) "International investment and international trade in the product cycle," *Quarterly Journal of Economics*, 80: 190–207.

Viner, J. (1955) *Studies in the Theory of International Trade*, London: Allen and Unwin.

Wilson, T., Sinha, R.P., and Castree, R. (1969) "The income terms of trade of developed and developing countries," *The Economic Journal*, 79 (316): 813–32.

Wood, A. (1991) "North-South trade and female labor in manufacturing: an asymmetry," *Journal of Development Studies*, 27 (2): 168–89.

—— (1994) *North-South Trade, Employment and Inequality: changing fortunes in a skill-driven world*, Oxford: Oxford University Press.

World Bank (2001) *World Development Indicators CDROM*, Washington, DC: World Bank.

5 The formal structure of a gender-segregated low-income economy

William A. Darity, Jr

Introduction

This chapter presents a compact formal framework for the analysis of interactions that take place in a low-income developing country characterized by a high level of gender segregation with respect to economic activity. The model is based directly upon the observations and insights advanced by researchers whose focus has been on the roles performed by women in developing countries, particularly the work of Elson (1991, 1993), Mbilinyi (1988), Lado (1992), Kennedy and Bouis (1989), and Tibaijuka (1994). Their findings are especially applicable to economic systems with a pronounced sexual division of labor in agrarian regions of sub-Saharan Africa.

This body of work was prompted, in part, by interest in exploring dimensions of structural adjustment typically ignored by development economists and by multilateral institutions such as the International Monetary Fund (IMF). While addressing the effects of structural adjustment, however, this body of work (and the model advanced here) goes beyond the ramifications of specific policy initiatives to suggest that there is a unique economic structure at play in these low-income regions.

The degree of gender segregation in tasks is, perhaps, more sharply drawn here than in many actual conditions where the model has applicability, but it is hoped the model will provide a basis for further investigations into the nature of economies of this type when modified appropriately. In this aggregative framework the community in question has two sectors of economic activity, a sector producing a cash-crop that can be exported and a sector producing household goods or social maintenance resources, or what otherwise might be called "subsistence." The cash-crop could be rice, tea, groundnuts, bananas, or tobacco in various parts of sub-Saharan Africa.

The gender division of labor operates at two levels. First, women are the sole workers in the social maintenance or "subsistence" sector. Men remain idle rather than assist with household chores. Women's output in the household sector is a composite commodity that includes growing and preparation of food for their families, childrearing, and the upkeep of the home.

Second, although both men and women work in smallholder export production, there is a partition between men and women's tasks in the cash-crop sector.

For example, males engage in "land preparation" which is identified as "men's work" while women engage in "other tasks such as transplanting and weeding" which is identified as "women's work" (Elson 1991). While there is no intrinsic difference in men's and women's abilities to perform one set of tasks or the other in the cash-crop sector, different efficiencies are associated with their efforts because the tasks are gender-typed.

Moreover, men control the income generated in smallholder export production. Correspondingly, they seek to determine the level of female participation in cash-crop production consistent with maximization of male incomes from the export activity. To the extent that they can exercise male power over a wife's and/or older, unmarried daughter's labor time, the scale of female labor available to cash-crop production will be higher.

Women also may willingly supply some effort *gratis*, as their husband or father increases his time devoted to the export sector's output, due to a spirit of interfamilial cooperation. On the other hand, women also may require some compensation to induce them to reduce their time devoted to household work and to increase the time devoted to export good production. Men pull women out of social maintenance activities; they can do so by dint of male authority, by dint of women's cooperativeness with spouse or father, by dint of wage payments, or, more generally, by the combined effect of all three factors (see Collier 1990 and the essays in Gladwin (ed.) 1991).

In this model, a nearby village offers a market where consumer or investment goods can be purchased. Male investment activity over time can augment the stock of tools, equipment, and animal power available to enhance production in the export sector. In the abstract time period of the model, the flow of new additions to this stock of labor-augmenting goods, called "capital" if one prefers, is so small that the stock is treated as fixed.

Males also may invest in the household sector, using a portion of their income to buy goods from the village market that ease women's tasks in subsistence production. Again, of course, the men do not deign to lend a hand directly. Finally, male income will be devoted to purchases of pure luxury items from the village market.

Women use their incomes for two types of purchases. Either they buy luxury goods or they invest in the household sector. In either case as long as all categories of expenditure increase with rising incomes, that is, all three categories represent "normal" goods, we can ignore luxury consumption altogether in what follows.

The efficiency of female production in the subsistence sector is endogenous for three reasons. Female efficiency in the provision of social maintenance resources can suffer as women devote more and more hours to cash-crop production. They must extend the overall length of their workday because they must still produce a threshold minimum of household output, sufficient to meet the customary provisions that the men expect as well as enough to at least sustain themselves and their families physiologically. Moreover, fewer hours devoted to household production means less task specialization among women and also lower efficiency. The contrasting two effects arise from the possible efficiency-enhancing effects of village market purchases of goods for the household sector out of both women's and men's incomes.

For simplicity, it is assumed that the total number of male and female hours of awake time is fixed. Awake time is divided between work and leisure. The model also abstracts from any direct role for government. This may not be unrealistic because of the comparative spatial distance between a community of this type and an urban-based national government. Still, it is not difficult to indicate how the model can be modified to introduce the effects of policies pursued by the national government. The effects of a devaluation as part of a national structural adjustment package that has the expected effect of raising export demand will be considered in detail.

The smallholder export sector

Equation (5.1) is the Cobb–Douglas technology representing the production function for the smallholder export sector. This constitutes the output of the cash crop. X_c is the quantity of the cash crop, M_c represents male labor in cash crop production, F_c represents female labor in the same sector, and K_c represents the stock of labor-augmenting resources, treated as fixed in the period of analysis:

$$X_c = M_c^\alpha F_c^\beta K_c^\gamma \tag{5.1}$$

It is assumed that the sum of the exponents α and β is less than unity.

Equation (5.2) indicated that total female awake time, $\overline{F}$, is divided between cash crop production, F_c, social maintenance or subsistence production, F_s, and leisure, L:

$$\overline{F} = F_c + F_s + L \tag{5.2}$$

Women's leisure time is squeezed as participation in cash-crop production expands. Any male time not devoted to cash-crop production is devoted exclusively to leisure.

The next equation of the model depicts the special nature of the female labor supply process to the export sector:

$$F_c = CM_c^\sigma (w/p_v)^\rho \quad C \geq 1, \sigma \geq 0, \rho \geq 0 \tag{5.3}$$

The term C is a scale factor that represents the prevailing level of male control over female labor time in this community. When $C = 1$, males exercise no power over the allocation of women's work time; when $C > 1$, male power becomes operative in dictating the split of women's time between the export sector and household work. Interpret C, then, as the male social coercion parameter vis-à-vis women.

The sensitivity of female labor supply to male employment in the cash-crop sector represents an opposite effect, the extent of female cooperation with a husband or a father's efforts to raise output in the sector. If σ, the elasticity of female employment in cash crop production with respect to male employment is zero, females offer no uncompensated, uncoerced labor to export production. The higher the value of σ the easier it is for men to get women to work in the fields without asserting male authority or paying higher compensation to women.

The variable w is the money wage rate and P_v is the given price of goods available in the village. Women's labor supply in cash-crop production responds positively to a higher real wage calculated in terms of village goods. Thus, equation (5.3) captures all three factors: coercion, cooperation, and compensation. As we will see later, such a framework is amenable to old-fashioned marginalist techniques but provides some interesting results, nonetheless.

Male and female incomes

The objective men have is to maximize male income, Y_M. Male income is the difference between the money value of the cash crop and the compensation paid to women:

$$Y_M = P_c X_c - w F_c \tag{5.4}$$

where P_c is the money price of the cash crop, also given from the perspective of the farmers. Men will seek to maximize (5.4) by selecting the level of their own activity in the export sector, M_c, and the money wage paid to women, w.

Substituting equations (5.1) and (5.3) into (5.4) and differentiating Y_M with respect to M_c and w yields:

$$Y_M = P_c M_c^\alpha [C M_c^\sigma (w/p_v)^\rho]^\beta K_c^y - w_c M_c^\sigma (w/p_v)^\rho \tag{5.5}$$

$$\frac{\partial Y_M}{\partial M_c} = (\alpha + \beta\sigma) P_c \frac{X_c}{M_c} - \sigma w \frac{F_c}{M_c} \tag{5.6}$$

$$\frac{\partial Y_M}{\partial W} = \beta\rho P_c X_c W - (\rho + 1) F_c \tag{5.7}$$

Each of the expressions has a straightforward interpretation. In (5.6) the marginal contribution of male employment to male incomes is determined by the difference between the total effect of increased male employment on the money value of cash-crop production and the money cost of the additional female labor. The bracketed expression $(\alpha + \beta\sigma)$ weights the money value of the average product of male labor in the first component of (5.6). It consists of the sum of the elasticity of export output with respect to male labor and the product of the elasticity of export output with respect to female labor supply and the elasticity of female labor supply with respect to male employment (the cooperation effect). The latter elasticity also weights the female wage multiplied by the female–male employment ratio in cash crops as the second component of (5.6).

In (5.7) the marginal effect of an increase in the female wage on male incomes can be viewed as the difference between the gain in output value prompted by the increased female employment (the compensation effect) net of the direct cost associated with increased female employment. Here the elasticity of female cash-crop employment with respect to the real wage figures prominently. In both (5.6) and (5.7) the coercion effect C is embedded in both the output variable, X_c, and the female labor supply variable, F_c.

Setting (5.6) and (5.7) equal to zero for a maximum permits solutions to be derived for the equilibrium levels of male employment, M_c^*, and the female wage, w^*:

$$w^* = \left\{ \frac{\rho+1}{\rho} D^{-(\alpha+\sigma\beta-\sigma)} (\beta P_c C^\beta K_c^\gamma)^{-1} P_v^\rho \, ^{(1-\beta)} \right\}^R \tag{5.8}$$

$$M_c^* = \left\{ \frac{\rho+1}{\rho} D^{-(\alpha+\sigma\beta-\sigma)} (\beta P_c \, C^\beta K_c^\gamma)^{-1} P_v^\rho \, ^{(1-\beta)} \right\}^{RQ} \tag{5.9}$$

$$D = \left[\frac{1}{J P_c C^\beta (1/P_v)^{\rho\beta} K_c^Y} \right]^{[1/(\alpha+\sigma\beta)]}$$

$$J = \left(\frac{\sigma}{\alpha + \sigma\beta} \right)$$

$$Q = \frac{1-\rho\beta}{\alpha + \sigma\beta}$$

$$R = \frac{1}{Q(\alpha + \sigma\beta) + (\rho\beta - 1 - \rho)}$$

With the equilibrium values of w^* and M_c^* in hand, given the prevailing level of male control over female labor time and the prevailing price of goods in the village, the equilibrium amount of women's work time in cash-crop production is determined:

$$F_c^* = C M_c^* (w^*/P_v)\rho \tag{5.10}$$

Female income from smallholder export production, Y_F, is also determined:

$$Y_F = w^* F_c^* \tag{5.11}$$

(For further discussion of solutions for w^* and M_c^*, see Appendix.)

The subsistence sector

The production conditions in the household sector are depicted as follows:

$$S = E \cdot F_s \tag{5.12}$$

"Subsistence" output, S, is the product of an efficiency factor, E, and the amount of women's work time devoted to subsistence production.

The efficiency factor is endogenized as follows:

$$E = E(F_c, Y_F/P_v, Y_M P_v) \quad E_1 < 0, E_2 > 0, E_3 < 0 \tag{5.13}$$

The efficiency of housework declines as more hours of women's awake time are devoted to export sector production, rises as female incomes increase and rises as male incomes increase, the latter two measured in terms of command over village goods.

Using (5.2), equation (5.12) can be rewritten as follows:

$$S = E(F_c, Y_F/P_v, Y_M/P_v) \cdot (\bar{F} - F_c - L) \tag{5.14}$$

Note that as female work time is reallocated toward cash-crop production, the squeeze must take place on women's leisure (recreation, rest, and recuperation). This is because a threshold amount of household goods must be provided to reproduce the community according to customary standards. Men must be "fed" what men expect to be "fed" as first claimants on subsistence. Women receive a residual after the men's needs are met:

$$S_F = S - \bar{q}\bar{M} \tag{5.15}$$

Equation (5.15) indicates that female subsistence consumption is dictated by what is left after men take their share. $\bar{M}$ represents total male awake time, and $\bar{q}$ is the community norm for male consumption of subsistence per waking hour. If $\bar{z}$ represents the minimum amount of female consumption of social maintenance resources per waking hour to maintain normal physiological existence, then the following condition must be true:

$$S_F \geq \bar{z}\bar{F} \tag{5.16}$$

The presumption here is generally $\bar{z} < \bar{q}$.

Condition (5.15) means, in turn:

$$E(F_c, Y_F/P_v) \cdot (\bar{F} - F_c - L) \geq \bar{q}\bar{M} + \bar{z}\bar{F} \tag{5.17}$$

Again, depending upon community norms, this constraint need not be absolutely binding. It will be relaxed, first, by women receiving less than $\bar{z}$ in average subsistence consumption, thereby facing health dangers. Under encroaching famine conditions, male priority would lead to women suffering first.

If women devote more hours to cash-crop production there is one unambiguous adverse effect on subsistence production: the adverse effect on scale associated with the negative efficiency effect attributable to the increased length of the female workday (and the accompanying loss of leisure) along with the decreased specialization. Whether this adverse effect dominates the efficiency gains associated with the household investment goods from the village market provided by the women themselves or by the men is the critical question. As the range of village goods that can raise efficiency in the social maintenance sector will be wider the greater is infrastructural development. Obviously, many appliances common to US or British kitchens cannot be used without electricity.

Absolute hours devoted to household production will not decline as long as there is still "free" or leisure awake time that can be squeezed downward. But women must continue to maintain sufficient hours in social maintenance work to meet the threshold requirements. As cash-crop production expands, women necessarily have a longer and longer workday. If the scale effect captured by the partial derivative E is dominant, efficiency will decline. With female hours in household production relatively unchanged, there will be a drop in subsistence output. Since men have the initial claim on subsistence output, there could be circumstances in which women are pulled so sharply into cash-crop production that women's average consumption of subsistence is driven perilously close to $\bar{z}$ or even below $\bar{z}$. Gender-specific nutritional deficiencies can arise despite an export boom in a community of this type if the pressure on female labor time in the household sector cannot be offset by village resources purchased with incomes generated in the export sector.

Effects of a currency devaluation

What, then, are the potential effects of an IMF-mandated structural adjustment package in this type of an economy? Consider specifically the effects of a devaluation of the domestic currency. The standard justification for such a policy is to promote foreign export demand. If the policy does prompt such a response, it will be manifest in the economy modeled here by a rise in P_c, the money price of cash crops.

Under reasonable parameterizations (i.e. technological and labor supply parameters stay within empirically plausible bounds), a higher price of cash crops will lead men simultaneously to raise their own hours devoted to the export sector and the wage paid to women. Tedious differentiation of (5.8) and (5.9) with respect to P_c demonstrates this result. The effect will be a movement of women's work hours toward the export sector. The greater the success of domestic currency devaluation in raising the relative price of cash crops, the greater the pressure on female labor time in the subsistence sector. Once more, if the higher income for both males and females associated with the rise in P_c does not result in an offsetting gain in efficiency through greater access to village resources, efficiency and output will fall in the household sector. Women will bear a disproportionate brunt of the drop in subsistence output. It is precisely when there is a highly successful effort to promote exports through a devaluation that gender-specific health disadvantages are more likely to rise.

It also can be shown easily that a rise in the price of village goods under similar parameterizations will have exactly the opposite effects. After all, the parameter P_v enters both (5.8) and (5.9) in an inverse fashion with P_c. Both w^* and M_c^* will fall in response to an increase in P_v, leading to a reverse pattern: a decline in output in the export sector but greater efficiency and output in the subsistence sector.

If there is a high foreign import content of goods available in the village market, the currency devaluation will have precisely this effect on P_v. A rise in P_v coincident with a rise in P_c could mitigate the upward pressure on women's total labor time driven by their shift toward cash-crop production. The shift would be muted by the higher price of village goods. Of course, both female and male command over village goods also would be reduced. Underlying gender relations certainly have profound implications for the effects of at least this prong of a structural adjustment program.

Conclusions

Thus far the model has been analyzed under the premise of maintenance of a stable regime of gender relations. But there are avenues for exploration of comparative statics of changes in gender relations. The most obvious is a change in the degree of male control over female labor which can be considered by a variation in C, the scale parameter that captures the level of coercive influence men exercise over women's time.

Suppose the coercive influence becomes greater. If men have a relatively strong preference for leisure they not only could reduce the money wage they pay women, but they also could reduce their own labor time, particularly if the increased coercive effect dominates the cooperation effect. Regardless of whether men reduce or increase their own labor time, the ratio F_c/M_c will rise as a consequence of the rise in C.

But C is more likely to trend downward over time as gender relations move toward greater equality. In this case, men would find their incomes maximized by working longer hours and by paying women a higher money wage. In a community where C is trending downward, male priority over subsistence consumption should diminish also. The likelihood of women being subjected to nutritional deprivation during an export boom would be lowered as well. Three effects would come into play that would benefit female health status: (a) women are less readily drawn into cash-crop production, thereby having less of an adverse efficiency effect on subsistence production; (b) the higher wage per female in cash-crop production can provide greater access to village goods that may substitute for the lost hours; and (c) the diminution of male priority over subsistence means women need not wait until male requirements are met fully before partaking in consumption.

In this model women have no alternative source of money income aside from working in the fields with their fathers or husbands. But the money income they obtain from cash-crop production is discretionary and a source of female independence. Women could accumulate resources to develop other options to facilitate migration to the village or city to attempt to take up other employment, to provide schooling opportunities for daughters, or to gain access to additional land or tools to grow their own cash crops and have direct control over the income from cash-crop production. Gender-specific government policies such as subsidies and cheap credit arrangements for women's farming enterprises could aid women in developing their own nonsubsistence farming activities. But these programs are unlikely to be adopted or maintained if a structural adjustment package mandates a sharp deficit reduction accompanied by cuts in social programs.

Such changes would raise the money wage men would have to pay to their female relatives. Indeed, if women move into their own smallholder export activity *en masse*, the strict gender separation in farming tasks would have to break down. The time/work burden in a gender-segregated, low-income economy falls disproportionately on women. A prevailing structure of gender rules concerning work, consumption, and authority makes this the case. The breakdown of that structure opens the door to other possibilities, even the possibility that men might contribute significantly to household production. But that is a yet to be realized revolution in high-income countries with considerably lower levels of gender-segregation in employment.

Appendix 5.A Formally modeling a gender-segregated economy: a reply to Campbell and Warner

Campbell and Warner (1997) have presented a thoughtful critique of my original analysis (Darity 1995). They identify two major problems. First, Campbell and Warner complain that my model "offers no explicit treatment of the woman negotiating her wages and places direct determination under the control of the man who is maximizing his income." They even argue that my model implies that maximization of male incomes means setting female compensation at zero. Second, Campbell and Warner complain that my model is "underspecified" in the formal sense that there is no internal maximum possible from the exercise developed in my paper.

Their first complaint is not substantive; their second complaint is correct. With respect to the first complaint, equation (5.3) constitutes a female labor supply equation in the Cobb–Douglas form. The real compensation (w/p_y) for women enters the equation with exponent ρ. The exponent ρ could be the outcome of custom, tradition, or even nonsymmetric intergender bargaining, given relative male dominance, the latter as Campbell and Warner prefer. But an explicit exploration of the game-theoretic/bargaining foundations for the economic outcomes in societies of this type is the subject matter for another paper. Moreover, if men were to set $w = 0$, female labor supply would vanish and, given the gender division of labor, no cash crops production or male income could be generated.

With respect to the second complaint, Campbell and Warner are right. When I set up the exercise, I sought the solution for optimal values of the female wage, w, and the amount of labor supplied by men for cash crops production, M_c. But since I tried to solve by direct substitution with manic inversion of exponents rather than driving to set up the system in matrix notation, I never detected the impossibility of deriving a nontrivial solution. Because the system was nonlinear and because I assumed the system had a solution through direct substitution, I never contemplated displaying the first-order conditions in matrix notation. Therefore, I evidently "forced" a solution, despite the insolubility of the notationally simplified version of my system Campbell and Warner present as:

$$JX = D \tag{5.A.1}$$

where

$$J = \begin{bmatrix} (\alpha + \sigma\beta)A - \sigma B \\ \rho\beta A - (\rho + 1)B \end{bmatrix}, \quad X = \begin{bmatrix} M_c^{\alpha + \sigma(\beta - 1)} \\ w^{1 + \rho(1 - B)} \end{bmatrix}, \quad \text{and} \quad D = \begin{bmatrix} 0 \\ 0 \end{bmatrix}$$

$$A \equiv P_c C^\beta K_c^\gamma (1/P_v)^{\rho\beta}$$

$$B \equiv C(1/P_v)\rho \tag{5.A.2}$$

The central technical problem is the fact that D is the zero vector, so that neither matrix inversion nor Cramer's rule yield a nontrivial solution. If the system were re-specified so that a constant term appeared in either the upper or lower cell of the D vector then, in principle, the system would have nonzero solutions for M_c and w. But it is unlikely that a re-specified system could be linearized and written in matrix notation. Direct substitution still would have to be used as the method of solution; at least an internal maximum would be feasible.

One route out of the impasse is to follow Campbell and Warner's inclination to treat the male optimization problem as inclusive of an old-fashioned labor–leisure choice. Suppose men in this community had a utility function in three arguments:

$$U = U(Y_M, M_c, w/P_v) \quad U_1 > 0, \; U_2 < 0, \; U_3 < 0 \tag{5.A.3}$$

In equation (5.A.3) men gain utility from additional income, disutility from increased labor (or decreased leisure), and disutility from paying women higher real compensation. The latter effect arises, apart from any reduction in male incomes that might be associated with a higher female wage, because higher real incomes for women can mean their exercise of greater independence.

The Lagrange equation now can be formed, again using Campbell and Warner's notational simplification:

$$L = U(Y_M, M_c, w/P_v) + \lambda\left[Y_M - AM_c^{\alpha + \sigma\beta} w^{\rho\beta} BM_c^\alpha w^{\rho+1}\right] \tag{5.A.4}$$

First-order conditions for a maximum are:

$$\frac{\partial L}{\partial Y_M} = U_1 + \lambda = 0 \tag{5.A.5}$$

$$\frac{\partial L}{\partial M_c} = U_2 - \lambda[(\alpha + \sigma\beta)AM_c^{(\alpha+\sigma\beta-1)}w^{\rho\beta} - \sigma BM_c^{\sigma-1}w^{\rho+1}] = 0 \tag{5.A.6}$$

$$\frac{\partial L}{\partial w} = U_3 - \lambda[\rho\beta AM_c^{\alpha+\sigma\beta}w^{\rho\beta-1} - (\rho+1)BM_c^{\sigma}w^{\rho}] = 0 \tag{5.A.7}$$

$$\frac{\partial L}{\partial \lambda} = Y_M - AM_c^{\alpha+\sigma\beta}w^{\rho\beta} + BM_c^{\sigma}w^{\rho+1} = 0 \tag{5.A.8}$$

By using expressions (5.A.5), (5.A.6), and (5.A.7) and by eliminating λ we arrive at the following two-equation system in two unknowns, M_c and w:

$$-U_1/U_2 = [(\alpha + \sigma\beta)AM_c^{(\alpha+\sigma\beta-1)}w^{\rho\beta} - \sigma BM_c^{(\sigma-1)}w^{(\rho+1)}]^{-1} \tag{5.A.9}$$

$$-U_1/U_3 = [\rho\beta AM_c^{\alpha+\sigma\beta}w^{\rho\beta-1} - (\rho+1)BM_c^{\sigma}w^{\rho}]^{-1} \tag{5.A.10}$$

Equation (5.A.9) captures the labor-leisure tradeoff and equation (5.A.10) captures the male income-female wage tradeoff at the optimum for men. Capacity to solve the system for optimal values of M_c and w depends upon the specific form given to the male utility function.

Aesthetically, I prefer an alternative route that involves a modest extension of my original model. This idea evolved in conversations with Korkut Ertürk. Simply deduct from men's income a sum proportionate to the amount of labor they supply. This could be interpreted as a male "psychic" cost of leisure forgone, if one so desires, or it could capture some inefficiency in generating income as men devote more hours to cash crops production. Net male income now is defined as follows:

$$Y_M = P_c X_c = wF_c - gM_c \quad g > 0 \tag{5.A.11}$$

The term gM_c represents the male income lost due to the "expense" men incur in devoting more labor to cash crops production. Note that males do not consider any costs associated with increased female labor devoted to cash crops production, ignoring, for example, the adverse impact on household or subsistence production. Thus, what is optimal for males plainly need not be optimal for the community as a whole.

Once again using Campbell and Warner's notational simplification (5.A.11) can be rewritten as:

$$Y_M = AM_c^{\alpha+\sigma\beta}w^{\rho\beta} - BM_c^{\sigma}w^{\rho+1} - gM_c \tag{5.A.11'}$$

First-order conditions for a male maximum now become:

$$\frac{\partial Y_M}{\partial M_c} = (\alpha + \sigma\beta)AM_c^{\alpha+\sigma\beta-1}w^{\rho\beta} - \sigma BM_c^{\sigma-1}w^{\rho+1} - g = 0 \tag{5.A.12}$$

$$\frac{\partial Y_M}{\partial w_c} = \rho\beta AM_c^{\alpha+\sigma\beta}w^{\rho\beta-1} - (\rho+1)BM_c^{\sigma}w^{\rho} = 0 \tag{5.A.13}$$

Dividing (5.A.12) by $M_c^{\sigma-1}w^{\rho\beta}$ and (5.A.13) by $M_c^{\sigma}w^{\rho\beta-1}$ by yields:

$$(\alpha+\sigma\beta)AM_c^{\alpha+\sigma(\beta-1)} - \sigma Bw^{1+\rho(\beta-1)} = gM_c^{1-\sigma}w^{-\rho\beta} \tag{5.A.12'}$$

$$\rho\beta AM_c^{\alpha+\sigma(\beta-1)} - (\rho+1) - Bw^{1+\rho(1-\beta)} = 0 \tag{5.A.13'}$$

Equations (5.A.12') and (5.A.13') are used to solve for w and M_c.
Barring another error the solutions are the following:

$$w^* = \left[\frac{H}{gR^{1/U(1-\sigma)}}\right]^{Q/T} \tag{5.A.14}$$

$$M_c^* = R^{1/U}w^*Q/U$$

$$R \equiv \frac{(\rho+1)B}{\rho\beta A}; \quad Q \equiv 1 + \rho(1-\beta)$$

$$U \equiv \alpha + \sigma(\beta-1); \quad H \equiv [(\alpha+\beta)AR - \sigma B]$$

$$T \equiv [Q/U(1-\sigma) - \rho\beta] \tag{5.A.15}$$

Obviously, these closed form solutions are messy, but they do provide a consistent basis for the findings I presented in my paper. For example, the price of cash crops, P_c, and the price of village goods, P_v, do indeed enter (5.A.14) and (5.A.15) in an inverse fashion and an increase in each will lead to opposite effects on w^* and M_c^*. Just as I suggested in my paper, a rise in P_c will tend to promote a rise in both w^* and M_c^*; the reverse effect will follow from an increase in P_v. But the effect of either price change on w^* is stronger and less ambiguous than the effect on M_c^*.

Note also the effect of the new parameter g that captures any losses in net income for men due to increased male labor devoted to cash crops production. A larger value of g will necessarily depress both the equilibrium values of labor, M_c^*, and women's real compensation, w^*, as long as the exponential term T/Q is positive.

At the core of the model is the characterization of the female labor supply process as decomposable into three effects: coercion, cooperation, and compensation. Of particular importance in determining outcomes in the model are the relative magnitudes of the parameters α, β, σ and ρ, α, and β are the elasticities of cash crops output with respect to inputs of male and female labor respectively, while δ and ρ are the elasticities of female labor supply with respect to male employment and the real wage for women. At least now the analysis can be performed with equilibrium values of w^* and M_c^* truly in "hand."

References

Campbell, D. and Warner, J. (1997) "Formally modeling a gender-segregated economy: a response to William Darity, Jr.," *World Development*, 25 (12): 2155–8.

Collier, P. (1990) "Gender aspects of labor allocation during structural adjustment," unpublished manuscript, Oxford: Oxford Unit for the Study of African Economics, Oxford University.

Darity, W. (1995) "The formal structure of a gender-segregated low-income economy," *World Development*, 23 (11): 1963–8.

Elson, D. (1991) "Male bias in macroeconomics: the case of structural adjustment," in D. Elson (ed.), *Male Bias in the Development Process*, Manchester: Manchester University Press.

—— (1993) "Gender-aware analysis and development economics," *Journal of International Development*, 5 (2): 237–47.

Gladwin, C. (ed.) (1991) *Structural Adjustment and African Women Farmers*, Gainesville: University of Florida Press.

Kennedy, E. and Bouis, H. (1989) "Traditional cash crop schemes effects on production, consumption and nutrition: sugarcane in the Philippines and Kenya," unpublished manuscript, Washington, DC: International Food Policy Research Institute.

Lado, C. (1992) "Female labor participation in agricultural production and the implications for nutrition and health in rural Africa," *Social Science and Medicine*, 34 (2): 787–807.

Mbilinyi, M. (1988) "The invention of female farming systems in Africa: structural adjustment in Tanzania," workshop on Economic Crisis, Household Strategies and Women's Work, Ithaca, NY: Cornell University.

Tibaijuka, A. (1994) "The cost of differential gender roles in African agriculture: a case study of smallholder banana-coffee farms in the Kagera Region, Tanzania," *Journal of Agricultural Economics*, 45 (1): 69–81.

6 Macroeconomic effects of reducing gender wage inequality in an export-oriented, semi-industrialized economy

Robert A. Blecker and Stephanie Seguino

Introduction

Until recently, macroeconomic models were constructed as if gender differences were irrelevant for aggregate economic performance. Even today, only a handful of macro models have been developed in which gender differences play any role (Darity 1995; Ertürk and Çağatay 1995). This chapter presents a macro model of one specific situation in which the gender dimension can be argued to be significant for aggregate economic outcomes: the case of "export-led growth" in semi-industrialized economies (SIEs) in which the export industries rely heavily on low-paid, female labor.

A large literature argues that women's low wages have been a stimulus to growth in many of the most successful cases of export-led development, such as South Korea, Hong Kong, and Taiwan (Deyo 1989; Hsiung 1996). Research suggests that the low female wages in these and other countries' export sectors are not explained entirely by women's relatively lower productivity or human capital. Rather, they are largely attributable to gender discrimination embedded in traditional gender norms and social practices combined with women's segregation into export sector employment and the repression of labor organization by state-corporate alliances (Ward 1988; Cheng and Hsiung 1994). These views imply a serious problem for efforts to enhance gender equity in SIEs: if women are able to raise their wages relative to men's, the result could be a decline in export competitiveness and a slowdown in the country's growth rate. In this case, gender equity may not be compatible with growth in an export-oriented SIE.

This chapter addresses this set of issues by constructing "structuralist" macro models in the sense of Taylor (1983, 1991): models that assume the "stylized facts" characterizing the main features of a historically specific economic situation and can be used to investigate the logical implications of those assumptions for the effects of various types of economic change. The main stylized fact that motivates the present analysis is the gender division of labor that is enforced in the labor markets of many, if not most, developing countries that export manufactures, in which female manufacturing workers face employment barriers that result in their segregation in export-sector jobs at lower wages than male workers receive in domestic industries.[1]

The models developed here build on existing two-sector models of SIEs with "home" and "export" products, and extend them to incorporate gender job segregation and differences in the wages paid to workers in the two sectors. In addition to this gender dimension, other stylized facts that will be reflected in the analysis include the following. First, SIEs are typically dependent on imports of capital goods and intermediate goods and their demand for such imports is price-inelastic. Second, many SIEs have manufacturing sectors characterized by excess capacity and, as a result, their industrial output levels are constrained by effective demand as well as by the availability of necessary imported inputs. Third, domestic manufactures in SIEs are often highly oligopolistic with rigid price-cost margins, while export-oriented manufactures are typically more competitive and have more flexible price-cost margins due to their need to "price to market" in order to compete in global markets. Fourth, although historically many manufacturing industries in developing countries produced exclusively for export markets, there is increasing production in some of these industries for domestic markets, particularly in middle-income SIEs.

Both of the models developed here are short-run models that take capital stocks and other slowly adjusting variables as given. The first model assumes that nominal wages are rigid for institutional reasons and the exchange rate is fixed, while the second model allows wages to be flexible and also introduces a managed exchange rate regime assuming that the government targets the real exchange rate when nominal wages rise.

The static model with rigid wages and a fixed exchange rate

This section presents a short-run, two-sector macro model of a SIE with gender differences between the workers in the two sectors (home and export goods).[2] This model is used to identify the conditions under which an exogenous rise in female wages has a contractionary or expansionary effect on the outputs of the two goods, and hence on male and female employment, holding male wages and the exchange rate fixed. This specification is motivated by the possible existence of nominal wage rigidities in many SIEs due to factors such as minimum wage laws, union wage bargaining (with long-term contracts), and/or social norms governing gender wage differentials. We also assume here that the exchange rate is fixed for simplicity.

The home product (H) is used for both domestic consumption and investment; for simplicity, it is not exported. It is produced using variable inputs of male labor and imported intermediate goods. The export product (X) is a pure consumption good that is produced primarily for export, but which may also be consumed at home. It is produced by variable inputs of female labor and imported intermediate goods. The price equations for the two goods are:

$$P_H = \tau(w_m a_H + e P_n{}^* n_H), \quad \tau > 1 \tag{6.1}$$

$$P_X = \varphi(w_f a_X + e P_n{}^* n_X), \quad \varphi > 1 \tag{6.2}$$

where τ and φ are the price-cost margins (equal to one plus the mark-up rate in each sector); w_m and w_f represent male and female nominal wage rates, respectively; a_i is the labor coefficient in sector i ($i = H, X$); n_i is the intermediate input coefficient in sector i ($i = H, X$); P_n^* is the world price of intermediate inputs; and e is the nominal exchange rate (domestic currency price of foreign exchange). All the input–output coefficients and P_n^* are exogenously fixed, along with both wage rates and the exchange rate. We assume that $w_f < w_m$ for consistency with the stylized facts. Although this does not matter formally to the analysis when wage rates are exogenously fixed, it will matter when we analyze flexible wages in the section "Short-run dynamics with flexible nominal wages and a managed exchange rate" later.

The home sector margin (τ) is assumed to be rigid due to protectionist barriers, government subsidies, and a highly concentrated oligopolistic structure (none of which are modeled explicitly here). The export-sector margin (φ) is assumed to be flexible in response to international competitive pressures, and given the intensely competitive nature of the export markets we assume that the price-cost margins adjust instantaneously to try to maintain market shares. The X-sector margin is determined by the following constant-elasticity function:

$$\varphi = \Phi \rho_X^\theta \tag{6.3}$$

where $\rho_X = eP_X^*/P_X$ is the real exchange rate for exports, P_X^* is the foreign currency price of competing products from other countries, $\Phi > 1$ is the domestic firms' "target" profit margin (a constant), and $\theta > 0$ is the elasticity of the price-cost margin with respect to ρ_X.

Essentially, θ is inversely related to the degree of "exchange rate pass-through": the higher is θ, the more domestic exporters squeeze their profit margins in response to a currency appreciation, and the less the appreciation is passed through into export prices. To see this more clearly, (6.2) and (6.3) can be combined to yield:

$$\varphi = \Phi^{1/(1+\theta)} \varepsilon^{\theta/(1+\theta)} \tag{6.4}$$

where $\varepsilon = \rho_X \varphi = eP_X^*/(w_f a_X + eP_n^* n_X)$ is the ratio of the price of foreign export-competing goods (converted to domestic currency units) to the unit costs (average variable costs) of domestic export goods. The degree of exchange rate pass-through is measured by $1 - [\theta/(1-\theta)] = 1/(1-\theta)$, that is, pass-through is full when $\theta = 0$ and $\varphi = \Phi$ is a constant, and approaches zero in the limit as θ approaches infinity and φ becomes more and more sensitive to ε.

Nominal national income is divided between total wages, W, and profits, R, assuming for simplicity that there is no government spending or taxation:

$$Y = W + R \tag{6.5}$$

Total wages are the sum of the wages earned by each gender in their respective sector:

$$W = w_m a_H H + w_f a_X X \tag{6.6}$$

where H and X denote the quantities of output of home and export goods, respectively. Total profits are the sum of the profits received in each sector:

$$R = R_H + R_X \tag{6.7}$$

with

$$R_H = (\tau - 1)(w_m a_H + eP_n{}^* n_H) H \tag{6.8}$$

$$R_X = (\varphi - 1)(w_f a_X + eP_n{}^* n_X) X \tag{6.9}$$

With regard to international trade, the small country assumption (infinitely elastic demand for a country's exports at a given world price) is not generally valid for SIE exporters because of product differentiation between different SIE suppliers. We therefore assume that good X is an imperfect substitute for competing foreign products, and hence exports of X have a finite (positive) price elasticity ψ:

$$E_x = A\rho_X^{\psi} \quad A>0, \ 0<\psi<\infty \tag{6.10}$$

The constant term $A > 0$ incorporates foreign income effects on the demand for exports, which are exogenous and can be suppressed for convenience.

Import demand is rigidly tied to domestic production and investment and is completely price-inelastic. Assuming there are no imports of consumption goods, nominal import demand equals the domestic currency value of imports of intermediate goods and capital goods:

$$eP_n{}^*(n_H H + n_X X) + eP_I{}^* I_M \tag{6.11}$$

where $P_I{}^*$ is the foreign-currency price of imported investment goods and I_M represents the quantity of imported investment goods. We assume that imported investment goods are a fixed proportion $\mu > 0$ of home investment goods, that is, $I_M = \mu I_H$,[3] in which case (6.11) becomes

$$eP_n{}^*(n_H H + n_X X) + eP_I{}^* \mu I_H \tag{6.11a}$$

Turning to domestic expenditures, we specify functions for private consumption and investment. Assuming that wage and profit recipients have different propensities to spend, and allowing for some domestic consumption of the "export" good, we have four consumption functions.[4] Using C_{ij} for real consumption of good j ($j = H, X$) by income recipients i ($i = W, R$), we have the following expressions for nominal consumption expenditures. For workers,

$$P_H C_{WH} = (1 - \alpha) c_W W \tag{6.12}$$

$$P_X C_{WX} = \alpha c_W W \tag{6.13}$$

where α is the fraction of their consumption spending on good X. For profit recipients,

$$P_H C_{RH} = (1 - \beta) c_R R \tag{6.14}$$

$$P_X C_{RX} = \beta c_R R \tag{6.15}$$

where β is the percentage of their spending on good X. Both α and β are assumed to be constant for simplicity. The parameters c_W and c_R are the marginal propensities to consume out of wage and profit income, respectively, assuming $1 \geqslant c_W > c_R \geqslant 0$.

Investment expenditures are assumed to be a function of profits in the two sectors (the sectoral destination of the investment is not specified in the model). In the present case, since the total amount of desired investment spending has to cover both domestic and imported investment goods, the investment function is written as follows:

$$eP_I^* I_M + P_H I_H = P_H I_0 + b_1 R_H + b_2 R_X \tag{6.16}$$

where the left-hand side is total investment expenditures on both types of investment goods and the right-hand side is the investment demand function, in which I_0 is a constant term (measured in real terms and reflecting Keynesian animal spirits) and b_1, $b_2 > 0$ measure the responsiveness of domestic investment to profits in the two sectors.[5] Using the assumption of a fixed proportion $\mu = I_M / I_H$, (6.16) can be rewritten in terms of expenditures on home investment goods as follows:

$$P_H I_H = \left[P_H I_0 + b_1 R_H + b_2 R_X \right] / (\rho_M \mu + 1) \tag{6.16a}$$

where $\rho_M = eP_I^*/P_H$ is the real exchange rate for imports of investment goods.

Equilibrium in the two commodity markets is given by the following conditions:

$$H = C_{WH} + C_{RH} + I_H \tag{6.17}$$

$$X = C_{WX} + C_{RX} + E_X \tag{6.18}$$

The equilibrium condition for overall goods market clearing (national income equals aggregate demand) can be written in nominal terms as:

$$W + R = P_H (C_{WH} + C_{RH}) + P_X (C_{WX} + C_{RX}) + P_H I_H + P_X E_X \\ - eP_n^* (n_H H + n_X X) \tag{6.19}$$

where imported investment goods have been netted out of both investment demand and imports.

This model can be solved as follows.[6] Given that both sectors are "fixprice" industries,[7] the two key variables that adjust in the short run are the quantities of output H and X; all other endogenous variables (such as W, R, I_H, I_M, and Y) have to be derived as functions of H and X. In order to obtain two independent

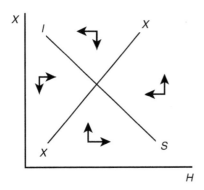

Figure 6.1 Equilibrium outputs and adjustment dynamics with rigid nominal wages.

functions in H and X, we can use any two of the three equations (6.17) to (6.19); the third can be derived from the other two. For present purposes, we use the national income identity (6.19), conceptualized as the saving-investment equilibrium condition (i.e. an "IS curve," although not a traditional one), together with equation (6.18) for X-sector market-clearing (which we call the "XX curve"). If the market for X clears then the market for H must also clear by Walras' Law so that (6.17) will also be satisfied.

The IS and XX curves are illustrated in Figure 6.1. The IS curve slopes down because, if output of either good rises, this creates an excess aggregate supply of goods (excess of saving over investment), and to restore goods-market equilibrium it is necessary for output of the other good to fall, *ceteris paribus*. That is, the IS curve shows the trade-off between the quantities of the two goods that can be produced at the same level of aggregate demand; the point along this trade-off at which the economy operates is then determined by relative demand for the two goods, as reflected in the XX curve. The XX curve slopes up because, if output of H rises, this generates additional wage and profit income, part of which is spent on consumption of X, and hence more X is also produced (assuming that the X-sector does not hit a capacity constraint).[8] There is excess supply in the market for X above and to the left of the XX line, and excess demand below it; there is excess aggregate demand below and to the left of the IS line, and excess aggregate supply above it. The short-run dynamics of the system are as shown in Figure 6.1 and the equilibrium is a locally stable focus in the neighborhood of the equilibrium point.

Comparative statics of increased female wages

The model developed in the previous section can be used to analyze the comparative static effects of exogenously increasing the female wage rate w_f, holding all other factors (including the male wage rate w_m) constant.[9] In the context of institutionally rigid wages, this goal might be achieved by raising the minimum wage, or by extending minimum wage guidelines to smaller firms that employ mainly female workers. Alternatively, w_f might increase suddenly as a result of women workers' gains following a successful strike and the negotiation of a new contract, or due to a change in social gender norms that allows women to earn higher wages relative to men.

The comparative static effects of raising w_f operate through three distinct "channels": (1) a relative price effect (the relative price of export goods P_X/P_H increases, and there is a real appreciation or decrease in the real exchange rate $\rho_X = eP_X^*/P_X$); (2) a gender redistribution effect (the women's real wage rises, and the men's real wage falls as long as $\alpha > 0$);[10] and (3) a class redistribution effect (the price-cost margin φ is squeezed by higher wages in the X-sector, thus reducing the profit share in that sector). The effects that operate through these three channels then depend on the values of the various parameters in the model, especially: the proportion of wage income spent on export goods (α), the different propensities to consume out of wage and profit income ($c_W > c_R$), the "footloose capital" effect in the investment function (b_2), the price elasticity of export demand (ψ), and the "profit-squeeze" effect on the X-sector price-cost margin (θ).

Table 6.1 lists the three main possible cases (I through III).[11] In the pessimistic Case (I), export markets are very price-competitive (the price elasticity ψ is relatively high) and there is little home consumption of these goods (α is low). The profit squeeze effect θ and the footloose capital effect b_2 are either both high or both low. The XX curve is relatively flat in this case, and a rise in w_f causes both the IS and XX curves to shift downward. Equilibrium output of X (and hence women's employment) definitely falls, while the change in equilibrium output of H (and hence men's employment) is ambiguous. The effects on total employment ($a_X X + a_H H$) and real income Y/P_H are ambiguous, but likely to be negative as long as H does not increase too much (and definitely negative if H falls along

Table 6.1 Comparative static effects of increasing the women's wage rate

Case	Description	Parameter values[a]					Effects on output[b]	
		c_W	α	ψ	θ	b_2	H	X
I	Pessimistic	moderate $(c_W > c_R)$	low	high, $>>1$	high/ low[c]	high/ low[c]	?	−
II	Cooperative, optimistic	high $(c_W >> c_R)$	low	moderate, but >1	high	low	+	?
III	Equalizing but conflictive	high $(c_W >> c_R)$	high	low, possibly <1	high	low	?	+

Notes

a Combinations of parameter values that together are sufficient to make each case occur; no individual parameter value shown by itself is sufficient to make a particular case obtain.

b Signs of the partial derivatives, $\partial H/\partial w_f$ and $\partial X/\partial w_f$, respectively. The effects on male employment ($a_H H$) and female employment ($a_X X$) have the same signs as the effects on H and X, respectively.

c The combination of *either* a high θ and a high b_2 *or* a low θ and a low b_2 can help to make Case I occur.

with X). Essentially, the higher women's wage causes a relatively large loss of export demand that is not offset by a large increase in domestic demand. Consumption does not rise much from the redistribution of income toward wages because c_W is only moderately higher than c_R. A large profit squeeze effect (high θ) causes a steep decline in investment (high b_2); alternatively, a small profit squeeze effect (low θ) results in only a small decrease in investment (low b_2).

Case II assumes that: there is a large profit squeeze effect (high θ); the footloose capital effect is small (low b_2); there is a large difference between the propensities to consume out of wages and profits ($c_W \gg c_R$); and export demand is only moderately price-elastic (i.e. ψ is only slightly greater than 1 – perhaps because of high quality export products). In this case, IS shifts up and to the right, since the redistribution of income toward wages boosts aggregate demand by more than the reduction in exports depresses it, while XX shifts downward (assuming α is low), which requires that the increase in domestic consumption of X is not large enough to outweigh the loss of export sales. The equilibrium level of H rises, while the change in equilibrium X is ambiguous. Total employment ($a_X X + a_H H$) and real national income Y/P_H are likely to rise, assuming the H sector is larger. Since both genders gain in some respect (women get higher real wages and men get more jobs), we call Case II "cooperative" or "optimistic." However, if one thinks that the combination of a relatively high θ with a relatively low ψ is implausible (why should firms flexibly adjust their price-cost margins if higher prices induce relatively little loss of export sales?) then this case may be difficult to achieve.

Case III is similar to II, except that export demand must be relatively price-inelastic ($\psi < 1$) and/or the workers' share of their consumer expenditures on the export good (α) must be relatively large. Then, both XX and IS can shift upward. The equilibrium level of X definitely rises, because of the strong boost in domestic consumption of X and relatively small loss of export sales, while the change in equilibrium H is ambiguous. Total employment ($a_X X + a_H H$) and real national income Y/P_H may either rise or fall. Women definitely gain in terms of employment as well as wages; men may either gain or lose jobs but their real wage definitely falls since they consume significant amounts of the export goods that have risen in price. Because women gain largely at the expense of men, we call this the "equalizing but conflictive" case, but again the combination of a low ψ and high θ may be implausible.

Short-run dynamics with flexible nominal wages and a managed exchange rate

This section considers a model in which nominal wages adjust endogenously in response to changes in labor market conditions in the short run. Assuming that labor markets are not auction markets, these adjustments are not instantaneous, but rather take place with lags due to institutional factors such as the need to renegotiate contracts. Because the forces that influence female and male wages differ, we model male and female wage rates as distinct endogenous variables that adjust separately in response to conditions in the markets for male and female labor, respectively. However, these two markets are not independent of each other, but rather are linked through various channels embodying household-level gender relations, such as the effect of the level of men's wages on women's labor supply decisions.

Flexible nominal wages influence prices through the mark-up pricing equations (6.1) and (6.2), and thus affect real exchange rates. Assuming that governments of SIEs are not indifferent to the resulting changes in export competitiveness, it is also necessary to model adjustments in the nominal exchange rate that can prevent the real exchange rate from getting too far out of line. Historically, most SIEs have either pegged or managed their exchange rates. One common arrangement is a "crawling peg," in which the nominal exchange rate is fixed at any point in time but is adjusted gradually over time (Williamson 1981). Although crawling pegs have fallen into disfavor since the Mexican and Asian financial crises of the 1990s, most SIEs continue to manage their exchange rates and a crawling peg will be assumed here as an analytically convenient specification.

The lagged adjustments in nominal wages and exchange rates can be assumed to occur in a relatively short time frame, that is, periods of one to two years or less, while other variables that adjust in the long run (e.g. capital stocks and technological coefficients) can be held constant. Thus, we can analyze the short-run dynamics of prices and distribution within a given framework of capital, technology, and institutions. In this analysis, we focus on two ratios that have to stabilize in order to reach a steady-state equilibrium in the short run: the ratio of female to male wages, $\omega = w_f/w_m$, and the real exchange rate for exports, defined previously as $\rho_X = eP_X^*/P_X$.[12]

To facilitate the dynamic analysis, we re-solve the static model from the second section for the equilibrium levels of H and X as functions of the two state variables, ω and ρ_X, using a simplified version assuming no intermediate imports ($n_H = n_X = 0$).[13] This results in reduced form solutions that can be written in implicit form as

$$H = H(\rho_X, \omega) \qquad (6.20)$$
$$-/? \ ?/+$$

$$X = X(\rho_X, \omega) \qquad (6.21)$$
$$+ \ ?$$

where the likely signs of the partial derivatives are shown underneath the corresponding variables.[14] In the solution for H, there are two alternative cases, with signs separated by slashes beneath equation (6.20). In one case, a real devaluation is contractionary for home goods production ($H_\rho < 0$), because the redistribution toward profits reduces consumption demand enough to outweigh the increase in export demand, but the effect of a higher relative female wage on home goods production (H_ω) is ambiguous in sign. In the second case, H_ρ is ambiguous in sign because a real devaluation can be either expansionary or mildly contractionary for the H-sector, while H_ω is positive because an increase in the female relative wage ω boosts consumption of the home good. In the X function (6.21), $X_\rho > 0$ definitely holds because a real depreciation directly increases exports, while X_ω is ambiguous in sign because of the offsetting effects of higher domestic consumption and reduced export competitiveness.

To simplify the dynamics, we continue to take τ, a_X, and a_H as exogenously given, and still assume that the export sector margin (φ) adjusts instantaneously to maintain export competitiveness according to (6.3). Using these assumptions along with the simplifying assumption of no intermediate imports ($n_H = n_X = 0$) in (6.1) and (6.2), the domestic relative price P_X/P_H converges to a constant level in the steady state. The dynamics of this model are then described by differentiating the definitions of ω and ρ_X logarithmically with respect to time, which yields

$$\hat{\omega} = \hat{w}_f - \hat{w}_m \tag{6.22}$$

$$\hat{\rho}_X = \hat{e} + \hat{P}_X^* - \hat{P}_X \tag{6.23}$$

where a circumflex denotes the instantaneous rate of change of the variable. Using (6.3) and the simplifying assumptions stated earlier, (6.23) can be expressed as

$$\hat{\rho}_X = \left[\hat{e} + \hat{P}_X^* - \hat{w}_f\right](1 + \theta)^{-1} \tag{6.23a}$$

Setting $\hat{P}_X^* = 0$ for convenience, we need only specify adjustment equations for the two nominal wage rates and the nominal exchange rate in order to complete the model.

Nominal wage increases for both women and men workers are assumed to depend on the bargaining power of each vis-à-vis their employers. Workers of each gender try to achieve a target level of their real wage by negotiating for increases in their nominal wage; the degree to which they can obtain nominal wage increases is influenced by the tightness of the labor market for each gender. We assume that, due to social institutions including possible discriminatory practices of firms or governments, women and men not only have different target real wages, but also different abilities to respond to the target-actual wage gaps and labor market tightness.

The two labor markets are assumed to be linked together in two direct ways, reflecting the asymmetrical nature of gender relations in a typical SIE, in addition to the indirect linkages that are implicit in the static model (e.g. consumption demand for each other's products). First, while the men's real wage target is exogenously set (e.g. by the power of male trade unions), the women's target is the men's real wage and they negotiate for nominal wage increases depending on the degree to which their own real wage falls short of the real male wage.[15] Second, since women's market income is often supplementary in male-headed households, female labor supply is modeled as a negative function of the male real wage. As male wages fall, female members of the household may engage in "distress sales" of their labor in order to maintain the family's standard of living.[16] Male labor supply, in contrast, is modeled as exogenous for simplicity.

Reflecting these considerations, the rate of growth of the female wage is determined by

$$\hat{w}_f = \gamma_1[(w_m - w_f)/P_C] + \gamma_2[a_X X - L_f^s(w_m/P_C)] \tag{6.24}$$

where $\gamma_1, \gamma_2 > 0$ are constant parameters reflecting female workers' bargaining power in terms of their ability to respond to labor market conditions;[17] the term multiplying γ_1 is the gap between the target female wage (i.e. the male real wage) and the actual female wage; $P_C = P_H^{(1-\alpha)}P_X^{\alpha}$ is a consumer price index with geometric expenditure weights $(1-\alpha)$ and α on H and X goods, respectively; $a_X X$ is the demand for female labor; and $L_f^s(\cdot)$ is the female labor supply, with $L_f^{s\prime} < 0$. Changes in the male wage rate are determined by

$$\hat{w}_m = \delta_1[\overline{W}_m - w_m/P_c] + \delta_2(a_H H - L_m^s) \tag{6.25}$$

where $\delta_1, \delta_2 > 0$ are constant parameters reflecting male workers' bargaining power, $\overline{W}_m$ is the exogenous target male real wage, $a_H H$ is the demand for male labor, and L_m^s is the exogenously given male labor supply.

The crawling peg policy is modeled by assuming that the monetary authorities adjust the nominal peg continuously in order to keep the real exchange rate for exports from deviating too far from a target level.[18] Thus, the nominal exchange rate is determined by the reaction function

$$\hat{e} = \lambda(\bar{\rho} - \rho_X) \tag{6.26}$$

where λ is the speed of adjustment and $\bar{\rho}$ is the target real exchange rate.

Substituting (6.24) to (6.26) into (6.22) and (6.23a), assuming $\hat{P}_X^* = 0$, using the price equations (6.1) and (6.2) with $n_H = n_X = 0$, the flexible markup rule (6.3), the definitions of P_C, ω, and ρ_X, and the static solutions (6.20) and (6.21), we obtain the following system of equations:

$$\hat{\rho}_X = \{\lambda(\bar{\rho} - \rho_X) - [\gamma_1(1-\omega)/\xi(\rho_X,\omega)] - \gamma_2[a_X X(\rho_X, \omega)$$
$$- (L_f^s/\xi(\rho_X, \omega))]\} (1+\theta)^{-1} \tag{6.27}$$

$$\hat{\omega} = [\gamma_1(1-\omega)/\xi(\rho_X, \omega)] + \gamma_2[a_X X(\rho,\omega) - (L_f^s/\xi(\rho_X, \omega))]$$
$$- \delta_1[\overline{W}_m - (1/\xi(\rho_X, \omega))] - \delta_2[a_H H(\rho_X,\omega) - L_m^s] \tag{6.28}$$

where $\xi(\rho_X, \omega) = (\tau a_H)^{1-\alpha}(\Phi a_X)^{\alpha} \rho_X^{\theta\alpha} \omega^{\alpha}$ for notational convenience. Equations (6.27) and (6.28) can be written in implicit form as (with likely signs of the partial derivatives below the corresponding variables):[19]

$$\hat{\rho}_X = Q(\rho_X, \omega) \tag{6.27a}$$
$$\quad\;\; - \;\; +$$

$$\hat{\omega} = Z(\rho_X, \omega) \qquad\qquad\qquad\qquad\qquad\qquad (6.28a)$$
$$\quad\;\; ? \;\;\; -$$

Equations (6.27) and (6.28) or, equivalently, (6.27a) and (6.28a) constitute a system of two simultaneous, nonlinear, first-order differential equations, the solution of which requires linearization around the steady-state equilibrium where $\hat{\rho}_X = \hat{\omega} = 0$, using the method of Taylor expansion. Note that the three variables for which agents have "targets" in equations (6.24) to (6.26) – the women's real wage, the men's real wage, and the real exchange rate – will *not* generally be at their target levels in the steady state. Given that labor demand cannot exceed labor supply for either gender, and assuming $\hat{\rho}_X^* = 0$, a steady-state equilibrium with positive inflation will be characterized by $\hat{e}_X = \hat{w}_f = \hat{w}_m > 0$ with $\rho_X < \bar{\rho}$, $w_f < w_m$, and $w_m/P_C < \bar{W}_m$. Thus, female workers, male workers, and the monetary authorities will all find their aspirations frustrated, but their efforts to pursue their respective targets will maintain positive cost-push, wage-price inflation with continuous nominal exchange-rate adjustments in the steady state.

Given the signs of the partial derivatives shown in (6.27a) and (6.28a), the linear approximation to $\hat{\rho}_X = 0$, must slope upward, but the linear approximation to $\hat{\omega} = 0$ can slope either upward or downward in the neighborhood of the equilibrium, creating three possible cases (labeled A through C and shown in Figures 6.2 through 6.4, respectively).

The slope of $\hat{\omega} = 0$ depends on the sign of Z_ρ: if $Z_\rho > 0$, then $\hat{\omega} = 0$ slopes up (Cases A and B); if $Z_\rho < 0$ then $\hat{\omega} = 0$ is downward sloping (Case C). The equilibrium is definitely a (locally) stable focus in Case C, where $\hat{\omega} = 0$ slopes down, while in Cases A and B local stability depends on which of the two upward-sloping isoclines is steeper.[20] In Case A, $\hat{\rho}_X = 0$ is steeper than $\hat{\omega} = 0$, and the equilibrium is a (locally) stable node; this case assumes that the crawling peg is adjusted rapidly, a depreciation is expansionary, and the women's labor supply response is relatively weak. In Case B, assuming the opposite conditions, $\hat{\omega} = 0$ is steeper than $\hat{\rho}_X = 0$ and the equilibrium is a saddle point.

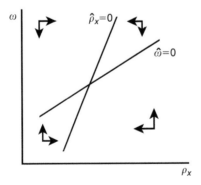

Figure 6.2 Dynamic model: Case A, Stable Node Equilibrium.

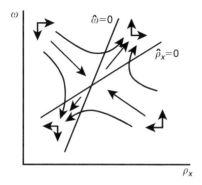

Figure 6.3 Dynamic model: Case B, Saddle Point Equilibrium.

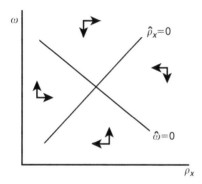

Figure 6.4 Dynamic model: Case C, Saddle Focus Equilibrium.

   The saddle point Case B is of particular interest and requires some discussion. The saddle point must be regarded as an unstable equilibrium in this model, since neither ρ_X nor ω is a "jump variable" that could be expected to automatically move the economy onto one of the two convergent paths. The instability in this case arises in part from strongly contractionary effects of a devaluation, which imply that as the real exchange rate ρ_X rises, home goods output and male employment fall, and therefore the men's wage falls relative to the women's wage so that ω rises; with women's real wages now closer to their target, women moderate their nominal wage increases, and hence ρ_X rises even further by (6.27). This case is more likely to occur if there is a strong women's labor supply response, so that as the men's real wage falls (due to the devaluation) women enter the labor force in large numbers, thereby depressing their own wage increases and making ρ_X rise even faster. This case also requires relatively slow adjustment of the nominal peg (i.e. a relatively low λ), so that the monetary authorities do not act fast enough to appreciate the currency (or slow its rate of depreciation) in nominal terms to offset the moderation in women's wage increases in the export sector.

The unstable paths leading away from the saddle point equilibrium in Figure 6.3 have interesting economic interpretations. The paths moving up and to the right represent export-led booms, in which currencies are chronically undervalued and women workers in export sectors are moving in the direction of closing the gender gap[21] due to tight labor market conditions that enhance their bargaining power. The paths moving down and to the left resemble a Latin American-style balance-of-payments crisis, in which the currency becomes highly overvalued and exports stagnate – and if export-sector workers are mainly women, the gender gap would be expected to rise. An obvious policy remedy for such instability suggested by this model is to increase the speed of adjustment of the exchange rate (λ).

Finally, we examine the comparative dynamics of the model for the two stable Cases A and C; the results are summarized in Table 6.2. First, consider the implications of increased bargaining power for women, made possible, for example, through improved female education, greater organizing efforts of female workers, or more democratic rights for women. This can be modeled as a rise in γ_1, that is, a greater ability of women to win nominal wage increases in order to keep their real wages close to their target (i.e. the men's real wage). This causes $\hat{\omega} = 0$ to shift up and $\hat{p}_X = 0$ to shift to the left. In Case C, the steady-state level of ω definitely rises (the gender gap is reduced) while the change in the steady-state real exchange rate p_X is ambiguous. In Case A, the effects on both variables are ambiguous in general, but it is likely that ω rises while p_X falls (the real exchange rate appreciates) under plausible conditions.[22]

Second, consider the effects of a devaluation policy, in the sense of an increase in the monetary authority's target real exchange rate $\bar{p}$. A rise in $\bar{p}$ causes $\hat{p}_X = 0$ to shift to the right, with no shift in $\hat{\omega} = 0$. The steady-state real exchange rate definitely rises (i.e. there is a real depreciation), but the effects on the steady-state relative female wage ω are ambiguous and depend on the slope of $\hat{\omega} = 0$. If a real depreciation is contractionary for the *H*-sector ($H_\rho < 0$), exports are highly responsive to the exchange rate ($X_\rho >> 0$), and the real wage effects are weak (the $\alpha\theta$ terms in Z_ρ are low), so that $Z_\rho > 0$ and $\hat{\omega} = 0$ slopes up (Case A), then equilibrium ω rises (the gender gap is reduced). But if a depreciation is expansionary for

Table 6.2 Comparative dynamic results

Increase in	Case	Shift in		Effect on[a]	
		$\hat{\omega} = 0$	$\hat{p}_X = 0$	ω	p_X
Women's bargaining	A (Figure 6.2)	up	left	$+$[b]	$-$[b]
power (γ_1)	C (Figure 6.4)	up	left	$+$	?
Real exchange	A (Figure 6.2)	none	right	$+$	$+$
rate target ($\bar{p}$)	C (Figure 6.4)	none	right	$-$	$+$

Notes
a Signs of the total derivatives of ω and p_X with respect to γ_1 and $\bar{p}$ in comparisons across steady-state equilibria. See text for discussion of the alternative cases.
b See note 22 for the conditions under which these signs result.

home goods ($H_\rho > 0$), the export response is small, and the real wage effects are strong ($\alpha\theta$ terms are high), so that $Z_\rho < 0$ and $\hat{\omega} = 0$ slopes down (Case C), then equilibrium ω falls (the gender gap worsens).

Thus, a devaluation policy has ambiguous effects on the gender gap. In spite of the stimulus to export production and women's employment, the female–male wage ratio may either rise or fall depending mainly on how much exports increase (and thus how much women's employment rises), the degree to which the higher exchange rate reduces real wages by increasing the prices of export goods consumed at home, and whether men's employment rises or falls (and hence whether they get a demand-side stimulus to their wages to offset the higher prices of exported consumer goods that otherwise reduce their real wage).

Conclusions

The models in this chapter shed light on the conditions under which gender equity can be enhanced for female workers in export-oriented SIEs without jeopardizing those countries' growth or sacrificing employment of either men or women. When nominal wages are rigid and the exchange rate is fixed, an exogenous rise in the women's wage rate need not reduce (and may even increase) employment of male or female workers, but only under certain stringent conditions. These conditions include: a relatively low price elasticity of exports, a high elasticity of price-cost margins with respect to international competitive pressures in the export sector, a wide gap between the marginal propensities to consume out of wage and profit income, and relatively large domestic consumption of the export good. If these conditions do not hold, then the fears of the pessimists are likely to be valid, at least in the short run.

When nominal wages are flexible and the exchange rate follows a crawling peg, a variety of short-run dynamic outcomes are possible. In the saddle point case, it is possible to have an export-led boom in which the gender gap is reduced while the real exchange rate depreciates – or, alternatively, stagnant exports and a rising gender gap with a chronically overvalued exchange rate. In the stable cases, structural changes or policy initiatives are identified that can potentially narrow the gender gap under certain conditions, including a rise in the monetary authority's real exchange rate target and an increase in women's bargaining power. Thus, altering the policy environment and the structure of gender relations can relieve some of the trade-offs between women's wage gains and export competitiveness that otherwise inhibit a narrowing of the gender wage gap.

Appendix 6.A Mathematics of the short-run static solutions

The model with fixed nominal wages and a fixed exchange rate

Using equations (6.1) to (6.2), (6.5) to (6.10), (6.12) to (6.15), and (6.16a) in (6.18) and (6.19), the short-run model can be reduced to the following two equations for the IS and XX curves, respectively, each written to show the condition for excess demand to equal zero:

$$- \{(1 - c_W)(1 - v_H) + [1 - c_R - b_1/(\rho_M \mu + 1)](\tau - 1) + v_H\}H$$

$$- \{(1 - c_W) + (1 - v_X) + [1 - c_R - b_2/(\rho_M \mu + 1)](\varphi - 1) + v_X\}\Omega X$$

$$+ [\tau I_0 /(\rho_M \mu + 1)] + A\varphi^{1 - \psi}\varepsilon^{\psi}\Omega = 0 \qquad (6.A.1)$$

$$[\alpha c_W (1 - v_H) + \beta c_R(\tau - 1)]H$$

$$- [\varphi - \alpha c_W (1 - v_X) - \beta c_R(\varphi - 1)]\Omega X + A\varphi^{1 - \psi}\varepsilon^{\psi}\Omega = 0 \qquad (6.A.2)$$

where φ is determined by equation (6.4), $v_H = eP_n^* n_H / (w_m a_H + eP_n^* n_H)$ and $v_X = eP_n^* n_X / (w_f a_X + eP_n^* n_X)$ are the shares of intermediate import costs in the average variable costs of each sector, and $\Omega = (w_f a_X + eP_n^* n_X)/(w_m a_H + eP_n^* n_H)$ is the ratio of average variable costs in the X sector to those in the H sector.

For notational convenience, we write (6.A.1) and (6.A.2), respectively, in implicit form as

$$F(H, X; w_f) = 0 \qquad (6.A.3)$$

$$G(H, X; w_f) = 0 \qquad (6.A.4)$$

where H and X are endogenous and w_f (the wage rate of the female workers in the export sector) is the exogenous variable that we wish to vary. Although these equations are linear in H and X, they are nonlinear in w_f and therefore the model has to be solved by total differentiation of (6.A.1) and (6.A.2) with respect to all three variables, which yields the matrix equation:

$$\begin{bmatrix} F_H & F_X \\ G_H & G_X \end{bmatrix} \begin{bmatrix} dH \\ dX \end{bmatrix} = \begin{bmatrix} -F_{w_f} dw_f \\ -G_{w_f} dw_f \end{bmatrix} \qquad (6.A.5)$$

with $F_H < 0$, $F_X < 0$, $G_H > 0$, and $G_X < 0$. The slope of the IS curve is $-F_H/F_X < 0$, while the slope of the XX curve is $-G_H/G_X > 0$. Local stability of the equilibrium is guaranteed by the fact that $tr\ \mathbf{J} < 0$ and $|\mathbf{J}| = F_H G_X - G_H F_X > 0$, where $\mathbf{J}$ is the 2×2 Jacobian matrix on the LHS of (6.A.5). The equilibrium must be a stable focus, with dynamics as shown in Figure 6.1 in the text.

To derive the comparative static results, the displacements in the IS and XX curves are determined by the two partial derivatives in the vector on the right-hand side (RHS) of equation (6.A.5), that is, $\partial F/\partial w_f$ and $\partial G/\partial w_f$. If either of these partial derivatives is positive, the corresponding curve shifts up (vertically upward for XX, and to the right for IS); if either is negative then the curve shifts down (vertically downward for XX, to the left for IS). From equations (6.A.1) and

(6.A.2), after considerable simplification, these partial derivatives can be expressed as follows:

$$-F_{w_f} = -\frac{\partial F}{\partial w_f} = \left[\{-\phi[1-c_R-b_2/(\rho_M\mu+1)] \right.$$

$$+ (1+\theta)[c_W-c_R-b_2/(\rho_M\mu+1)]\} X$$

$$\left. + A(1-\psi)\varphi\left(\frac{\varepsilon}{\Phi}\right)^{\frac{\psi}{1+\theta}}\right]\left(\frac{1-v_X}{1+\theta}\right)\frac{\Omega}{w_f}$$

$$-G_{w_f} = -\frac{\partial G}{\partial w_f} = \left\{ [-\phi(1-\beta_{c_R}) + (1+\theta)(\alpha_{c_w}-\beta_{c_R})]X \right.$$

$$\left. + A(1-\psi)\varphi\left(\frac{\varepsilon}{\Phi}\right)^{\frac{\psi}{1+\theta}}\right\}\left(\frac{1-v_X}{1+\theta}\right)\frac{\Omega}{w_f}$$

These partial derivatives are used in solving the system of equations (6.A.5) using Cramer's Rule, which yields the total derivatives

$$dH/dw_f = [-F_{w_f}G_X + G_{w_f}F_X]/|\mathbf{J}|$$
$$dX/dw_f = [-G_{w_f}F_H + F_{w_f}G_H]/|\mathbf{J}|$$

which show the changes in the equilibrium levels of H and X corresponding to the shifts in the intersection of the IS and XX curves.

Case I is shown in Figure 6.A.1 (and is described in the section "Comparative statics of increased female wages"). Here, a rise in w_f causes both the IS and XX curves to shift downward, causing equilibrium output of X (and hence women's employment) to fall, while the change in equilibrium output of H (and hence men's employment) is ambiguous.

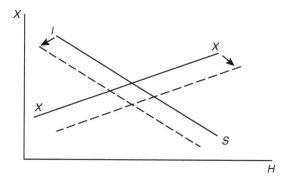

Figure 6.A.1 Effects of increased female wages: Case I, pessimistic.

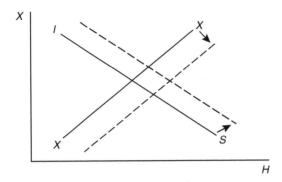

Figure 6.A.2 Effects of increased female wages: Case II, cooperative/optimistic.

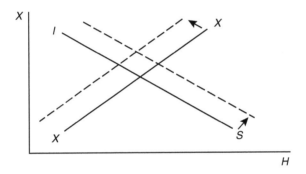

Figure 6.A.3 Effects of increased female wages: Case III, equalizing but conflictive.

Case II, the cooperative or optimistic scenario, is shown in Figure 6.A.2. A higher female wage causes the IS curve to shift upward while XX shifts downward. The equilibrium level of H (and men's employment) rises and the change in equilibrium X (and women's employment) is ambiguous.

Finally, Case III (equalizing but conflictive) is shown in Figure 6.A.3. Under the conditions outlined in the text, a higher female wage causes both XX and IS to shift upward. In this case, the equilibrium level of X rises, while the change in equilibrium H is ambiguous. Women definitely gain in terms of employment as well as wages; men may lose or gain jobs but their real wages definitely fall. Total employment and real national income may either rise or fall.

Simplified model with the female–male wage ratio and real exchange rate as state variables

For the analysis of short-run dynamics in the section "Short-run dynamics with flexible nominal wages and a managed exchange rate," we use a simplified static model with no intermediate imports in which ω and ρ_X are treated as state variables. Setting $v_H = v_X = 0$ in equations (6.A.1) and (6.A.2) and using equation (6.3) plus the definitions of the ratio of female to male wages (ω) and the real exchange rate for exports (ρ_X), and also noting that $\rho_M = k\omega\rho_X^{1+\theta}$ where $k = \Phi a_X P_I^*/\tau a_H P_X^* > 0$, the equations for the IS and XX curves can be written as functions of ω and ρ_X as follows (in the form excess demand equals zero):

$$- \{(1 - c_W) + [1 - c_R - b_1/(k\omega\rho_X^{1+\theta}\mu + 1)] (\tau - 1)\}H$$
$$- \{(1 - c_W) + [1 - c_R - b_2/(k\omega\rho_X^{1+\theta}\mu + 1)] (\Phi\rho_X^\theta - 1)\}(a_X/a_H)\omega X$$
$$+ [\tau I_0/(k\omega\rho_X^{1+\theta}\mu + 1)] + A\Phi\rho_X^{\theta+\psi} (a_X/a_H)\omega = 0 \tag{6.A.6}$$

$$[\alpha c_W + \beta c_R(\tau - 1)]H$$
$$- [\Phi\rho_X^\theta - \alpha c_W - \beta c_R(\Phi\rho_X^\theta - 1)](a_X/a_H)\omega X$$
$$+ A\Phi\rho_X^{\theta+\psi} (a_X/a_H)\omega = 0 \tag{6.A.7}$$

or, in implicit form,

$$F(H, X; \rho_X, \omega) = 0 \tag{6.A.8}$$
$$G(H, X; \rho_X, \omega) = 0 \tag{6.A.9}$$

The Jacobian matrix corresponding to the system of equations (6.A.8) and (6.A.9) is

$$\mathbf{J} = \begin{bmatrix} F_H & F_X \\ G_H & G_X \end{bmatrix}$$

with $F_H < 0$, $F_X < 0$, $G_H > 0$, and $G_X < 0$. With the determinant $|\mathbf{J}| = F_H G_X - G_H F_X > 0$ and the trace $tr\,\mathbf{J} < 0$, short-run stability is guaranteed.

The partial derivatives of (6.A.8) and (6.A.9) with respect to ρ_X and ω are as follows:

$$F_\rho = \frac{\partial F}{\partial \rho_X} = (\theta + \psi)A\Phi\omega\rho_X^{\theta+\psi-1}(a_X/a_H) - [1 - c_R - b_2/(k\omega\rho_X^{1+\theta}\mu + 1)]$$

$$\times (a_X/a_H)\theta\Phi\,\rho_X^{\theta-1}\,\omega X - \frac{\mu(1+\theta)k\omega\rho_X^\theta}{(k\omega\rho_X^{(1+\theta)}\mu + 1)}[b(\tau - 1)H$$

$$+ b_2(\Phi\rho_X^\theta - 1)/(a_X/a_H)\omega X + \tau I_0]$$

The first term in F_ρ is the effect of a real depreciation in stimulating export demand, which is positive. The second term is the effect of higher profits in the X sector on national saving (net of induced investment), due to the increase in the X-sector profit margin, and is negative. The third term is the reduction in domestic investment spending due to the increased cost of imported investment goods following a depreciation, and is also negative. Thus, F_ρ is ambiguous in sign, and is positive if a depreciation has a net expansionary effect on excess demand (if the first term dominates) and is negative if it has net contractionary effects (the second two terms dominate).

$$F_\omega = \frac{\partial F}{\partial \omega} = A\Phi\, \rho_X^{\theta+\psi}\,(a_X/a_H) - \left\{(1-c_W)+\left[1-C_R\right.\right.$$

$$\left. - b_2\,/(k\omega\,\rho_X^{1+\theta}\mu+1)]\,(\Phi\,\rho_X^\theta-1)\right\}(a_X/a_H)X - \frac{\mu k \rho_X^{1+\theta}}{\left(k\omega\,\rho_X^{1+\theta}\mu+1\right)^2}$$

$$\times\left[b_1(t-1)H+b_2(\Phi\,\rho_X^\theta-1)(a_X/a_H)\omega X+\tau I_0\right]$$

In spite of a few differences, F_ω is very similar to F_ρ and is likely to have the same sign.

$$G_\omega = \frac{\partial G}{\partial \omega} = A\Phi\,\rho_X^{\theta+\psi}\,(a_X/a_H) - \left[\Phi\rho_X^\theta - \alpha c_W - \beta_{C_R}(\Phi\,\rho_X^\theta-1)\right](a_X/a_H)$$

This derivative looks ambiguous in sign, but using (6.A.7) it can be seen that this is equivalent to $G_\omega = -(\alpha c_W + \beta c_R)H/\omega \le 0$, with $G_\omega < 0$ as long as either α or β is positive (i.e. as long as there is any home consumption of the export good), and this is what we will assume. Finally,

$$G_\rho = \frac{\partial G}{\partial \rho} = \left[(\psi+\theta)A\,\rho_X^{\theta+\psi-1} - (1-\beta_{C_R})X\theta\,\rho_X^{\theta-1}\right](a_X/a_H)\Phi\omega$$

While this appears ambiguous, since this derivative represents the direct effects of a real depreciation on excess demand *in the market for the exported good*, we assume that the positive first term in the brackets dominates and $G_\rho > 0$.

The preceding partial derivatives are then used in the Cramer's Rule solutions for the effects of changes in ω and ρ_X on outputs of H and X, represented in implicit form by equations (6.20) and (6.21) in the text. These solutions are as follows:

$$H_\rho = dH/d\rho_X = (-F_\rho G_X + F_X G_\rho)/|\,\mathbf{J}\,|$$
$$H_\omega = dH/d\omega = (-F_\omega G_X + F_X G_\omega)/|\,\mathbf{J}\,|$$
$$X_\rho = dX/d\rho_X = (-F_H G_\rho + F_\rho G_H)/|\,\mathbf{J}\,|$$
$$X_\omega = dX/d\omega = (-F_H G_\omega + F_\omega G_H)/|\,\mathbf{J}\,|$$

Analysis of signs of partial derivatives in dynamic equations

Assumed signs of the partial derivatives of (6.27a) and (6.28a) are based on the following analysis. The own-effects of increases in ρ_X are given by

$$Q_\rho = \partial\hat\rho_X/\partial\rho_X = \{-\lambda-[\gamma_1\theta\alpha\,(1-\omega)/\xi(\rho_X,\,\omega)\rho_X]$$
$$- \gamma_2[a_X X_\rho - (\theta\alpha\,L_f^{s\prime}/\xi(\rho_X,\omega)\rho_X)]\}(1+\theta)^{-1}$$

A rise in ρ_X induces the monetary authorities to reduce the rate of nominal depreciation at the speed of adjustment λ, which lowers $\hat{\rho}_X$. A rise in ρ_X also allows the X-producers to raise their profit margins by (6.3), thereby reducing the gap between the men's and women's real wages, and hence induces women workers to raise their money wages more slowly (the γ_1 term), which in turn makes ρ_X rise more rapidly (assuming $1 - \omega > 0$, that is, a positive gender wage gap).

In addition, assuming that a devaluation increases X output ($X_\rho > 0$), a rise in ρ_X stimulates demand for women's labor, which allows them to win higher wage increases (depending on women's bargaining strength γ_2), which in turn lead to a lower $\hat{\rho}_X$. Finally, the positive labor supply response of women as male wages fall (assuming $L_f^{s'} < 0$) causes female wages to rise more slowly and $\hat{\rho}_X$ to rise faster. In order for increases in ρ_X to be self-stabilizing (i.e. $Q_\rho < 0$), the first and third of these four effects must dominate the other two; this requires assuming a relatively small effect of a devaluation on real wages (i.e. low θ and/or α),[23] a relatively high speed of adjustment of the crawling peg (λ), and/or a relatively strong X-output effect of a devaluation ($X_\rho \gg 0$, which in turn requires a relatively high export elasticity ψ).

The cross-effect of increases in ω on $\hat{\rho}_X$ is given by

$$Q_\omega = \partial\hat{\rho}_X/\partial\omega = \{\gamma_1[1 + (\alpha(1 - \omega)/\omega)]/\xi(\rho_X\,\omega)$$

$$- \gamma_2[a_X X_\omega + (\alpha\,L_f^{s'}/\xi(\rho_X,\,\omega)\omega)]\}(1 + \theta)^{-1}$$

The γ_1 term represents the fact that a higher ω brings the women's real wage closer to their target (the male real wage), and thus induces women workers to seek smaller money wage increases, which implies a higher $\hat{\rho}_X$. The first term in the bracket after γ_2 is ambiguous in sign since X_ω is ambiguous. In the second term in that bracket, the positive women's labor supply response to the decline in the male real wage (again assuming $L_f^{s'} < 0$) dampens female wage growth, causing a higher $\hat{\rho}_X$. Assuming that X_ω is not too positive,[24] we conclude that $Q_\omega > 0$.

The opposite cross effect (Z_ρ) is ambiguous in sign:

$$Z_\rho = \partial\hat{\omega}/\partial\rho_X = \gamma_2 a_X X_\rho - \delta_2 a_H H_\rho + [\gamma_2 L_f^{s'} - \gamma_1(1 - \omega) - \delta_1]$$

$$\times [\theta\alpha/\xi(\rho_X,\omega)\rho_X]$$

The first term, which is the effect of increased demand for women's labor on female wage increases, is positive assuming $X_\rho > 0$. The second term, which is the effect on the demand for men's labor and therefore on male wage increases, is ambiguous since H_ρ is ambiguous as discussed earlier. The third term reflects the various effects of the reductions in real wages (of both genders) induced by a depreciation, all of which are negative. The lower male real wage leads to an increase in women's labor supply (since $L_f^{s'} < 0$), which reduces women's ability to win wage increases. Also, a smaller real wage gap relative to men induces women to seek smaller wage increases (assuming $\omega < 1$), while a lower men's real wage induces men to seek higher wage increases (in pursuit of their fixed target) – all of which tend to make ω rise more slowly. If a real depreciation is contractionary for the home goods sector ($H_\rho < 0$), exports are highly responsive to the exchange rate ($X_\rho >> 0$, or ψ is relatively high), and the various real wage effects are relatively weak (because α or θ is small), then $Z_\rho > 0$. But under the opposite conditions, $Z_\rho < 0$ can result, and therefore we consider both cases for the sign of Z_ρ.

Finally, the own-effect of ω is:

$$Z_\omega = \partial\hat{\omega}/\partial\omega = \gamma_2 a_X X_\omega - \delta_2 a_H H_\omega + \{[\gamma_2 L_f^{s\prime} - \delta_1 - \gamma_1(1-\omega)](\alpha/\omega) - \gamma_1\}$$

$$\times [1/\xi(\rho_X, \omega)]$$

The first two terms (effects on the demand for female and male labor, respectively) are each ambiguous in sign, since both X_ω and H_ω are ambiguous. The last term is definitely negative, however, since all the terms inside the braces are negative. Assuming that the negative last term dominates the ambiguous first two terms (i.e. X_ω is not too positive and H_ω is not too negative) it seems safe to assume that $Z_\omega < 0$.

Notes

1 Several factors may contribute to discriminatorily low wages for women, including crowding of women into a limited range of jobs and practices such as the marriage ban that limits women's job tenure. See Hou (1991), Seguino (1997), and Standing (1989).

2 The modeling approach used here builds on the two-sector framework in Krugman and Taylor (1978), but also borrows features from Blecker (1989, 1996), Dutt (1990), and Taylor (1983). Krugman and Taylor did not allow for domestic consumption of the export good, as we do here.

3 This specification could be rationalized, for example, by assuming that I_M consists of machinery that is not produced domestically in a SIE, while I_H consists of factory buildings produced by domestic labor with imported intermediate goods.

4 We do not distinguish saving and consumption behavior by gender because there is less clear evidence on how women and men differ in this regard. For one empirical study on the impact of a gender wage redistribution on aggregate savings, however, see Seguino and Floro (2003).

5 The coefficient b_2 reflects the openness of a country to inflows and outflows of "footloose capital," which makes investment in any particular SIE responsive to the relative profitability of its export production compared with that of other SIEs.

6 The mathematical solution of this model is outlined in the appendix to this chapter.

7 Although there is a flexible price-cost margin in the X-sector, this does not generally imply that P_X is flexible enough to clear the market for X without quantity adjustments by producers.

8 This effect would not be present if there were no home consumption of X ($\alpha = \beta = 0$), in which case output of X would be determined solely by supply-and-demand conditions in the export market independently of H production, and the XX curve would be a horizontal line.

9 We give an intuitive presentation of the comparative statics here; the mathematics underlying the results are discussed in the appendix.

10 This assumes that the men's nominal wage stays fixed, which implies that the price of home consumption goods P_H also stays fixed, so that even if women workers buy a combination of home and exported goods their real wage necessarily rises. Also, note that the price of exported goods P_X rises less than proportionally to the rise in the women's wage w_f due to the "profit squeeze" effect in equation (6.3). Male workers lose as long as they buy any export goods.

11 Logically, there is a fourth possible case, in which XX shifts up while IS shifts down. We cannot think of a plausible combination of parameter values in which this would occur.

12 The adjustments in the real exchange rate for imports of investment goods ρ_M are linearly dependent on the adjustments in ρ_X and ω, and hence do not have to be modeled separately. To see this, note that since $\hat{\rho}_M = (1 + \theta)\hat{\rho}_X + \hat{\omega}$, ρ_M will be stationary when $\hat{\rho}_X = \hat{\omega} = 0$, assuming that both foreign goods prices (P_I^* and P_X^*) are constant for convenience.

13 This simplification is intended to focus on the dynamics of labor costs in relation to export competitiveness, but may affect the results insofar as it eliminates the effect of currency depreciation in increasing costs of imported intermediate goods.

14 For mathematical details on the simplified static model see the appendix.

15 Women may target real male wages because they view men's wage payments as nondiscriminatory, and hence as a benchmark for their own wage aspirations, or else because they consider gender wage equality as an objective to be pursued. Alternatively, women's wages could be modeled as a function of female wages in export sectors in other SIEs. While foreign female wages are not modeled explicitly here, they do influence domestic women's wages indirectly insofar as they affect foreign competing export prices (P_X^*) and the real exchange rate ρ_X.

16 This negative effect of the male wage on female labor supply will be weaker in situations where women workers are more independent, such as in female-headed households or in the case of daughters who have migrated to urban areas and are living on their own.

17 Factors that affect women's bargaining power may also include discriminatory behavior or gender stereotyping by employers, which may deny women greater access to a wide array of jobs. Also, if women have less access to secondary and higher education this may limit their employment options and hence reduce their bargaining power.

18 The assumption of a real exchange rate target used here is similar to Aghevli (1981).

19 The signs of these partial derivatives are analyzed in the appendix.

20 Formally, considering the Jacobian matrix of the system (6.27a) and (6.28a), the local stability condition is a negative trace ($Q_\rho + Z_\omega < 0$) and a positive determinant ($Q_\rho Z_\omega - Z_\rho Q_\omega > 0$). The saddle point occurs when $Q_\rho Z_\omega - Z_\rho Q_\omega < 0$, which is equivalent to $\hat{\omega} = 0$ being steeper.

21 Although it looks like ω increases indefinitely on the upward paths in Figure 6.3, and thus ω could reach or even exceed unity (thus eliminating or reversing the gender gap), this figure represents only the local dynamics in the neighborhood of an equilibrium with $\omega < 1$, and hence all we can say is that ω is rising but not whether or not it will reach or exceed unity.

22 The condition for equilibrium ω to rise in Case A, in which $Z_\rho > 0$, is $Z_\rho > (1 + \theta)Q_\rho$, which can be interpreted as implying that a devaluation must not be excessively contractionary, that is, H_ρ must not be too negative (although $H_\rho < 0$ must hold in order for $Z_\rho > 0$). The condition for equilibrium ρ_X to fall is $Q_\omega < -Z_\omega/(1 + \theta)$; this same condition applies in both Cases A and C.

23 Note that in the special cases where either $\theta = 0$ (a fixed markup in the X-sector) or $\alpha = 0$ (no home consumption of the export good), the two positive terms vanish and $Q_\rho < 0$ definitely.

24 Note that a strongly positive X_ω would require the equalizing but conflictive case, in which raising the women's wage raises their own employment, to hold in the static model.

References

Aghevli, B. (1981) "Experiences of Asian countries with various exchange rate policies," in J. Williamson (ed.), *Exchange Rate Rules: the theory, performance and prospects of the crawling peg*, New York: St. Martin's Press: 298–318.

Blecker, R.A. (1989) "International competition, income distribution and economic growth," *Cambridge Journal of Economics*, 13: 395–412.

—— (1996) "The New Economic Integration: structuralist models of North–South trade and investment liberalization," *Structural Change and Economic Dynamics*, 7: 321–45.

Cheng, L. and Hsiung, P.-C. (1994) "Women, export-oriented growth, and the state: the case of Taiwan," in J. Aberbach, D. Dollar, and K. Sokoloff (eds), *The Role of the State in Taiwan's Development*, Armonk, NY: M.E. Sharpe: 321–53.

Darity, W., Jr (1995). "The formal structure of a gender-segregated low-income economy," *World Development*, 23: 1963–68.

Deyo, F. (1989) *Beneath the Miracle: labor subordination in the new Asian industrialism*, Berkeley: University of California Press.

Dutt, A.K. (1990) *Growth, Distribution, and Uneven Development*, New York: Cambridge University Press.

Ertürk, K. and Çağatay, N. (1995) "Macroeconomic consequences of cyclical and secular changes in feminization: an experiment in gendered macromodeling," *World Development*, 23: 1969–77.

Hou, J. (1991) "Wage comparison by gender and the effect of segregation: the case of Taiwan," *China Economic Review*, 2: 195–214.

Hsiung, P.-C. (1996) *Living Rooms as Factories: class, gender, and the satellite factory system in Taiwan*, Philadelphia, PA: Temple University Press.

Krugman, P. and Taylor, L. (1978) "Contractionary effects of devaluation," *Journal of International Economics*, 8: 445–56.

Seguino, S. (1997) "Gender wage inequality and export-led growth in South Korea," *Journal of Development Studies*, 34: 102–32.

Seguino, S. and Floro, M. (2003) "Does gender matter for aggregate saving? An empirical analysis," *International Review of Applied Economics*, 17: 147–66.

Standing, G. (1989) "Global feminization through flexible labor," *World Development*, 17: 1077–95.

Taylor, L. (1983) *Structuralist Macroeconomics*, New York: Basic Books.

—— (1991) *Income Distribution, Inflation, and Growth*, Cambridge, MA: MIT Press.

Ward, K. (1988) *Women Workers and Global Restructuring*, Ithaca, NY: International Labor Relations Press.

Williamson, J. (ed.) (1981) *Exchange Rate Rules: the theory, performance and prospects of the crawling peg*, New York: St. Martin's Press.

Part III

Impacts of trade on gender inequality

7 Modeling the effects of trade on women, at work and at home

Comparative perspectives

Marzia Fontana

Introduction

Trade reforms have uneven effects on women and men in developing countries. These effects further vary depending on socioeconomic characteristics, sector, and geographical region. The use of gender as a category of analysis makes it possible to better understand these patterns and to help in the formulation of equitable policies.

Feminist approaches emphasize the need to redefine the realm of economic analysis to include the nonmarket sphere of social reproduction as well as the market sphere of production. The many unpaid services provided within households, such as caring for the children and other dependents, are not only vital for social well-being and human development, but also supplied mainly by women. To make these services visible is an important ingredient of a gender-aware economic model. In addition, it allows consideration of more constraints and interactions than with standard approaches.

Trade liberalization that creates more jobs in female-intensive exporting sectors also destroys jobs in sectors producing import-substitutes. The lost jobs may or may not be female, but even if they are male, women members of the households of the men concerned may be adversely affected, either by reduction of consumption or by being forced to take paid work in addition to domestic commitments, including child-rearing. Even if increased employment involves a rise in women's labor market force participation, this may be at the expense of the time they can devote to caring for their families, or of their leisure, their sleep, and their health.

As these examples show, a full assessment of the impact of trade on women's well-being must take into account interactions among different dimensions and analyze how changes in the market economy influence, and are influenced by, behavior in the unpaid sector. Computable general equilibrium (CGE) models, with their emphasis on linkages and feedbacks effects, provide such a framework. These models are often used to analyze the distributional impact of trade policies but almost all of them neglect the gender dimension.

Fontana and Wood (2000) construct a CGE model that distinguishes female from male labor and includes household work and leisure as sectors, in addition to market activities. This chapter develops their work empirically and methodologically. It applies the Fontana and Wood approach to Bangladesh and Zambia. These two countries have different resource endowments, labor market institutions, systems of property rights, and sociocultural norms, thus making comparison interesting. The chapter also discusses the strengths and limitations of this modeling approach in relation to other methods in the gender-and-trade literature. The analysis in this chapter involves three different levels of comparison: between social accounting matrices (SAMs), between simulations, and between methods.

The following section compares the two gender-aware social accounting matrices from Zambia and Bangladesh that are then used to simulate the effects of tariff abolition in the section "Comparison of simulations." The section "Comparison of methods" analyses model results in the context of other nonmodeling approaches. The final section concludes.

Comparison of SAMs

Sub-Saharan Africa and South Asia are markedly different in their export structure, with Africa's exports heavily concentrated on primary products and South Asia's exports consisting mainly of labor-intensive manufactures. These differences largely reflect differences in the two regions' combination of human and natural resources relative to other regions (Mayer and Wood 2001; Wood and Mayer 2001). Zambia and Bangladesh are no exception to these patterns. In Zambia the main export is copper, which constitutes almost 80 percent of total foreign exchange earnings, while in Bangladesh the main export is ready-made garments (RMG), which provides over 60 percent of total foreign earnings.

Traditionally, women's participation in market activities in Bangladesh has been low and confined to a narrow range of casual jobs on the margins of the labor market. However, since the establishment of the garment factories in the 1980s, significant changes in female labor force participation have taken place. These are documented in a rich literature (Zohir 1998; Kabeer 2000; Sobhan and Khundker 2001). Women's contribution to agriculture is significant but still little studied, as women in this sector work mostly as unpaid family labor on activities carried out within the homestead.

In Zambia, colonial policies encouraged male labor migration to the cities and discouraged female migration, with a resulting high proportion of female-headed households in rural areas who face particular constraints as producers and are over-represented among poor small farmers (Moore and Vaughan 1994). Non-staple food crops are women's sole responsibility but most crops are grown with both male and female labor. In urban areas women are heavily concentrated in informal sector occupations.

The gendered social accounting matrices for Bangladesh and Zambia described in this section both refer to a similar time period, 1994 for Bangladesh and 1995 for Zambia. They were constructed by integrating existing data sets with additional information on the gender structure of the economy, both in the labor market and at the household level. The innovative feature of these two SAMs is the addition of social reproduction and leisure activities. Social reproduction includes services provided within households for own-consumption, which the standard System of National Accounts (SNA) defines as "economic" but not "productive" (United Nations 1993), such as: cooking and cleaning; care of children, the sick, and the elderly; repairing the house, furniture, and clothes; and personal, social, and community support services. Leisure is the time that remains after market-oriented and social reproduction work (net of time for sleeping, eating, and personal hygiene assumed to be 10 hours for both men and women).[1] In countries like Bangladesh and Zambia, where unemployment and underemployment are common, people often work fewer hours than they would wish and hence their "leisure" should more accurately be interpreted as idle time. Throughout the chapter the category of nonwork is referred to as "leisure." This is just a label used for convenience.

Labor inputs are measured in terms of hours rather than persons. The output in social reproduction and leisure is derived by valuing labor, for each skill and gender category, at its average market wage (considered to be the opportunity cost of each worker's time), assuming that nonmarket sectors use neither capital nor land nor intermediate inputs. The estimated outputs of social reproduction and leisure appear in the SAM both in the production accounts and in final demand (as part of household consumption).

The limitations of this approach should be noted. Setting the opportunity cost equal to the market wage assumes no constraints on people's ability to sell their time in the labor market. In the presence of market failures each individual's subjective price for her time would no longer be equal to its market price, leading to different behavior than with perfect markets. These aspects are further discussed in Fontana (2003).

Table 7.1 compares the export structure and the employment distribution of the female labor force in the two SAMs. It shows that exports are quite concentrated in both countries and that the proportion of the female labor force employed by the export sectors is higher in Bangladesh than in Zambia. Manufactures constitute about 92 percent of total exports in Bangladesh and account for about 11 percent of female market employment. In Zambia, copper constitutes about 78 percent of exports but employs less than one percent of the female labor force. In both Bangladesh and Zambia more than 60 percent of women work in agriculture, a sector with few exports (and probably, in both countries, with few prospects of becoming a leading export sector). Women work also in services (30 percent of the female labor force is in services in Zambia and 20 percent in Bangladesh) but are mostly concentrated in sectors that are nontraded and often informal (trading services, such as fruit vendors, and transport in Zambia and domestic services in Bangladesh).

Bangladesh is far more populous than Zambia, with an adult population of about 63 million compared with 3 million in Zambia. This big difference in the

Table 7.1 Export composition and gender structure of the labor force in Bangladesh and Zambia (%)

	Bangladesh		Zambia	
	Total exports	*Female market employment*	*Total exports*	*Female market employment*
Primary products[a]	8.1	68.9	81.2	64.4
Of which copper	0.0	0.0	78.4	0.3
Manufactures	91.9	11.2	8.6	6.3
Of which garments	60.8	6.4	n.a.	n.a.
Services	0.0	19.9	10.2	29.3
Total	100.0	100.0	100.0	100.0

Source: 1994 Bangladesh and 1995 Zambia gendered SAMs.

Note
a SITC definition (includes processed primary).

Table 7.2 Female/male wage gap by educational level

	No educ.	*Prim. educ.*	*Sec. educ.*	*Post educ.*
Bangladesh				
Average female hourly wages as percentage of male wages	48	54	45	70
Market employment (million hours per year)				
Female	133	47	22	11
Male	302	184	113	84
Zambia				
Average female hourly wages as percentage of male wages	65	59	95	95
Market employment (million hours per year)				
Female	906	2,471	232	36
Male	557	2,365	814	106

Source: 1994 Bangladesh and 1995 Zambia gendered SAMs.

size of the two countries is reflected in their different degree of openness. The share of exports and imports in GDP is higher in Zambia (77 percent) than in Bangladesh (20 percent). Hence one would expect the impact of changes in trade policies on the domestic labor market to be smaller in Bangladesh than in Zambia.

In Bangladesh the educational distribution of the adult population is more unequal not only across educational categories but also across sexes: average years of schooling for women are about 66 percent of average years for men in Bangladesh, and 74 percent in Zambia. Gender inequality is larger in Bangladesh than in Zambia also as far as wages are concerned. Table 7.2 shows that women with no education earn less than 50 percent of what men of the same group earn in Bangladesh compared with 65 percent in Zambia. The gender wage gap narrows with tertiary education in both Bangladesh and Zambia, to 70 percent and 95 percent respectively. The smaller gap in earnings between female and male workers with university education can be explained by the fact that most highly educated women in both countries are employed by the public sector, where gender disparities in wages are less marked than in other sectors. This information should, however, be taken with caution as reliable data on wages are not available. Wage estimates from various labor force surveys had to be adjusted in both SAMs to correct for discrepancies between value added data and employment data.[2]

As shown in Table 7.3, on average, the adult population of both Bangladesh and Zambia spend about 38 percent of time on leisure and 62 percent working. There are, however, differences between the two countries in how the work is distributed between the market and the household, with people in Bangladesh spending 28 percent of the time on market work compared with 43 percent in Zambia, and 34 percent on social reproduction compared with 19 percent in Zambia. These different patterns mainly reflect women's lower market participation in Bangladesh, which results in more time overall being devoted to household work. Men spend the same share of time on market work in the two countries (42 percent) but spend longer hours without working in Zambia (52 percent of total time compared with 42 percent in Bangladesh). A possible interpretation is that, because of rigid sociocultural norms that encourage women to stay within the homestead, in Bangladesh men are more likely to get involved in household tasks such as food shopping, or anything else that involves "being seen." Fafchamps and Quisumbing (1999) find this type of specialization in rural Pakistan, where men dominate in "outside" housekeeping tasks such as firewood collection or

Table 7.3 Allocation of time between market and nonmarket activities (%)

	Total	Female	Male
Bangladesh			
Market	27.8	13.3	42.0
Social reproduction	34.4	53.2	16.1
Leisure	37.8	33.6	41.9
Total	100.0	100.0	100.0
Zambia			
Market	43.4	44.9	42.0
Social reproduction	18.5	32.9	5.7
Leisure	38.1	22.2	52.3
Total	100.0	100.0	100.0

Source: 1994 Bangladesh and 1995 Zambia gendered SAMs.

visiting the market. It is not certain whether the time allocation surveys for the two countries adopt the same definition of household work.[3] These different patterns, however, are consistent with other evidence on time allocation in South Asia and Sub-Saharan Africa (Ilahi 2000).

Tables 7.4 and 7.5 show that the skill and gender composition of both market and nonmarket sectors varies between Bangladesh and Zambia. Of the two nonmarket sectors, social reproduction is somewhat more female-intensive in Zambia (female time is 84 percent of total labor time) than in Bangladesh (76 percent of total). Moreover, while in Zambia social reproduction is more female-intensive than any market sector, in Bangladesh there is one market sector, garments, which is more female-intensive than social reproduction (83 percent of total time is female).[4] The garment sector is also the most export-oriented sector (88 percent of its output is exported) and one of the most labor-intensive sectors (labor accounts for 77 percent of total value added).

The most female-intensive sectors in Zambia are the agricultural sectors, especially food and livestock (in which 70 percent of total time is female) and

Table 7.4 Educational and gender structure of SAM sectors, Bangladesh

	Shares of sectoral employment (% of female labor)				Females (% of total labor)
	No educ.	Prim. educ.	Sec. educ.	Post educ.	
Grains	59	26	12	4	17
Commercial crops	57	28	11	4	3
Livestock and horticulture	61	25	11	3	47
Fishing	36	17	28	19	29
Food processing	48	26	18	9	30
Garments	43	34	17	7	83
Other textiles	31	35	20	14	12
Other manufacturing	37	31	20	12	16
Infrastructure	48	27	12	13	5
Trade	30	29	24	18	5
Transport	56	26	11	7	1
Public services	5	8	17	70	20
Financial services	3	9	13	75	6
Domestic services	48	25	17	9	43
All market sectors	49	26	15	11	24
All social reproduction	55	23	14	8	76
All leisure	50	25	15	10	44
All	51	25	15	9	49

Source: 1994 Bangladesh SAM.

Table 7.5 Educational and gender structure of the SAM sectors, Zambia

	Shares of sectoral employment (% of female labor)				Females (% of total labor)
	No educ.	Prim. educ.	Sec. educ.	Post educ.	
Maize	7	88	5	0	54
Commercial crops	6	94	0	0	41
Horticulture and groundnuts	19	54	24	4	60
Food and livestock	60	40	0	0	70
Fishing and forestry	12	78	10	0	7
Mining	10	45	41	4	7
Labour-intensive mfg	7	31	57	5	43
Capital-intensive mfg	43	49	7	1	4
Construction and utilities	20	80	0	0	3
Trade and transport	18	46	33	4	51
Public services	35	49	15	1	29
Market services	6	36	52	6	32
All market sectors	7	22	53	18	49
All social reproduction	20	65	14	2	84
All leisure	25	55	18	3	27
All	19	54	24	4	47

Source: 1995 Zambia SAM.

horticulture and groundnuts (60 percent). These sectors are the least skill-intensive sectors in the market economy in Zambia (although on average they are more skill-intensive than similar sectors in Bangladesh, reflecting the higher average educational level of the workforce in Zambia). Other relatively high female-intensive sectors in Zambia are trade and transport, with female time being 51 percent of total time. The same sectors in Bangladesh are very male-intensive (less than 5 percent of total time is female). Mining, which is by far the most open sector in Zambia (more than 93 percent of its output is exported), is highly male-intensive, with a female share in total time of only 7 percent. Mining is also the most capital-intensive sector (capital contributes 86 percent of total value added). The full details of the sectoral structure of Bangladesh and Zambia are shown in Table 7.6.

Comparison of simulations

The previous section has highlighted several differences between Zambia and Bangladesh. Although the two countries have similar production structures (particularly the shares of both agriculture and manufacturing in GDP), they differ in the sectoral composition of their foreign trade. The degree of their integration

Table 7.6 Sectoral structure of Bangladesh and Zambia

	Net output (% of GDP)	Labor (% of tot VA)	Export intensity[a]	Import penetration[a]	Tariff revenue (% of imports)
Bangladesh					
Grains	8.8	54.8	—	2.3	12.5
Commercial crops	3.6	33.2	0.1	6.6	2.0
Livestock and horticulture	6.9	44.5	0.2	1.9	8.5
Fishing	2.8	6.3	10.0	—	—
Food processing	4.5	13.1	1.4	1.8	61.4
Garments	1.5	84.9	87.5	8.2	4.1
Other textiles	2.7	72.2	18.5	28.3	11.8
Other manufacturing	3.9	42.2	1.9	45.8	20.8
Infrastructure	12.2	17.5	—	—	—
Trade	16.7	76.6	—	—	—
Transport	14.5	35.4	—	—	—
Public services	12.2	32.2	—	—	—
Financial services	5.5	20.4	—	—	—
Domestic services	3.9	92.7	—	—	—
All market sectors	100.0	43.6	11.4	19.6	18.4
All social reproduction	36.6	100.0	—	—	—
All leisure	52.6	100.0	—	—	—
Total	189.2				—
Zambia					
Maize	4.3	69.5	4.3	15.0	3.1
Commercial crops	1.4	55.6	15.6	16.9	0.4
Horticulture and groundnuts	5.6	90.6	2.9	2.7	21.0
Food and livestock	6.7	80.7	1.9	4.7	18.6
Fishing and forestry	4.8	55.7	—	0.2	15.9
Mining	17.3	13.9	93.3	23.3	20.3
Labor-intensive manufacturing	9.6	51.7	4.0	13.0	11.8
Capital-intensive manufacturing	3.1	35.2	9.1	65.0	14.1
Construction and utilities	6.4	17.7	10.1	0.2	19.5
Trade and transport	20.6	57.9	—	7.7	13.4
Public services	7.3	77.1	—	—	—
Market services	13.0	52.8	8.6	25.2	13.4
All market	100.0	50.9	16.5	20.3	13.4
All social reproduction	20.8	100.0			
All leisure	67.8	100.0			
Total	188.6				

Source: 1994 Bangladesh and 1995 Zambia SAMs.

Note
a Export intensity is measured as the share of exports in gross output and import penetration is measured as the share of imports in domestic use.

Table 7.7 Tariffs and openness (%)

	Bangladesh	Zambia
Average tariff rate	18.4	13.4
Tariffs as share of government revenue	30.7	30.0
Imports as share of GDP	12.1	41.0
Exports as share of GDP	7.5	36.1

Source: 1994 Bangladesh and 1995 Zambia SAMs.

into world markets varies – with Zambia being more open than Bangladesh – and so does the female intensity of their internationally traded sectors – with export sectors employing more women in Bangladesh than in Zambia. It is to be expected therefore that the same trade policies would have different gendered outcomes in the two countries.

A computable general equilibrium model applied to the Bangladesh and Zambia SAMs is used to analyze the effects of abolition of all tariffs. Both Bangladesh and Zambia have, on average, moderate levels of protection. As shown in Table 7.7, the average tariff rate, measured by the ratio of total tariff revenue to total imports, is about 18 percent in Bangladesh and about 13 percent in Zambia. Tariffs constitute approximately 30 percent of total government revenue in both countries. However, the degree of tariff dispersion is higher in Bangladesh, ranging from 2 percent in commercial crops (mainly jute, sugar, and tea) to more than 61 percent for food processing (due to very high protection in the edible oil sector). In Zambia the tariff ranges from almost zero in commercial crops (cotton, sugar, tobacco, and coffee) to 21 percent in horticulture and groundnuts.

The model is explained in detail in Fontana (2003). A brief description of closures and exogenously specified elasticity parameters is provided in this chapter. The production function in the model is a three-level constant elasticity of substitution (CES) function. At the lowest level, for each educational category, female labor and male labor of the same skill are aggregated into composite labor. To reflect the rigidity of gender roles, particularly within the household, female/male substitution is limited by setting the value of the elasticities to −0.5 in the market sectors and −0.25 in social reproduction and leisure.

The production function has an intermediate level which aggregates the four educational types of composite labor, with a substitution elasticity of −0.5, into one larger labor bundle. This larger labor bundle is the "output" of the reproduction and leisure sectors. In the market sectors, the production function has an upper level which combines composite labor with capital and land to produce net output (which is then combined in fixed proportions with intermediate inputs to make gross output). The value of the substitution elasticity at the upper level ranges from −0.5 in agriculture to −0.8 in manufacturing and services. The full set of elasticities used in the simulations is provided in Table 7.8.

Table 7.8 Values of substitution elasticities in the CES production function

	Market	Nonmarket	Agric.	Manuf.	Serv.
Lower level (Labor by gender for each educational group)	0.5	0.25			
Intermediate level (Labor by education)	0.5	0.5			
Upper level (Labor and nonlabor factors)			0.5	0.8	0.8

Source: Model simulations.

The treatment of foreign trade in the model is such that buyers in each sector divide their expenditure between imports and domestically produced goods in shares which vary in response to changes in the ratio of domestic to import prices. Likewise, producers in each sector divide their output between the home and the export markets in shares which vary with the ratio of domestic prices to export prices. These CES import functions and export constant elasticity of transformation (CET) functions partially insulate domestic prices from world prices, unlike more standard trade models in which the domestic prices of traded goods are strictly determined by world prices. The elasticity of substitution in both these functions is set at -2.0 in agriculture, -1.5 in manufacturing, and -0.8 in services.[5]

As for the macro closures, the balance of trade is fixed and the level of exports and imports adjust through changes in the real exchange rate. Alternative options would include quantity clearing (net borrowing adjusts) or rationing (scarce foreign exchange is somehow allocated between sources of demand). Government consumption in each sector is fixed in real terms, as is the demand for investment goods. It is assumed that loss of revenue from imports is fully recovered by increasing direct taxes by a uniform number of percentage points for all income recipients, hence spreading the burden uniformly across households and enterprises. Alternative government account closure rules would be possible. Assuming increases in indirect taxes or flexible government consumption would lead to important differences in the distributional effects of trade liberalization, in terms of both income and gender. The savings–investment balance is achieved through adjusting the household propensity to save.

As for the factor market closures, the assumption is that the supply of capital and land in each sector is fixed, but labor is mobile, so that supply to each sector responds freely to demand, within limits set by the fixed total supplies of female and male labor. Alternative rules in the labor market could be also modeled: for instance, wage determination mechanisms that reflect bargaining between workers and employers (Taylor 1989), or formal unemployment.

The macro closures and the factor market closures, as well as the elasticities for factor substitution and foreign trade, are set the same for both Bangladesh and Zambia and might not be realistic. The objective of the experiments in this chapter was to emphasize differences in outcomes driven exclusively by differences in the initial socioeconomic structure of the two countries rather than by differences in behavioral parameters. The implications of alternative closures for simulation results will be examined in future work.

The simulation results described in the following pages are analyzed with particular attention to: (1) changes in the allocation of female labor between employment in the market economy, social reproduction, and leisure and (2) the female wage rate, both absolute and relative to male wages. While the labor categories are identical in the two countries, the classification of production sectors and household types differs between them. To make comparison of results easier, changes are reported for aggregated categories. Details of more disaggregated results and other experiments can be found in Fontana (2003).

Abolition of tariffs plus depreciation of the real exchange rate

When all tariffs are removed, the total volume of imports increases by 3.5 percent in Zambia and by 14.7 percent in Bangladesh. Imports increase the most in manufacturing, but also in female-intensive agriculture in Zambia, and in manufacturing other than garments in Bangladesh, as these were previously the most protected sectors. In both cases the trade balance is restored by a depreciation of the exchange rate, which is greater in Zambia (7.6 percent) than in Bangladesh (0.6 percent). This has partly to do with the supply elasticity of the export sectors, which is greater in Bangladesh than in Zambia because of the much larger share of labor value added in garments as compared with mining.[6]

As a result of the exchange rate depreciation, exports rise in both countries, mainly in garments in Bangladesh, and in mining and in male-intensive agriculture in Zambia.

These changes in exports and imports cause domestic market output to increase in both countries by about 0.5 percent as shown in Table 7.9. The sectors which expand the most are manufacturing in Bangladesh and mining in Zambia (i.e. the export sectors). Within the Bangladesh manufacturing sector, garments rise while

Table 7.9 Effects of tariff abolition on output (percentage changes from the base)

	Bangladesh	Zambia
Market of which:	0.5	0.6
Agriculture	−0.2	0.4
Mining	—	1.8
Manufacturing	3.2	0.1
Services	0.2	0.4
Social reproduction	−0.2	−0.3
Leisure	−0.3	−0.7

Source: Model simulations.

food, beverages, and tobacco, and other manufacturing decline. Manufacturing in Zambia is unchanged, because of offsetting changes in the capital-intensive sector, which declines, and in the labor-intensive sector, which slightly increases. Agriculture declines marginally in Bangladesh while it increases in Zambia, due to higher production of male-intensive commercial crops and maize, while output in both female-intensive sectors – food staples and horticulture – falls.

The corollary of higher market production is an output fall in social reproduction and leisure. The effect of tariff elimination accompanied by exchange rate depreciation sufficient to restore the trade balance is to reduce the average price of internationally traded relative to non-internationally traded goods and services. In both countries, market sectors expand and nonmarket sectors that are neither internationally nor domestically traded contract. The decline is higher in leisure than in social reproduction, since the consumption of leisure is more responsive to price changes than that of household work. Leisure, a male-intensive activity, declines in Zambia more than in Bangladesh, because its opportunity cost increases more in the former country than in the latter, reflecting a larger rise in male wages. The increase in total output (both market and nonmarket) is 0.2 percent in Bangladesh and negligible in Zambia.[7]

Because of the different gender composition of the expanding and contracting sectors in the two countries, the increase in female market labor force participation in the experiment is larger in Bangladesh than in Zambia and so is the rise in female wages. Effects across educational groups also vary between the two countries.

Employment in the garment sector in Bangladesh rises by about 37 percent for both women and men, but the absolute increase is higher for women than for men, because of their much larger initial share. Reflecting the educational composition of the garment sector's female labor force, the increase in market employment is largest for women with primary and secondary education, and less significant for the highly skilled. Market participation of uneducated female workers rises only by 1 percent, as the increase in their garment employment is partly offset by a decline in their time inputs in grain production. A shift in employment from agriculture to the manufacturing sector could have potentially significant positive effects, even when net increases in participation are slight, as this sector generally offers better working conditions than agriculture. Time spent in social reproduction by women with primary and secondary education declines on average by about 0.4 percent, while their leisure time declines more. A similar pattern, although smaller in magnitude, can be observed for female workers with both higher education and no education. Because the abolition of tariffs causes a significant expansion of the most female-intensive sector in the Bangladesh economy, the economy-wide demand for female labor rises more than the demand for male labor, and hence the wage rate of women increases both absolutely and relative to men. The rise is largest for women with primary and secondary education as described in Table 7.10.

Because the impact of the elimination of tariffs combined with exchange rate depreciation on internationally traded market goods raises the average demand for market goods relative to nonmarket goods, female market employment rises

Table 7.10 Effects of tariff abolition on employment and wages, Bangladesh (percentage changes from base)

	Female no educ.	Female prim. educ.	Female sec. educ.	Female post educ.	Total female	Total male
Employment						
All market sectors	1.4	3.1	3.4	2.2	2.1	0.3
of which:						
Grains	−1.7	−2.0	−1.9	−1.7	−1.8	−1.4
Commercial crops	1.7	0.0	1.5	1.7	1.6	2.0
Livestock and	0.2	−0.1	0.0	0.2	0.1	0.5
horticulture						
Fishing	0.6	0.3	0.3	0.6	0.5	0.8
Food processing	−2.8	−3.1	−3.0	−2.8	−2.9	−2.6
Garments	36.8	36.4	36.5	36.8	36.6	37.1
Other textiles	10.5	10.2	10.2	10.5	10.4	10.7
Other manufacturing	−13.0	−13.3	−13.2	−13.0	−13.1	−12.9
Infrastructure	0.2	−0.1	—	0.2	0.2	0.4
Trade	0.5	0.2	0.2	0.5	0.4	0.7
Transport	0.7	0.4	—	0.7	0.6	0.9
Public services	0.2	−0.1	−0.1	0.2	0.1	0.3
Financial services	—	−0.1	0.0	0.2	0.1	0.3
Domestic services	0.0	−0.4	−0.3	−0.1	−0.1	0.1
All social reproduction	−0.2	−0.4	−0.4	−0.2	−0.3	−0.1
All leisure	−0.3	−0.5	−0.5	−0.4	−0.4	−0.3
Hourly wages						
Absolute	1.8	2.9	2.5	1.7		
Relative to males[a]	0.9	1.8	1.4	0.5		

Source: Simulation results.

Note

a This is the difference between the absolute percentage change for females and the absolute percentage change for males. A positive value indicates that the female/male wage gap has narrowed.

in Zambia too, and so does the female wage rate, but by a smaller proportion than in Bangladesh. An important difference, however, is that in Zambia the gender wage gap widens, instead of narrowing as in Bangladesh. This is because mining and commercial crops, the sectors that expand the most as a result of tariff elimination in Zambia, are male-intensive.

The increase in market labor force participation in Zambia is small on average for all educational groups. As shown in Table 7.11, employment rises the most (1.1 percent) for female workers with no education, because of expansion of commercial crops, and for women with secondary education, whose largest sectoral increase is in mining. While for this latter group the rise in market participation is entirely at the expense of their leisure, with only a negligible change in time spent on household work, for the former the decline in nonmarket time is by 0.5 in social reproduction and by more than one percent in leisure. Although social reproduction and leisure decline on average, there are differences between some

Table 7.11 Effects of tariff abolition on employment and wages, Zambia (percentage changes from base)

	Female no educ.	Female prim. educ.	Female sec. educ.	Female post educ.	Total female	Total male
Employment						
All market sectors	1.1	0.4	1.1	0.6	0.7	1.1
of which:						
Groundnuts and horticulture	0.0	0.1	—	—	0.1	−0.2
Commercial crops	6.7	0.0	—	—	6.7	6.4
Food and livestock	−0.4	−0.3	—	—	−0.3	−0.6
Fishing and forestry	0.6	0.8	1.0	0.7	0.8	0.5
Maize	2.3	2.4	—	—	2.4	2.1
Infrastructure	5.7	5.8	6.0	5.7	5.9	5.5
Mining	13.8	14.0	14.2	13.9	14.1	13.7
Labor-intensive manufacturing	0.8	0.9	1.1	0.8	0.8	0.5
Capital-intensive manufacturing	−1.8	−1.7	−1.5	−1.8	−1.6	−2.0
Market services	0.9	1.0	1.2	0.9	1.1	0.7
Trade and Transport	0.5	0.6	0.8	0.6	0.6	0.3
Public services	0.1	0.2	0.4	0.1	0.3	−0.1
All social reproduction	−0.5	−0.4	0.0	−0.1	−0.4	−0.4
All leisure	−1.1	−0.9	−0.4	−0.2	−0.8	−0.8
Hourly wages						
Absolute	1.0	0.8	0.4	1.0		
Relative to males	−0.8	−0.5	−1.1	−0.3		

Source: Simulation results.

(rich) households, where nonmarket time rises, and other (poor) households, where it falls. Women of the same skill experience either a decline or a rise in their time inputs on household work and leisure, depending on the type of household they belong to. In Zambia women with higher education are concentrated in rich households, while women with less education mainly belong to poor ones, so the decline in female nonmarket time is larger for the latter than for the former. The impact on wages too differs between these two groups of female workers, with gains being smaller for the higher educated.

Changes in the functional distribution of income favor female labor over male labor and labor over land and capital in Bangladesh, while in Zambia nonlabor factors gain more than labor factors, and capital gains more than land.

Figure 7.1 provides a summary of effects. In Bangladesh women gain in terms of higher market employment and wages. Importantly, it is not only their absolute wages that increase, but also their wages relative to men. In Zambia, absolute

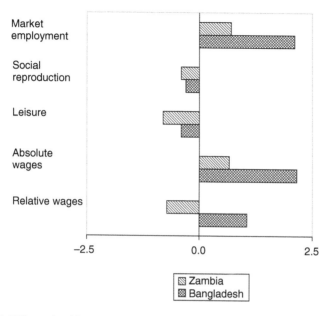

Figure 7.1 Effects of tariff abolition on female employment and wages (average across all educational groups).

income gains are smaller than in Bangladesh while the gender wage gap widens. In both Bangladesh and Zambia, however, higher female market employment means that women spend less time on caring for families and on leisure. This decline in nonmarket time is more marked in Zambia than in Bangladesh. In Bangladesh, the narrowing of the gender wage gap, and thus the increase in the opportunity cost of female workers' time relative to that of male workers, encourages some substitution of male for female labor in social reproduction, potentially leading to a more equitable allocation of tasks within the household. These results are of course partly driven by the assumptions in the model. In some specific households and sociocultural contexts, the intra-household division of labor might not be at all responsive to economic incentives because of strong gender norms.

When the same experiment is run assuming a higher price elasticity of social reproduction (as a proxy for greater flexibility in the allocation of women's time), the effect is a larger outflow of female labor from social reproduction both in Bangladesh and in Zambia. However, the way in which women's time is released from the household and reallocated to other activities varies between the two countries. In Zambia commercial crops and maize, the production of which increases as a result of tariff abolition, are more female-intensive than leisure, so most of the female time released from social reproduction is spent on working more in agriculture. Conversely in Bangladesh, because leisure is more female-intensive than most market sectors, the time freed up from household work mainly attenuates the decline in women's leisure time. Other variants of the experiments show, too, that changing the value of gender-related parameters matters for the overall impact of tariff abolition.[8] The effects can be positive or negative for equality, depending on the gender composition of the nonmarket sectors relative to market sectors, and on the extent and nature of the gender wage gap.

Comparison of methods

Many different methods can be used to analyze the gender effects of economic reforms: qualitative methods, econometric methods, and modeling methods. Each of these methods includes in turn a variety of approaches. For example, some econometric studies use time-series analysis while others are based on panel data analysis. Single-country static general equilibrium models, such as those used in this chapter, are only one of many types of models. Modeling can be at the household level, country level, or global level; could focus on specific sectors or on the whole economy; and be either dynamic or static. Each approach has strengths and weaknesses. No single method or discipline can provide all the answers and often a combination of tools is the best solution.[9] Validating model results with studies from other methods can also significantly strengthen their influence on policy (Devarajan and Robinson 2002).

This section compares the model results described in the previous sections with other work in the gender and trade literature. The first part highlights results that are the same as with other methods. The second part discusses ways in which the modeling approach contributed to a better understanding of the impact. The third part examines aspects that the Bangladesh and Zambia models did not cover. Some of these limitations are specific to the models used in this chapter, while others are characteristic of CGE modeling in general.

Results in common with other methods

The simulation findings that trade liberalization plus exchange rate depreciation raises female employment and wages in a labor-abundant country like Bangladesh but is not as beneficial for women in a natural resource-abundant country like Zambia are consistent with other evidence. Several studies – mainly case studies of specific sectors or firms, and some cross-country econometric analyses – show that the growth of export-oriented manufacturing, especially in South and Southeast Asia, has created many jobs for women, at wages which, though lower than those of men, are higher than they could have earned in the alternative forms of work open to them. Very little research exists on the impact of trade on women in mineral-rich countries like Zambia.

The SAMs and CGE models in this chapter expose reasons for the differences in impact. They clearly show where women are located in the economy, and highlight the mechanisms through which changes in the domestic prices of imports and exports affect a country's output structure and hence its factor demand (and wages). Thus in Bangladesh, where the main export is female-intensive (and low-skill-intensive), women benefit when trade liberalization is coupled with exchange rate depreciation. Conversely in Zambia, where the main export is a mineral resource that is highly capital and male-intensive in production, women are disadvantaged by tariff elimination even if coupled with exchange rate depreciation.

An important point made in feminist economics research (most notably by Elson 1991) is that increases in female market employment might be at the expense of the time women devote to caring for their families, or, more likely, of their leisure. It often results in heavier work burdens and a decline in well-being. By incorporating social reproduction and leisure sectors, the model used in this chapter addresses these concerns and operationalizes them numerically.

The responsiveness of the gender division of labor to changes in economic incentives – for example, how much time women spend on household activities falls in response to improvements in their market wage or employment opportunities – varies depending on a wide range of social and cultural norms. In an analysis of foreign direct investment in Indonesia, Braunstein (2000) discusses how family structures and institutional contexts influence female labor supply. She suggests that women heads of households with few job alternatives available to them may be prepared to work for much lower pay than women in patriarchal households and that wives' reservation wages for subcontracted homework are likely to be lower than those for waged employment outside the home. Although not all of these interesting dimensions and nuances can be represented explicitly in the CGE framework, some can be implicitly captured by the value of key parameters in the model: for instance, the elasticity of substitution between male and female labor in market and nonmarket production, and the price elasticity of demand for social reproduction. Depending on the values assigned to these key parameters, the magnitudes of the effects of the experiments have been shown to vary, which is important to consider when designing policies.

Results not attainable by other methods

The gendered CGE models of Bangladesh and Zambia provide an integrated framework for the analysis of the effects of trade on women which allows consideration of more constraints and interactions than is possible using other methods.

Most existing research on the gender impact of trade liberalization examines specific firms or sectors in isolation, or only one aspect of welfare, and hence does not provide sufficient analysis of linkages among different dimensions. Partial equilibrium analysis assumes that repercussions from one market to another will be slight and neglects the indirect effects that change in one sector may have on prices, output, and employment in other sectors (both market and nonmarket). Such approaches cannot produce an accurate measurement of net outcomes – it would not be possible to know whether, for example, the number of female jobs that are destroyed in sectors producing import-substitutes would be greater than the number of female jobs created in female-intensive exporting sectors, or whether the positive effect on well-being from higher wages and market employment would be more than offset by the negative impact on it from reduced leisure.

Moreover, the use of a partial sectoral method to assess the impact of a trade shock in a non-female-intensive sector would likely lead to the conclusion that the shock did not have any gender implications, even though the indirect effects on women were substantial. Most studies of the manufacturing sector in Bangladesh and elsewhere explore effects at the household level (e.g. Zohir 1998; Hewett and Amin 2000), but do not consider linkages with the rest of the market economy. Some of the African agricultural studies (for instance, Kennedy 1994 on Kenya; Kumar 1994 on Zambia; Katz 1995 on Guatemala) do, however, go beyond a single-sector approach, since they examine the effects of commercialization of certain crops on the food production sector, on other nonfarm activities, and on consumption as well as income – important steps towards a general equilibrium analysis.

One of the most important advantages of CGE modeling over other existing methods is its ability to include a wide range of macroeconomic, sectoral, and social impacts and to provide economy-wide quantification of these effects. It is important to know whether effects of a specific policy measure are big or small and what are the main causal chains. By providing a simulation laboratory for controlled experiments, CGE models improve our understanding of the many ramifications induced by a shock and highlight the strength of various forces at work.

By contrast with the sectoral studies, more conventional CGE models permit analysis of both direct and indirect effects of trade policies. However, by excluding the household and leisure sectors, they disregard important broader welfare implications and are likely to yield inaccurate results about the impact of such reforms on standard market variables.

Model limitations and suggestions for further research

The Bangladesh and Zambia CGE models shed no light on whether gains in female employment from greater trade openness would be sustained over time. Recent studies based on time-series analysis (e.g. Kusago and Tzannatos 1998; Joekes 1999) point to a decline in women's share in the manufacturing labor force of several middle-income countries (such as Mexico, Malaysia, and South Korea) – a phenomenon often referred to as "de-feminization" of employment. Female workers do not seem able to maintain their position within the industrial workforce as the composition of exports moves toward more technologically sophisticated goods or shifts to other low-wage countries. Changes over time in gender patterns of production have been observed also in some African agriculture–these too, often, to women's disadvantage. Evidence seems to suggest that, as the prospects for market sales of a crop rise, more men tend to move into its production, for example, groundnuts in Zambia (Wold 1997). On a more positive note, case studies of Bangladesh (Zohir 1998; Kabeer 2000) suggest that increasing female employment has the potential to change families' attitudes toward considering daughters as assets instead of liabilities. These long-term changes are likely to affect strategic gender interests in important ways and are better captured by other methods, such as time-series econometrics and qualitative case studies.

Time-series analysis indicates dynamic processes of gender patterns of work. This brings attention to "surprises" – or deviations from expected trends, some of which could not be anticipated by a model. For a better understanding of the nature of, and reasons for, these "surprises," qualitative approaches are particularly valuable. Qualitative methods add depth and nuances to the analysis that could not be captured by any of the quantitative methods.

The model used in this analysis is a single-period static model and assumes labor endowments and production technology to be fixed.[10] In principle, however, CGE models can be made dynamic. For instance, the potential positive long-term effect of trade expansion on female education in Bangladesh could be captured in the model by considering a sequence of equilibria whereby in each period the skill level of the female labor force is updated, and the extent of this change is a function of increases in female-intensive production or a similar such hypothesis. Changes in the productivity of the labor force over time could also be made a function of the level of social reproduction provided in each period. Importantly, this would offer an opportunity to link explicitly the productivity of the labor force to the provision of care. Insights from the medical and sociological literature (e.g. studies on the impact of maternal care on children's nutritional status and their school attainments (Quisumbing 2003)) could significantly contribute to a better design of such a model.

The Bangladesh and Zambia models were not able to establish conclusively whether rises in female employment and earnings translate into welfare gains for women. This is because the CGE approach used in this chapter does not take into account the nature of production relations and the unequal distribution of power and resources between different people.

An intricate web of institutions and norms mediates individuals' access to resources and its translation into impact, which in-depth qualitative research is better able to explain. Several anthropological and sociological studies, for example, suggest that, in general, women are more likely to exercise control over the proceeds of their labor when it is carried out in forms of production which are independent of male household members and in social relationships outside the familial sphere (Benería and Roldan 1987). Kabeer (2000) provides an interesting example of this in her study of the effects of the clothing industry on two different groups of Bangladeshi women, one working in factories in Dhaka and one involved in home-based work in East London. While in Bangladesh the regularity of the wages from the factory jobs, and the location of the work outside the control of male relatives, has increased women's influence on household decisions, in London, the organization of work around home-based piecework has meant that the empowering effects have been weak. The CGE model, in its current formulation, would record in both cases an increase in female income, without detecting any difference in outcomes arising from differences in women's ability to control resources.

A more fully developed model of the household based on bargaining behavior could redress some of these limitations. Game-theoretic approaches – which introduce the idea of preference heterogeneity, bargaining power divergences, and individual resource control – are increasingly used to model household decision-making (e.g. Smith and Chavas 1999; Warner and Campbell 2000). Collective household models have the advantage that they allow consideration of unequal intra-household resource allocation. However, they take the rest of the economy as given and thus neglect feedback effects.

Ideally, if data were available, a fully developed household model could be nested within a CGE model. This would allow consideration of more interactions between macro and micro dimensions than other approaches, but would have the disadvantage of high computational complexity. Another option could be to keep a simpler CGE structure, but to develop an independent household module outside the model to be used for postsimulation calculations. This might be easier to implement, but should be used only when feedback effects are known to be small.

The Bangladesh and Zambia models allow for gender differences in labor markets by specifying different degrees of mobility among labor categories, and different levels of substitution between female and male workers across sectors. If better data were available, a more fully developed characterization of the labor market could be developed – for example, different mechanisms for wage determination or distinguishing between formal and informal activities.

Recent work attempts to measure the extent of the informal sector and of women's contribution to GDP generated by this sector in various developing countries (most notably Charmes 2000). However, statistical information is still sparse. The effects of informal employment on poverty and gender outcomes will evidently vary depending on the type of activities in which workers are involved. The scattered evidence seems to suggest Zambia has a more female-intensive informal sector than Bangladesh (in Bangladesh informal female workers are mostly concentrated in domestic services, while the large informal transport and marketing sector is predominantly male), but there is no clear indication on the nature of prevailing activities and their linkages with other household and market activities.

One possible working hypothesis for modeling formal and informal labor markets could be to assume an increasing wage-employment curve in the formal sector, with wages in the informal sector set to absorb all the labor not employed in the formal sectors. If sufficient information were available, the probability of being unemployed could be estimated separately for men and women as a function of a set of socioeconomic characteristics and this used to adjust key labor market parameters in the model.

A shortcoming of CGE models more generally is to disregard the process required to move from the initial to the final equilibrium state, thus ignoring adjustment costs. For example, women who lose their jobs in import-substituting industries might not be able to take advantage of newly created opportunities elsewhere in the economy in the short run, or not at all, if adequate training and assistance is not provided or there are severe constraints to their physical mobility. Some studies of displaced workers (e.g. Benería 1998) provide information by gender on the circumstances of their layoffs, availability of retraining, length of their unemployment spells, quality of any new employment available to them, and other impacts at the family level. The value of these studies is to highlight important short-term effects neglected by the modeling approach.

Finally, CGE models cannot say anything about women's and men's perceptions and feelings. Subjective happiness is a concept that covers many more aspects of human welfare than the standard concept of utility based on revealed preferences (for a review see Frey and Stutzer 2002). "Oddly, while economists generally think that people are the best judges of their own welfare, they resist asking people directly how they feel" (Ravallion 2001 cited in Kanbur 2001a). Research needs to incorporate the possibility that, in some cases, women might not enjoy their higher income if they face increased social tensions as a result of taking paid work. In other cases, women might derive important psychological benefits from paid work that more than compensate for the loss of leisure time and any social censure. Even as regards taking care of children and the elderly in the household, perceptions across individual women might vary from feeling happy to feeling overburdened. Addressing these problems requires information which is not found in conventional economic analysis but on which there is a growing literature in other disciplines (e.g. Chen 1997; Mohamed and Rajan 2003).

Conclusions

The CGE model used in this chapter provides useful insights into the gendered economic outcomes of tariff liberalization that could not have emerged using other approaches. It is applied comparatively to Bangladesh and Zambia. Simulation results highlight how differences in the socioeconomic structure of the two countries shape the way in which trade expansion affects gender inequalities. The finer level of detail in the gender disaggregation of factors, sectors, and households also permits a better understanding of how the differential impact of policy changes on female and male workers varies, depending on whether or not the workers concerned have education, live in urban areas or in rural areas, and are or are not head of their households.

More importantly, by including consideration of the time devoted to caring activities and to the amount of leisure that people enjoy, the modeling approach used in this chapter provides a broader understanding of the welfare effects of policy compared with conventional CGE models.

In the experiments run with the Bangladesh and Zambia models no attempt is made to construct a single index of well-being. The effects of certain policy shocks are often ambiguous and emphasize that while there might be gains in some dimensions there might be losses in others.

For example, an increase in female earnings from greater participation in the market economy might on balance reduce social welfare if it also resulted in a substantial decline in leisure time for women. Whether women are better-off with more cash income and less leisure depends on whether they have chosen this outcome or been forced into it. Similarly, whether the decline in social reproduction has a negative impact on the production of human capabilities depends on the extent to which substitutes (for instance, paid child care) exist.

No single approach can provide all the answers to these questions and, hence, the main recommendation of this chapter is that a combination of methods be applied. Methodological tools other than CGE models are useful for exploring those dimensions of the gender impact of trade – such as subjective well-being or sector-specific changes – that by their very nature require more in-depth and more qualitative analyses than what the modeling can offer. Other methods can also be valuable in informing modeling choices. A constant "dialogue" between methodologies should be encouraged in which insights from one approach are used to enrich, or challenge, findings from another approach.

Notes

1 Some studies suggest that time spent eating and sleeping responds to changes in economic variables with effects on labor productivity (Biddle and Hamermesh 1990) and might also vary by gender (Zaman 1995 on Bangladesh). In the current SAMs, however, for simplicity, differences in time spent on personal care by men and women are all captured by differences in leisure time.

2 This is a common problem when constructing SAMs, since information for different accounts is derived from various sources which do not always use same definitions and measurements.

3 Estimating the allocation of women's and men's time between market and nonmarket activities was not easy, as data on time-use, in both Bangladesh and Zambia, are sparse and cover neither all tasks nor all geographical areas (no detailed time-use study was available for the urban areas, for example). Subsistence agriculture is included in market work.

4 This is true also when social reproduction is considered by household type, with the sole exception of social reproduction in rural female-headed households, in which female time is 92 percent of the total.

5 Elasticity values of -0.8 are considered "medium low," -1.5 "medium high," and -3.0 "very high" (Sadoulet and de Janvry 1995).

6 Since the assumption in the model is that labor is a mobile factor while the supply of capital and land in each sector is fixed, a sector that uses large inputs of labor relative to land and capital is able to increase more easily its output in response to price changes.

7 It is important to reemphasize that the choice of market-clearing mechanisms is a key determinant of model behavior. In the experiments described in this section, changes in the production structure of both Bangladesh and Zambia are driven mostly by the assumption that the trade balance is restored through a depreciation of the exchange rate. Moreover, the model is constructed so that loss of revenue from imports is recovered fully by increasing direct taxes. This portrays a more optimistic scenario than what many developing countries actually experience with trade liberalization. The objective of the simulations was not to be "realistic" but simply to emphasize differences in outcomes resulting from different initial gendered structures.

8 However, the effects of changes in these parameter values are rather weak.

9 For a useful discussion on how/when to integrate qualitative and quantitative methods in development research see Kanbur (2001a,b).

10 Changes in production methods or labor endowments could of course be simulated as part of an experiment.

References

Benería, L. (1998) "The impact of industrial relocation on displaced workers: a case study of Cortland, NY," *Community Development Reports, Research Briefs & Case Studies*, 6 (1), Ithaca, NY: Cornell Community and Rural Development Institute.

Benería, L. and Roldan, M. (1987) *The Cross-Road of Class and Gender*, Chicago, IL: University of Chicago Press.

Biddle, J. and Hamermesh, D. (1990) "Sleep and the allocation of time," *Journal of Political Economy*, 98 (5): 922–43.

Braunstein, E. (2000) "Engendering foreign direct investment: household structures, labour markets and the international mobility of capital," *World Development*, 28 (7): 1157–72.

Charmes, J. (2000) "Size, trends and productivity of women's work in the informal sector," paper presented at the annual IAFFE conference, Istanbul, August 15–17, 2000.

Chen, M. (1997) *A Guide for Assessing the Impact of Micro-enterprise Services at the Individual Level*, Mimeo: USAID.

Devarajan, S. and Robinson, S. (2002) "The influence of computable general equilibrium models on policy," TMD Discussion Paper No. 98, Washington, DC: International Food Policy Research Institute (IFPRI).

Elson, D. (1991) *Male Bias in the Development Process*, Manchester: Manchester University Press.

Fafchamps, M. and Quisumbing, A.R. (1999) "Social roles, human capital, and the intra-household division of labour: evidence from Pakistan," FCND Discussion Paper No. 73, Washington, DC: IFPRI.

Fontana, M. (2003) "The gender impact of trade liberalization in developing countries," unpublished PhD thesis, IDS at the University of Sussex.

Fontana, M. and Wood, A. (2000) "Modelling the effects of trade on women, at work and at home," *World Development*, 28 (7): 1173–90.

Frey, B.S. and Stutzer, A. (2002) "What can economists learn from happiness research?" *Journal of Economic Literature*, 40 (2): 402–35.

Hewett, P. and Amin, S. (2000) "Assessing the impact of garment work on quality of life measures," New York: Population Council.

Ilahi, N. (2000) "The intra-household allocation of time and tasks: what have we learnt from the empirical literature?" Gender and Development Working Paper Series 13, Washington, DC: World Bank.

Joekes, S. (1999) "Gender, property rights and trade: constraints to Africa growth," in K. King and S. McGrath (eds), *Enterprise in Africa: between poverty and growth*, Oxford: Centre of African Studies.

Kabeer, N. (2000) *The Power to Choose: Bangladeshi women and labour market decisions in London and Dhaka*, London: Verso.

Kanbur, R. (2001a) "Economics, social science and development," *World Development*, 30 (3): 477–86.

—— (ed.) (2001b) "Qual-quant: qualitative and quantitative poverty appraisal-complementarities, tensions and the way forward," contributions to a workshop held in Ithaca, NY: Cornell University, March 15–16, 2001.

Katz, E. (1995) "Gender and trade within the household: observations from rural Guatemala," *World Development*, 23 (2): 327–42.

Kennedy, E. (1994) "Effects of sugarcane production in Southwestern Kenya on income and nutrition," in J. von Braun and E. Kennedy (eds), *Agricultural Commercialisation,*

Economic Development and Nutrition, Baltimore, MD: The Johns Hopkins University Press for IFPRI.

Kumar, S.K. (1994) "Adoption of hybrid maize in Zambia: effects on gender roles, food consumption and nutrition," IFPRI Research Report No. 100, Washington, DC: IFPRI.

Kusago, T. and Tzannatos, T. (1998) "Export processing zones: a review in need of update," HDDSP Discussion Paper No. 9802, Washington, DC: World Bank.

Mayer, J. and Wood, A. (2001) "South Asia's export structure in a comparative perspective," *Oxford Development Studies*, 29 (1): 5–29.

Mohamed, E. and Rajan, S.I. (2003) "Gender and mental health in Kerala," paper presented at the second meeting of the MIMAP Gender Network, Bangkok, January 14–17, 2003.

Moore, H.L. and Vaughan, M. (1994) *Cutting Down Trees: gender, nutrition, and agricultural change in the northern province of Zambia*, Portsmouth, NH: Heinemann, Lusaka: University of Zambia Press.

Quisumbing, A. (ed.) (2003) *Household Decisions, Gender and Development: a synthesis of recent research*, Baltimore and London: The Johns Hopkins University Press.

Sadoulet, E. and de Janvry, A. (1995) *Quantitative Development Policy Analysis*, Baltimore, MD: The Johns Hopkins University Press.

Smith, L. and Chavas, J. (1999) "Supply response of West African agricultural households: implications of intra-household preference heterogeneity," FCND Discussion Paper No. 69, Washington, DC: IFPRI.

Sobhan, R. and Khundker, N. (2001) *Globalisation and Gender: changing patterns of women's employment in Bangladesh*, Dhaka: The University Press.

Taylor, L. (1989) *Stabilization and Growth in Developing Countries: a structuralist approach*, New York: Harwood Publishers.

United Nations (1993) "System of national accounts 1993," Studies in Methods, Series F 2/Rev 4, New York: UN Statistical Division.

Warner, J.M. and Campbell, D.A. (2000) "Supply response in an agrarian economy with non-symmetric gender relations," *World Development*, 28 (7): 1327–40.

Wold, B.K. (1997) *Supply Response in a Gender-Perspective: the case of structural adjustment in Zambia*, Oslo: Statistics Norway.

Wood, A. and Mayer, J. (2001) "Africa's export structure in a comparative perspective," *Cambridge Journal of Economics*, 25 (3): 369–94.

Zaman, H. (1995) "Patterns of activity and use of time in rural Bangladesh: class, gender, and seasonal variations," *The Journal of Developing Areas*, 29 (3): 371–88.

Zohir, S.C. (1998) "Gender implications of industrial reforms and adjustment in the manufacturing sector of Bangladesh," unpublished PhD thesis, Economics and Social Studies, Manchester: University of Manchester.

8 Mature export-led growth and gender wage inequality in Taiwan

Günseli Berik

Introduction[1]

Taiwan is arguably the most successful practitioner of the export-led growth model, which is an important contributor to the accelerated globalization process of the late twentieth century. It was one of the first countries to adopt this model and to achieve sustained growth rates based on manufacturing for export. Since the late 1970s Taiwan has sought to maintain and strengthen its international competitiveness by adapting its industrial structure to the changes in the global economy. It has moved beyond labor-intensive manufacturing toward a more capital-intensive industrial base and a diversified export structure. Since the mid-1980s, there has also been a rapid increase in overseas investment by Taiwanese firms, primarily in the Southeast Asian economies. This study evaluates the implications of this second-stage or mature phase of Taiwan's export-led growth strategy for gender wage inequality in manufacturing industry.

The study contributes to the feminist economics project of engendering the investigation of the export-led growth model. Economists' evaluations of Taiwan's record focus on genderless macroeconomic aggregates and, with few exceptions (cf. Galenson 1979; Liu 1989; Fields 1992, 1994; Ranis 1995), pay little attention to labor market outcomes. These studies praise Taiwan's success in maintaining high growth rates and a stable macroeconomic environment while reducing income inequality among households. However, income inequality between men and women has not received attention in these evaluations. Feminist anthropologists and sociologists, on the other hand, have analyzed the important role women workers played in the success of export-led growth in Taiwan (Gallin 1990; Cheng and Hsiung 1994; Hsiung 1996), and the impact of paid employment outside the home on women's status and intra-family distribution (Diamond 1979; Arrigo 1980; Kung 1983; Greenhalgh 1985). But most of these small-scale studies focus on the early phase of export-led growth. Moreover, they describe the *process* whereby gender inequalities are maintained, but do not link gendered *outcomes* in the labor market to economic variables at either the industry or macroeconomic levels. Feminist economists have begun to fill this research lacuna by assessing the cost of macroeconomic success in the newly industrializing economies (Berik 1995; Seguino 1996, 1997a,b; Zveglich *et al.* 1997). These studies have found persistent gender wage inequalities, despite the closing of gender gaps in education, and have raised doubts about the export-led model's ability to improve women's economic status relative to men. The present study refines the empirical methodology necessary for evaluating the gendered impact of restructuring in such macroeconomic success stories or "miracles."

Recent studies that attempt to explain rising wage inequality between skilled and unskilled workers in industrial countries in terms of technological change and changing trade patterns do not use gender as a category of analysis (cf. Wood 1994; Freeman 1995). Conversely, research on gender wage inequality in the US is not informed by a global awareness (O'Neill and Polachek 1993; Blau and Kahn 1997; Blau 1998). The present study is one of the first to integrate the analysis of gendered labor market outcomes with the analysis of trade and capital flows and of technological change. Using data for 22 manufacturing industries over the 1984–93 period this study estimates an empirical model on the determinants of gender wage inequality and the wage rates of women and men.

Globalization, export-led growth, and gender inequalities in manufacturing

The main concern of feminist research on the processes of economic globalization has been the gendered employment and income effects of the implementation of the neoliberal (also known as "supply-side") model in both Third World and industrial countries (Berik 2000). This research has problematized the implications for women of the structural shift away from industry to services and the trade-induced manufacturing job losses and income insecurity in industrial countries (Cohen 1987; Connelly *et al.* 1995; Greene and Hoffnar 1995). In the case of the Third World the focus has been on the effects of the Structural Adjustment Programs that have ushered in the neoliberal model (cf. Beneria and Feldman 1992; Bakker 1994; Sparr 1994). This research has shown that the model's imperative to be export-oriented brings about the rapid expansion of employment opportunities for women, and absorbs increasing numbers of women, who are pressed for jobs as a result of worsening living standards.

The feminist literature that specifically focuses on export-orientation has evaluated the typical scenario of export manufacturing based on labor-intensive, low-skill, standardized production processes, and explained the high proportion of women among the employed in terms of the lower unit-labor costs attained with women workers (Elson and Pearson 1981; Standing 1989). In turn, the labor-cost advantage provided by women is shown to be the outcome of concerted efforts by governments and firms to enact employment and hiring rules that discriminate against women and to mobilize gender ideals and stereotypes that justify women's concentration in unskilled, low-paying, high-turnover jobs (Elson 1995; Seguino 1997a). Thus, gender wage inequality is perpetuated either by women's crowding into a limited set of occupations and industries and/or employer and government-sanctioned discrimination against women in wage-setting in industries or occupations dominated by women. These arguments, known as the "crowding" and "discrimination" hypotheses, were put forth initially by feminist economists as explanations for the negative relationship between female share of employment and wage levels in a closed economy framework (Bergmann 1974; Treiman and Hartmann 1981).

The empirical focus of the feminist literature on export-orientation has mainly been the trend in gender composition of employment (Çağatay and Berik 1990; Stichter 1990; Joekes 1995). Case studies and cross-country evidence have documented the association of export-orientation with the rise in female share of employment (Wood 1991; Çağatay and Özler 1995). However, this trend also appears to have been stalled or reversed in the few economies that have moved beyond labor-intensive export manufacturing. Studies have found that rising capital intensity, technological upgrading, and improvement in the quality of export products were accompanied by a secular decline in women workers' share of manufacturing employment (Acevedo 1990; Joekes 1995; Pearson 1995). The main explanation for this decline is employer discrimination against hiring women in the new, higher-paid, skill-intensive jobs and capital-intensive production processes. The upgrading of skills with technological change leads to a reduction in the share of jobs requiring less-skilled labor. This process entails a decline in the demand for women's labor as some production jobs disappear while others are redefined as "technical" jobs and become "men's" jobs (Cockburn 1985; Goldstein 1989; Acevedo 1990; Pearson 1995). In addition, there is evidence that the diffusion of just-in-time organizational innovations is leading to a de-feminization of manufacturing employment as men emerge as the more flexible, cost-effective workers compared to women (Roldan 1993).

In contrast to the empirical attention given to gender composition of employment, there are very few studies on the implications of export-oriented growth for gender wage inequality. Seguino (1997b) presents evidence on the East Asian newly industrializing economies that shows that sustained export-led growth since the 1960s has brought about, at best, a negligible decline in gender wage inequalities.

Econometric investigations of gender wage inequalities mostly apply the standard human capital model to various institutional settings and generally attribute a sizable portion of the gender wage inequality to wage discrimination against women (cf. Anker and Hein 1986; Gannicott 1986; Pscharapoulos and Tzannatos 1992; Horton 1996; Zveglich *et al.* 1997).

The alternative to the microeconomic approach is to examine either the interindustry variation in wages (cf. Dickens and Katz 1987) or the industry-level determinants of male and female earnings (Hodson and England 1986). This approach shifts the emphasis away from labor supply to labor demand character-istics and is better suited to examine the impact of macroeconomic and trade policies on gender wage inequality. Seguino's research on gender inequalities in East Asia has utilized this alternative approach. She has examined the crowding hypothesis in Korean manufacturing industries and found that the industry-relative earnings are negatively affected by the female share of employment (Seguino 1997a). Similarly, in a comparative study of Korea and Taiwan, Seguino (1996) explained the widening gender wage gap in Taiwan (versus a slow closing of the gap in Korea) by the greater international mobility of capital in Taiwan, which weakens women workers' bargaining power. While the context of both empirical studies is export-oriented economies, neither study has examined the effect of export-orientation at the industry-level on wage levels or gender wage inequality.

In this study, I apply the industry-level approach and consider the separate effects of not only export-orientation but also a number of other characteristics that represent the industrial underpinnings of restructuring. The contributions of the present study are two-fold. I focus on not only gender wage inequality but also on women's and men's wages, thereby highlighting the forces that drive the gender wage inequality. This methodology provides a more complete analysis than studies that use either the average industry wage or the gender wage ratio as the sole dependent variable. Second, by using disaggregated data and choosing the industry as the unit of analysis, the present study provides a stronger empirical foundation for various arguments on the determinants of gender wage inequality. For example, it examines whether or not export-orientation has an adverse effect on women's wages and gender wage inequality over and above the wage-depressing effects of female industrial crowding or labor intensity of production.

Mature export-led growth in Taiwan

The Taiwan economy began its shift toward second-stage export-led growth in the late 1970s. This followed a short period of import-substitution in the 1950s, and the export-led growth strategy based on labor-intensive manufactures in the 1960s. Following the 1974–5 recession, which hit Taiwan's export industries hard, the government made efforts to shift Taiwan's manufacturing base away from exclusive reliance on labor-intensive exports toward more capital- or technology-intensive exports and to upgrade product quality in order to maintain Taiwan's international competitiveness. Government policies supported the upgrading of technology, emphasized technical training, implemented infrastructure projects, and created research parks for R&D. In the 1980s, additional measures were taken to encourage R&D and to train technical personnel (Wang and Tsai 1995).

These policies produced the anticipated results. There has indeed been a significant increase in the capital intensity of manufacturing and a diversification of exports, and Taiwan has ascended to a leading role in world production in electronics (Riedel 1992; DGBAS 1996a; Mathews 1996). During the 1980s and 1990s, the electrical and electronics products industry continued to be the leading generator of export earnings, while there was a shift away from apparel and miscellaneous manufactures toward machinery and transportation equipment industries as major sources of export earnings.[2] There was also significant increase in the export-orientation (defined here as the share of exports in gross sectoral output) of the electronics, machinery, textiles, precision equipment industries, while the apparel, miscellaneous manufactured goods, and nonmetal minerals industries became far less export-oriented.[3] From 1981 to 1993, manu-factured exports grew at an impressive average annual rate of 12.3 percent, and on the whole, manufacturing industry became slightly more open to trade (UNCTAD 1995; DGBAS 1996b).

From the mid-1980s onward, the relocation of labor-intensive industrial production out of Taiwan became an additional force transforming the manufacturing industry. While larger firms sought to develop high technology industries with short product cycles on Taiwan, smaller and more export-oriented firms began to shift the production of commodities in which Taiwan was losing its export competitiveness to lower labor-cost sites in Southeast Asia (Ranis 1992; San 1992). Rising labor costs in Taiwan, growing foreign exchange surplus, and the appreciation of the currency were the major factors underlying this relocation of production. However, the timing of the significant increase in overseas investment was based on the liberalization of financial markets and foreign exchange in 1985 (Chen 1992; Lee 1992).[4] Greater openness to foreign direct investment by host countries in Southeast Asia during the 1980s (as part of their implementation of the neoliberal model) provided an additional incentive for capital exports (San 1992).

The impact of overseas foreign direct investment on the industrial structure of Taiwan is difficult to sort out, in view of the trade-inducing effects of some of this investment on the very sectors from which it emanates and the variety of motivations underlying the relocation overseas. Thus far, the industrial restructuring process since the mid-1980s appears to have resulted in limited and selective deindustrialization in labor-intensive industries (Chen and Chen 1995). Between 1986 and 1994, when the annual average growth rate of manufacturing real GDP was 9 percent, apparel, leather, wood and bamboo products, and miscellaneous manufacturing were the only industries that experienced an absolute decline in their real GDP (DGBAS 1996b). Nonetheless, after 1987, manufacturing industry experienced a relative and absolute decline in employment. While it is still the largest employer in the economy, manufacturing's share of jobs declined from its peak level of 35 percent in 1987 to 28 percent in 1994 (DGBAS 1998), and as detailed in the next section, women workers have disproportionately borne the brunt of these employment losses.

Mature export-led growth and gender inequalities in Taiwan's manufacturing industry

In the period after 1980, three trends characterize the gendered employment and earnings patterns in manufacturing industries. First, there was a slow and steady decline in women's share of employment from 1982 onward. This share peaked in 1981, following a dramatic rise over the initial phase of export-led growth (1961–72) and a slow rise during the 1970s (Berik 1995). Figure 8.1 shows that the decline after 1982 was driven by the decrease in the share of women among wage workers. The female share of wage workers declined from 52 percent in 1982 to 45 percent in 1996, while their share among salaried workers remained nearly constant (around 35 percent) throughout this period. Figure 8.2 shows that the decline in female share of wage workers was driven by the larger increase in men's employment compared to women's employment in the early 1980s, and a sharper decline for women after 1987. There was an absolute decline in the

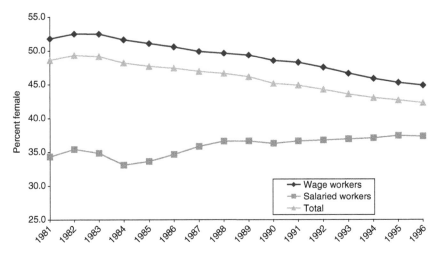

Figure 8.1 Female share of manufacturing employment, 1981–96.

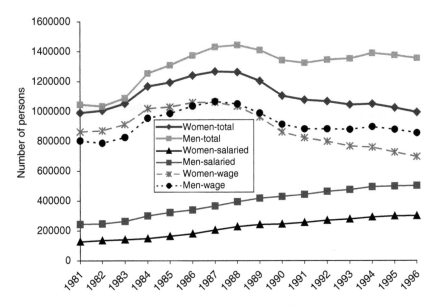

Figure 8.2 Employment trends in manufacturing industry, 1981–96.

number of both men and women wage workers after 1987. By 1996 women's wage employment had dropped well below the level of 1981, while men's employment was still above its 1981 level. By contrast, there was a steady increase in the numbers of both women and men salaried workers during this period, resulting in a shift in the employment structure away from wage workers toward salaried workers.

This shift in employment structure is reflected in a second measure, the ratio of wage workers to salaried workers, which has declined particularly dramatically for women (Figure 8.3). This ratio is likely to be highly correlated with the production–nonproduction worker ratio or the share of office jobs in total employment, both of which are used as proxies for the skill composition of labor force in industrial country research (Hodson and England 1986; Cline 1997). Unfortunately, establishment survey data for Taiwan do not include an occupational breakdown of wage and salaried workers that would allow us to establish a direct link with the occupational structure. In empirical research on industrial countries, the decline in the production–nonproduction worker ratio is interpreted as an indicator of "skilling" of labor (i.e. that fewer production workers per nonproduction worker are needed to produce), and this process is proposed as an explanation for the rise in wage inequality between skilled and unskilled workers (Freeman 1995; Feenstra 1998). The relative contribution of technological change and trade-induced decline in the demand for production workers to the rise in wage inequality continues to be a matter of dispute. However, as Feenstra (1998) forcefully argues, the two effects are likely to be working together and may be statistically indistinguishable. Indeed, in the case of Taiwan, one could interpret the decline of the wage-salaried worker ratio as a manifestation of job restructuring, which has as its contributors the large-scale relocation of production to Southeast Asia in the most labor-intensive industries, the trade-displacing effects of some of this offshore production, and domestic technological change. A disproportionate loss of production jobs for women and their smaller gains in salaried jobs would explain the sharper decline in the wage-salaried worker ratio for women observed in Figure 8.3. Such an account of the gendered employment effects of restructuring is also consistent with the employment trends observed in Figure 8.2.

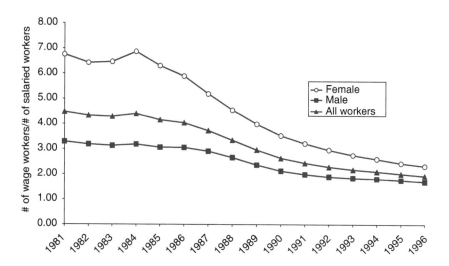

Figure 8.3 Waged-salaried worker ratio.

The third trend is the widening of the earnings inequality between men and women wage workers (Figure 8.4), which is consistent with a relative decline in demand for female labor.[5] Between 1983 and 1992, when nominal earnings of both men and women wage workers rose, the average monthly gender earnings ratio of wage workers declined from a high of 71 percent to 62 percent. After 1992 there was a slight rise in the gender earnings ratio to 65 percent, due to the slower growth in nominal earnings of men relative to women. Gender earnings inequality among salaried workers was greater in 1981 (63 percent) and this inequality increased slightly (to 61 percent). Greater earnings inequality among salaried workers could be due to the more pronounced occupational segregation by sex among the salaried workers relative to wage workers (i.e. the concentration of men in higher-paying professional, administrative, and technical jobs and of women in lower-paying clerical jobs).[6] Interestingly, gender wage inequalities in the manufacturing industry increased against the backdrop of a narrowing of the overall educational gap between men and women during this period.[7]

These gendered employment and earnings trends took place in the context of a high level of segregation of male and female workers across industries. The top three employers of women in manufacturing industries accounted for around one-half of women's employment, while the top three employers of men employed one-third of the male workers.[8] Table 8.1 summarizes the characteristics of manufacturing industries grouped on the basis of female share of wage workers over the 1984–93 period. On average, in comparison with male-intensive industries, female-intensive industries were more labor-intensive, more export-oriented, had lower labor productivity, lower gender wage inequality, and accounted for a higher share of Taiwan's export earnings from manufacturing. The wage-salaried worker

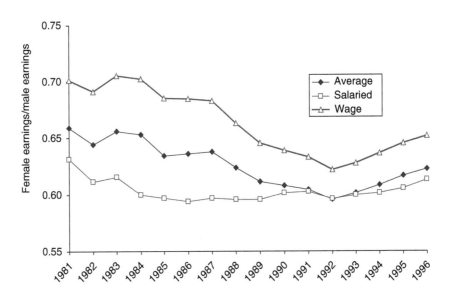

Figure 8.4 Gender earnings ratio in manufacturing industry, 1981–96.

Table 8.1 Characteristics of female-intensive and male-intensive industries[a]

Characteristics[b]	Female-intensive industries[c] (N = 80)[d]	Male-intenesive industries[c] (N = 140)[d]
Capital intensity (1,000 NT$/employee)**	584.5	921.9
Labor productivity (NT$/employee)**	36,081	59,932
Wage-salaried worker ratio	3.5	3.3
Export-orientation (Exports as a share of output) (%)***	48.0	23.0
Industry share of manufactured exports (%)***	11.0	4.4
Percent of industries where outward foreign direct investment as a share of GDP exceeds 0.5%	42.8	35.3
Percent of industries where average firm has more than 60 employees	3.23	6.44
Gender wage ratio (%)***	75	69

Notes

a "Female-(male-)intensive" is defined as industries where women's (men's) share of wage workers was greater than 50 percent in each year during the 1984–93 period. Accordingly, the female-intensive industries are the apparel, tobacco, textile, leather, plastics, electrical/electronics, precision instruments, miscellaneous manufacturing industries, and the male-intensive industries are the food, wood products, furniture, paper, printing, industrial chemicals, chemical products, petroleum and coal, rubber, nonmetal minerals, basic metal, fabricated metal, machinery, transport equipment industries.

b See Table 8.2 for definitions and data sources of all variables, except labor productivity and industry share of manufactured exports. Labor productivity is measured as the value of average monthly output in 1991 constant NT$ per equi-employed employee, and the data are reported in DGBAS (1995). Industry share of exports data are based on UNCTAD (1995).

c Mean values for 1984–93, weighted by size of total industry employment.

d The sample size is equal to the number of industries times the number of years.

, * denote that the hypothesis of equality of means is rejected at the 5 percent and 1 percent levels, respectively (two-tailed tests).

ratio, outward foreign direct investment as a share of sectoral GDP (OFDI/GDP), and firm size were not significantly different between the female-intensive and male-intensive industries.

In sum, during the 1981–96 period of restructuring in Taiwan, gender wage inequality among wage (i.e. blue-collar, production) workers increased as women's share of wage workers declined. By contrast, there has been virtually no change in either variable for the salaried (i.e. white-collar, nonproduction) workers. Against this backdrop of aggregate trends, I will pursue a disaggregated analysis of gender wage inequality among *wage* workers using panel data for 22 industries of the manufacturing sector for the 1984–93 period.[9]

The determinants of gender wage inequality: estimation and results

The empirical model presented here seeks to identify the effect of industry characteristics on gender wage inequality among wage workers in manufacturing industry. Since the changes in the gender wage inequality are driven by changes in men's and women's wages, the empirical model consists of two independent wage equations for women and men, and a gender wage ratio equation derived from these two equations. In each equation, the independent variables and the number of observations are identical. Thus,

$$\ln(Wage)_{it} = \beta_0 + \beta_1 \ln(Export/Output)_{it} + \beta_2(OFDI/GDP)_{it}$$
$$+ \beta_3 \ln(Capital/Labor)_{it} + \beta_4 \ln(Wage/Salaried)_{it}$$
$$+ \beta_5 \ln(Female\ Share)_{it} + \beta_6(Female\ Reserve)_i$$
$$+ \beta_7\ (Firm\ Size)_i + u_{it}$$

where *Wage* is defined as the average hourly real wages of women and men, and the gender wage ratio, respectively, in the three equations of the model. The gender wage ratio is the ratio of female to male average hourly real wage rates. The variable i is the industry subscript ($i = 1, \ldots, 22$), t is the year subscript ($t = 1983, \ldots, 1994$), making each observation an industry-year, and u_{it} is the random disturbance term. The variables used in the regression analysis are defined and their data sources identified in Table 8.2.[10]

The first four explanatory variables capture various facets of Taiwan's restructuring process that are the outcome of strategies to maintain and strengthen industry international competitiveness: export-orientation, overseas investment, technological change, and job restructuring. The last three variables control the effects of female crowding, female reserve labor supply, and firm size.[11] Descriptive statistics on these variables are reported in Table 8.3.

The value of exports as a share of sectoral gross output (*Export/Output*) measures the export-orientation of sector, which is expected to be associated with lower industry average wages, given the greater pressures to maintain or achieve international competitiveness. However, its effect on the gender wage ratio is theoretically ambiguous. There are no studies that inform hypotheses on the relative effects of export-orientation on men's and women's wages.

The relative importance of outward foreign direct investment in a given industry is captured by a dummy variable (*OFDI/GDP*), which takes the value of 1 in years when its value exceeds one-half percent of the sectoral GDP and is zero otherwise. The available data measure the volume of foreign direct investment *approved* by the government, not the actual amount. Since these figures are highly volatile from one year to another, and approved investment may be realized gradually, it is more appropriate to treat *OFDI/GDP* as a dummy rather than a continuous variable.[12] I adopted a very low benchmark value in view of the significant underestimation of the volume of overseas investment in official Taiwanese data.[13] While funds for overseas investment in a particular industry do not necessarily emanate from that industry, nonetheless, where such overseas investment is sizable, one would expect the domestic industry to pay lower wages due to weaker labor demand. Within an industry, the relative effects of *OFDI/GDP* on men's and women's wages will depend on women's relative vulnerability to layoffs, that is, their relative bargaining power. That, in turn,

Table 8.2 Variables and data sources

Variables	Description	Sources[a,b]
Dependent variables		
Women's real hourly earnings	(Average monthly earnings/monthly hours worked)/industry WPI	Monthly earnings and hours from *Yearbook of Earnings and Productivity* (1994), (1996); wholesale price index is
Men's real hourly earnings		from *Quarterly National Income Statistics in Taiwan Area* (1996b) [22]
Gender wage ratio	Women's real hourly earnings/men's real hourly earnings	
Independent variables		
Export/Output[c]	Exports/Industry gross output	*Input–Output Tables* (1984), (1986), (1989), (1991), (1994) [18]
OFDI/GDP	Outward foreign direct investment (in NT$)/Nominal GDP of industry	*Investment Commission, 1998* [15]; *National Income in Taiwan Area 1995* [22]
Capital/Labor	Value of real net fixed capital stock per employee	*Yearbook of Earnings and Productivity* (1996a) [18]
Wage/Salaried	Number of wage workers/number of salaried workers	*Yearbook of Earnings and Productivity* (1990), (1994), (1996a) [22]
Female share	Share of women among *wage* workers	*Yearbook of Earnings and Productivity* (1991a), (1994), (1996) [22]
Female reserve	(Women unpaid family workers + own account workers)/Total female employment in industry	*Yearbook of Manpower Survey Statistics, 1990* (1991) [22]
Firm size	Number of employees per firm in industry	*The Report on 1991 Industrial and Commercial Census* (1993) [22]

Notes
a DGBAS is the reporting agency for each statistical source. See References for full citations.
b Numbers in parentheses refer to the level of disaggregation of the data (i.e. the number of industrial sectors) used by the reporting source.
c Missing values for this variable were estimated by fitting a trend line to the observations for 1984, 1986, 1989, 1991, 1994.

depends on the nature of jobs staffed by women and men workers and the gendered pattern of layoffs. If women in these industries are in less-skilled jobs, have less seniority, or face institutional barriers that prevent them from acquiring seniority, then one would expect women to be laid off in greater numbers and face stronger downward pressure on their wages in comparison with men. This would lead us to expect negative effects not only on men's and women's wages but also on the gender wage ratio.

Table 8.3 Means and standard deviations of variables

Variables	Mean	Standard deviation
Female real hourly earnings (in 1991 constant NT$)	68.1	23.4
Male real hourly earnings (in 1991 constant NT$)	96.2	36.0
Gender wage ratio (%)	71.9	6.3
Export/Output (%)	36.1	18.0
Outward foreign direct investment/GDP 　($> 0.5\%$ = 1) (%)	40.6	
Capital intensity (1,000 NT$/worker)	745.4	915.6
Wage-salaried worker ratio	3.4	1.2
Female share of wage workers (%)	49.2	19.2
Female reserve (size of reserve $> 10\%$ = 1) (%)	31.2	
Firm size (average employment > 60 = 1) (%)	3.2	

Source: See Table 8.2.

Note
Mean values for 1984–93, weighted by size of industry total employment (N = 220).

The capital intensity of production (*Capital/Labor*) is the technology variable and a proxy for labor productivity. A high level of capital investment is expected to increase worker productivity and make possible the payment of higher wages. Its effect on gender wage inequality depends on whether there is a gender difference in workers' ability to translate higher productivity into higher wages. The literature suggests that men are better able to bargain for or are granted greater wage increases than women (cf. Hartmann 1979). If this is true, then we expect a higher capital-labor ratio to be associated with a lower gender wage ratio (i.e. greater gender wage inequality).[14]

The ratio of wage-salaried workers (*Wage/Salaried*) in a given industry captures the job restructuring that may be driven by technological change, changing trade structure, or both. If, as noted earlier, a lower wage-salaried worker ratio is interpreted as a proxy for greater skill level of sector, then a lower ratio is expected to be associated with higher average industry wages. Thus, we expect the wage-salaried worker ratio to be negatively related to both women's and men's wages. However, the effect on the gender wage ratio is likely to be positive. This follows from my observations on Figures 8.2 and 8.3 that the wage-salaried worker ratio is on the decline and is accompanied by a fall in demand for female relative to male workers. This implies that in the course of the job restructuring or skilling process women's wages may rise less than men's, and thereby increase gender wage inequality.

The share of women among wage workers (*Female Share*) tests for the crowding and employer discrimination arguments, both of which predict a negative relationship between the female share of employment and the average wage. In the former case this is due to the wage-depressing effects of women's industrial crowding and in the latter case because the preponderance of women in a given industry gives employers the license to pay lower wages. Originally, these arguments were formulated for and found empirical support at the occupational level. At the industry level, however, the results are mixed. For Korea, Seguino (1997a) found that a higher female share depresses the average industry wage, while Hodson and England (1986) did not find a statistically significant effect of gender composition of employment on either men's or women's wages at the industry level. In keeping with this literature, my expectation is that a high female share will depress the wages of men as well as women in the industry. Of particular interest are the relative magnitudes of the impact on men's and women's wage rates, which determine the direction of change in gender wage inequality.

In addition to female crowding within, female crowding outside the registered establishments is also likely to affect wage levels and gender wage inequality. Thus, the model includes a dummy variable (*Female Reserve*) to estimate the impact of the female employment in each industry outside the registered manufacturing establishments covered by the Employee Earnings Survey (see note 10). Using household survey data, I defined the female reserve labor supply variable on the basis of the share of women unpaid family workers and own account workers in total female employment in each industry. This, in part, is the labor force examined by Hsiung (1996). She argues that the state-sponsored program of "living room factories" implemented after 1978 was designed to mobilize the labor of housewives to work out of their homes for subcontractors. The creation of this female reserve labor supply is arguably an integral component of Taiwan's mature export-led growth strategy.[15] The existence of a sizable female reserve is expected to temper wage increases for women and (depending on the substitutability between women and men) for male workers employed in registered establishments in those industries. If the female reserve is a weak substitute for this group of men, then *Female Reserve* will be negatively related to the gender wage ratio. A cut-off level of 10 percent is used to distinguish between industries that have a sizable female reserve labor supply and those where this reserve is either nonexistent or small.[16] In the context of the present industry-level analysis this measure is superior to the *economy-wide* unemployment rate, which is commonly used as a measure of surplus labor.

Finally, the model includes *Firm Size*, which is measured as a dummy variable constructed on the basis of the average number of employees per firm in industry, *i*. Taiwan is well-known for the predominance of small and medium enterprises in its manufacturing industry. Here, industries for which the average firm size is 60 or more employees are classified as those with large firms, for which the variable takes on the value of 1. Tobacco, petroleum and coal products, and industrial chemicals are the only industries in which the average firm size is large. Large firms are expected to generate higher revenues per worker due to economies of scale, which may translate into higher wage rates in industries with larger average firm size. As with the capital–labor ratio, the effect of average firm size on gender wage inequality depends on whether there is a gender difference in workers' ability to secure higher wages on the basis of greater firm revenues.

The model is estimated using year fixed effects in order to capture the variation across the years.[17] In estimation, observations are weighted by total sectoral employment since there are significant differences in industry size. The results are reported in Table 8.4. Because the estimated model is in logarithmic form the regression coefficients are elasticities. The estimated coefficient of each variable in the gender wage ratio equation is, by definition, equal to the difference between the respective coefficients in the female and male wage equations.[18]

The estimated wage equations explain nearly all of the variation in women's and men's wages, with R^2s of 0.93 and 0.96, respectively. The results for the women's wage equation indicate that, with the exception of the wage-salaried worker ratio, all coefficients have the expected signs. Export-orientation, female share of employment, female reserve labor supply, and *OFDI/GDP* reduce women's wages, while capital–labor ratio and firm size raise them, all as predicted.[19] The inverse relationship between export-orientation and women's wages in a multiple regression framework provides a stronger foundation for feminist arguments concerning the effects of export-orientation. Export-orientation is associated with lower wages for women over and above the adverse effects of female crowding inside and outside the registered manufacturing establishments, and when skill composition, productivity, and firm size are controlled for.[20] The positive sign on the wage-salaried worker ratio coefficient suggests that women's wages are higher where this ratio is higher. This means that as the industry

Table 8.4 Determinants of women's and men's wages and the gender wage ratio in Taiwan's manufacturing industry, 1984–93 (with fixed year effects)

	Women's wage rate (log of hourly real wage)	Men's wage rate (log of hourly real wage)	Gender wage ratio (log of female–male wage ratio)
ln(*Export/Output*)	−0.040	−0.062	0.022
	(0.023)*	(0.016)***	(0.014)
OFDI/GDP (>0.5% = 1)	−0.022	−0.011	−0.012
	(0.014)	(0.011)	(0.007)
ln(*Capital/Labor*)	0.023	0.020	0.003
	(0.012)*	(0.010)**	(0.007)
ln(*Wage/Salaried*)	0.072	−0.093	0.165
	(0.028)**	(0.023)***	(0.018)***
ln(*Female share*)	−0.104	−0.153	0.049
	(0.027)***	(0.020)***	(0.016)***
Female Reserve (>10% = 1)	−0.066	−0.028	−0.038
	(0.016)***	(0.014)**	(0.012)***
Firm Size (*large* = 1)	0.133	0.139	−0.006
	(0.073)*	(0.061)**	(0.032)
R^2	0.93	0.96	0.58
N	220	220	220

Notes
Standard errors are reported in parentheses.
***, **, * denote that the value is significant at the 99, 95, 90 percent probability levels. The results are White-corrected for heteroskedasticity.

occupational mix shifts from wage to salaried workers the pay of women wage workers is declining.

The signs of the estimated coefficients of the men's wage equation are also consistent with my expectations.[21] The results show that employment in export-oriented industries brings a wage penalty not only for women but also for men. Compared to men who work in more domestic market-oriented industries, men in relatively export-oriented industries are paid lower wages. Moreover, the wage penalty is greater for men than for women (i.e. a wage reduction of -0.062 percent for men versus -0.040 percent for women for each percent increase in export-orientation). A similarly surprising result concerns the relative magnitudes of the impact of female share on men's and women's wages. Men are more adversely affected than women from working in industries with a higher share of women (a wage penalty of -0.152 and -0.104 percent, respectively). Thus, each of these variables has a positive effect on the gender wage ratio. The estimated elasticities of the gender wage ratio with respect to export-orientation and female share are 0.022 and 0.049, respectively.

Another surprising result concerns the differing effects of the wage-salaried worker ratio on men's and women's wages. While women benefit from being employed in industries with a higher wage-salaried worker ratio, men are disadvantaged by it. As a result, the wage-salaried worker ratio is strongly positively related to the gender wage ratio. This suggests that the decline in the wage-salaried worker ratio is associated with a new pattern of occupational segregation among *wage* workers that places women in lower paying jobs compared to men. In the absence of data on the occupational breakdown among wage workers it is not possible to examine whether or not this is the case. However, this study shows that the decline in wage-salaried worker ratio observed in Figure 8.3 represents an alarming trend for women and a beneficial one for men wage workers.

It is noteworthy that a higher outward foreign direct investment as a share of GDP (*OFDI/GDP*) is associated with greater wage inequality, albeit the coefficient is not statistically significant. While this result is consistent with Seguino (1996), the two studies are not directly comparable because of methodological differences. Most important among these is that Seguino's work was based on *economy-wide* measures of international capital-mobility instead of industry-level data and it pooled data for Taiwan and Korea. It should also be pointed out that the levels of statistical significance reported by Seguino for this variable are dramatically higher than what I found for Taiwan. In view of the quality and limitations of the underlying foreign direct investment data (see notes 12 and 13), however, this result warrants further examination in future research.

Finally, large firm size provides women and men equal payoff and does not have an important effect on wage inequality. Capital–labor ratio has a larger positive impact on women's wage and consequently reduces wage inequality, although this result is not statistically significant at the conventional levels. Working in industries that have a sizable female reserve labor supply increases gender wage inequality because women's wages are more adversely affected than men's wages. The latter result suggests the weak substitutability of women reserve workers for men employed in registered establishments.

On the whole, estimating a three-equation model, which explores the determinants of the wages of men and women as well as the gender wage ratio, provides considerable information on the factors underlying wage determination compared to estimating a single gender wage ratio equation. This approach provides a more adequate exploration of the gender dimension of wage inequality, highlighting the effects of industry characteristics on men's as well as women's wages. It shows, for example, that export-orientation has an adverse effect on men's as well as women's wages, a result that is not obvious (and obscured) if the focus is solely on women's wages, average industry wages, or the gender wage ratio. The results pertaining to the female share and export-orientation variables suggest that feminist economists' concern about gender wage inequality cannot be limited to women's standing relative to men, but that the level and direction of change in men's wages are equally relevant. Women's smaller losses relative to men's losses cannot be good news.

Conclusion

This study investigated the effects of Taiwan's changing role in the global economy after 1980 on gender wage inequalities. During this period, Taiwan's manufacturing industry underwent transformations that were shaped by the forces of domestic technological restructuring and growing investment outflow to Southeast Asia.

At the aggregate level, this period was characterized by employment losses in manufacturing industry, a relative shrinking of the sector, and a shift in the job opportunities in manufacturing industry from wage to salaried employment. Against this backdrop, women wage workers experienced a disproportionate loss of employment opportunities. While this loss is not necessarily negative (since female intensity of manufacturing employment is often an indicator of women's secondary status in the labor market (Joekes 1995)), the growing gender wage inequality that accompanied these trends suggests that the emerging employment opportunities in manufacturing did not improve the economic status of women relative to men.

Using an industry-level approach, I examined the separate effects of export-orientation, overseas investment by Taiwanese firms, skill composition, and capital intensity, after controlling for female share of industry employment, female reserve labor supply, and average firm size. This analysis showed that between 1984 and 1993 working in more export-oriented sectors adversely affected both women's and men's wages. Greater wage penalty of export-orientation on men compared to women contributed to greater wage equality in these industries. This result suggests that lower wages, even without gender wage inequality, may be sufficient for export competitiveness. Outward foreign direct investment did not have an important effect on either wage levels or gender wage inequality. Further investigation of the effect of overseas investment using more complete investment data (which include investment approvals in China after 1991) may provide more robust results.

This study also found that technological restructuring during this period did not improve the relative economic status of women. Higher capital intensity improved women's wages marginally more than men's, leaving women's relative economic status virtually unchanged. On the other hand, women wage workers were losers in absolute and relative terms from the trend toward growing importance of salaried jobs in manufacturing industry. This result is consistent with earlier feminist analyses of the implications of technological change, product upgrading, and redefinition of job titles.

Two features of the empirical methodology considerably strengthen the explanatory power of this analysis. First, using an empirical model that examined the determinants of women's and men's wages as well as gender wage inequality allowed us to identify the sources of change in gender wage inequality and to make sense of some of the puzzling effects on the gender wage ratio, such as the positive effects of export-orientation and female share of employment. These results suggest that determining the *absolute* changes in men's and women's economic status as well as changes in women's economic status *relative* to men yields more insights in evaluating changes in gender inequalities. Second, using industry-level data at a finer level of aggregation than is usual helped establish sharper statistical links between gendered economic outcomes and the character-istics of the export-oriented model that is undergoing restructuring. This investigation showed that export-orientation, labor-intensity, smaller firm size, and female crowding within and outside registered establishments were the industry characteristics that had separate, negative effects on women's wage levels. The same industry characteristics adversely affected men's wages as well, albeit the magnitude of some of these effects differed by gender. The wage-salaried worker ratio was the only industry characteristic that had opposite effects on men and women's wages. Whether the magnitude and direction of these wage effects of restructuring are short-lived are questions that need to be investigated in the future. Nonetheless, feminist analysis of Taiwan's economic success in the 1984–93 period shows that the underlying restructuring process is neither gender- nor class-neutral.

Notes

1 Early versions of this chapter were presented at the ASSA meeting in New York City in January 1999 and the IAFFE Conference in Ottowa in June 1999. This study is part of a larger research project on gender inequalities in Taiwan's economic development process. I owe many individuals thanks in acquiring or processing the data over the years of the gestation of this project. In particular, I wish to thank Tsung-wu Ho, Detlef Kotte, David Kucera, Ebru Kongar, Soner Songül, and Vedat Aslan. I thank Martha MacDonald and two anonymous referees of *Feminist Economics* for useful comments and suggestions. Special thanks are due to Cihan Bilginsoy. I also gratefully acknowl-edge support from the University Research Committee of the University of Utah. I alone bear the responsibility for any errors.
2 In 1983, the top four sources of export earnings (as a share of manufactured exports) were electronics (17 percent), apparel (10 percent), miscellaneous manufactures (10 percent), and textile (9 percent) industries. In 1993 the largest shares of export

earnings were generated by electronics (20 percent), machinery (20 percent), textiles (11 percent), and transportation equipment (9 percent) industries (author's calculations based on UNCTAD (1995)). For this analysis, I grouped the export data based on the annual trade data reported at the four-digit level SITC (revision 2) according to three-digit level ISIC (revision 2).

3 I calculated exports as a share of sectoral gross output from input–output tables (DGBAS, various years). Apparel was the most open sector in 1984 when 65 percent of its output was exported. By 1994 this share declined to 49 percent. Over this period, the electronics industry increased its share of exported output from 45 to 67 percent, textiles from 23 to 54 percent, machinery from 20 to 50 percent, and precision equipment from 64 to 77 percent.

4 Approved overseas investment remained less than one percent of Taiwan's gross fixed capital formation until 1988, after which it rose dramatically (author's calculations based on DGBAS (1989, 1998) and Investment Commission (1998)). Commentators agree that even the dramatic rise in overseas Taiwanese investment reflected in these statistics is a gross underestimate of the actual investment figures (Lee 1992; Chen 1992; San 1992).

5 Over the 1984–93 period, the trends in time-adjusted earnings ratios (i.e. corrected for gender differences in hours worked) were nearly identical to the trends in unadjusted ratios in Figure 8.4 (for the 1981–96 period). Moreover, both trends are consistent with trends revealed by the household survey data, which indicate a widening of gender earnings inequality among workers with less than a high school degree from 1978 to 1992 and a stagnant wage inequality for high school and college graduates (Zveglich *et al.* 1997).

6 Household survey data indicate a high degree of sex segregation in white-collar occupations. In 1993, for example, 27 percent of the male employees in the manufacturing industry were in professional and administrative occupations while only 12 percent of the women were in these occupations. By contrast, 14 percent of women and 3 percent of men were clerical workers. The same data also show that women accounted for 77 percent of clerical and 39 percent of the professional and administrative jobs (DGBAS 1994b). This data source does not include an occupational breakdown of production occupations.

7 Between 1981 and 1993, average years of schooling increased from 7.49 years to 9.24 years for men and 5.27 years to 7.8 years for women, thereby narrowing the gap from 2.2 years to 1.3 years (DGBAS 1998).

8 In 1981, the top three employers of women were textiles, electronics, plastics, and top employers of men were electronics, fabricated metal products, transport equipment industries. By 1996, fabricated metal products had replaced plastic products as the third largest employer of women and the basic metals industry had replaced transport equipment as the third largest employer of men. Electronics and textiles are also among the industries with the highest female shares of employment (DGBAS 1996a).

9 Data constraints regarding gender-differentiated hours determined the period of the regression analysis. The 22 industries are food processing, tobacco, textiles, apparel, leather products, wood products, furniture, paper, printing, industrial chemicals, chemical products, petroleum and coal, rubber, plastics, nonmetal minerals, basic metals, fabricated metals, machinery, electrical/electronics, transport equipment, precision instruments, and miscellaneous manufacturing.

10 The earnings and employment data used in this analysis come from the monthly establishment surveys (Employee Earnings Surveys) conducted from 1972 onward and reported in DGBAS (1990, 1994a, 1996a). The employees in the Employee Earnings Survey include white-collar and blue-collar workers, permanent, temporary, contract workers and apprentices with pay, who work in either private or government establishments. The employee category *excludes* own-account workers, unpaid family workers, and contract workers who work on a piece-rate basis outside establishments. The survey covers all registered establishments, including ones that employ less than five workers.

In the survey, all establishments employing more than 200 workers are surveyed. The rest of the establishments are divided into six strata and surveyed by random sampling. See DGBAS (1990: 740) for details of the sampling methodology.

11 While various aspects of the restructuring process are interrelated, only export-orientation and capital intensity (i.e. capital–labor ratio) is highly correlated (-0.76). In addition, firm size is correlated with export orientation (-0.65) and the capital–labor ratio (0.68). These statistical relationships are consistent with observations that export-oriented firms are smaller and use more labor-intensive technologies.

12 The years in which *OFDI/GDP* fell short of the benchmark value but where the preceding and subsequent years' values were high were also designated as *OFDI/GDP* = 1 years. This definition was adopted so as to take into consideration the lagged effects of outward flow of investment on the wage determination process in a given industry. The regression results reported in Table 8.4 were found to be not sensitive to the use of either this definition over a more rigid one or a dichotomous measure over a continuous one.

13 Comparison of Taiwan's official data on approved overseas investment with the host country figures indicates that the former figures are substantially lower. Due to under-reporting of overseas investment by small and medium-sized enterprises, in some years the investment total reported in Taiwanese statistics equals only 5 percent of the host government figures on incoming Taiwanese investment (San 1992)!

14 Labor productivity is an alternative variable to capital intensity. The correlation coefficient between the two variables over the 1984–93 period is 0.93, and in alternative regressions they yield very similar results. Here, only the results based on regressions that include capital intensity are reported.

15 The effects of this program may be seen in the rise of both the proportion of women who are employed as unpaid family workers and the share of women among unpaid family workers. The share of unpaid family workers among women employed in the manufacturing industry rose from a low of 4.6 percent in 1981 to 7 percent in 1990 (where it also stood in 1996). Likewise, the share of women among unpaid family workers in manufacturing rose from a low of 55.4 percent in 1976 to 72 percent in 1990 (and 77 percent in 1996) (Cheng and Hsiung 1994; and author's calculations based on DGBAS 1991, 1997).

16 I identified these sectors on the basis of household survey data reported in DGBAS (1991). Among the 22 industries, the industries where the size of the female reserve supply of labor is greater than 10 percent are the food, wood products, printing, basic metals, fabricated metals, machinery, and miscellaneous manufacturing industries. In 1990 the proportion of female reserve supply was 25 percent in fabricated metals, 21 percent in food, 19 percent each in printing and machinery, 12 percent in wood products, and 11 percent each in basic metals and miscellaneous manufacturing. The female reserve ratios calculated for 1996 (which falls beyond the period used in the regression analysis) also yield the same set of industries (with the exception of miscellaneous manufacturing), as having a sizable share of female reserve labor (DGBAS 1997).

17 The empirical model does not include the usual controls for labor quality due to the lack of industry-level data on average worker characteristics. Published gender-differentiated education data for Taiwan, for instance, is available only for the country as a whole and therefore it is not possible to determine the industry-level variability of educational attainment and its impact over these years. Nonetheless, I estimated another set of regressions (without year fixed effects) that includes average years of schooling of men and women. This specification yielded schooling as a highly significant variable but did not alter the results otherwise. This suggests that the year fixed effects adequately capture the impact of rising educational level over the period under consideration (see note 7). The results of this alternative specification are available from the author upon request.

18 If female share and export-orientation are influenced by the male and female wage rates, then the model may be subject to simultaneity problem. In view of this possibility, I estimated alternative regressions using one-period lagged values of female share and export-orientation (instead of their current values). This alternative specification did not alter the results reported in Table 8.4, which suggests that a serious simultaneity problem does not exist. The results of this alternative specification are available from the author upon request.

19 All estimated coefficients, except *OFDI/GDP*, are statistically significant at least at the 90 percent probability level.

20 Note that the estimated coefficients are statistically significant despite the relatively high correlation coefficients between export-orientation, capital–labor ratio, and firm size noted earlier (see note 11).

21 Again, all estimated coefficients, except *OFDI/GDP*, are statistically significant at least at the 90 percent probability level.

References

Acevedo, L. (1990) "Industrialization and employment: changes in the patterns of women's work in Puerto Rico," *World Development*, 18 (2): 231–55.

Anker, R. and Hein, C. (eds) (1986) *Sex Inequalities in Urban Employment in the Third World*, New York: St. Martin's.

Arrigo, L.G. (1980) "The industrial work force of young women in Taiwan," *Bulletin of The Concerned Asian Scholars*, 12 (2): 25–38.

Bakker, I. (ed.) (1994) *The Strategic Silence: gender and economic policy*, London: Zed.

Beneria, L. and Feldman, S. (eds) (1992) *Unequal Burden: economic crisis, persistent poverty and women's work*, Boulder, CO: Westview.

Bergmann, B. (1974) "Occupational segregation, wages and profits when employers discriminate by race or sex," *Eastern Economic Journal*, 1: 103–10.

Berik, G. (1995) "Growth with gender inequity: manufacturing employment in Taiwan" Processed, Economics Department, University of Utah.

—— (2000) "Globalization," in J. Peterson and M. Lewis (eds), *The Elgar Companion to Feminist Economics*, Cheltenham: Edward Elgar.

Blau, F.D. (1998) "Trends in the well-being of American women, 1970–95," *Journal of Economic Literature*, 36 (1): 112–65.

Blau, F.D. and Kahn, L. (1997) "Swimming upstream: trends in the gender wage differential in the 1980s," *Journal of Labor Economics*, 15 (1, Part 1): 1–42.

Çağatay, N. and Berik, G. (1990) "Transition to export-led growth in Turkey: is there a feminization of employment?," *Review of Radical Political Economics*, 22 (1): 115–34.

Çağatay, N. and Özler, S. (1995) "Feminization of the labour force: the effects of long-term development and structural adjustment," *World Development*, 23 (11): 1883–94.

Chen, T.-J. (1992) "Determinants of Taiwan's Direct Foreign Investment: the case of a newly industrializing country," *Journal of Development Economics*, 39: 397–407.

Chen, T.-J. and Chen, Y.-P. (1995) "Foreign Direct Investment and deindustrialization: the case of Taiwan," *Journal of Industry Studies*, 2 (1): 57–68.

Cheng, L. and Hsiung, P.-C. (1994) "Women, export-oriented growth, and the state: the case of Taiwan," in J.D. Aberbach, D. Dollar, and K.L. Sokoloff (eds), *The Role of the State in Taiwan's Development*, Armonk and London: M.E. Sharpe.

Cline, W.R. (1997) *Trade and Income Distribution*, Washington, DC: Institute for International Economics.

Cockburn, C. (1985) *Machinery of Dominance: women, men and technical know-how*, London: Pluto.

Cohen, M.G. (1987) *Free Trade and the Future of Women's Work*, Toronto: Garamond.

Connelly, P., Li, T.M., MacDonald, M., and Parpart, J.L. (1995) "Restructured worlds/restructured debates: globalization, development and gender," *Canadian Journal of Development Studies*, Special Issue: 17–38.

Diamond, N. (1979) "Women and industry in Taiwan," *Modern China*, 5 (3): 317–40.

Dickens, W.T. and Katz, L.F. (1987) "Inter-industry wage differences and industry characteristics," in K. Lang and J. Leonard (eds), *Unemployment and the Structure of Labor Markets*, Oxford and New York: Basil Blackwell.

Directorate General of Budget, Accounting and Statistics (DGBAS) (1989) *National Income in Taiwan Area*.

—— (1990) *Yearbook of Earnings and Productivity 1990, Taiwan Area, Republic of China*.

—— (1991) *Yearbook of Manpower Survey Statistics, Taiwan Area, Republic of China 1990*.

—— (1993) *The Report on 1991 Industrial and Commercial Census: Taiwan-Fukien Area, The Republic of China, Vol. 3 Manufacturing (Enumeration Period: April–June 1992)*.

—— (1994a) *Yearbook of Earnings and Productivity 1994, Taiwan Area, Republic of China*.

—— (1994b) *Yearbook of Manpower Survey Statistics 1993, Taiwan Area, Republic of China*.

—— (1995) *The Trends in Labor Productivity, Taiwan Area, Republic of China*.

—— (1996a) *Yearbook of Earnings and Productivity 1996, Taiwan Area, Republic of China*.

—— (1996b) *Quarterly National Income Statistics in the Taiwan Area, Republic of China, 1961–95*.

—— (1997) *Yearbook of Manpower Survey Statistics, Taiwan Area, Republic of China 1996*.

—— (1998) *Statistical Yearbook 1998*.

—— (Various years) *Input-Output Tables*.

Elson, D. (1995) "Male bias in macroeconomics: the case of structural adjustment," in D. Elson (ed.), *Male Bias in the Development Process*, Manchester: Manchester University Press.

Elson, D. and Pearson, R. (1981) "The subordination of women and the internationalization of factory production," in K. Young, C. Wolkowitz, and R. McCullagh (eds), *Of Marriage and the Market*, London, Boston, Melbourne, and Henley: Routledge and Kegan Paul.

Feenstra, R.C. (1998) "Integration of trade and disintegration of production in the global economy," *Journal of Economic Perspectives*, 12 (4): 31–50.

Fields, G.S. (1992) "Living standards, labor markets and human resources in Taiwan," in G. Ranis (ed.), *Taiwan: from developing to mature economy*, Boulder, CO: Westview.

—— (1994) "Changing labor market conditions and economic development in Hong Kong, the Republic of Korea, Singapore, and Taiwan, China," *The World Bank Economic Review*, 8 (3): 395–414.

Freeman, R.B. (1995) "Are your wages set in Beijing?" *Journal of Economic Perspectives*, 9 (3): 15–32.

Galenson, W. (1979) "The labor force, wages and living standards," in W. Galenson (ed.), *Economic Growth and Structural Change in Taiwan*, Ithaca, NY: Cornell University Press.

Gallin, R.S. (1990) "Women and the export industry in Taiwan: the muting of class consciousness," in K. Ward (ed.), *Women Workers and Global Restructuring*, Ithaca, NY: Cornell/ILR Press.

Gannicott, K. (1986) "Women, wages, and discrimination: some evidence from Taiwan," *Economic Development and Cultural Change*, 34 (4): 721–30.

Goldstein, N. (1989) "Silicon glen: women and semi-conductor multinationals," in D. Elson and R. Pearson (eds), *Women's Employment and Multinationals in Europe*, London: Macmillan.

Greene, M. and Hoffnar, E. (1995) "Gender earnings inequality in the service and manufacturing industries in the U.S.," *Feminist Economics*, 1 (3): 82–95.

Greenhalgh, S. (1985) "Sexual stratification: the other side of growth with equity in East Asia," *Population and Development Review*, 11 (2): 265–314.

Hartmann, H. (1979) "Capitalism, patriarchy, and job segregation by sex," in Z. Eisenstein (ed.), *Capitalism, Patriarchy and the Case for Socialist Feminism*, New York: Monthly Review.

Hodson, R. and England, P. (1986) "Industrial structure and sex differences in earnings," *Industrial Relations*, 25 (1): 16–32.

Horton, S. (1996) *Women and Industrialization in Asia*, New York: Routledge.

Hsiung, P.-C. (1996) *Living Rooms as Factories*, Philadelphia, PA: Temple University Press.

Investment Commission, Ministry of Economic Affairs (1998) *Statistics on Overseas Chinese and Foreign Investment, Technical Cooperation, Outward Investment, Outward Technical Cooperation, Indirect Mainland Investment*.

Joekes, S.P. (1995) "Trade-related employment for women in industry and services in developing countries," Occasional Paper 5, Geneva: United Nations Research Institute For Social Development.

Kung, L. (1983) *Factory Women in Taiwan*, Ann Arbor, MI: University of Michigan Press.

Lee, J.S. (1992) "Capital and labor mobility in Taiwan," in G. Ranis (ed.), *Taiwan: from developing to mature economy*, Boulder, CO: Westview.

Liu, P.K.C. (1989) "Employment, earnings, and export-led industrialization in Taiwan," *Economic Review* (Taipei): 248–49, (March-April 1989): 4–15, (May-June): 7–29.

Mathews, J.A. (1996) "High technology industrialization in East Asia," *Journal of Industry Studies*, 2 (2): 1–67.

O'Neill, J. and Polachek, S. (1993) "Why the gender gap in wages narrowed in the 1980s," *Journal of Labor Economics*, 11 (1, Part 1): 205–28.

Pearson, R. (1995) "Male bias and women's work in Mexico's Border Industries," in D. Elson (ed.), *Male Bias in the Development Process*, Manchester: Manchester University Press.

Psacharopoulos, G. and Tzannatos, Z. (1992) *Case Studies on Women's Employment and Pay in Latin America*, Washington, DC: World Bank.

Ranis, G. (1992) "From developing to mature economy: an overview," in G. Ranis (ed.), *Taiwan: from developing to mature economy*, Boulder, CO: Westview.

—— (1995) "Another look at the East Asian miracle," *The World Bank Economic Review*, 9 (3): 509–34.

Riedel, J. (1992) "International trade in Taiwan's transition from developing to mature economy," in G. Ranis (ed.), *Taiwan: from developing to mature economy*, Boulder, CO: Westview.

Roldan, M. (1993) "Industrial restructuring, deregulation and new JIT labour processes in Argentina: towards a gender-aware perspective?" *IDS Bulletin*, 24 (2): 42–52.

San, G. (1992) "Taiwanese corporations in globalization and regionalization," Technical Papers No. 61, Paris: OECD.

Seguino, S. (1996) "Economic liberalization, export-led growth, and gender wage differentials in South Korea and Taiwan," paper prepared for presentation at a Joint ASE/IAFFE session at the 1997 ASSA Meetings in New Orleans, Louisiana, January 3–6.

—— (1997a) "Gender wage inequality and export-led growth in South Korea," *Journal of Development Studies*, 34 (2): 102–32.

—— (1997b) "Export-led growth and the persistence of gender inequality in the Newly Industrialized Countries," in J. Rives and M. Yousefi (eds), *Economic Dimensions of Gender Inequality: a global perspective*, Westport, CT: Praeger.

Sparr, P. (ed.) (1994) *Mortgaging Women's Lives: feminist critiques of structural adjustment*, London and New Jersey: Zed.

Standing, G. (1989) "Global feminization through flexible labour," *World Development*, 17 (7): 1077–95.

Stichter, S. (1990) "Women, employment and the family: current debates," in S. Stichter and J.L. Parpart (eds), *Women, Employment and the Family in the International Division of Labour*, Philadelphia, PA: Temple University Press.

Treiman, D. and Hartmann, H. (eds) (1981) *Women, Work and Wages: equal pay for jobs of equal value*, Washington, DC: National Academy Press.

United Nations Conference on Trade and Development (UNCTAD) (1995) *International Trade Statistics (4-digit SITC), Taiwan*, Unpublished, in electronic form.

Wang, J.-C. and Tsai, K.-H. (1995) "Taiwan's industrial technology policy measures and an evaluation of R&D promotion tools," *Journal of Industry Studies*, 2 (1): 69–82.

Wood, A. (1991) "North–South trade and female labour in manufacturing: an asymmetry," *Journal of Development Studies*, 27 (2): 168–89.

—— (1994) *North–South Trade, Employment and Inequality: changing fortunes in a skill driven world*, Oxford: Oxford University Press.

Zveglich, J., van der Meulen Rodgers, Y., and Rodgers III, W.M. (1997) "The persistence of gender earnings inequality in Taiwan, 1978–92," *Industrial and Labor Relations Review*, 50 (4): 594–609.

9 Export-led industrialization and gender differences in job creation and destruction

Micro evidence from the Turkish manufacturing sector

Şule Özler

Introduction[1]

Much has been written on women's integration into the industrialization process in semi-industrialized countries, ever since Boserup (1970) emphasized that women were marginalized under import substitution policies. There is now an extensive literature linking export-led industrialization with feminization of the labor force.[2] A key message of this literature is that in semi-industrialized countries, export-led industrialization has increased women's employment opportunities, and thus their income and autonomy.[3] At the same time, however, there are numerous illustrations of the precariousness of women's employment resulting from factors such as poor work conditions and low pay.[4] The purpose of this study is to contribute to this literature by investigating gender differences in job creation and job reallocation across sectors by their trade orientation. As we discuss later, our focus on gender differences in job creation across sectors by trade orientation enables us to address issues relevant to the process through which feminization of the workforce takes place. Measuring job reallocation, on the other hand, is a way of quantifying gender differences in vulnerable employment.

There are two views on the underlying processes that lead to increased employment opportunities for women during export-led industrialization.[5] According to one view, increased exports to industrialized countries shift demand toward those sectors where women have been traditionally employed (Wood 1991). Thus, new employment opportunities for women are to be found in export-oriented industries. Other interpretations of feminization are based on the notion that women constitute a "cheap" source of labor.[6] Elson (1996) argues that the changing nature of jobs, as reflected in increased flexibility and deskilling, leads to a decline of positions that were previously held by men, and increased job opportunities for women. Standing (1989, 1999), on the other hand, argues that the declining strength of labor market insiders have enabled employers to substitute women's "cheap" labor for that of men, leading to a decline of jobs that were previously held by men.[7] This set of explanations challenges the view that industrialization based on trade expansion and market flexibility expands existing employment opportunities. It suggests that even in sectors that are not traditionally female-intensive, employment opportunities for women have increased relative to men.

Empirical studies that link the female share of employment and export-led industrialization use various methodologies and data at different levels of aggregation. In some studies, cross-country time series comparisons are made, through an inspection of overall trends (Standing 1989, 1999), or through the use of an econometric framework (Wood 1991; Çağatay and Özler 1995).[8] There are also numerous case studies on countries from different regions, which focus on export processing zones, broad sectors of the economy, or sub-sectors of the manufacturing industry.[9]

Most studies use aggregate, as opposed to plant level data.[10] One advantage of using plant level data to investigate job creation processes is that it permits identifying and quantifying the conditions under which workers are integrated into the workforce. In particular, it allows for measurement of job reallocation rates. Industry level studies, with their focus on net job changes, cannot identify the degree of job reallocation (simultaneous job creation and destruction) that may be taking place in an industry. A high level of job reallocation, in the process of creating a given level of net jobs, is an indicator of the high degree of uncertainty experienced by the workforce.[11] Thus, gender-based measures of job reallocation rates are important indicators of gender differences in job vulnerability.

In this study we investigate gender differences in net job creation rates and gross job reallocation rates using a data set collected by the State Institute of Statistics (SIS) in Turkey for the period of 1986–96. Net job creation rates are calculated as the difference between gross job creation rates and gross job destruction rates, where gross job creation is a weighted sum of employment gains at expanding and new establishments within a sector (where the weights are average employment shares of plants in a given sector). Similarly, gross job destruction is a weighted sum of employment losses at dying and shrinking establishments within a sector. Gross job reallocation rates are the sum of gross job creation and gross job destruction rates.

The period is well suited for our purposes, as it follows the initiation of export-led industrialization policies in Turkey.[12] A particular advantage of using this data set for our purposes is that employees are classified by gender at varying skill levels, thus enabling gender comparisons at a given skill level. The data analyzed in this study include private manufacturing establishments.

Our analysis indicates important differences in net job creation and gross job reallocation rates by worker groups for the manufacturing industry as a whole. Though creation and destruction rates differ by skill level (*unskilled*, *skilled*, and *nonproduction*) for workers of the same gender, larger gaps stem from gender differences for workers at the same skill level. In fact, the most striking aspect of our results is that net job creation rates, as well as gross job reallocation rates in each skill category, are higher for females than for males. Among skilled workers, the biggest gender gap is observed in net job creation rates: the average annual net job creation rate is 5.76 percent for skilled females in contrast to 1.69 percent for skilled males. The biggest gender gap in gross job reallocation rates is observed for skilled workers, as well. The gross job reallocation rate for skilled females, which is 87.8 percent, is about twice that of skilled males.

These findings hold even when industries are categorized according to their trade orientation. That is to say, irrespective of a sector's trade orientation, net job creation and gross job reallocation rates for females at every skill level are higher than those of their male counterparts. Across sectors, gross job reallocation rates, or the ratio of gross job reallocation rates of females to males at a given skill level, differ only slightly. Net job creation rates show a more discernable difference across industries. In particular, net job creation rates in the export sector are higher than they are in the import-competing sectors for all worker groups. However, the net job creation rate for female production (nonproduction) workers relative to their male counterparts is higher (lower) in the import-competing sector than it is in the export sector. Since female production (nonproduction) workers constitute a smaller (larger) share of employees in import-competing sectors, the results indicate that relative net job creation rates for females are somewhat higher where females constitute a relatively smaller fraction of the workforce.

Overall, the high net job creation rates for females in export industries have contributed to the feminization of the labor force in Turkey. However, opening the economy to international competition, privatization, and deregulation appear to have resulted in higher net job creation for women across sectors with different trade orientations. Thus, the changing nature of jobs and increased flexibility in the economy appears to be largely behind the increased feminization of the labor force in manufacturing (Standing 1989, 1999; Elson 1996).

Before concluding that Turkey has successfully integrated women into the workforce, it is important to note two caveats. First, in every sector of the economy, females experience significantly higher job uncertainty, as measured by gross job reallocation rates. Second, despite high annual net job creation rates, females still hold a small fraction of private manufacturing jobs. Even though the female share of total employees increased by about six percent over the period under consideration, the share of females rose to only 22 percent by 1996.

Economic policies and employment generation

In January 1980 the government introduced a short-term stabilization program in response to a severe balance of payments crisis. The scope of the reforms was extended in the following years as Turkey embarked on an ambitious trade liberalization program to overhaul the country's inward-looking development strategy.

In order to increase exports from its very low level of $2.9 billion in 1980 (less than 5 percent of GNP), the government implemented export promotion measures, including direct export subsidies, tax rebates, export credits, simplification of export procedures, and maintaining a competitive real exchange rate. The establishment of the Turkish Eximbank in 1987 provided greater support for exports, and credits and guarantee programs targeted the sectors with high export potential.

Total export subsidies provided by the government through the new export promotion system amounted to 17.2 percent of exports in 1980. Uygur (1998) calculates that, even with a slight decline in subsidies in the second half of 1980s, total subsidies through direct payments, export credits, duty and tax allowances never fall below 20 percent until 1994. The export support regime was modified in 1996 to comply with the customs code of the European Community, and Turkey's other international commitments.

In addition to explicit export support measures, the government deliberately followed a policy of real devaluation of the Lira in the early 1980s so that Turkish products would become more competitive in both international and domestic markets. But, because of cost-push inflation generated by devaluation, the government discontinued the devaluation-based exchange rate policy. Although the Lira appreciated by 34 percent in real terms in the second half of the 1980s, exports continued to increase and reached $13 billion in 1990.

The government opened the capital account in 1989 in order to attract foreign portfolio investors and increase the funds available to finance public sector borrowing. With a liberalized capital account, coupled with a controlled exchange rate regime, Turkey attracted large sums of foreign capital flows in the first half of 1990s. However, during this period, the Turkish Lira became overvalued. As direct and indirect export subsidies declined, and the real devaluation policy was phased out, export performance stalled throughout the 1990s. Only recently, following the worst economic crisis that hit the country in decades, have Turkey's exports revived.

Detailed export data reveal that not only have total exports increased, there has also been a significant change in the composition of exports (using four-digit SITC categories) over time. Following the Customs Union with the EU in 1996, intra-industry trade has increased substantially. Moreover, those products that were not high in the export list have over time climbed up the ladder, probably produced by plants that had not hitherto been involved in export production.

Turkey has also undergone a number of policy changes to eliminate import barriers, including reducing quantitative restrictions and tariffs. The changes in quantitative restrictions resulted in considerable elimination of trade barriers. Krueger and Aktan (1992) suggested that the wedge between the domestic and international price of imports imposed by quantitative restrictions was 50 percent in 1980, declining by 10 percent every year, so that it was zero by 1986.

The 1984 import program also entailed significant changes in the tariff structure. Tariffs on imports of intermediate and capital goods were reduced. Though tariffs were increased on imports of consumer goods and goods that would compete with domestically produced manufacturing goods, this did not lead to an increase in over-all nominal protection rates, because imports of the goods in these categories were severely restricted before 1984. The output-weighted average nominal tariff rate for the manufacturing industry stood almost unchanged from 75.8 percent in 1983 to 76.9 percent in 1984 but declined to 40 percent in 1990 and 20.7 percent in 1994.

The data

This study employs a data set collected by the Turkish State Institute of Statistics (SIS) for the Turkish manufacturing industry. SIS periodically conducts the Census of Industry and Business Establishments (CIBE).[13] In addition, the SIS conducts Annual Surveys of Manufacturing Industries (ASMI) at establishments with 10 or more employees.[14] The set of addresses used during ASMI are those obtained during CIBE years. In addition, in every non-census year, addresses of newly opened private establishments with 10 or more employees are obtained from the chamber of industry.[15] For this study we use a sample that matches plants from CIBE and ASMI for the 1986–96 period.[16] We focus only on *private establishments*. The resulting sample of private manufacturing plants contains a total of 97,415 plant years.

The plants are classified at the three-digit level by trade orientation into three groups: *nontradable, import competing,* and *export* (see Table 9.1) The classification

Table 9.1 Industry trade orientation classification

	Number of employees			Mean	Standard deviation
	3-digit industry	*Number of plant years*	*Employment shares*		
Import-competing					
Tobacco	314	140	0.002	149	255
Leather prod.	323	1,569	0.008	43	58
Wood prod.	331	2,178	0.012	46	57
Paper	341	1,500	0.014	79	104
Printing	342	2,232	0.016	59	180
Ind. Chemicals	351	885	0.018	169	420
Other chemic.	352	2,725	0.033	102	168
Petroleum der.	354	309	0.005	125	185
Plastic	356	3,680	0.022	51	84
Nonmetal-min.	369	6,443	0.051	66	107
Iron and steel	371	2,878	0.033	98	205
Nonfer. Metals	372	1,339	0.011	70	138
Metal prod.	381	7,726	0.055	59	102
Elec. Machin.	383	4,233	0.056	112	275
Transport eq.	384	3,915	0.069	149	460
Other	390	1,095	0.007	51	59
Exports					
Food	311	12,236	0.106	73	177
Other food	312	2,799	0.020	60	91
Beverages	313	751	0.010	113	141
Textiles	321	13,172	0.230	147	337
Apparel	322	12,625	0.104	70	121
Footware	324	1,074	0.006	46	62
Furniture	332	1,547	0.009	48	81
Rubber prod.	355	1,567	0.016	87	214
Ceramics	361	472	0.013	226	389
Glass	362	691	0.016	197	439
Nontradable					
Nonelec. machin.	382	6,853	0.053	66	205
Professional eq.	385	781	0.005	54	68

Source: Author's calculations based on data from the Census of Industry and Business Establishments (CIBE) and the Annual Surveys of Manufacturing Industries (ASMI), 1986–96.

Table 9.2 Employment by trade orientation

	Number of plant years	Employment shares	Number of employees	
			Mean	Standard deviation
Import-competing	42,847	0.41	89	178
Export	46,934	0.53	107	205
Nontradable	7,634	0.06	60	137

Source: Author's calculations based on data from the Census of Industry and Business Establishments (CIBE) and the Annual Surveys of Manufacturing Industries (ASMI), 1986–96.

is based on industry level data on exports, imports, and production, and it is undertaken by Erlat (1998) using the criterion of Krueger *et al.* (1981).[17] Since a fairly large period is covered, the fact that some sectors might have switched classification may be a source of concern. However, the classification is generally stable through the 1980s, as reported in Erlat (1998).

Table 9.2 presents some basic statistics on employment by trade orientation. As can be seen in the first column, the export sector has the highest number of observations (46,934), closely followed by the import-competing sector. Nontradables, on the other hand, account for only about eight percent of total observations. The second column reports employment shares of these industries. Only 6 percent of all employees are in nontradable sectors. The employment share of import-competing sectors is 41 percent, and the employment share of export sectors is 53 percent. Average plant size, measured by average number of employees, varies considerably across these industry groups. Plant size is close to 90 among import-competing industries and 106 among export industries. As can be observed by a comparison of average size with its standard deviation, there is a large degree of variation across three-digit industries within each sector by trade orientation.

In order to show how worker composition changes across industries, we create six worker ratios, which differ by skill level and gender. The surveys contain a question asking the number of employees in subcategories of production and nonproduction workers, by gender. Nonproduction workers are composed of management staff, bureau workers, and others. Production workers are divided into four groups: high-level technical personnel, medium-level technical personnel, foremen, and workers.

We aggregated some of these groups to create three groups of employees for each gender. First is the *nonproduction worker* category, which is an aggregation of its subgroups. To obtain the second and third groups we divide production workers into *skilled workers*, which includes the foremen category, and high- and medium-level technical personnel, and *unskilled workers*, which includes employees from all other production workers.

Table 9.3 reports the distribution of workers *across* sectors by trade orientation. Although nontradable sectors are included for completeness, due to their small share of workers we focus primarily on a comparison of the other two sectors. The most

Table 9.3 Worker ratios

	Unskilled female	Unskilled male	Skilled female	Skilled male	Nonprod. female	Nonprod. male
A. Distribution across sectors						
Import-competing	0.16	0.45	0.31	0.49	0.44	0.44
Export	0.82	0.48	0.66	0.43	0.5	0.5
Nontradable	0.02	0.07	0.03	0.08	0.06	0.06
B. Distribution within a sector						
Import-competing	0.07	0.56	0.009	0.13	0.05	0.19
Export	0.26	0.47	0.015	0.07	0.04	0.13
Nontradable	0.05	0.59	0.007	0.14	0.04	0.18
Manufacturing	0.17	0.51	0.01	0.11	0.04	0.16

Source: Author's calculations based on data from the Census of Industry and Business Establishments (CIBE) and the Annual Surveys of Manufacturing Industries (ASMI), 1986–96.

striking feature of these worker shares is that the export sectors employ 82 percent of all the unskilled females and 66 percent of all the skilled females in the manufacturing industry. The share of skilled and unskilled male production workers does not differ nearly as substantially between the export and import-competing sectors.

Table 9.3 also presents the distribution of employees *within* sectors by trade orientation, as well as for the manufacturing sector as a whole. Again, the most notable difference across industry groups by trade orientation concerns the share of female workers. In particular, import-competing sectors have a significantly lower share of unskilled females in comparison to the others. Unskilled females constitute 7 and 15 percent of all employees in import-competing and export sectors, respectively. Overall, export sectors are more female-intensive and less skill-intensive compared to import-competing sectors. The female share of employees across all skill levels is about 13 percent in import-competing sectors but 21 percent in export sectors. Female and male unskilled workers together are 63 percent of import-competing sectors but 69 percent of export sectors. Thus, as in many other developing countries, export-oriented sectors in Turkey are unskilled-worker-intensive and feminized.

Examination of the distribution of workers across industries, as well as the distribution of workers within industry groups by trade orientation, suggests the presence of large gender/skill differences. We next turn to investigating whether the job creation process is merely reproducing the existing gender/skill distributions or showing tendencies that alter the existing distributions.

Job creation, destruction, and reallocation

Definitions

In defining job creation and destruction measures, we adopt the methodology in Davis and Haltiwanger (1990). Let us denote employment at plant i in year t by x_{it}, and define average employment as: $ax_{it} = (x_{i,t} + x_{i,t-1})/2$. The growth rate of employment at plant i in period t, g_{it}, is defined so that it is symmetric around zero and lies in the closed interval $[-2, 2]$ where $g_{it} = -2$ corresponds to the death of a plant, and $g_{it} = 2$ corresponds to the birth of a plant. Using the notation introduced here, the growth rate is:[18]

$$g_{it} = (x_{i,t} - x_{i,t-1})/ax_{it} \qquad (9.1)$$

Gross job *creation* is a weighted sum of employment gains at expanding and new establishments within a sector (where the weights are average employment shares of plants in a given sector). Similarly, gross job *destruction* is a weighted sum of employment losses at dying and shrinking establishments within a sector. The *gross job creation rate* in sector s at time t, and the *gross job destruction rate* in sector s at time t are expressed as:

$$Creation_{s,t} = \Sigma\ g_{it}\ (ax_{it}/AX_{st}) \qquad Destruction_{s,t} = \Sigma\ |g_{it}|\ (ax_{it}/AX_{it}) \qquad (9.2)$$
$$i \epsilon E_{s,t} \qquad\qquad\qquad i \epsilon E_{s,t}$$
$$g_{it} > 0 \qquad\qquad\qquad g_{it} < 0$$

where, $E_{s,t}$ is the set of establishments in s at time t, and AX_{st} is the average sector employment defined analogously to average establishment employment. Sectors could be defined based on three-digit SIC codes, plant sizes, trade orientation, or other features. To obtain the creation rate for the whole sample, the weighted sum of $Creation_{s,t}$ is calculated, whereby the weights are average employment shares of the sectors. It is, of course, possible to separate *Creation* into gross job creation generated by *entry* of new plants and gross job creation generated by size adjustments of continuing plants. Similarly, *Destruction* can also be decomposed into the part that arises from plant closures (*exit*) and size adjustments of continuing plants.

It is important to note that we observe only plant-level employment and hence cannot determine whether a given level of employment in two different points in time for the same plant represents a new employment position, or continuation of an existing employment position. Thus, these measures of creation and destruction represent lower bounds on true creation and destruction rates. Using these measures, we can calculate the *net* job creation rate as the difference between *creation* and *destruction*. Gross job reallocation is calculated as the sum of job creation and destruction and denoted by *sum*.[19]

Job creation and destruction for all workers

Several studies on industrialized as well as developing countries have shown that jobs are simultaneously created and destroyed (e.g. see Davis and Haltiwanger 1990; Roberts 1996; Levinsohn 1999). Furthermore, the evidence indicates that even modest rates of net job creation are associated with high rates of gross job reallocation. Before investigating gender/skill differences, we present the results for all workers and compare the average magnitudes for Turkey with other countries. This comparison gives us a benchmark for evaluating whether the changes in the job creation process in Turkish manufacturing are large or small.

Job creation, destruction, net job creation, and gross job reallocation rates for the private manufacturing sector as a whole are reported in Table 9.4. As can be seen in the first row of Table 9.4, when all employees are considered, the annual average *creation* rate is 14.44 percent and the *destruction* rate is 11.78 percent, leading to a *net* job creation rate of 2.66 percent. This rate, based on our sample, is higher than the 2 percent total employment growth rate based on the Labour Force Surveys (during the 1989–97 period) but lower than the 3.3 percent annual population growth rate for those who are 12 years old and over during the same period.[20] As such, the average net employment generation of the manufacturing sector has been disappointing. This message is consistent with the few studies that analyze employment shifts in the post-1980 period.[21] For example, Taymaz (1999) reports an average 2.2 percent annual growth for manufacturing employment in the 1980–93 period, in comparison to 4.8 percent for the 1969–80 period.

Sum, the gross reallocation rate for all employees, as reported in column four, row one of Table 9.4, is 26.2 percent. To put this magnitude in perspective, note that the net job creation rate is 2.66 percent during this period. Thus, the net job creation rate in Turkey (similar to other developing countries) hides a large degree of job reallocation. For example, in his study of Chile, Colombia, and Morocco, Roberts (1996) finds gross job reallocation rates ranging between 25 and 31 percent. These magnitudes are about 30 percent higher than those observed in Canada and the US.

Table 9.4 Jobs for all workers

	Creation	Destruction	Net	Sum
A. All plants				
Manufacturing	14.44	11.78	2.66	26.22
Import-competing	13.65	12.28	1.37	25.94
Export	15.14	11.35	3.79	26.48
Noncompeting	13.74	12.29	1.45	26.03
	Entry	Exit	NetE/NetC[a]	SumE/SumC[b]
B. Entry and exit				
Manufacturing	1.44	1.02	0.19	0.10
Import-competing	1.08	1.05	0.02	0.09
Export	1.65	1.00	0.21	0.11
Noncompeting	1.04	0.94	0.07	0.08

Source: Author's calculations based on data from the Census of Industry and Business Establishments (CIBE) and the Annual Surveys of Manufacturing Industries (ASMI), 1986–96.

Notes
a NetE/NetC is computed as (entry − exit)/[(creation − entry) − (destruction − exit)].
b SumE/SumC is computed as (entry − exit)/[(creation − entry) − (destruction − exit)].

Results by trade orientation of industries are presented in the next three rows.[22] An important difference among the sectors is manifested in a comparison of their net job creation rates. The annual net job creation rate in export sectors is 3.79 percent, which is about 2.4 percent higher than import-competing and nontradable sectors. A comparison of gross creation rates and gross destruction rates across industry groups indicates that export industries differ in two respects: the gross creation rate is slightly higher and the destruction rate is slightly lower in export industries than the others. Thus, the net job creation rate in the export sectors is somewhat larger than the others.

There is no discernable difference, however, in gross job reallocation rates across industry groups by trade orientation (reported in the fourth column). It has been suggested that trade liberalization in developing countries may promote high turnover industries, thus creating more churning in the job market. For example, Levinsohn (1999) reports weak evidence for a higher net job creation rate accompanied by a somewhat higher (about six percent higher) gross reallocation rate in the export sector in his study of Chile. This pattern is plausible for developing countries with export sectors that are labor-intensive, which involves relatively low start-up costs. The fact that this pattern does not generalize to Turkey may be due to differences in policies implemented in Chile and Turkey through their trade reform episodes. In Turkey, trade reforms included various types of subsidies to the export sector, which may have contributed to lower gross job destruction rates for that sector and gross reallocation rates that are similar to other sectors.

The creation and destruction rates reported earlier include size adjustments of continuing plants, as well as the entry and exit of plants. The importance of entry and exit may differ across industries based on the importance of the sunk cost of entry and exit in those industries. To assess the significance of entry and exit in the Turkish manufacturing sector, we report job creation rates generated by entering plants only and job destruction rates generated by exiting plants only, under entry and exit in the first two columns of Table 9.4. A comparison of these magnitudes with total creation and destruction rates indicates that entry and exit play a rather insignificant role.

To further assess the role of entry and exit, column three of Table 9.4 reports the ratio of net job creation generated by entry and exit to net job creation generated by size adjustments of continuing plants. The ratio is 19 percent for the manufacturing sector as a whole, but it varies considerably across sectors. The ratio of net changes from entry and exit to net changes from size adjustments in continuing plants is only 2 percent for import-competing sectors, but, as would be expected, it is considerably larger for the export sectors. Nevertheless, entry and exit play a smaller role in net job creation in the Turkish manufacturing sector in comparison to some other countries at similar levels of development. For example, Roberts (1996) reports that net job creation due to entry and exit was double the size of net job creation created by continuing plants in Chile, Colombia, and Morocco.

Given the small share of entry in job creation and the small share of exit in job destruction, it is not surprising to find that the ratio of gross reallocation generated by entry and exit to gross reallocation generated by size adjustments in continuing plants is also small. This ratio is 10 percent, as reported in column four of Table 9.4, and does not vary across sectors. Again, this ratio is low in comparison to the 41–89 percent range for other developing countries reported in Roberts (1996). Government policies that subsidize inefficient plants, factors that constrain entry, such as credit rationing, trade policies that influence the rate of entry of new firms, as well as uncertainty of feature market conditions that may result from macroeconomic instability, are among the reasons that can lead to entry/exit having a relatively small role in the employment creation process in Turkey's manufacturing industry.

Gender and skill differences in manufacturing sector

We now turn to differences in the job creation and destruction process for the six skill, gender worker groups. Table 9.5 reports job creation and destruction rates and the consequent net job creation and gross job reallocation rates for the manufacturing sector as a whole. A comparison of gross job creation rates across employee groups, presented in column one, highlights significant gender and skill differences. First, female job creation rates vary more across skill groups than male job creation rates. Second, within each skill group, gross job creation rates for females are higher than for males. Both of these observations also hold for job destruction rates, reported in column two.

The net job creation rate for females in each skill category is also higher than for males, as can be seen in column three of Table 9.5. The net job creation rate for females is highest in the nonproduction workers category, where it is more than twice that of males. The biggest gender disparity is observed for skilled workers, where the 5.76 percent net job creation rate for females is more than three times that of males. The lowest disparity is for unskilled workers, with the net job creation rate for females being less than twice that of males. Overall, despite the disappointing average net job creation rate of private manufacturing

Table 9.5 Job creation and destruction by skill and gender

| | Manufacturing as a whole | | | |
	Creation	*Destruction*	*Net*	*Sum*
Unskilled female	25.33	21.55	3.78	46.88
Unskilled male	19.0	17.0	2.0	36.0
Skilled female	46.79	41.03	5.76	87.82
Skilled male	24.0	22.31	1.69	46.31
Nonprod. female	30.47	23.84	6.63	54.31
Nonprod. Male	20.93	18.18	2.75	39.11

Source: Author's calculations based on data from the Census of Industry and Business Establishments (CIBE) and the Annual Surveys of Manufacturing Industries (ASMI), 1986–96.

plants during the period under consideration, there are important differences in employment generation across worker groups.[23] Net job creation rates for non-production workers are significantly higher than for production workers. More notably, female net job creation rates, controlling for skill levels, are significantly higher than male job creation rates.[24]

Gross reallocation rates of female jobs are also significantly higher than gross reallocation rates of male jobs, as can be seen in column four of Table 9.5. The average gross job reallocation rate for unskilled female workers is 46.8 percent, while it is 36 percent for unskilled male workers, yielding a ratio of 1:3. The gender gap in gross job reallocation rates for nonproduction workers is about the same, with a female to male ratio of 1:4. The largest gender gap is for skilled workers; the female reallocation rate (87.8 percent) is 1.9 times the size of the male reallocation rate (46.3 percent).[25]

That gross job reallocation rates of female jobs are much higher than the rates for male jobs indicates that females experience greater churning in the labor market. This is an important piece of evidence suggesting the precarious nature of female jobs. High gross reallocation rates for females are not unique to Turkey. In a closely related study, Levinsohn (1999) examines job reallocation rates for females and males in Chile but without controlling for their skill levels and the differences between blue-collar and white-collar workers. Levinsohn reports that gross job reallocation rates are significantly higher for females in comparison to males and attributes this to gender differences rather than to skill differences. Though the interpretation is likely to be correct because the gender gap in reallocation rates is substantially higher than the skill gap in reallocation rates, it is important to control for skill levels while measuring the gender gap.

Gender and skill differences by trade orientation

The results presented so far indicate that the net job creation rate is higher in export-oriented sectors than others; they also indicate that net job creation rates for females are higher than males in every skill group when the manufacturing sector is considered as a whole. We next turn to investigating whether the high net job creation rate for females is limited to export-oriented sectors. Table 9.6 reports net job creation rates for each of the six worker groups by industries' trade orientation. (Even though the results for nontradable sectors are reported, the discussion focuses on export and import-competing sectors.) Similar to the manufacturing industry considered as a whole, the net job creation rate for females is higher than males in every skill category in import-competing, as well as in export industries. Thus, the evidence suggests that, independent of the sector's trade orientation, net job creation rates are higher for females than for males.

To assess the difference in relative net job creation rates between the two sectors for each gender/skill group, columns seven through nine of Table 9.6 present the ratio of female net job creation rates to male net job creation rates. There is weak evidence suggesting that among production workers the female net

Table 9.6 Gender differences by trade orientation

	(1)	(2)	(3)	(4)	(5)	(6)	(7)	(8)	(9)
	Un-skilled female	Un-skilled male	Skilled female	Skilled male	Nonprod. female	Nonprod. male	Ratio (1)/(2)	Ratio (3)/(4)	Ratio (5)/(6)
A. Net job creation rates									
Import-competing	1.40	0.71	4.36	0.86	4.90	2.61	1.96	5.07	1.87
Export	4.19	3.50	6.35	2.87	8.29	2.96	1.20	2.21	2.80
Noncompeting	7.00	0.53	6.89	0.36	5.80	2.46	13.33	19.07	2.36
B. Gross job reallocation rates									
Import-competing	55.50	35.57	81.89	43.86	49.32	37.51	1.56	1.87	1.32
Export	45.03	36.80	89.74	48.44	58.89	40.79	1.22	1.85	1.44
Noncompeting	53.66	35.37	105.39	50.21	53.50	40.50	1.52	2.10	1.32

Source: Author's calculations based on data from the Census of Industry and Business Establishments (CIBE) and the Annual Surveys of Manufacturing Industries (ASMI), 1986–96.

job creation rate is higher than the male rate in import-competing industries, where representation of females is smaller. The job creation rate for unskilled females is 1.96 times that of unskilled males in the import-competing sectors. The comparable number for the export sector, where the unskilled female group is relatively large, is 1.20. The difference is more pronounced for skilled females (see column eight). For nonproduction workers the ratio is larger in export sectors than in import-competing sectors. Recalling that 5 percent of workers in import-competing sectors are nonproduction females, in comparison to the 4 percent in export sectors (Table 9.3), it is striking that the female net job creation rate is higher than the male rate even though female representation is smaller.

The findings described here suggest support for the "cheap labor" hypothesis advanced by Elson (1996), and Standing (1999). It is true that job creation rates are higher in export sectors for all worker groups. It is also true that females constitute a larger share of employees in export sectors, so that changes in this sector contribute more to changes in the manufacturing sector as a whole. However, measured with relative female to male net job creation rates, the tendency is toward increased feminization irrespective of trade orientation of sectors.

The finding regarding gross job reallocation rates for the entire manufacturing sector also holds for import-competing and export sectors individually: in every skill group, there is more job churning for females in comparison to males, as can be seen in Table 9.6. Columns seven through nine present ratios of female gross job reallocation rates to male gross job reallocation rates in each skill group. Differences between sectors are less pronounced in comparison to net job creation comparisons.

We next investigate whether entry and exit play a more prominent role for certain worker groups than others. Though the role of entry and exit in net job

Table 9.7 Gender differences by plant entry and exit

	(1) Creation	(2) Destruction	(3) Entry	(4) Exit	(5) NetE/NetC[a]	(6) SumE/SumC[b]
A. Unskilled females						
Import-competing	28.45	27.05	2.43	2.27	0.12	0.11
Export	24.61	20.42	3.03	2.10	0.29	0.12
Noncompeting	30.33	23.33	1.85	1.35	0.08	0.04
B. Unskilled males						
Import-competing	18.14	17.43	1.67	1.68	−0.01	0.13
Export	20.15	16.65	2.47	1.73	0.27	0.12
Noncompeting	17.95	17.42	1.57	1.55	0.30	0.05
C. Skilled females						
Import-competing	43.13	38.77	2.39	1.96	0.11	0.09
Export	48.05	41.69	4.46	3.28	0.23	0.10
Noncompeting	56.14	49.25	3.29	2.55	0.12	0.03
D. Skilled males						
Import-competing	22.36	21.50	2.31	2.41	−0.10	0.15
Export	25.66	22.78	3.45	2.71	0.35	0.14
Noncompeting	25.29	24.92	2.56	2.53	0.09	0.06
E. Nonproduction females						
Import-competing	27.11	22.21	2.83	2.19	0.15	0.15
Export	33.59	25.30	3.88	2.33	0.23	0.14
Noncompeting	29.65	23.85	3.36	2.41	0.20	0.07
F. Nonproduction males						
Import-competing	20.06	17.45	1.91	1.82	0.04	0.13
Export	21.87	18.91	2.61	1.90	0.30	0.14
Noncompeting	21.48	19.02	2.29	2.07	0.10	0.06

Source: Author's calculations based on data from the Census of Industry and Business Establishments (CIBE) and the Annual Surveys of Manufacturing Industries (ASMI), 1986–96.

Notes
a NetE/NetC is computed as (entry − exit)/[(creation − entry) − (destruction − exit)].
b SumE/SumC is computed as (entry − exit)/[(creation − entry) − (destruction − exit)].

creation is relatively small in comparison to those generated by continuing plants, it seems to work in the direction of increasing the trend toward the convergence noted earlier. In particular, in import-competing sectors, where females are fewer in numbers, the ratio of net job creation generated by entry/exit to that created by continuing plants is larger for females than for males. (This can be seen in column five of Table 9.7.)[26] In export sectors, on the other hand, the ratio of net job creation generated by entry/exit to that created by continuing plants is on average larger for males than it is for females.[27] The role of entry and exit in generation of gross job reallocation does not differ by gender/skill groups.

Since high gross job reallocation is a pronounced aspect of gender differences in the job creation process we examine this with an alternative measure of job stability. Specifically, we consider the persistence of the job creation and destruction process. To be precise, the persistence of job creation at plants is measured by calculating what percentage of jobs created between the years $t-1$ and t are still present in year $t+1$. Similarly, the persistence of job destruction is measured as the percentage of jobs lost between $t-1$ and t, and yet still not present in year $t+1$.[28] The persistence percentages by trade orientation are reported in Table 9.8. Job creation persistence percentages for males in each skill category and across sectors are higher than for females, with one exception: only female unskilled jobs in the export industries have slightly higher creation persistence. In the import-competing sector, for example, almost 60 percent of jobs created for skilled males in a given year are likely to exist two years later, in contrast to the 40 percent for skilled females. To compare sectors, we present ratios of the female to male ratio of creation persistence. The ratio is higher where representation of females is higher. For example, skilled female to male creation persistence is 69 percent in import-competing sectors where skilled females constitute 0.9 percent of all workers, while it is 76 percent in export sector where skilled females constitute 1.5 percent of all workers. Job destruction persistence percentages presented in Table 9.8 are lower for males in each skill category than their female counterparts. This finding holds across all sectors.

Both the gross job reallocation rates and job creation and destruction persistence percentages indicate that women face less secure positions, independent of the trade orientation of the industries where they are employed. These findings suggest that females may constitute a flexible reserve of labor. One way to ascertain if this is the case is to investigate how the job creation process changes over business cycles. If women constitute a flexible reserve, they will be drawn into the labor market

Table 9.8 Gender differences in job creation and destruction

	(1) Un- skilled female	(2) Un- skilled male	(3) Skilled female	(4) Skilled male	(5) Nonprod. female	(6) Nonprod. male	(7) Ratio (1)/(2)	(8) Ratio (3)/(4)	(9) Ratio (5)/(6)
A. Job creation									
Import- competing	59.24	67.04	40.83	59.14	59.71	63.66	0.88	0.69	0.94
Export	67.52	65.88	42.84	56.58	56.07	61.72	1.02	0.76	0.91
Noncompeting	60.99	66.60	34.97	53.50	59.15	60.68	0.92	0.65	0.97
B. Job destruction									
Import- competing	85.42	79.68	90.76	82.66	83.41	77.78	1.07	1.10	1.07
Export	83.15	80.15	92.01	82.65	80.46	75.91	1.04	1.11	1.06
Noncompeting	83.74	81.69	94.38	83.21	82.90	76.75	1.03	1.13	1.08

Source: Author's calculations based on data from the Census of Industry and Business Establishments (CIBE) and the Annual Surveys of Manufacturing Industries (ASMI), 1986–96.

during upturns and expelled during downturns relatively more easily than men.[29] In fact, in support of this hypothesis, Özler (2001) finds that net job creation rates fell more quickly for skilled and unskilled females in comparison to males as the economy headed into a recession, and then recovered before their male counterparts during the upturns.[30]

To summarize, the export sector, with its high net job creation rate for females, contributes to the feminization of the labor force. This pattern is strengthened by the entry of new plants. However, net job creation for females is higher than for males in the import-competing sectors as well. At the same time, gross job reallocation rates are higher for females irrespective of skill levels, or trade orientation of sectors, indicating that the precarious nature of female jobs is pervasive throughout manufacturing industries.

Concluding remarks

The contribution of this study to the existing literature can be summarized as follows. The literature, described in the introduction to this chapter, has focused on gender differences in net job creation and concluded that trade liberalization has led to feminization of the labor force. Increasing involvement of women in the labor force is seen by some to facilitate gender equality. At the same time, others point out that the conditions under which women are integrated into the labor market, in terms of pay, social environment, and so forth, are poor. In this study we quantify one of these dimensions by focusing on gross job reallocation. Our findings indicate that while female net job creation rates are significantly higher than male net job creation rates, female gross job reallocation rates are also significantly higher than male rates at every skill level. Since gross job reallocation rate is an indication of the volatility of jobs, this suggests that female jobs are significantly less stable.

Second, this chapter contributes to the literature on employment shifts in the Turkish economy during its export-led industrialization phase. Consistent with earlier studies, we find that the average net job creation rate is lower than the growth rate of the working age population. Despite this, our study indicates that there are important differences in employment generation across worker groups. The net job creation rate for nonproduction workers is significantly higher than for production workers. Similarly, female net job creation rates, controlling for skill levels, are significantly higher than male job creation rates.

Third, this chapter contributes to plant level studies on jobs not only by introducing evidence from Turkey, but also by bringing gender differences into focus. Among the earlier studies, Levinsohn (1999) discusses gender differences based on a comparison of all females with all males. The advantage of our study is that we compare males and females in the same skill groups. In fact, we find the largest gaps, both in net job creation and gross job reallocation, are among skilled males and skilled females. This would be very difficult to identify in a simple comparison of all males and females, since females are largely in unskilled jobs, and they hold a smaller share of skilled jobs.

Notes

1 I would like to thank Lourdes Benería, Nilüfer Çağatay, Caren Grown, Dani Rodrik, Erol Taymaz, and Insan Tunali for helpful comments. This work has benefited from a financial grant from the Economic Research Forum for the Arab Countries, Iran and Turkey. The contents and recommendations do not necessarily reflect the views of the Economic Research Forum. The database used in this study is the Turkish State Institute of Statistics (SIS) Industrial Analysis Data Base 1999/1. I would like to thank many at the SIS for their efforts in establishing the procedures that has allowed me to use the data set at the SIS premises, and for providing me with the data set. Among those are President Sefik Yildizeli, former President Omer Gebizlioglu, Vice President Nurgul Ogut, Emine Kocberber, Selmin Altin, Ilhami Mintemur, Ali Gunes, and Akin Bodur.
2 See UN (1999) for a recent summary.
3 There is also some evidence suggesting that the association of increased intensity of female employment with export-oriented industrialization might be reversed (see, for example, Berik (2000) and Joekes and Weston (1994)). Where it is observed, the reversal is attributed to introduction of new technologies, skill upgrading of export producers, and reorganization of production, especially multitasking of flexible labor engaged in high-performance production.
4 See UN (1999) and Benería (2001).
5 Women's availability for paid employment in the manufacturing sector is also attributed to several different factors. "Push factors" refer to women's participation in paid employment due to increased family income insecurity during structural adjustment programs (Benería 1992). Kabeer (1995) notes that women's entry into the workforce is in response to a variety of needs and incentives, not only to support family income. Daughters' choice of factory employment in the face of opposition from parents, for example, is interpreted as their route to personal liberation (Wolf 1992). See Özler (1999) for an overview of this literature.
6 Pearson 1998: 5 – "'cheap' labor is deconstructed beyond wage levels to include employee protection, employer's contribution to social wage, taxation, investment and working conditions in combination with non-militancy, docility and manual dexterity and conscientious application to often monotonous production process."
7 Nevertheless, the basic argument rests on outsiders replacing insiders, which is the view that Elson (1996) takes issue with.
8 Wood (1991) estimates female share only as a function of the export ratio. Çağatay and Özler (1995) use a framework that incorporates other economic and demographic factors and information on implementation of adjustment programs as potential explanatory variables, in addition to changes in export performance.
9 References to many case studies can be found in Çağatay and Berik (1991) and UN (1999).
10 See, for example, Özler (2000 and 2001).
11 Plant level studies on developing countries document that within an industry a substantial amount of job creation and destruction takes place simultaneously (see, for example, Roberts (1996) on Chile, Colombia, and Morocco, and Levinsohn (1999) on Chile). For examples of studies on industrialized countries using similar methodologies see Davis and Haltiwanger (1990) and Dunne *et al.* (1989) on the US, and Baldwin *et al.* (1998) on Canada and the US.
12 The reforms began in 1980. See Celasun and Rodrik (1990) for the chronology of the programs.
13 Since the formation of the Turkish Republic, CIBE has been conducted seven times (in 1927, 1950, 1963, 1970, 1980, 1985, and 1992).
14 SIS also collects data on establishments with less than 10 employees. However, up to 1992 data on these establishments were collected only during CIBE years. Since then, SIS has collected annual data for establishments with less than 10 employees using a sampling method.

15 Plant entry can be observed in every year of the sample. Though not reported here, in the CIBE years, we observe a larger number of new plants and a higher fraction of smaller plants. Both of these observations reflect the concerted effort by the SIS to include all establishments in the CIBE years (Özler (2001)).

16 The ASMI and CIBE data are available in a machine-readable form starting from 1980. For this study we limited the sample for the post-1985 period for two reasons: (1) in the years prior to 1986 the quality of data on the gender breakdown of employees is less reliable and much work is needed for its improvement, and (2) the gender breakdown of employees is not available for plants with less than 25 employees in the years prior to 1985. For a description of the matching procedure and other features of data preparation see Özler (2001).

17 The criterion is based on the difference between domestic consumption C and production Q per unit of consumption: $T = (C-Q)/C$. Using $C \equiv Q-X+M$, T is calculated as $T = (M-X)/(Q-X+M)$, where M is imports, X is exports. Obviously, if a sector is a net exporter, then $T < 0$. The analysis in Erlat (1998) leads her to use 0.40 as a cutoff value to separate nontradables from import competing sectors. The sectors with T values between 0 and 0.40 are classified as import competing and those with T values greater than 0.40 as nontradable.

18 The g measure is monotonically related to the conventional growth rate measure G, defined as the change in employment scaled by lagged employment. The two measures are linked by the identity $G \equiv 2g/(2-g)$.

19 *Sum* is the upper bound on gross job reallocation rate. It represents an upper bound because some workers move from shrinking to growing establishments. To obtain a lower bound and eliminate the possibility of double counting one can compute *max* = max |*creation, destruction*|.

20 The number is based on the 1989 and 1997 Labor Force Surveys. During this period, the population growth rate for the 15–64 group was 3.4 percent.

21 Among these, Celasun (1989) and Senses (1994) address employment performance in the broad sectors of the economy, and Yenturk (1997), Taymaz (1999), and Erlat (1999) investigate employment patterns for detailed subsectors in the private manufacturing industry.

22 Multiplication of the net creation rate reported for each sector by its respective manufacturing employment share reported in Table 9.2 yields the manufacturing industry net creation rate.

23 Multiplication of the net creation rate reported for each worker group by its respective manufacturing employment share reported in the last row of Table 9.3 yields the manufacturing industry net creation rate.

24 It is important to note that this has taken place in the context of declining labor force participation among working age women. The movement of women out of the labor force is attributed to migration from rural to urban areas (see Bulutay (1995) and Tunali (1997)). This decline is attributed to both cultural and economic factors. An important economic factor influencing the decision to stay home appears to be the decline in wage-earning opportunities for women in urban areas, especially those with low education.

25 This finding, that the gender gap for skilled workers is higher than the gender gap for unskilled workers, is primarily due to differences between females with different skill levels. The gross job reallocation rate of skilled females is 41 percent higher than unskilled females, while the rate of skilled males is only 10 percent higher than unskilled males.

26 Entry and exit lead to net job destruction for unskilled and skilled male workers, even though the net destruction rate is small in comparison to the net job creation from continuing plants. In contrast, the net job creation rate generated by entering and exiting plants for females (skilled and unskilled) is about 11–12 percent of the continuing plant net creation rate.

27 Though the ratio is slightly higher for unskilled females in comparison to males, it is larger by a greater margin for other skill groups.

28 Plant level job creation percentage, JCPP, and plant level destruction percentage, JDPP, in year t, are:

$$JCPP_t = \begin{cases} 1 & \text{if } L_t > L_{t-1} \text{ and } L_{t+1} \geq L_t \\ \dfrac{(L_{t+1} - L_{t-1})}{(L_t - L_{t-1})} & \text{if } L_t > L_{t-1} \text{ and } L_{t+1} > L_{t+1} > L_{t-1} \\ 0 & \text{otherwise,} \end{cases}$$

$$JDPP_t = \begin{cases} 1 & \text{if } L_t < L_{t-1} \text{ and } L_{t+1} \leq L_t \\ \dfrac{(L_{t-1} - L_{t+1})}{(L_{t-1} - L_t)} & \text{if } L_t < L_{t-1} \text{ and } L_t < L_{t+1} < L_{t-1} \\ 0 & \text{otherwise.} \end{cases}$$

where, L_{t-1}, L_t, and L_{t+1} are employment in plant in years $t-1$, t, and $t+1$, respectively. Thus, persistence percentages are undefined in the first and last years of the sample (we choose the time interval for persistence to be two years in order not lose more observations).

29 See Humphries (1988).

30 Levinsohn (1999) reports similar results in his comparisons of white-collar and blue-collar workers.

References

Baldwin, J., Dunne, T., and Haltiwanger, J. (1998) "A comparison of job creation and destruction in Canada and the United States," *The Review of Economics and Statistics*, 80 (3): 347–56, August.

Benería, L. (1992) "The Mexican debt crisis: restructuring the economy and the household," in L. Beneria and S. Feldman (eds), *Unequal Burden: economic crises, persistent poverty and women's work*, Boulder, CO: Westview Press.

—— (2001) *Changing Employment Patterns and the Informalization of Jobs: general trends and gender dimensions*, Mimeo: Cornell University.

Berik, G. (2000) "Mature export-led growth and gender wage inequality in Taiwan," *Feminist Economics*, 6 (3): 1–26.

Boserup, E. (1970) *Women's Role in Economic Development*, New York: St. Martin's Press.

Bulutay, T. (1995) *Employment, Unemployment and Wages in Turkey*, Ankara: ILO and SIS.

Çağatay, N. and Berik, G. (1991) "Transition to export-led growth in Turkey: is there a feminization of employment?" *Review of Radical Political Economics*, 22: 115–34.

Çağatay, N. and Özler, S. (1995) "Feminization of the labor force: the effects of long-term development and structural adjustment," *World Development*, 23: 1883–94.

Celasun, M. (1989) "Income distribution and employment aspects of Turkey's post-1980 adjustment," *METU Studies in Development*, 16: 1–31.

Celasun, M. and D. Rodrik (1990) "Debt adjustment and growth: Turkey," in J. Sachs and S. Collins (eds), *Developing Country Debt and Economic Performance*, vol. 3, Chicago and London: University Chicago Press.

Davis, S. and Haltiwanger, J. (1990) "Gross job creation and destruction: microeconomic evidence and macroeconomic implications," *NBER Macroeconomics Annual*, V: 123–68.

Dunne, T., Roberts, M., and Samuelson, L. (1989) "Plant turnover and gross employment flows in the U.S. manufacturing sector," *Journal of Labor Economics*, 7 (1): 48–71.

Elson, D. (1996) "Appraising recent developments in the world market for nimble fingers," in A. Chhachhi and R. Pittin (eds), *Confronting State, Capital and Patriarchy: women organizing in the process of industrialization*, Basingstoke: Macmillan.

Erlat, G. (1998) "Foreign trade and employment in Turkey," in *Labor Statistics*, State Institute of Statistics, Ankara, Turkey.

—— (1999) "Measuring the impact of trade flows on employment in the Turkish manufacturing industry," ERC Working Paper Series No. {99/12}, Middle East Technical University, Ankara.

Humphries, J. (1988) "Women's employment in restructuring America: the changing experience of women in three recessions," in J. Rubery (ed.), *Women and Recessions*, London and New York: Routledge and Kegan Paul.

Joekes, S. and Weston, A. (1994) *Women and the New Trade Agenda*, New York: UNIFEM.

Kabeer, N. (1995) "Necessary, sufficient or irrelevant? Women, wages and intra-household power relations in Bangladesh," IDS Working Paper No. 25, Institute of Development Studies, University of Sussex.

Krueger, A. and Aktan, O. (1992) "Swimming against the tide: Turkish trade reforms in the 1980s," *International Center for Economic Growth*, San Francisco, CA: ICS Press.

Krueger, A., Lary, H.B., Monson, T., and Akrasanee, N. (eds) (1981) *Trade and Employment in Developing Countries I: individual studies*, Chicago, IL: University of Chicago Press.

Levinsohn, J. (1999) "Employment responses to international liberalization in Chile," *Journal of International Economics*, 47: 321–44.

Özler, S. (1999) "Globalization, employment and gender," *Background Papers: Human Development Report*, New York: UNDP.

—— (2000) "Export-orientation and female share of employment: evidence from Turkey," *World Development*, 28 (7): 1239–48.

—— (2001) "Gender differences in job creation and destruction over business cycles: micro evidence from Turkish manufacturing sector," in T. Bulutay (ed.), *Wages and Wage Income Distribution*, ILO and State Institute of Statistics, Ankara, Turkey.

Pearson, R. (1998) "Feminist visions of development: research analysis and policy," London and New York: Routledge.

Roberts, M. (1996) "Employment flows and producer gross job reallocation," in M. Roberts and J. Tybout (eds), *Producer Heterogeneity and Performance in the Semi-Industrialized Countries*, Oxford: Oxford University Press.

Senses, F. (1994) "Labor market response to structural adjustment and institutional pressures: the Turkish case," *METU Studies in Development*, 21: 405–48.

Standing, G. (1989) "Global feminization through flexible labor," *World Development*, 17: 1077–95.

—— (1999) "Global feminization through flexible labor: a theme revisited," *World Development*, 27 (3): 583–602.

Taymaz, E. (1999) "Trade liberalization and employment generation: the experience of Turkey in the 1980s," ERC Working Paper Series No. {99/12}, Middle East Technical University, Ankara.

Tunali, I. (1997) "To work or not to work: an examination of female labor force participation rates in Turkey," *Annual Conference of Economic Research Forum*, Beuirut.

United Nations (1999) "World survey on the role of women in development: globalization gender and work," New York.

Uygur, E. (1998) "Export policies and export performance: the case of Turkey," in Raed Safadi (ed.), *Opening Doors to the World: a new trade agenda for the Middle East*, Cairo: International Development Research Centre and Economic Research Forum.

Wolf, D. (1992) *Fctory Daughters: gender, household dynamics and rural industrialization in Java*, Los Angeles: University of California and Oxford University Presses.

Wood, A. (1991) "North–South trade and female labor in manufacturing: an asymmetry," *Journal of Development Studies*, 27 (2): 168–89.

Yenturk, N. (1997) "Turk imalat sanayiinde ucretler, istihdam ve birikim," Istanbul: Friedrich Ebert Vakfi.

10 Gender segregation and gender bias in manufacturing trade expansion

Revisiting the "Wood Asymmetry"

David Kucera and William Milberg

Introduction[1]

Does globalization have a gender bias? Wood (1991) found an apparently fortunate asymmetry: trade between developed and developing countries corresponded with an increased female intensity of employment in developing countries and had no noticeable negative symmetric effect on the female intensity of employment in the traded-goods sector of industrialized countries. As Wood noted, the asymmetry is particularly striking because it contradicts the findings of research done in the mid-1980s. Schumacher (1984), using 1977 data, found that a representative (and trade-balance neutral) bundle of imports and exports between six European Union countries and developing countries had a distinct positive effect on male employment and negative effect on female employment. And Baldwin (1984) found that women make up a disproportionately large share of workers displaced by foreign trade. Though at odds with both theoretical prediction and prior empirical evidence, Wood's asymmetry result has received surprisingly little attention. In this chapter we revisit the Wood Asymmetry, using more recent and disaggregated data (22 manufacturing industries) for 10 OECD countries for the 1978–95 period. We use factor content analysis to calculate changes in male and female employment associated with trade expansion. We find that in most of the countries in the sample (in particular Australia, Canada, Japan, the Netherlands, and the USA) trade expansion with non-OECD countries resulted in employment declines that disproportionately affected women. In most continental European countries in our sample (France, Germany,[2] and Italy) there was little or no gender bias in the decline in employment associated with the expansion of non-OECD trade.

Analysis at the industry level shows that in almost every case the gender bias of non-OECD trade is associated with developments in the textiles, apparel, leather, and leather goods industry. The high female percentage of employment in this industry indicates that gender segregation plays an important role in the gender bias of employment effects from non-OECD trade expansion. But given the strikingly high correlation in the female percentage of employment by industry across the sample of OECD countries, we conclude that the differences in gender bias observed across countries are not the result of gender segregation but due mainly to differences in trade performance in the textiles, apparel, leather, and leather goods industry.

Our results constitute a reversal of the Wood Asymmetry, most likely because our study covers a different time period. We consider the period 1978–95, while Wood analyzed the period 1960 through the mid-1980s. At the same time, our results raise another puzzle – a strong negative cross-country correlation within the 1978 to mid-1990s period between the magnitude of gender bias resulting from non-OECD trade and the decline in the relative female intensity of manufacturing employment. We attribute this result to the relative importance of domestic (as opposed to international trade) factors related both to female employment directly and to demand changes occurring as part of the long-term process of economic growth.

Manufacturing trade expansion and the female intensity of production

The last 20 years have seen the rapid expansion of world trade relative to output, that is, the trade share. Despite globalization, most of world trade continues to be among OECD countries. But an important contributor to the growing world trade share has been a rapid increase in import penetration by developing countries into the OECD. Table 10.1 shows the rise in import penetration in manufacturing from 1970 to 1995 for 10 countries. Import penetration rose over the period for every country. The figures are then broken out into trade with other OECD countries and with non-OECD countries.[3] The rise in import

Table 10.1 Import penetration for manufacturing industries, 1970–95 (imports as a percentage of domestic consumption)

	World	*OECD*	*Non-OECD*
Australia			
1970	16.3	15.1	1.2
1978	21.2	18.0	3.1
1990	23.8	19.8	4.1
1995	31.7	25.5	6.2
Canada			
1970	24.6	23.7	0.8
1978	30.9	29.7	1.2
1990	37.2	34.9	2.4
1995	49.7	46.3	3.4
Denmark			
1970	41.1	39.0	2.1
1978	42.4	40.1	2.4
1990	50.7	47.8	3.0
1995	52.4	49.3	3.1
France			
1970	14.7	13.4	1.4
1978	19.4	17.9	1.5
1990	29.6	27.3	2.3
1995	32.0	29.1	2.9

Table 10.1 Continued

	World	*OECD*	*Non-OECD*
Germany			
1970	13.4	12.0	1.4
1978	17.7	15.9	1.8
1990	25.0	22.6	2.4
1995	27.2	23.9	3.3
Italy			
1970	13.6	12.0	1.6
1978	17.3	15.6	1.6
1990	21.3	19.1	2.2
1995	27.2	24.2	3.0
Japan			
1970	4.0	2.9	1.1
1978	4.1	2.7	1.4
1990	6.8	4.5	2.3
1995	7.7	4.8	2.9
Netherlands			
1970	40.4	38.6	1.9
1978	49.0	46.4	2.7
1990	66.9	64.0	2.8
1995	70.7	66.5	4.2
UK			
1970	14.2	12.2	2.0
1978	22.5	20.2	2.3
1990	31.3	28.6	2.7
1995	36.7	33.0	3.8
USA			
1970	5.3	4.2	1.1
1978	8.5	6.3	2.2
1990	14.5	10.2	4.3
1995	17.9	11.9	6.0

Source: OECD *STAN Database for Industrial Analysis*, 1998a; OECD, *Bilateral Trade Database*, 1998b.

Note
Germany refers to the former West Germany except for 1995, for which trade data includes regions of the former East Germany.

penetration with non-OECD countries exceeded that with other OECD countries for each of these countries.

What have these trends in world manufacturing trade and especially North–South trade meant for the demand for male and female labor? Wood (1991) finds no clear relation between changes in manufacturing import penetration and female intensity of manufacturing relative to female intensity in the nontradeables sector (with female intensity defined as the number of females divided by the number of males multiplied by 100 and the nontradeables sector defined by Wood as all sectors except agriculture, manufacturing, and mining).

Wood notes (p. 176), "Surprisingly, given the expected effects of expanded North–South trade, [the results] show that there was not a general decline in the female intensity of developed-country manufacturing during 1960–85." He then breaks out blue-collar and white-collar employment and finds exactly the opposite of what he expected: female intensity for white-collar manufacturing employment fell relative to that in the nontradeables sector and for blue-collar workers, "where trade would be expected to have had more of an adverse impact," relative female intensity of manufacturing employment rose (Wood 1991: 180).

More recent data on the female percentage of manufacturing employment, presented in Table 10.2, appears consistent with Wood's asymmetry. In all countries except France, Germany, and the UK, the female percentage of manufacturing employment rose between 1978 and 1995. The female percentage of manufacturing employment is remarkably stable in the face of serious manufacturing trade deterioration. In this case the exceptions truly prove the rule: Germany and France are two of the countries which, as described later, do not show a gender bias from trade with non-OECD countries over this period.

The problem is that trade effects on female intensity in manufacturing have likely been swamped by domestic institutional forces regarding the decline of the male–female wage gap and changes in educational attainment, household relations, and family leave and health care policies of the private and public sectors. As Wood himself admits:

> Needless to say, other things affecting female labor supply and demand have not in fact been equal. Economic, social, legal and cultural changes have altered the availability of women for paid work and the willingness of employers to hire them. Moreover, these changes have occurred at varying speeds and to varying extents in different countries.
>
> (Wood 1991: 169)

Wood's response is to control for these other factors by normalizing the female intensity in manufacturing by female intensity of employment in the nontradeables sector. We do the same exercise for the 1978–94 period, normalizing the female percentage of manufacturing employment by the female percentage of employment in nontraded goods sectors. The results are summarized in Table 10.3. These ratios show a decline in the relative female percentage of manufacturing for all countries except Denmark. This is quite different from Wood's results, and we attribute that to the fact that we are looking at a different time period. For the more recent period that we are considering, the direct effects of trade on female employment resulting from the surge in developing country import penetration have had more time to work through. Moreover, and perhaps more important, the structural changes regarding female participation and sectoral demand have also played out over a longer period of time than the 1960 to mid-1980s period that Wood analyzed.

Table 10.2 Female percentage of manufacturing employment, 1975–97

	Australia	Canada	Denmark	France	Germany	Italy	Japan	Netherlands	UK	USA
1975		24.7	28.2	30.9	30.1		31.8	15.6	29.8	28.7
1976	26.0	25.8	28.5	30.9	30.0		32.7	14.8	29.3	29.5
1977	25.5	25.0	27.9	31.1	29.8	31.4	33.7	14.7	29.6	29.9
1978	25.4	25.6	28.3	31.0	30.1	31.3	34.4	15.2	29.5	30.4
1979	25.4	26.6	30.2	31.1	29.9	31.7	33.7	15.5	29.7	30.7
1980	25.3	26.9		30.9	30.4	32.1	34.0	16.3	29.4	31.1
1981	25.3	26.9	29.2	30.7	30.1	32.8	34.5	16.3	28.8	31.4
1982	25.3	27.2		30.6	29.5	32.9	34.1	16.4	28.7	31.9
1983	25.2	28.3	30.6	30.7	28.7	32.8	34.8	15.7	28.8	32.4
1984	25.6	28.2	31.3	30.8	28.9	32.8	34.9	16.2	29.3	32.5
1985	25.9	27.8	31.6	30.8	29.1	32.8	35.2	16.1	29.6	32.4
1986	26.3	28.7		30.7	28.8	32.7	35.4	16.2	29.7	32.6
1987	26.6	28.6		30.6	29.1	32.9	35.2	17.1	30.0	32.9
1988	27.0	28.6		30.4	28.9	32.8	35.3	18.4	30.2	32.9
1989	27.1	28.7		30.4	28.6	33.3	36.1	18.2	30.2	33.0
1990	28.0	28.8		30.5	29.8	33.6	36.1	19.6	30.2	32.9
1991	28.2	28.6		30.6	29.5	33.1	36.0	19.8	30.1	33.0
1992	28.0	28.7		30.5	29.5	32.7	35.7	20.2	30.1	32.9
1993	26.9	28.0		30.5	28.6		35.7	20.7	30.0	32.8
1994	27.2		32.4		28.7	31.7	35.1	19.8	29.7	32.7
1995	27.4		30.8		28.7		34.9	20.8	29.3	32.4
1996			31.4		28.6			20.9	28.8	32.2
1997			31.1		28.4			21.7		32.1

Source: ILO Yearbook of Labour Statistics, various years. Missing years were not published in this source.

Note

Germany refers to the former West Germany.

Table 10.3 Relative female intensity of employment, 1978–94

	Australia	Canada	Denmark	France	Germany	Italy	Japan	Netherlands	UK	USA
Female intensity of employment in manufacturing										
1978	34.0	34.4	39.4	45.0	43.1	45.5	52.5	17.9	41.7	43.7
1994	38.0	38.8	47.9	44.9	42.4	46.5	54.0	24.8	42.3	48.5
Female intensity of employment in nontraded goods sectors										
1978	71.1	76.5	97.5	77.3	71.6	41.6	61.3	53.8	93.6	84.2
1994	100.4	96.1	107.4	98.2	82.0	49.2	67.4	85.7	120.2	106.4
Ratio of female intensity of employment in manufacturing-to-nontraded goods sectors										
1978	0.48	0.45	0.40	0.58	0.60	1.09	0.86	0.33	0.45	0.52
1994	0.38	0.40	0.45	0.46	0.52	0.95	0.80	0.29	0.35	0.46
Difference	−0.10	−0.05	0.04	−0.12	−0.08	−0.15	−0.05	−0.04	−0.09	−0.06

Source: ILO *Yearbook of Labour Statistics*, various years.

Notes
Female intensity is defined as the number of female employees divided by the number of male employees in percent terms; nontraded goods sectors are defined as nonagricultural sectors minus manufacturing and mining; mining data are unavailable for Canada; all data are for paid employment, excluding self-employed and unpaid family workers; for Canada and France, data are for 1978 and 1993. For Germany, data are for 1978 and 1990.

Because of the presence of these well-known structural factors, we do not take the Table 10.3 figures as a necessary indication of a gender bias in the employment effects of changing trade patterns. A more direct measure of the gendered employment effects of trade expansion is one that Wood himself championed in his later work: factor content analysis (Wood 1994). We turn now to this approach, and return in the conclusion to the question of how to reconcile the results of Table 10.3 both with the Wood Asymmetry and with the cross-country gender bias pattern that the factor content analysis reveals.

Factor content algorithms

In keeping with much of the literature on employment effects of trade, we calculated the change in factor content resulting from a change in the structure of international trade.[4] As with Sachs and Shatz (1994: 28), the change in trade structure for each industry over the period from 1978 to 1995 is defined as follows:

$$T = [X^{95} - (X^{95}(x^{78}/x^{95}))] - [M^{95} - (M^{95}(m^{78}/m^{95}))] \tag{10.1}$$

where T is the vector of changes in total trade intensity, X, M are the vectors of export and import values, respectively, and, x, m are the vectors of export and import propensities, respectively. Export propensity, for example, is total exports divided by domestic production in the industry. Superscripts refer to the beginning and end of the period.[5]

The trade expansion vector gives the difference between actual export and import levels at the end of the period and what these levels would have been at the end of the period if the sectoral export and import propensities had remained constant over the period. That is, the trade expansion vector is the difference between actual net exports at the end of the period and counterfactual net exports, more clearly shown when equation (10.1) is rewritten as follows:

$$T = (X^{95} - M^{95}) - (X^{78} - M^{78})(Q^{95}/Q^{78}) \tag{10.2}$$

where Q is the vector of domestic production.

Since T is a measure of the effect of trade changes on final demand, total employment gains or losses resulting from the change in the structure of trade are given by:

$$L = \hat{E}[(I - A)^{-1}T] \tag{10.3}$$

Where L is the vector of changes in total employment associated with a change in the structure of world trade, $\hat{E}$ is the diagonal matrix of labor coefficients (employment per unit of output), I is the identity matrix, and A is the technical coefficients matrix. The female labor embodied in a given change in total trade structure is given by the following

$$L^f = \hat{G}L \tag{10.4}$$

where L^f is the vector of change in female employment associated with a change in the structure of trade, and, $\hat{G}$ is the diagonal matrix of female coefficients of employment (number of female employees divided by the number of total employees).

The residual is the change in male employment:

$$L^m = [1 - \hat{G}]L \tag{10.5}$$

where L^m is the vector of change in male employment associated with a change in the structure of trade.

Since our interest is mainly in North–South trade, we define the non-OECD trade intensity vector as follows:

$$T_n = [X_n^{95} - (X_n^{95}(x_n^{78}/x_n^{95}))] - [M_n^{95} - (M_n^{95}(m_n^{78}/m_n^{95}))] \tag{10.6}$$

where the subscript n refers to non-OECD trade and all else is as defined in (10.1). The employment changes for non-OECD trade may then be written as follows:

$$L_n = \hat{E}[(1 - A)^{-1}T_n] \tag{10.7}$$

$$L_n^f = \hat{G}L_n \tag{10.8}$$

$$L_n^m = [1 - \hat{G}]L_n \tag{10.9}$$

Employment effects of trade expansion

The employment effects of trade expansion are summarized in Table 10.4. Input–output data are from OECD (1995); output, total employment, and price deflator data are from OECD (1998a); and trade data are from OECD (1998b). Data on the female percentage of employment are from UNIDO (1999) and country sources.[6] The total effects of world trade relative to our counterfactual base-year trade position are largest for the USA, Japan, and the UK. Average annual employment is estimated to decline by over two million workers in the USA, 849,000 workers in Japan, and 651,000 workers in the UK as a result of world trade. The figure for the USA is larger than the 1.2 million found by Sachs and Shatz (1994: 7), but their calculation covered only the 1978–90 period. A number of countries had an increase in labor demand as a result of trade. Trade is estimated to have increased employment by 176,000 workers in the Netherlands, by 105,000 in Denmark, by 89,000 in Italy, and by 69,000 in Canada. Germany's trade was largely neutral for employment, with a loss of 15,000 workers (with magnitudes in worker years).

The large share of these employment effects accounted for by non-OECD trade is striking, especially given the still low *level* of import penetration by non-OECD countries, as shown in Table 10.1. For the USA, non-OECD trade accounted for

Table 10.4 Employment effects from trade of manufactures: absolute numbers (number of employees in worker years)

	Total	Male	Female
Australia (1978–92)			
World trade	−125,386	−93,927	−31,458
OECD trade	−94,965	−77,169	−17,796
Non-OECD trade	−30,421	−16,758	−13,663
Canada (1978–95)			
World trade	69,406	87,565	−18,159
OECD trade	280,025	221,000	59,025
Non-OECD trade	−210,619	−133,435	−77,184
Denmark (1978–94)			
World trade	105,492	73,431	32,061
OECD trade	126,087	85,156	40,931
Non-OECD trade	−20,595	−11,725	−8,870
France (1978–95)			
World trade	−85,627	−49,465	−39,122
OECD trade	92,471	58,368	25,389
Non-OECD trade	−178,099	−107,833	−64,511
Germany (1978–90)			
World trade	−14,996	−2,140	−12,856
OECD trade	412,340	303,973	108,367
Non-OECD trade	−427,336	−306,113	−121,223
Italy (1978–94)			
World trade	88,830	43,074	45,756
OECD trade	195,330	128,243	67,087
Non-OECD trade	−106,500	−85,169	−21,331
Japan (1978–95)			
World trade	−848,953	−436,795	−412,158
OECD trade	−273,556	−151,108	−122,448
Non-OECD trade	−575,397	−285,686	−289,710
Netherlands (1978–95)			
World trade	175,775	148,002	27,773
OECD trade	259,432	212,549	46,883
Non-OECD trade	−83,657	−64,547	−19,110
UK (1978–94)			
World trade	−651,041	−447,467	−203,574
OECD trade	−205,730	−147,002	−58,728
Non-OECD trade	−445,311	−300,465	−144,846
USA (1978–95)			
World trade	−2,026,870	−1,163,044	−863,826
OECD trade	−736,779	−513,726	−223,054
Non-OECD trade	−1,290,091	−649,319	−640,772

Source: OECD *STAN Database for Industrial Analysis*, 1998a; OECD *Bilateral Trade Database*, 1998b; OECD *Input–Output Database*, 1995. See notes to Table 10.6 for sources on female percentage of employment.

Table 10.5 Employment effects from trade of manufactures: relative to 1978–80 manufacturing employment (%) and measures of gender bias

	Relative to 1978–80 manufacturing employment (%)				Measures of gender bias	
	Total	Male	Female	Female – Male (%)	$((F^{95}/M^{95})/(F_{nt}^{95}/M_{nt}^{95}) - 1)*100$	$((F^{78} + T_f)/(M^{78} + T_m) - (F^{78}/M^{78}))*100$
Australia (1978–92)						
World trade	-10.40	-10.45	-10.28	0.16	1.02	0.06
OECD trade	-7.88	-8.58	-5.82	2.77	3.34	1.03
Non-OECD trade	-2.52	-1.86	-4.46	-2.60	-2.30	-0.90
Canada (1978–95)						
World trade	3.83	6.55	-3.84	-10.39	-10.81	-3.44
OECD trade	15.47	16.52	12.49	-4.03	-7.04	-1.22
Non-OECD trade	-11.63	-9.97	-16.34	-6.36	-4.36	-2.50
Denmark (1978–94)						
World trade	21.30	20.95	22.15	1.20	-4.23	0.41
OECD trade	25.46	24.29	28.28	3.99	-2.19	1.32
Non-OECD trade	-4.16	-3.34	-6.13	-2.78	-1.66	-1.19
France (1978–95)						
World trade	-1.56	-1.31	-2.29	-0.98	-1.35	-0.45
OECD trade	1.69	1.55	1.49	-0.06	-0.03	-0.03
Non-OECD trade	-3.25	-2.86	-3.78	-0.91	-1.30	-0.43
Germany (1978–90)						
World trade	-0.17	-0.03	-0.53	-0.49	-0.51	-0.19
OECD trade	4.62	4.69	4.43	-0.26	-0.20	-0.09
Non-OECD trade	-4.79	-4.72	-4.96	-0.24	-0.31	-0.09

Italy (1978–94)						
World trade	1.51	0.99	2.98	1.99	2.40	0.70
OECD trade	3.32	2.95	4.37	1.42	1.56	0.49
Non-OECD trade	−1.81	−1.96	−1.39	0.57	0.82	0.21
Japan (1978–95)						
World trade	−6.12	−4.79	−8.67	−3.88	−2.72	−2.12
OECD trade	−1.97	−1.66	−2.57	−0.92	−0.63	−0.49
Non-OECD trade	−4.14	−3.13	−6.09	−2.96	−2.16	−1.59
Netherlands (1978–95)						
World trade	17.16	17.13	17.34	0.21	−0.65	0.03
OECD trade	25.33	24.60	29.27	4.67	6.09	0.70
Non-OECD trade	−8.17	−7.47	−11.93	−4.46	−4.09	−0.89
UK (1978–94)						
World trade	−8.92	−8.46	−10.11	−1.65	−1.73	−0.69
OECD trade	−2.82	−2.78	−2.92	−0.14	−0.07	−0.05
Non-OECD trade	−6.10	−5.68	−7.20	−1.51	−1.73	−0.61
USA (1978–95)						
World trade	−9.92	−8.22	−13.74	−5.52	−4.23	−2.67
OECD trade	−3.60	−3.63	−3.55	0.08	0.47	0.04
Non-OECD trade	−6.31	−4.59	−10.19	−5.60	−4.81	−2.61

Sources: OECD *STAN Database for Industrial Analysis*, 1998a; OECD *Bilateral Trade Database*, 1998b; OECD; *Input–Output Database*, 1995. See notes to Table 10.6 for sources on female percentage of employment.

Notes

Measures of gender bias: the first measure is column 3 minus column 2; the second is the ratio of female-to-male employment with trade (i.e. based on actual employment in endpoint years) divided by the ratio of female-to-male employment with no trade (i.e. based on actual employment in endpoint years minus trade effects (columns 2 and 3 of Table 10.4)) minus one (as a percentage); the third is the ratio of female-to-male employment in 1978–80 plus trade effects (columns 2 and 3 of Table 10.4) divided by the ratio of female-to-male employment in 1978–80 (as a percentage).

1.29 million of the 2.03 million decline. For the UK and Japan, the non-OECD share is even higher. For France and Germany, increases in labor demand from trade with other OECD countries were more than offset by declines in labor demand brought about by trade expansion with non-OECD countries.

To better understand the magnitude of the employment effect and to address the question of gender bias, we calculated the employment effects in manufacturing as a percentage of the average total male and female manufacturing employment for the 1978–80 period. Table 10.5 gives the percent change in total male and female manufacturing employment from manufacturing trade expansion by country for world trade, non-OECD trade, and OECD trade.[7] The decline in the USA is 9.9 percent of total manufacturing employment.[8] Australia is the most negatively affected of the countries in our sample, with labor demand in manufacturing falling by 10.4 percent. The UK decline was 8.9 percent and for Japan the decline was 6.1 percent of manufacturing employment. The figure for Japan is surprising given their well-known export success. Using similar methods, Kucera (1998) finds that Japan is estimated to have gained employment from both world and OECD trade for the 1970–91 period, with estimated losses from non-OECD trade. Results for the 1978–91 period are similar to those for the 1978–95 period, indicating that Japan's negative employment effect is driven by weaker trade performance after the late 1970s.

The big success stories among these countries are Denmark, the Netherlands, and Canada, whose trade performance brought an increase in employment of 21.3, 17.2, and 3.8 percent respectively compared to the counterfactual. This may seem surprising in light of the high levels of import penetration in these countries, especially Denmark and the Netherlands (see Table 10.1). The explanation is that import penetration figures alone largely veil the role of export performance. For each of these three countries, and only these countries among the 10 in our study, the export propensities for world trade of manufactures rose more rapidly than import propensities in the 1978–95 period.

We present three ways of calculating the gender bias of the employment effects, and they are presented in Columns 4 through 6 of Table 10.5. In the first measure (Column 4), gender bias is captured by the simple difference in the percentage changes for male and female employment. The second measure (Column 5) is a proportional change indicator constructed by dividing the female-to-male employment ratio with trade (based on actual employment in endpoint years) by the female-to-male employment ratio with no trade (i.e. based on the actual employment in endpoint years minus trade effects from Columns 2 and 3 of Table 10.4), subtracting one, and multiplying by 100.[9]

If we arbitrarily designate a difference between male and female employment changes of greater than two percentage points to constitute a "gender bias," we see that for most of the countries in the sample, world trade did not have a gender-biased employment effect over the period from 1978–95. Only Canada, Japan, and the USA experienced such a bias and in each case it was against female employment. For trade expansion with other OECD countries, there was a gender bias in the employment effects for four countries (Australia, Canada, Denmark, and the Netherlands). Of these, only the Canadian bias is against women's employment, and this was a case of employment *gains* from trade: the bias was that male employment gains exceeded female employment gains by four percentage points.

If we consider non-OECD trade – the focus of the Wood study – then the number of countries that experienced gender-biased employment effects from trade expansion jumps to six: Australia, Canada, Denmark, Japan, the Netherlands, and the USA. In each case there is an employment decline and it is female employment that is estimated to fall disproportionately.

The spirit of these results is largely unchanged if we use the proportional change measure of gender bias (Column 5) and assign the designation "gender bias" to any change of greater than 2 percent. The cross-country results are unchanged except for Denmark, which now falls below the threshold.[10]

Tests of robustness

The input–output technique underpinning the factor content analysis has come under a variety of criticisms. To address these criticisms, we use some alternative estimates of employment effects. These alternatives also allow a test of the robustness of the results presented in Tables 10.4 and 10.5. One criticism is that the analysis does not account for technological change, an assumption that will directly impact the labor productivity figures and thus the measured employment effects.[11] To address this concern we recalculated all employment effects using average labor and technical coefficients over the 1978–95 period. The use of the average labor and technical coefficients led to the expected increase in all estimates of absolute employment effects (since it is based on lower productivity) but did not alter the nature of gender bias. In fact, cross-country differences in the two methods are very highly correlated with differences in productivity growth in manufacturing as a whole.

A second concern is that because trade volumes in some industries are highly volatile – lumpy – and thus it may be problematic to capture trade trends with export and import propensities in endpoint years. To address this we recalculated the employment effects excluding industries for which trade is highly volatile because of its lumpiness, where, for instance, a large order may take place every few years. These industries include shipbuilding and repairing, other transport (which includes railway cars), aircraft, and petroleum and coal products.[12]

The exclusion of industries with highly volatile trade data had little effect on the results, with the exception of Australia. For Australia, very large employment gains are estimated to occur in the petroleum and coal products industry, in which the female percentage of employment is very low. As a consequence, the gender bias of non-OECD trade drops considerably with the exclusion of trade-volatile sectors, from minus 2.6 to minus 1.2 percentage points.

A third criticism of factor content analysis is its failure to account for changes in labor market conditions over the period under study. To address this concern, we adjusted for the change in the female percentage of manufacturing employment

Table 10.6 Female percentage of manufacturing employment by industry

ISIC code and industry		Australia 1989	Canada 1990	Denmark 1990	France 1988	Germany 1990	Italy 1991	Japan 1990	Netherlands 1986	UK 1990	USA 1990	Unweighted average
31	Food, beverages and tobacco	31.0	32.3	43.4	35.6	42.2	26.5	54.5	23.5	39.0	32.5	36.1
32	Textiles, apparel, leather and leather goods	63.1	66.4	70.6	65.1	60.5	62.8	68.7	42.2	61.4	66.8	62.8
33	Wood products and furniture	16.6	16.5	24.4	29.1	20.8	23.3	30.8	9.7	18.8	22.2	21.2
34	Paper, paper products and printing	34.0	30.2	35.7	35.6	27.9	24.7	31.4	22.1	33.3	38.1	31.3
351 + 352 − 3522	Industrial chemicals	25.5	26.2	31.7	21.0	22.9	15.8	26.0	14.9	24.6	26.7	23.5
3522	Drugs and medicines	46.9	38.6	52.6	46.6	51.4	25.1	26.0	25.0	42.8	44.9	40.0
353 + 354	Petroleum and coal products	5.9	21.0	10.7	4.9	13.0	8.2	13.3	10.0	10.2	16.3	11.3
355 + 356	Rubber and plastic products	30.2	26.1	36.1	28.9	28.6	25.3	38.6	13.8	29.9	35.1	29.2
36	Nonmetallic mineral products	10.7	19.1	24.0	19.2	21.9	16.6	25.0	6.9	14.2	19.7	17.7
371	Iron and steel	7.3	7.7	16.0	8.4	8.5	6.8	10.9	6.9	6.8	10.1	9.0
372	Nonferrous metals	7.9	10.7	23.6	14.3	15.2	10.4	20.3	0.0	9.8	18.3	13.0
381	Fabricated metal products	17.3	17.8	21.7	18.5	22.0	17.3	26.9	8.2	18.1	22.2	19.0
382−3825	Nonelectrical machinery	13.3	19.6	20.5	19.2	15.7	13.5	20.5	8.0	16.1	18.4	16.5
3825	Office and computing machinery	32.5	32.9	28.8	32.7	30.1	24.8	41.9	16.0	24.0	34.2	29.8
383−3832	Electrical apparatus, other	31.7	29.8	36.0	34.2	31.8	29.3	41.9	16.0	29.2	42.9	32.3
3832	Radio, TV, and communication equipment	43.3	40.5	43.9	34.2	46.4	32.4	41.9	16.0	30.7	41.7	37.1

3841	Shipbuilding and repairing	7.7	8.9	9.4	14.3	6.0	4.1	18.5	6.3	8.4	13.8	9.7
3842 + 44 + 49	Other transport	4.2	7.6	20.3	14.3	11.5	9.8	18.5	6.3	7.5	21.9	12.2
3843	Motor vehicles	15.7	23.0	16.7	17.7	15.2	14.4	18.5	6.3	11.6	19.4	15.9
3845	Aircraft	10.8	20.7	15.0	14.3	14.1	10.3	18.5	6.3	12.2	22.6	14.5
385	Professional goods and precision instruments	47.5	40.5	43.2	19.2	40.2	38.0	37.9	22.2	31.9	41.4	36.2
39	Jewelry, musical instruments, toys, and sporting goods, misc.	33.9	41.7	50.3	N/A	50.4	54.1	49.6	19.3	44.6	46.4	43.4
3	Total female percentage of employment	27.1	28.5	33.9	30.6	27.1	27.3	36.3	16.2	28.2	32.9	28.8
	Male employment (in thousands)	774	1,505	338	2,931	5,194	2,000	7,348	804	3,445		12,792
	Female employment (in thousands)	288	600	173	1,293	1,926	751	4,190	155	1,353		6,285
	Total employment (in thousands)	1,061	2,105	511	4,223	7,120	2,751	11,538	959	4,798		19,077
	Manufacturing employment as a share of total civilian employment	14.9	16.0	22.8	21.6	31.6	22.1	24.1	19.3	25.5	18.0	21.6
	Female percentage of labor force	40.7	44.2	46.1	42.6	40.8	36.9	40.6	34.8	42.9	44.7	41.4

Source: For male and female employment: Australia, Denmark, Germany, Italy, and the United Kingdom: UNIDO *Industrial Statistics Database*, 1999; Canada: Statistics Canada *Labor Force Survey*; France: Ministere de l'Economie, des Finances et du Budget *Annuaire Statistique de la France*, 1990; Japan: Japan Ministry of Labor *Yearbook of Labor Statistics*, 1990; Netherlands: ILO *Yearbook of Labour Statistics*, 1988; United States: Bureau of Labor Statistics *Employment, Hours, and Earnings*, *United States, 1990–1995*. Source for manufacturing employment as a share of total civilian employment and female percentage of labor force: OECD *Historical Statistics, 1960–1995*.

Notes

Year represents year of input–output data from OECD Input–Output Database, 1995, or, in the case of France and Italy, nearest available year for which male–female employment data are available. (Input–output data is for 1990 for France and 1985 for Italy.); "—" under "ISIC Code and Industry" indicates subtraction; there are duplicate data for some industries in France, Japan, and the Netherlands, when data for these industries are combined in the original data sources.

between 1978 and the year of the female coefficients of employment (most often 1990), as follows:

$$L^f = \hat{G}[(I-A)^{-1}T](i^{78}/i^{90})$$
(10.10)

where i^{78} and i^{90} refer to female percentage of manufacturing employment. Thus if the female percentage of employment rose between 1978 and 1990 (as it did in all countries except Germany and France), the female employment effects are adjusted downward.[13] This allows us to abstract from changes in nontrade factors, including changes on the supply side of the labor market and demand effects of domestic origin. The adjustments, however, are small and the revised results are essentially unchanged from those presented in Table 10.5, especially the measure given in Column 5 of Table 10.5, with Denmark not experiencing a gender bias in the employment effect of manufacturing trade over the period.[14]

Industry-level analysis

What is driving these relatively robust results of the gender bias in employment effects of non-OECD trade expansion? For any given industry, female employment effects can be broken into four components: (a) labor productivity (the inverse of labor coefficients); (b) female percentage of employment; (c) trade imbalances and; (d) trade propensity changes. We can see these four components in the factor content algorithm. Writing out the full expression for female employment effects from non-OECD trade (by combining expressions (10.6)–(10.8)) gives the following:

$$L_n^f = \hat{G}\{\hat{E}\,[[(I-A)^{-1}][X_n^{95} - (X_n^{95}(x_n^{78}/x_n^{95})) \\ -(M_n^{95} - (M_n^{95}(m_n^{78}/m_n^{95})))]]\}$$
(10.11)

Gender bias could thus result from an industry profile in which some industries have a combination of disproportionately high female percentage of employment ($\hat{G} * 100$), low productivity ($I/\hat{E}$), large trade imbalances (X_n^{95}, M_n^{95}) or high growth of the import propensity relative to export propensity ((x_n^{78}/x_n^{95}), (m_n^{78}/m_n^{95})).

Table 10.6 shows the female percentage of employment by industry for each of the 10 OECD countries under consideration, in the base year provided by the year of the input–output data. With the exception of the Netherlands, the female percentage of employment for all of manufacturing was between 27.1 and 36.3 percent.[15] Within this narrow band of averages there is enormous variation across industries. On average (across the 10 countries) the most female-intensive industries are textiles, apparel, leather, and leather goods (62.8 percent), jewelry, musical instruments, toys and sporting goods (43.4 percent), drugs and medicines (40.0 percent), radio, TV, and communication equipment (37.1 percent), professional goods and precision instruments (36.2 percent), and food, beverages, and tobacco (36.1 percent). The least female-intensive industries were iron and steel (9.0 percent), shipbuilding and repairing (9.7 percent), petroleum and coal products (11.3 percent),

Table 10.7 Correlation coefficients for female percentage of manufacturing employment in 22 industries

									Mean:	0.90
Canada	0.94									
Denmark	0.93	0.91								
France	0.86	0.84	0.91							
Germany	0.93	0.93	0.97	0.88						
Italy	0.86	0.91	0.91	0.86	0.91					
Japan	0.82	0.84	0.86	0.84	0.86	0.90				
Netherlands	0.92	0.92	0.90	0.87	0.87	0.84	0.82			
UK	0.93	0.93	0.97	0.93	0.96	0.91	0.88	0.94		
USA	0.95	0.94	0.95	0.90	0.93	0.92	0.87	0.90		0.95
	Australia	Canada	Denmark	France	Germany	Italy	Japan	Netherlands	UK	

Source and Note: See Table 10.6.

other transport (12.2 percent), and nonferrous metals (13.0 percent). One possible explanation for the cross-country variation in gender bias is the differences in the female intensity of production. But we can quickly rule this out because of the strikingly high correlation across countries of the cross-industry variations in the female percentage of employment – at 0.90 on average, with all coefficients significant at the one-percent level – as shown in Table 10.7.[16] We leave the explanation of these correlation coefficients to future research and simply reiterate here that they indicate that gender segregation cannot account for cross-country variation in trade-based gender bias – since relative female intensities are essentially identical across the 10-country sample.[17]

Our results on gender bias then appear to be driven by a surprisingly simple phenomenon: the trade performance of the textiles, apparel, leather, and leather goods industry (which includes leather footwear). This industry is relatively labor-intensive, relatively female-intensive, and is a classically mature industry that has seen rapidly rising import penetration from non-OECD countries. To illustrate this point, we recalculated the factor content changes, this time excluding the textiles, apparel, leather, and leather goods industry. The results are reported in Table 10.8. The gender bias of non-OECD trade expansion is presented using three measures, as in Table 10.5. Using the same thresholds as before for the simple difference in percentage changes (Column 4) and the proportional change measure (Column 5), we see that the gender bias disappears in every case except that of Australia. And in almost every case (Canada, Denmark, Japan, the Netherlands, and the USA) the disappearance of the bias results from the difference in the effect on female employment resulting from the exclusion of this one industry – male employment effects being largely unchanged.[18]

The UK case is also instructive. There is no gender bias (by our definition) with or without the textiles, apparel, leather, and leather goods industry. But the exclusion of the industry from the factor content calculation results in a large swing from a slight employment effect against women's employment to a slight employment effect against men's employment. This simply reinforces our point about the importance of this one industry in our overall results: even in cases when the differential effect on male and female labor demand is small, the change

Table 10.8 Employment effects from trade of manufactures: excluding textiles, apparel, leather, and leather goods relative to 1978–80 manufacturing employment (%) and measures of gender bias

	Relative to 1978–80 manufacturing employment (%)				Measures of gender bias	
	Total	Male	Female	Female–Male (%)	$((F^{95}/M^{95})/(F_{nt}^{95}/M_{nt}^{95})-1)*100$	$((F^{78}+T_f)/(M^{78}+T_m)-(F^{78}/M^{78}))*100$
Australia (1978–92)						
World trade	−11.57	−11.08	−13.02	−1.95	−0.80	−0.74
OECD trade	−9.20	−9.29	−8.91	0.38	1.13	0.14
Non-OECD trade	−2.37	−1.78	−4.11	−2.32	−2.06	−0.81
Canada (1978–95)						
World trade	6.46	7.84	2.56	−5.28	−6.45	−1.73
OECD trade	15.17	16.39	11.71	−4.68	−7.69	−1.42
Non-OECD trade	−8.71	−8.55	−9.16	−0.60	0.46	−0.23
Denmark (1978–94)						
World trade	20.17	20.41	19.60	−0.81	−6.14	−0.28
OECD trade	22.57	22.88	21.84	−1.04	−7.19	−0.35
Non-OECD trade	−2.40	−2.46	−2.24	0.22	0.71	0.10
France (1978–95)						
World trade	−0.33	−0.61	0.10	0.72	0.96	0.33
OECD trade	1.73	1.58	1.58	0.00	0.06	0.00
Non-OECD trade	−2.07	−2.19	−1.47	0.72	0.89	0.33
Germany (1978–90)						
World trade	0.39	0.31	0.60	0.29	0.31	0.11
OECD trade	4.38	4.55	3.94	−0.60	−0.57	−0.22
Non-OECD trade	−3.99	−4.24	−3.34	0.90	0.83	0.35

Italy (1978–94)						
World trade	0.06	0.17	−0.23	−0.39	−0.49	−0.14
OECD trade	1.95	2.17	1.32	−0.85	−1.20	−0.29
Non-OECD trade	−1.88	−2.00	−1.55	0.46	0.68	0.16
Japan (1978–95)						
World trade	−3.28	−3.33	−3.17	0.16	0.39	0.08
OECD trade	−1.29	−1.31	−1.26	0.05	0.14	0.03
Non-OECD trade	−1.98	−2.02	−1.91	0.11	0.25	0.06
Netherlands (1978–95)						
World trade	15.24	15.74	12.52	−3.22	−4.98	−0.52
OECD trade	20.36	21.01	16.89	−4.12	−6.80	−0.63
Non-OECD trade	−5.12	−5.26	−4.36	0.90	1.18	0.18
UK (1978–94)						
World trade	−6.46	−7.02	−4.98	2.04	3.03	0.84
OECD trade	−2.22	−2.43	−1.66	0.77	1.19	0.30
Non-OECD trade	−4.24	−4.59	−3.32	1.27	1.94	0.51
USA (1978–95)						
World trade	−6.21	−6.25	−6.11	0.14	0.78	0.07
OECD trade	−3.22	−3.43	−2.75	0.68	1.06	0.31
Non-OECD trade	−2.99	−2.82	−3.36	−0.54	−0.25	−0.25

Source: OECD *STAN Database for Industrial Analysis*, 1998a; OECD *Bilateral Trade Database*, 1998b; OECD *Input–Output Database*, 1995. See notes to Table 10.6 for sources on female percentage of employment.

Note

* See notes to Table 10.5 (except that trade employment effects in absolute terms are not shown for analysis excluding ISIC 32).

in the differential is large if we exclude the textiles, apparel, leather, and leather goods industry.

The reason that the textiles, apparel, leather, and leather goods industry plays such a crucial role is that it is both relatively labor-intensive and female-intensive, and in many countries had a large trade deficit along with a relatively rapid increase in import propensity relative to export propensity for non-OECD trade. As shown in Table 10.9, labor productivity in the industry is on average about one-half that of manufacturing as a whole. Moreover, the female percentage of employment in the industry is more than twice the average for manufacturing as a whole. Note that for both relative labor productivity and relative female intensity, the standard deviations of the 10-country sample are very small (0.12 and 0.20), with coefficients of variation of 0.21 and 0.09, respectively. This is not the case for trade deficits, as shown in Table 10.10. While all countries except Italy experienced a deterioration in the non-OECD trade balance for the industry over the sample period (Column 3), the relative extent of the deterioration varied considerably. The picture is also evident by looking at the trade propensities, shown in Table 10.11. Six countries experienced a greater increase in import propensity than export propensity while the other four actually had a greater increase in the export propensity compared to import propensity. The countries with a greater increase in import propensity are Canada, France, Japan, the Netherlands, UK, and USA – largely the same countries for which this industry mattered most in creating a gender bias from non-OECD trade.

Figure 10.1 is a scatter plot of the gender bias of the employment effect (Column 5 from Table 10.5) and the change in net exports relative to domestic consumption in the textiles, apparel, leather, and leather goods industry (Column 5 from Table 10.10), both as regards non-OECD trade. The relation is clearly positive: countries with better trade performance in this industry are those with less gender bias. The USA, Canada, the Netherlands, and Denmark, with among the largest deficits (relative to total trade) are those countries with the largest gender bias. The correlation coefficient of 0.73 is statistically significant at the five-percent level.

Note also that excluding the textiles, apparel, leather, and leather goods industry affects the measured bias from trade expansion with other OECD countries (Table 10.8). The bias disappears for Australia. The gender bias against men's employment for Denmark and the Netherlands is reversed and the balance instead becomes a bias against women's employment. This last result reflects that the direction of trade expansion in this industry differed strongly for trade within and outside the OECD.

A new puzzle?

The factor content analysis of gender bias in manufacturing employment due to trade (Table 10.5) confirms the results of the relative female intensity of manufacturing employment (Table 10.3) that there was a broadly shared gender bias in the employment effects of manufacturing trade expansion. On closer look, however, these two independently derived sets of results present a new puzzle. Specifically,

Table 10.9 Labor productivity and female percentage of employment in the textiles, apparel, leather, and leather goods industry

	Base year	Labor productivity (output/employee in millions of national currency in base year)			Female percentage of employment		
		ISIC 32	Total manufacture	Relative labor productivity (Column 1/Column 2)	ISIC 32	Total manufacture	Relative female percentage (Column 4/Column 5)
Australia	1989	0.08	0.13	0.64	63.09	27.12	2.33
Canada	1990	0.08	0.17	0.48	66.43	28.51	2.33
Denmark	1990	0.50	0.69	0.72	70.55	33.87	2.08
France	1988	0.49	0.81	0.61	65.11	30.61	2.13
Germany	1990	0.16	0.22	0.69	60.54	27.05	2.24
Italy	1991	76.37	113.48	0.67	62.76	27.31	2.30
Japan	1990	7.37	22.05	0.33	68.69	36.31	1.89
Netherlands	1986	0.18	0.28	0.62	42.22	16.16	2.61
UK	1990	0.03	0.06	0.48	61.37	28.20	2.18
USA	1990	0.08	0.15	0.50	66.80	32.95	2.03
Mean				0.58	62.76	28.81	2.21
Standard deviation				0.12	7.89	5.49	0.20
Coefficient of variation				0.21	0.13	0.19	0.09

Sources: OECD *STAN Database for Industrial Analysis*, 1998a; see notes to Table 10.6 for sources on female percentage of employment. For labor productivity "Base Year" represents year of input–output data from OECD Input–output Database (1995). For female percentage of employment, "Base Year" represents year of input–output data from OECD *Input–output Database* (1995), or in the case of France and Italy, nearest available year for which male–female employment data are available. (Input–output data are for 1990 for France and 1985 for Italy.)

Table 10.10 Trade deficits with non-OECD countries for the textiles, apparel, leather, and leather goods industry

	Base year	Trade deficit (in thousands of constant national currency in base year)			Trade deficit in 1993–5 as a percentage of total trade in 1993–5 $(X − M)/(X+M)*100$	Change in trade performance 1978–80 to 1993–5
		1978–80	1993–5	Percent change 1978–80 to 1993–5		
Australia	1989	−1,093	−1,314	20.22	−40.86	−1.36
Canada	1990	−1,800	−3,866	114.81	−92.78	−12.65
Denmark	1990	−2,879	−4,911	70.61	−68.27	−12.98
France	1988	−6,401	−24,158	277.42	−40.96	−8.70
Germany	1990	−10,774	−15,687	45.60	−57.96	−5.51
Italy	1991	−508,954	−379,688	−25.40	−3.03	0.28
Japan	1990	−41,903	−1,438,483	3332.86	−55.61	−9.68
Netherlands	1986	−1,612	−4,091	153.88	−61.95	−23.95
UK	1990	−1,356	−3,478	156.58	−65.35	−11.77
USA	1990	−8,030	−39,056	386.40	−68.60	−14.88
Mean				453.30	−55.54	−10.12
Standard deviation				1019.20	23.68	6.99
Coefficient of variation				2.25	−0.43	−0.69

Sources: OECD *STAN Database for Industrial Analysis*, 1998a; OECD *Bilateral Trade Database*, 1998b; OECD *Input–Output Database*, 1995. See notes to Table 10.6 for sources on female percentage of employment.

Notes

"Base Year" represents year of input–output data from OECD *Input–Output Database*, 1995; deficits represent three-year averages. For some countries, data do not run to 1993–5. See span of years following country headings in Tables 10.4, 10.5, or 10.8 in this regard. Trade performance is defined as net exports relative to domestic consumption in percent terms, or $((Xn − Mn)/(Q+M−X)) * 100$, where subscript n = non-OECD, X = exports, M = imports, and Q = domestic output, with change referring to the percentage point difference between the 1993–5 and 1978–80 periods.

Table 10.11 Export and import propensities with non-OECD countries for the textiles, apparel, leather, and leather goods industry (non-OECD exports and imports in relation to domestic production)

	Export propensity 1978–80	Export propensity 1993–5	Ratio of change (Column 2/ Column 1)	Import propensity 1978–80	Import propensity 1993–5	Ratio of change (Column 4/ Column 5)	Difference in ratios (Column 3 – Column 6)
Australia	0.031	0.100	3.19	0.162	0.238	1.46	1.73
Canada	0.008	0.012	1.46	0.113	0.319	2.81	−1.35
Denmark	0.030	0.072	2.40	0.189	0.384	2.03	0.36
France	0.036	0.092	2.53	0.063	0.220	3.51	−0.98
Germany	0.037	0.070	1.90	0.154	0.263	1.71	0.19
Italy	0.027	0.063	2.37	0.033	0.067	2.02	0.34
Japan	0.058	0.046	0.80	0.061	0.162	2.67	−1.87
Netherlands	0.101	0.158	1.57	0.279	0.674	2.41	−0.84
UK	0.046	0.061	1.31	0.111	0.291	2.62	−1.30
USA	0.033	0.059	1.79	0.090	0.318	3.54	−1.76
Mean	0.041	0.073	1.93	0.125	0.293	2.48	−0.55
Standard deviation	0.025	0.038	0.70	0.073	0.161	0.70	1.16
Coeff. of variation	0.607	0.524	0.36	0.583	0.548	0.28	−2.11

Sources: OECD *STAN Database for Industrial Analysis*, 1998; OECD *Bilateral Trade Database*, 1998b.

Notes

Export and import propensities represent three-year averages. For some countries, data do not run to 1993–5. See span of years following country headings in Tables 10.4, 10.5, or 10.8 in this regard.

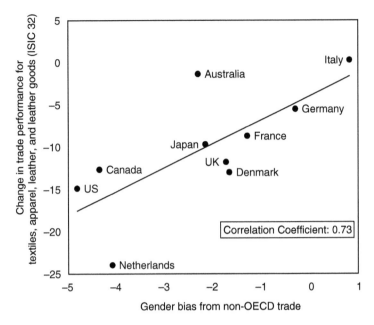

Figure 10.1 Gender bias from non-OECD trade and change in trade performance for textiles, apparel, leather, and leather goods.

Notes:
Gender bias from non-OECD trade is from column 5 of Table 5 and defined therein; trade performance is defined as net exports relative to domestic consumption in percent terms, or $((Xn-Mn)/(Q+M-X))$ * 100, where subscript n=non-OECD, X= exports, M=imports, and Q=domestic output, with change referring to the percentage point difference between the 1993–5 and 1978–80 periods.

those countries with a larger decline in the relative female intensity of manufacturing employment had a smaller gender bias as measured by the factor content analysis. To better compare these two approaches to the gender bias question, we calculated a new indicator of gender bias from the factor content data. This measure is the ratio of female-to-male employment in 1978–80 plus trade effects (Columns 2 and 3 of Table 10.4) minus the ratio of female-to-male employment in 1978–80 in percent terms. The measure is given in Column 6 of Table 10.5. Comparing this measure with the changes in relative female intensity (last row of Table 10.3) we find there is a negative cross-country correlation, with a correlation coefficient of −0.51. If we exclude Denmark from the calculation, the one country for which the relative female intensity of manufacturing employment rose, the correlation coefficient is −0.73.

How can we explain this apparent puzzle? Putting aside the question of data errors, we suggest that the answer lies in the failure to control for the myriad of social, political, demographic, and economic changes that determine the female intensity of manufacturing employment relative to female employment in non-traded sectors. Different labor market, health care, and family-related policies may play a role. Variations in industrial composition may matter. Also, women's employment is concentrated in the production of goods (food, beverages, and tobacco; textiles, apparel, leather, and leather goods) for which the income elasticity of demand is relatively low. This Engel's law effect creates a persistent relative demand shift away from women's manufacturing employment for reasons having nothing to do with foreign trade. Since we have not controlled for these structural changes in the female intensity data, we cannot expect this measure to be consistent, much less highly correlated, with a measure based on purely trade-related employment effects.

Conclusion: explaining national differences in gender bias

In this chapter we tried to measure the degree of gender bias in the employment effects of the expansion of international trade for 10 OECD countries. Focusing on trade with developing countries we found that in most cases a gender bias did exist. North–South trade of manufactures has in many industrialized countries reduced female employment relatively more than male employment. Globalization of production does not seem to be the win-win situation for Northern and Southern women workers found by Wood in his "asymmetry." Our results constitute a reconfirmation of the earlier studies by Schumacher and Baldwin.

The gender bias varied considerably across countries, however, and was nonexistent in some. How can we explain the cross-country differences in the effect of trade expansion on female employment? Given the high cross-industry correlation of female intensity among OECD countries, we must rule out a role for gender segregation. And given that the gender bias in most cases disappears completely when the textiles, apparel, leather, and leather goods industry is excluded from the analysis, the different national outcome is not the result of some broad-based increase in international outsourcing, which is typically identified as one of the key causes of expanding world trade. Instead, the results appear to hinge on the issue of how well a nation's textiles, apparel, leather, and leather goods industry responded to foreign competition. Those with a disproportionately large drop in female manufacturing employment as a whole are those countries that saw the worst trade performance in this industry. Italy, for example, is well-known for its continued importance in the international fashion industry. On the other hand, the USA experienced one of the largest increases in import penetration in that sector among industrialized countries, due in part to preponderance of large firms, in particular retailers, and their propensity for outsourcing (especially in Asia), and in part to its preferential treatment of Latin American and Caribbean nations in textiles trade.[19] For sure, the gradual phaseout of the Multifiber Arrangement under the Uruguay Round Agreement will have important implications for the gender bias of labor market changes in the future.

While our results appear, for now, to overturn the Wood Asymmetry, they seem to raise another paradox. Those countries with a larger gender bias according to the factor content analysis generally had a smaller decline in the relative female intensity of manufacturing employment. We explained this by appealing to a host of social and political forces that determine the female intensity of employment, the combined effect of which is likely to be very different from the effects of international trade *per se* relative to a narrowly defined counterfactual trade scenario.

Appendix 10.A Data notes

This study makes use of the OECD's *STAN Structural Analysis* databases, the *Input–Output Database* (1995) for input–output data, the *Bilateral Trade Database* (1998) for trade data, and the *STAN Database for Industrial Analysis* (1995, 1998) for output, total employment, and price deflator data (the last derived from data on value added in real and nominal terms, which are not provided for Australia in the 1998 edition and for which the 1995 edition is used). These datasets have the advantage of being largely standardized by industry classification, following what the OECD calls an "Adjusted ISIC Revision 2 Classification," for which there are 22 distinct manufacturing industries. The classification scheme is shown in Table 10.6 by both ISIC code and industry description.

The OECD *Input–Output Database* provides data only on the 10 countries considered in this paper. For the bulk of the analysis, input–output data are used for the most recent year available, usually 1990. These are the "Base Years" noted in Tables 10.9 and 10.10, which also show the deviations from 1990. For the construction of average technical coefficients for the 1978–95 period, technical coefficients derived from input–output data for the most recent year are averaged with technical coefficients derived from input–output data for the mid- to late-1970s (Australia 1974; Japan 1975; Canada 1976; Denmark, France, the Netherlands, and the USA 1977; Germany 1978, and the UK 1979). For Italy, input–output data are for 1985 only, and thus no analysis is done using average technical coefficients (only average labor coefficients). For Australia, Denmark, Germany, and the Netherlands, input–output data do not perfectly conform to the "Adjusted ISIC Revision 2 Classification." Thus data from the *STAN Database for Industrial Analysis* and *Bilateral Trade Database* are modified to match the input–output data for these countries whenever feasible. For Australia, ISIC 3832 also includes ISIC 3825; for Denmark, ISIC 382−3825 also includes ISIC 3825 and ISIC 3843 also includes 3842 + 44 + 49 and 3845; for Germany, ISIC 351 + 352 also includes ISIC 3522 and ISIC 383−3832 also includes ISIC 3832 (ISIC 3842 + 44 + 49 is omitted, as input–output data for it is spread among industries in such a way that a correction is not feasible); for the Netherlands, ISIC 371 also includes ISIC 372 and ISIC 383−3832 also includes ISIC 3832.

Regarding the definition of the OECD and non-OECD regions in the *Bilateral Trade Database*, the data documentation states: "The relatively new OECD member countries (Czech Republic, Hungary, South Korea, Mexico and Poland) are currently included in the Non-OECD" region.

Whenever possible, the analysis uses data from 1978–95. As a result of missing employment and production data, however, the analysis runs only to 1992 for Australia and 1994 for Denmark, Italy, and the UK. For Germany (i.e. the former

West Germany), trade data include regions of the former East Germany after 1990, and thus the analysis runs only to 1990. In addition, employment data in Australia for ISIC 3845 begin only in 1981; employment data in Japan for ISIC 3842 + 44 + 49 and ISIC 3825 begin only in 1984. Thus other data for these industries in these two countries are also truncated to match the shorter period. Employment and production data for ISIC 3842 + 44 + 49 are missing for all years for Australia, Canada, Denmark, the Netherlands, and the USA; employment and production data for ISIC 3845 are missing for all years for Denmark. These industries in these countries are thus excluded from the analysis.

Industry-level price deflators are used in the construction of average labor coefficients. Price data are missing for eight of the 10 countries for ISIC 3825, Office and Computing Equipment. Thus labor coefficients for the year of the input–output data are used for this industry.

For industry-level data on the female percentage of manufacturing employment, data for Australia, Denmark, Germany, Italy, and the UK are from the UNIDO *Industrial Statistics Database* (1999), for which data are classified by ISIC code. (For France and Netherlands, the UNIDO dataset does not provide data on the number of women employees; for Japan and the USA, UNIDO data are not available in the year of the most recent input–output data; for Canada, data from Statistics Canada is of equivalent quality to UNIDO data.) For Netherlands, data are from the ILO *Yearbook of Labour Statistics* and are also classified by ISIC code. For the other four countries, sources are noted in Table 10.6. Using the industry classifications provided in the country data sources, matches with the OECD data are shown in Table 10.A as follows (where "–" indicates subtraction).

Industry-level data on men and women's manufacturing employment (used to construct $\hat{G}$) are for the same year as the most recent year of input–output data, with two exceptions. For Italy, the data are for 1991 (the most recent input–output data is for 1985); for France, the data are for 1988 (the most recent input–output data is for 1990). UNIDO data do not go back to the 1978–80 period. Thus data from the ILO *Yearbook of Labour Statistics* are used to obtain the female percentage of employment for the manufacturing sector as a whole for the 1978–80 period, necessary for the estimates of gender bias in relation to average employment in 1978–80. There are some differences, generally very small, in the female percentage of manufacturing employment between the ILO and other data (from UNIDO and country sources). Thus adjustments are made to the average female percentage of employment for the 1978–80 period from the ILO data. The assumption is made that the difference between the ILO and other data in the 1978–80 period is proportionate to the difference in the year of the industry-level data on men and women's manufacturing employment. (That is, the average female percentage of employment for 1978–80 for the manufacturing sector as a whole is divided by f^{ilo}/f^{unido}, where the numerator stands for female percentage of employment from the ILO *Yearbook of Labour Statistics* and the denominator stands for the female percentage of manufacturing employment from the UNIDO dataset or country sources, with both terms for the manufacturing sector as a whole in the year of industry-level data on men and women's employment.)

Table 10.A Industry classification and OECD data

Adj. ISIC Rev. 2	Canada 1980 SIC	France (NAP 40)	Japan	USA 1987 SIC
31	101 − 122	02, 03	12 − 13	20, 21
32	171 − 249	18, 19	14, 15, 24	22, 23
33	251 − 269	20	16, 17	24, 25
34	271 − 284	21, 22	18, 19	26, 27
351 + 352 − 3522	371 − 379 − 374	11	20	28 − 283
3522	374	12	20	283
353 + 354	361, 369	4	21	29
355 + 356	151 − 169	23	22, 23	30
36	351 − 359	10	25	32
371	291 − 294	7	26	331, 332
372	295 − 299	8	27	333, 335, 336
381	301 − 309	13	28	34
382 − 3825	311 − 319	14	29	35 − 357
3825	336	15A	30	357
383 − 3832	331 − 333, 337 − 339	15A, 15B	30	36 − 366
3832	334, 335	15A, 15B	30	366
3841	327, 328	17	31	373
3842 + 44 + 49	326, 329	16	31	37 − (371 + 372 + 373)
3843	323 − 325	16	31	371
3845	321	17	31	372
385	391	14	32	38
39	392 − 399	N/A	33–34	39

This enables one to make best use of the continuity over time provided by the ILO data and the industry detail provided by data from UNIDO and country sources. In any case, the analysis is quite robust in this regard. The exception is Denmark, for which there are no years of overlap between the ILO and UNIDO data. Thus data for 1978–81 (data for 1980 are not published) are used straight from the ILO *Yearbook of Labour Statistics*.

Notes

1 We thank Hui Gao and Frank Schroeder for excellent research assistance and Richard Anker for suggesting the use of the UNIDO *Industrial Statistics Database*. This research was supported by a grant from the John D. and Catherine T. MacArthur Foundation.

2 Throughout this study, Germany refers exclusively to the former West Germany or the regions of the former West Germany, except as noted in Table 10.1 for 1995.

3 Throughout this study, the newer members of the OECD (the Czech Republic, Hungary, Poland, Mexico, and South Korea) are included among the non-OECD countries.

4 See, for example, Schumacher (1984), Sachs and Shatz (1994), Wood (1994), Lee and Schmitt (1996), and Kucera (1998).

5 The endpoints were calculated as three-year averages. Thus "78" refers to the average for 1978–80 and "95" refers to the average for 1993–5. These averages are used to account for the volatility of export and import propensities. In order to match the averages for export and import propensities and export and import levels in 1993–5,

three-year averages are also used for employment levels in the beginning of the period 1978–80 and the female percentage of employment for the manufacturing sector as a whole in the beginning of the period 1978–80, in regards to results in Tables 10.5 and 10.8, for instance. For some countries, data do not run to 1993–5. See span of years following country headings in Tables 10.4, 10.5, or 10.8 in this regard.

6 See Appendix 10.A for more information.

7 OECD trade is simply the difference between world and non-OECD trade.

8 This compares to the 5.9 percent decline found by Sachs and Shatz (1994: table 13).

9 A third measure of gender bias (shown in Column 6) is the ratio (in percentage terms) of female-to-male employment in 1978–80 plus trade effects (Columns (2) and (3) of Table 10.4) minus the ratio of female-to-male employment in 1978–80. This measure is most useful for a comparison with the Table 10.3 figures on the change in the relative female intensity of manufacturing employment. We discuss this comparison later.

10 Dropping Denmark from the group that experienced a gender bias employment effect from trade is also indicated by another calculation in which the employment effects were adjusted for changes in the female percentage of manufacturing employment. This exercise is discussed later.

11 See Leamer (1994) and the response in Wood (1995).

12 These industries were identified by examining the growth rates of exports and imports. The volatility of the petroleum and coal products industry is likely the result of price volatility. Indirect demands for these industries' output from other industries were included in the analysis, since these indirect demands have no bearing on the trade volatility of the four problematic industries.

13 Effects on male employment were taken as the difference between total and female employment changes.

14 Results of the exercises described in this and the previous paragraphs are available from the authors on request.

15 The low level of female participation in the Netherlands is partly explained by the fact that policies that support employment for mothers with children are very limited by European standards. See Gornick, Meyers, and Ross (1998, table 1).

16 Note that the Spearman correlation coefficient average is 0.88, with all coefficients again significant at the one-percent level.

17 Gender segregation is labor market segmentation along gender lines. We take wide variations in female intensity across industries to be an indication of gender segregation.

18 That is, we are comparing the non-OECD trade employment effects in Tables 10.5 and 10.8.

19 See Christerson and Appelbaum (1995) for a discussion of the determinants of outsourcing behavior in the USA apparel sector.

References

Baldwin, R. (1984) "Trade policies in developed countries," in R. Jones and P. Kenen (eds), *Handbook of International Economics*, vol. 1, Amsterdam: Elsevier Science Publishing: 571–620.

Christerson, B. and Appelbaum, E. (1995) "Global and local subcontracting: space, ethnicity, and the organization of apparel production," *World Development*, 23 (8): 363–74.

Gornick, J., Meyers, M., and Ross, K. (1998) "Public policies and the employment of mothers: a cross-national study," *Social Science Quarterly*, 79 (1): 35–54.

Kucera, D. (1998) "Foreign trade and men's and women's employment and earnings in Germany and Japan," CEPA Working Paper No. 9, New York: Center for Economic Policy Analysis (CEPA), New School University.

Leamer, E. (1994) "Trade, wages and revolving-door ideas," Working Paper No. 4716, Cambridge, MA: National Bureau of Economic Research.

Lee, T. and Schmitt, J. (1996) "Trade and income distribution: theory, new evidence, and policy alternatives," Washington, DC: Economic Policy Institute.

OECD (1995) *Input-Output Database*, Paris: OECD.

—— (1998a) *STAN Database for Industrial Analysis*, Paris: OECD.

—— (1998b) *Bilateral Trade Database*, Paris: OECD.

Sachs, J. and Shatz, H. (1994) "Trade and jobs in USA manufacturing," *Brookings Papers on Economic Activity*, 1: 1–84.

Schumacher, D. (1984) "North–South trade and shifts in employment," *International Labor Review*, 123 (3): 333–48.

UNIDO (1999) *Industrial Statistics Database*, Vienna: UNIDO.

Wood, A. (1991) "North–South trade and female labor in manufacturing: an asymmetry," *Journal of Development Studies*, 27 (2): 168–89.

—— (1994) *North–South Trade, Employment and Inequality: changing fortunes in a skill-driven world*, Oxford: Clarendon Press.

—— (1995) "How trade hurt unskilled workers," *Journal of Economic Perspectives*, 9 (3): 57–80.

11 Importing equality or exporting jobs?

Competition and gender wage and employment differentials in US manufacturing

Ebru Kongar

Introduction

Despite intense interest in the impact of trade expansion on men and women workers in US manufacturing sector, there are surprisingly few empirical studies, and available studies indicate contradictory findings. Focusing on the pre-NAFTA period, a few studies have found benign or positive effects of trade expansion on female share of manufacturing employment or decline in the gender wage gap (Wood 1991; Black and Brainerd 2004). These results are inconsistent with predictions of standard trade theory and other empirical studies. The widely accepted version of comparative advantage trade theory predicts relative losses for less-skilled workers in industrialized economies compared to skilled workers when trade expands. This prediction is supported by studies that show widening wage inequality between skilled and less-skilled workers in the US (Katz and Murphy 1992; Borjas and Ramey 1994, 1995). To the extent that women are the less-skilled workers in the US, they are expected to experience disproportionate job losses and wage declines as a result of the changing trade patterns. A number of empirical studies find evidence for the adverse effect of trade on relative employment opportunities of women in the traded (manufacturing) sector (Schumacher 1984; Katz and Murphy 1992; Kucera and Milberg 2000; Kucera 2001).

This study examines these contradictory findings by pursuing a gender- and class-(occupation)differentiated analysis of wage and employment effects of increased import competition in US manufacturing over the 1976–93 period. The specific objective of this chapter is to investigate whether the findings that trade expansion caused a decline in female share of US manufacturing employment can be reconciled with the finding that increased import competition reduced the gender wage discrimination in US manufacturing over the same period. Contrary to Black and Brainerd's (2004) importing equality argument, which interprets import expansion as an instrument of increased domestic competition among firms that has reduced the discriminatory wage differential enjoyed by male workers in concentrated industries, this study develops an alternative account of the decline in the gender wage gap. The decline in the gender wage inequality in import-impacted, concentrated sectors is unlikely to indicate a decline in discrimination against women workers. Rather, the fall in gender wage inequality is most likely the outcome of job losses and wage adjustments in response to increasing imports in concentrated industries that have led to an increase in women's wages, without an increase in relative demand for female labor.

International trade, wages, and employment

The Hecksher–Ohlin–Samuelson (H–O–S) theory of international trade predicts that trade expansion will increase relative demand for the factor of production that is intensively used in the production of goods in which the country has comparative advantage. Accordingly, in industrialized countries, trade expansion will increase demand for more-skilled workers compared to less-skilled workers. The opposite will hold in developing countries. Given that women comprise a disproportionate share of less-skilled workers both in industrialized and developing countries, trade expansion will reduce the relative demand for women in industrialized countries and increase it in developing countries.

There has indeed been an increase in women's share in employment in developing economies associated with trade liberalization, in particular, the shift to export orientation (Standing 1989, 1999; Çağatay and Berik 1990, 1994; Wood 1991; Joekes and Weston 1994; Çağatay and Özler 1995; Joekes 1995; Çağatay 1996; Mehra and Gammage 1999; Tzannatos 1999; Özler 2000). However, the so-called feminization of employment was not accompanied by an improvement in gender pay differentials. On the contrary, export-orientation in developing countries has been linked to persistent wage gaps (Seguino 1997; Berik 2000), even increases in the discriminatory wage differentials between men and women (Maurer-Fazio and Hughes 2002; Berik *et al.* 2004; Packard 2004).

The literature on the trade impact in industrialized countries, in general, and the US in particular, is gender-blind for the most part. Studies that tested the predictions of H–O–S theory found evidence of increasing skill differentials in wages and employment levels in the US. Specifically, although there is no consensus over its magnitude, there is now enough evidence to suggest that increasing trade expansion over the past several decades caused declines in relative demand for less-educated and experienced workers in the US economy (Bluestone and Harrison 1988; Bound and Johnson 1992; Katz and Murphy 1992; Murphy and Welch 1992; Berman *et al.* 1994; Bertola and Ichino 1995). There is also evidence to suggest that relative demand for production workers declined compared to nonproduction workers (Borjas *et al.* 1991; Katz and Murphy 1992; Borjas and Ramey 1994, 1995). The evidence on the impact of trade on relative demand for women, however, is mixed. In terms of the employment effects of trade, Wood (1991, 1994) found that trade expansion did not have the predicted reduction in the female share in manufacturing employment in industrialized countries. Wood's results were later challenged by several studies that showed that trade had more adverse effects on female employment compared to male employment in industrial countries (Schumacher 1984; Kucera and Milberg 2000; Kucera 2001). The segregated nature of manufacturing employment, specifically, concentration of women in import-competing industries and low-wage production occupations seems to have played a significant role in explaining the gender-differentiated effects of trade expansion. While trade-related job losses came disproportionately in female-intensive industries of textiles, apparel, leather goods, and footwear, male-intensive industries of machinery and chemicals have been identified as trade winners. Less-skilled women who predominate in the production occupations in textiles, apparel, leather goods, and footwear industries were identified as the group most adversely affected by import expansion in the US (Wood 1991; Katz and Murphy 1992; Kucera 2001).

For the most part, the focus of studies on the impact of trade on the wage structure of the US economy has been on skill differentials, rather than gender differentials in wages. While most of these studies tested whether H–O–S type linkages have been observed, some analyzed the impact of trade on wages within the framework of the rent sharing hypothesis (Borjas and Ramey 1994, 1995), where market structure plays a significant role in determining the impact of trade on relative wages. Using this framework, Borjas and Ramey (1994) found that, in concentrated industries, increased import competition reduced excess profits (rents) hence the wage premium associated with employment in these industries. In competitive industries, wages declined *indirectly* when less-skilled workers who lost their jobs in concentrated industries spilled over into the competitive industries.

A recent study by Black and Brainerd (2004), which has been highlighted by Bhagwati (2004) for showing the benefits of globalization, combined the rent sharing hypothesis with Becker's taste for discrimination theory and investigated the impact of increased import competition on discriminatory gender wage differentials in US manufacturing. According to this study, in concentrated industries, discriminatory wage differentials between men and women arise as rents are disproportionately shared by men as employers use excess profits to indulge in their "taste for discrimination" against women.[1] Extending Becker's definition of competition to include import competition, Black and Brainerd hypothesized that, as imports expand, rents will decline, reducing men's and women's wages. Men's wages will decline more than women's as men, in addition to the industry premium, will also lose the male premium in their wages. The gender gap will narrow. As increasing number of employers prefer cheaper female labor, women's share in employment will increase.

After controlling for gender differences in skill, Black and Brainerd test their hypothesis and find that increased import competition narrowed the residual gender wage gap in concentrated industries.[2] They interpret this finding as having support for the thesis that import competition reduced costly discrimination against women in concentrated manufacturing industries. However, they find no evidence for an increase in female share in employment as a result of increased competition, nor do they investigate whether the narrowing of the gender wage gap was driven by a larger decline in male wages, as predicted. Moreover, their results indicate that increased import competition led to an increase in the residual gender wage gap in competitive industries – a finding that contradicts their analytical framework where more competition is expected to erode discriminatory wage differentials, not exacerbate it. They attribute this finding to the impact of imports on unobservable skill differentials between men and women. Specifically, they argue that given the predominance of women among less-skilled workers, this finding is consistent with the prediction of H–O–S theorem that import expansion reduces relative wages of less-skilled workers compared to high-skilled workers. It is not clear why the residual gender wage gap captures gender differences in unobservable skills in competitive industries, and discriminatory wage differentials in concentrated industries.

Black and Brainerd's interpretation of the decline in the gender wage gap also contradicts the findings of several other studies that trade expansion led to an increase in discriminatory wage differentials between men and women (Maurer-Fazio and Hughes 2002; Berik *et al.* 2004; Packard 2004), and is inconsistent with the findings that trade expansion led to disproportionate job losses for women, in general (Schumacher 1984; Kucera and Milberg 2000; Kucera 2001), and low-wage women in production jobs, in particular (Katz and Murphy 1992).

These problems aside, even within the Beckerian framework, there is reason to doubt that discrimination against women declined in US manufacturing over the 1980s. The 1976–93 was a period of historically high unemployment rates in US manufacturing, where the unemployment rate did not fall below 5.1 percent and was an average of 7.4 percent.[3] Discrimination in hiring against women (and minorities) is more likely to decline if the labor market is tight enough (i.e. there is full employment), so that women (and minorities) can move up the hiring queue and discriminatory employers can thus be penalized, and not when there is substantial unemployment in the labor market (Shulman 1987). Substantial unemployment rates lead to an increase in the supply of (white) men in the hiring queue; women (and minorities) fall behind as more experienced (white) men are preferred by employers (Shulman 1987). This effect would be even stronger in an economic environment where there is a large increase in relative demand for more experienced workers – a characteristic of the US labor market in the 1980s. Within this labor market context, women are not likely to have moved up the hiring queue.

Trends in wages and employment in US manufacturing

Since the late 1970s, there has been an increase in relative demand for skilled workers (Berman *et al.* 1994; Bartel and Sicherman 1999). These shifts were due to increased import competition, automation of production processes, and skill-biased technological change (Bound and Johnson 1992; Katz and Murphy 1992). These factors affected production and nonproduction workers differently, favoring nonproduction workers. Increasing import competition is likely to reduce demand primarily for production workers since activities of nonproduction workers such as marketing, sales, and accounting may be complementary with production workers overseas (Katz and Murphy 1992), especially when increasing imports reflects an increase in outsourcing activities where production moves offshore leaving the shell of the company. Automation of production processes, commonly known as laborsaving technological change, also reduces demand primarily for production workers.

The trends in employment presented in Table 11.1 are consistent with declines in demand for less-skilled and production workers compared to their counterparts. Over the 1976–93 period, while manufacturing employment declined by 7 percent, high-wage workers increased their share in this shrinking sector.[4] The increase reflected a combination of absolute declines in employment in low-wage occupations and absolute increases in employment in high-wage occupations.

There are also significant differences in the experiences of production workers compared to their counterparts. In the low-wage category, while employment declined both in production and nonproduction occupations, the declines were larger in production occupations (Table 11.1). In the high-wage category, employment increased significantly in white-collar occupations (Table 11.1). These trends are consistent with the shifts in labor demand. The shifts in labor demand seem to have affected men and women differently. Between 1976 and 1993, both men's and women's employment declined in low-wage occupations (Table 11.1). The declines, however, were significantly larger for women. Employment in low-wage production occupations declined by 42 percent for women, and 19 percent for men. Similarly, employment in low-wage nonproduction occupations declined by 9 percent for women, and 3 percent for men. Women's employment in high-wage occupations – both production and nonproduction – increased dramatically, whereas men's employment in high-wage production employment declined by 11 percent.

Between 1976 and 1993, female share in manufacturing employment stayed nearly constant (Table 11.2), but the occupational composition of the female

Table 11.1 Change in manufacturing employment by occupation, 1976–93

	Percent change (1976–93)		
	Total (%)	*Men (%)*	*Women (%)*
Total	−6.7	−3.0	−9.0
Production	−21.2	−15.4	−31.2
High-wage	0.3	−10.9	118.8
Low-wage	−30.4	−18.8	−42.6
Nonproduction	17.6	10.5	31.0
High-wage	37.1	15.5	177.8
Low-wage	−6.7	−3.0	−9.0

Source: Author's calculations from March CPS data files.

Notes
High-wage production (blue-collar) occupations are precision production, craft, and repair. Machine operators, assemblers, inspectors are categorized as low-wage production occupations. High-wage nonproduction (white-collar) occupations are executive, administrative, managerial, professional specialty, technical, and related support occupations. Low-wage nonproduction occupations are: sales and administrative support, including clerical.

workforce changed significantly. In 1976, women were underrepresented in high-wage occupations (Table 11.3).[5] Between 1976 and 1993, occupational segregation by gender declined primarily as women moved out of low-wage production occupations and into traditionally male, high-wage nonproduction occupations. Declines in high-wage production occupations also contributed to the desegregation process (Table 11.1). The net result was not only a more integrated workforce but possibly also a narrower gender wage gap as suggested by several other studies (Katz and Murphy 1992; Blau and Kahn 1997).

Women's entry into traditionally male high-wage occupations is also likely to have contributed to the narrowing of the gender pay gap in the US.[6] Whether this was at least in part due to a trade-related decline in gender discrimination which increased employment opportunities in traditionally male occupations for women, as argued by Black and Brainerd (2004), is unknown.

Table 11.2 Female share in manufacturing employment by occupation, 1976–93

	1 Female share in employment		2 Change in female share in employment (1976–93)
	A 1976 (%)	B 1993 (%)	
Total	35.8	34.6	−0.01
Production	36.6	31.9	−0.05
High-wage	8.6	18.8	0.10
Low-wage	48.5	40.0	−0.09
Nonproduction	34.4	38.3	0.04
High-wage	13.3	27.0	0.14
Low-wage	60.6	59.0	−0.02

Source: Author's calculations from March CPS data files.

Table 11.3 Distribution of women and men across occupations 1976–93

	Women			Men		
	1976 (%)	1993 (%)	Change	1976 (%)	1993 (%)	Change
Production	68.1	52.9	−0.15	66.0	59.8	−0.06
High-wage	4.8	11.9	0.07	28.4	27.1	−0.01
Low-wage	63.3	41.0	−0.22	37.6	32.6	−0.05
Nonproduction	31.9	47.1	0.15	34.0	40.2	0.06
High-wage	6.8	21.4	0.15	24.9	30.8	0.06
Low-wage	25.1	25.7	0.01	9.1	9.5	0.00

Source: Author's calculations from March CPS data files.

Importing equality or exporting jobs

This section utilizes the methodology of Borjas and Ramey (1994) and Black and Brainerd (2004) and analyzes the trade-related trends in the residual gender wage gap. The analysis aims to reconcile the finding that increased import competition led to a decline in the residual gender wage gap in concentrated industries (Black and Brainerd 2004), with the findings that in import-competing industries of US manufacturing, there has been a disproportionate decline in women's employment (Katz and Murphy 1992; Kucera and Milberg 2000; Kucera 2001). The analysis explores the underlying mechanisms that explain the trade-related changes in gender wage differentials, and searches for an alternative interpretation of these changes that would be consistent across both concentrated and competitive industries of US manufacturing.

Methodology

The empirical models presented here test the hypotheses that increased import competition caused declines in the share of low-wage production workers among women, raised the average wages of women who remained, and thus narrowed the gender wage gap. To test these hypotheses, following Black and Brainerd (2004), a difference-in-differences methodology that conceptually groups the observations along the lines of market structure of an industry (i.e. noncompetitive versus competitive) and also import-intensity in an industry (i.e. import-impacted versus not import-impacted) is used.[7] In testing the effect of change in imports on the change in the residual gender wage gap, this conceptual grouping of industries is formalized by the following equation:[8]

$$\Delta_t(Gap_i) = \alpha + \beta_1 \Delta_t \, trade_i + \beta_2 \, m\_power_i$$
$$+ \beta_3 (\Delta_t trade * m\_power)_i + \beta_4 \, \Delta_t \, tech_i \qquad (11.1)$$

where $\Delta_t \, trade_i$ is the change in the import share in industry i, m_power_i is the price-cost margin in industry i in 1976 ($\Delta_t \, trade * m\_power)_i$ is the interaction term between $\Delta_t \, trade_i$ and m_power_i, and $\Delta_t \, tech_i$ is the change in real investment per labor in industry i.[9]

The dependent variable is the change in the residual gender wage gap over the 1976–93 period. Residual wages are calculated as follows: log earnings are first regressed on four categorical education variables, potential experience, potential experience squared, and indicator variables for nonwhite, marital status, region, and metropolitan status.[10] The average industry residual wage gap is then calculated as the difference between average industry residual wages of men and women for 1976 and 1993. In the estimation, following Black and Brainerd (2004), observations are weighted by the inverse of the 1993 sampling variance.

The change in import share variable measures the impact of trade on the residual gender wage gap in competitive (non-concentrated) industries. The focus variable is the interaction term between the market power variable and the trade variable.

This variable measures the marginal impact of trade on the residual gender wage gap in concentrated industries. A negative coefficient on this variable may be interpreted in two ways. According to Black and Brainerd (2004), it would lend support to the hypothesis that increased import competition led to a decline in gender wage discrimination in noncompetitive industries compared to competitive industries. Alternatively, it may be interpreted as the effect of disproportionate loss of employment for low-wage women, which increased the average wages of women who remained and thus narrowed the gender wage gap. The following two equations are estimated to see which mechanism is supported by the data:

$$\Delta_t(Wage_i^s) = \alpha + \beta_1 \Delta_t \, trade_i + \beta_2 \, m\_power_i$$

$$+ \beta_3(\Delta_t \, trade * m\_power)_i + \beta_4 \Delta_t \, tech_i \qquad (11.2)$$

where the dependent variable is the change in the residual wages of men and women in industry i over the 1976–93 period, and all the right-hand side variables are as defined in equation (11.1). The focus variable is again the interaction term between the market power variable and the change in import share variable. A positive coefficient in the female wage equation would not only indicate that increased exposure to import competition in noncompetitive industries might have led to a decline in the female share in employment in low-wage occupations but would also be inconsistent with the declining discrimination hypothesis. Similarly, a positive coefficient in the male wage equation would also be inconsistent with the declining discrimination hypothesis.

Finally, the following equation is estimated to investigate the impact of imports on the female share in employment and in low-wage production occupations in concentrated and competitive industries:

$$\Delta_t(\% \, Female_i) = \alpha + \beta_1 \Delta_t \, trade_i + \beta_2 \, m\_power_i$$

$$+ \beta_3(\Delta_t \, trade * m\_power)_i + \beta_4 \Delta_t \, tech_i \qquad (11.3)$$

where the dependent variable is change in the female share in employment in industry i over the 1976–93 period and all the right-hand side variables are as defined in equation (11.1). While increase in the female share in employment in concentrated industries would be consistent with the importing equality hypothesis, a decline in the female share would support the argument of this chapter.

The data

Earnings and employment data come from the Current Population Survey (CPS), March Annual Demographic Files for the survey years between 1977 and 1994.[11]

The trade data are from the National Bureau of Economic Research (NBER) Trade Database compiled by Robert Feenstra (1996). The impact of trade on an industry is measured using import shares that are calculated as the ratio of imports to domestic shipments. Imports are measured as the cost in freight value of imports.

The market power variable is the price-cost margin in an industry in 1976. It is calculated as "value added − labor costs/total sales." The interaction term between this variable and the trade variable measures the marginal impact of imports in noncompetitive industries.

The technological change variable is real investment per labor, which is calculated as real investment divided by employment.[12] The data on investment and employment are from the NBER Manufacturing Productivity database (1996). Technological change is expected to widen the gender wage gap for three reasons. First, several studies have found that skill-upgrading leads to a relative decline in demand for women compared to men as some production jobs disappear, while others are redefined as technical jobs and become men's jobs (Cockburn 1985; Acevedo 1990; Pearson 1995). Second, employer discrimination in hiring against women may also be exacerbated if technological performance of industries is a source of monopoly power (Galbraith and Calmon 1994), and hence excess profits that finance discrimination (Becker 1971). Third, women might be excluded from the training for such technologically sophisticated jobs due to the employers' prejudices of women's role as caretakers (Seguino 2005).

The data on domestic shipments, investment, employment, value added, labor costs, and total sales are from the NBER Manufacturing Productivity database (1996). The four-digit SIC coded industry-level trade, investment, and market power data are aggregated at the three-digit (CIC) level based on the 1980 Census definition. Industries in which female or male share in employment is less than 10 percent are excluded from the sample. These refinements to the data lead to 61 industries in the sample, which are listed in Appendix 11.A.

The 1976–93 period is chosen by Black and Brainerd because 1977 was the first year in which a relatively large number of metropolitan areas are identified in the CPS. Although the trade data are available through 1994, in their study, Black and Brainerd use 1993 as the end point after finding that their results were sensitive to the choice of 1994 earnings data as an endpoint, whereas results using 1991 and 1992 earnings data as endpoints were consistent with the results using 1993 earnings data as an endpoint. In this study, I also use 1993 as the endpoint both because it allows results to be comparable to those of Black and Brainerd and also because the post-NAFTA period represents a substantially different trade regime.

Estimation results

Table 11.4 reports the estimation results. Focusing on the interaction term, the negative and statistically significant coefficient indicates that increased import competition reduced the gender wage gap in concentrated industries relative to competitive industries (Column 1). Consistent with the exporting jobs hypothesis, the gender wage gap closed due to the increase in women's wages (Column 2), rather than a decline in male wages (Column 3). The coefficient on the interaction term in the female share in employment equation is negative, but statistically

Table 11.4 Regression results

Dependent variable	Change (1976–93)				
	1 *Residual gender wage gap*	*2* *Residual female wages*	*3* *Residual male wages*	*4* *Female share in employment*	*5* *Female share in low-wage prodution employment*
Constant	−0.228**	0.112	−0.116*	0.060	0.035
	(0.101)	(0.093)	(0.061)	(0.053)	(0.093)
Market power[a]	0.084	0.085	0.168	−0.156	−0.052
	(0.371)	(0.341)	(0.222)	(0.196)	(0.342)
Change in import share	2.211***	−2.417***	−0.206	0.008	1.410**
	(0.624)	(0.573)	(0.374)	(0.329)	(0.575)
Market power × Change in import share	−7.624***	8.950***	1.326	−0.399	−5.798***
	(2.377)	(2.183)	(1.425)	(1.253)	(2.188)
Change in real investment per labor	0.017***	−0.014**	0.003	0.002	−0.004
	(0.006)	(0.005)	(0.004)	(0.003)	(0.006)
Adj. R²	0.262	0.303	0.127	0.059	0.139
N	61	61	61	61	61

Notes
Standard errors are reported in parentheses.
***, **, * denote that the value is significant at the 99, 95, 90 percent probability levels. All observations are weighted by the inverse of the sampling variance.
a Market power is the price-cost margin in an industry in 1976.

significant indicating that the increase in women's wages was not coupled by an increase in female share in employment (Column 4). This result is consistent with the prediction that the increase in women's wages reflects changes in the occupational composition of the female workforce rather than an increase in relative demand for women due to declining gender discrimination. Moreover, increased import competition decreased the female share in low-wage production employment in concentrated industries (Column 5). This result is consistent with the prediction that increased import competition in concentrated industries reduced the gender wage gap. But, this reflects a decline in the female share in low-wage production employment rather than a decline in gender discrimination in these industries.

In competitive industries, the opposite results hold: the positive and statistically significant coefficient on the trade variable indicates widening of the gender wage gap as a result of increased import competition in competitive industries (Column 1). This is because increased import competition led to a decline in female wages in these industries (Column 2). Similar to concentrated industries, increased import competition in competitive industries does not seem to have had a significant impact on male wages (Column 3). The coefficient on the female share in employment is statistically insignificant (Column 4). Increased import competition increased the female share in employment in low-wage production occupations (Column 5).

Technological change, proxied by real investment per labor, is associated with a wider gender wage gap, as predicted (Column 1). Women earn less in sectors with higher real investment per labor (Column 2), but technological change does not have a significant impact on male earnings (Column 3). Neither the female share in employment nor the share of women among low-wage production workers seems to be affected by technological change (Columns 4 and 5). Lower wages for women might reflect exclusion of women from training for technologically sophisticated jobs.

Overall, these results suggest that employers in concentrated and competitive industries reacted differently to increased import competition. A plausible explanation for this difference is as follows: employers in both groups of industries attempted to reduce the wage bill in the face of increased international competition. In concentrated industries, the reduction in the wage bill was achieved through disproportionate layoffs of low-wage women. Outsourcing, specifically in the final assembly of reimported, outsourced production, may have preserved some jobs for men, which in turn may explain why men in these industries were hurt less than women in terms of job losses.[13] Concentrated and trade-impacted industries of computer/electronic products, electrical products, motor vehicles and parts, primary metal and miscellaneous manufacturing industries, which are concentrated and import-impacted industries, heavily outsourced their operations in the 1980s (USITC 1999; Burke *et al.* 2004). In the beginning of the 1976–93 period, these five industries employed more than two-thirds (74 percent) of the workforce in concentrated and trade-impacted industries in the sample. Moreover, the female share in low-wage production employment declined four times more in these industries compared to the remaining import-impacted concentrated industries. Consequently, the decline in the female share in low-wage production occupations in these industries accounted for 80 percent of the six percentage point decline in import-impacted concentrated industries.

Employers in competitive industries who could not (or did not) outsource their operations reacted to increased international competition by substituting lower-waged women for men in an attempt to reduce labor costs.[14]

Robustness checks

In 1976, unionization rates were higher in noncompetitive industries and among men, compared to their counterparts.[15] Hence, de-unionization of the manufacturing workforce over the 1976–93 period might have reduced the gender wage gap more in concentrated industries.[16] It is also possible that since unions reduce gender wage gaps (Hartmann *et al.* 1994), if unionization rates fell more in either competitive or noncompetitive industries, the gender wage gap would have increased more (or narrowed less) in those industries. To eliminate the possibility that changes in the gender wage gap that were

Table 11.5 Robustness checks

Dependent variable	Change (1976–93)		
	Residual gender wage gap	Female share in employment in high-wage occupations (1976–93)	
		Production	Nonproduction
Constant	−0.352**	0.159	0.127*
	(0.115)	(0.115)	(0.066)
Market power[a]	0.131	−0.324	−0.082
	(0.361)	(0.423)	(0.223)
Change in import share	2.078**	−0.110	0.036
	(0.610)	(0.711)	(0.428)
Market power × Change in import share	−6.980**	0.112	0.281
	(2.331)	(2.708)	(1.518)
Change in real investment per labor	0.017**	0.001	−0.001
	(0.006)	(0.007)	(0.003)
Change in unionization rate	−0.665*		
	(0.321)		
Adj. R^2	0.303	−0.041	−0.014
N	61	60	47

Notes
Standard errors are reported in parentheses.
**, * denote that the value is significant at the 95, 90 percent probability levels. All observations are weighted by the inverse the sampling variance.
a Market power is the price-cost margin in an industry in 1976.

previously attributed to imports in fact reflect unionization effects, change in unionization rate in US manufacturing over the 1976–93 period is included in equation 11.1.[17] The results are presented in Table 11.5 and show that the earlier results still hold.

The coefficient on the unionization rate variable is negative and statistically significant indicating that decline in unionization rates in US manufacturing over the 1976–93 period is associated with a rise in the gender wage gap. This is consistent with the findings in the literature that central wage setting institutions in general (Blau and Kahn 1995, 1996) and unions in particular reduce gender wage gaps (Hartmann *et al.* 1994).

There is no evidence of an increase in female share in concentrated industries that were exposed to international competition, as predicted by Becker's theory of discrimination. On the contrary, the findings show that, in these industries, increased import competition led to the de-feminization of low-wage production occupations. It, however, is possible that while increased import competition reduced the female share in low-wage production occupations, it increased it in high-wage occupations, which in turn led to the absence of any impact of import expansion on the female share in concentrated industries.[18] If this were the case, then it would be hard to refute the importing equality thesis. To test this hypothesis, equation (11.3) is estimated separately for high-wage production and nonproduction workers. The results reported in Table 11.5 do not support the hypothesis that increased import competition helped women enter high-wage occupations.[19] In fact, the model is a very poor fit to explain the variations in the female share in employment in these occupations.

Conclusions and future research

The results of this study show that, over the 1976–93 period faced with rising imports employers in import-impacted, concentrated sectors of US manufacturing were able to achieve cost reductions (i.e. reduce the wage bill) without increasing the relative demand for female labor. Quite the contrary, women low-wage production workers seem to have been disproportionately laid off in these industries without an offsetting increase in the proportion of women in high-wage occupations. The decrease in the female share in low-wage production employment brought up the average wages of women workers who remained in these sectors. It is likely that women's production jobs were lost to overseas workers, possibly contributing to a feminization of production workers beyond US borders. Outsourcing, specifically in the final assembly of reimported, outsourced production, may have preserved some jobs for men, which in turn may explain why men in these industries were hurt less than women in terms of job losses.

In competitive industries, on the other hand, employers seem to have reacted to increased international competition by substituting men with lower-waged women in an attempt to reduce labor costs. This can be inferred from the increase in the female share of low-wage production workers, which was associated with a significant decline in residual wages of women that led to a widening of the gender wage gap.

The findings suggest that in neither competitive nor concentrated sectors the average female share of employment changed as the import share rose. Instead, there has been a trade-induced defeminization among low-wage production workers in concentrated industries, which was associated with the closing of the gender wage gap. Rather than being an indication of reduced discrimination against women as claimed by Black and Brainerd, discrimination may have increased during this period. Disproportionate job losses are a likely indicator of a decline in cost of discrimination in a weak labor market, which enabled employers to continue and even intensify their discriminatory hiring (and firing) practices during this period. While rising import share may provide an incentive for employers to reduce costly discrimination, it is also a source of job destruction and therefore intensified job competition among workers that enables discrimination. Our findings support this interpretation of the mechanism for the decline in gender wage gap in concentrated, import-impacted industries. Hence, the findings of this study suggest that it is better to interpret increased international competition as a factor that increases job competition among and decreases the relative demand for low-wage production workers, rather than a competition stick that forces employers to reduce discrimination.

The policies that address the consequences of increased trade and relocation of US companies' offshore target retraining trade-displaced workers for employment in the growing sectors of the US economy, mainly the service sector.[20] However, while high-paying jobs were being lost in the manufacturing sector, new employment opportunities came in relatively low-wage categories in the growing service sector (Levy and Murnane 1992). There is an increasing concern regarding the effects of this increase in low-wage employment in the US economy. The shift in employment away from a male-dominated sector to a sector that provides employment opportunities primarily for women has been linked to narrowing of the gender wage gap in the US economy (Greene and Hoffnar 1995). However, recent findings show that, in the 1990s, the gender earnings gap within manufacturing declined and that, within services, it stayed nearly constant (Kongar 2005). The inter-sector difference in gaps closed in 1997, and by 1999, the gap was smaller in the manufacturing sector compared to the service sector. Hence, if these trends continue, deindustrialization is not likely to reduce the gender earnings gap in the US economy, in the future.

The findings of this study suggest that the differential impact of increased import competition on gender inequalities seems to arise from heavy outsourcing rather than the competitive structure of an industry. Future research that focuses on outsourcing activities rather than market structure is likely to shed more light into the gendered outcomes of increased international competition. Also, feminist research on the trade impact on gender inequalities in developing economies finds that existing gender inequalities played a significant role in shaping trade patterns in these economies (Çağatay 1996; United Nations 1999; Seguino 2000). Hence, the empirical framework presented here needs to be broadened to take into account both the gender-segregated nature of employment and the gender earnings differentials within manufacturing.

While there is no evidence for a significant impact on male wages of increased import competition, extending the analysis to include the post-NAFTA period might change this result. NAFTA exacerbated the trends in outsourcing of production jobs, causing significant job losses in male-dominated industries, such as the auto industry. Even when production stayed in the US, increasing unemployment among production workers in combination with employers' threats to locate offshore reduced the bargaining power of unions during wage negotiations (Bronfenbrenner 2000). If, in the post-NAFTA period, men's wages declined more than women's, the gender wage gap would have narrowed. Just like a decline in the gender wage gap due to disproportionate job losses for low-wage women, the narrowing of the gender wage gap through this mechanism would indicate illusory gains toward gender equality.

Appendix

Appendix 11.A Noncompetitive/competitive and import-impacted/not import-impacted industries

Noncompetitive industries[a]		Competitive industries	
CIC code	*Industry: not import-impacted*[b]	*CIC code*	*Industry: not import-impacted*
110	Grain mill products	100	Meat products
130	Tobacco manufacturers	101	Dairy products
140	Dyeing and finishing textiles, exc. wool and knit	102	Canned and preserved fruits, vegetables
171	Newspaper publishing and printing	111	Bakery products
182	Soaps, cosmetics	121	Misc. food prep. and kindred products
250	Glass and glass products	−12	
262	Misc. nonmetallic mineral and stone products	141	Floor coverings, except hard surfaces
280	Other primary metal industries	142	Yarn, thread, and fabric mills
291	Metal forgings and stampings	150	Misc. textile mill products
292	Ordnance	161	Misc. paper and pulp products
310	Engines and turbines	162	Paperboard containers and boxes
311	Farm and machinery equipment	172	Print., publish., allied, exc. newspapers
352	Aircraft and parts	180	Plastics, synthetics, resins
361	Railroad and locomotive equipment	181	Drugs
		190	Paints, varnishes, related products
		191	Agricultural chemicals
		192	Industrial and miscellaneous chemicals
		201	Misc. petroleum and coal products
		212	Misc. plastic products
		241	Misc. wood products
		242	Furniture and fixtures
		282	Fabricated structural metal products
		290	Screw machine products
		300	Misc. fabricated metal products
		341	Radio, TV, communications equip.
		370	Cycles and misc. transportation equip.
		372	Optical and health services supplies
CIC code	*Industry: import-impacted*	*CIC code*	*Industry: import-impacted*
210–11	Tires and inner tubes and other rubber products[c]	132	Knitting mills
252	Structural clay products	151	Apparel and accessories, except knit[c]
261	Pottery and related products[c]	152	Misc. fabricated textile products

(*Appendix 11.A continued*)

Noncompetitive industries[a]		Competitive industries	
CIC code	*Industry: import-impacted*	*CIC code*	*Industry: import-impacted*
272	Primary aluminum industries[c]		Footwear, except leather and
312	Construct., material handling machine	221	plastic[c]
		222	Leather products, except footwear[c]
321	Office and accounting machines[c]	281	Cutlery, hand tools, other hardware
322	Electronic computing equipment[c]	320	Metalworking machinery
340	Household appliances[c]	331	Machinery, except electrical
342	Electrical machinery, equipment supplies[c]	371	Scientific and controlling instruments[c]
351	Motor vehicles, motor vehicle equip.		
380	Photographic supplies and equipment[c]		
390–1	Misc. mfg. and toys, amusement sport. goods[c]		

Notes

a Following Black and Brainerd (2004), a competitive (noncompetitive) industry is defined as one where the four-firm concentration ratio was less (greater) than 40 percent in 1977.

b Following Black and Brainerd (2004), an import impacted industry is defined as one in which the import share increased by at least 10 percentage points between 1976 and 1993.

c These industries engage in outsourcing. Outsourcing is inferred from increasing export as well as import shares. An import-impacted industry is identified as outsourcing if, within that industry, export share increased by at least the manufacturing average of five percentage points, between 1976 and 1993.

Appendix 11.B Variables and data sources

Data	Years	Sources
Earnings[a]	1973–93	Current Population Surveys, March 1977–1994 Conducted by the Bureau of the Census for the Bureau of Labor Statistics. Washington: Bureau of the Census [producer and distributor]. Santa Monica, CA: Unicon Research Corporation [producer and distributor of CPS Utilities], 2001
Imports[b]/ Exports	1976–93	US World IM and X: National Bureau of Economic Research (NBER) Trade Database compiled by Robert Feenstra (1996) (1972 4-digit SIC version) Robert C. Feenstra, "NBER Trade Database, Disk 1: US Imports, 1972–1994: Data and Concordances," NBER Working Paper no. 5515, March 1996
Value of industry shipments investment[c]	1976–93	Bartelsman, Eric J., Randy A. Becker, and Wayne B. Gray. 2000. "NBER-CES

Appendix 11.B Continued

Data	Years	Sources
		Manufacturing Industry Database (1958–1996)." Database on-line. Available at http://www.nber.org/nberces/nbprod96.htm
Unionization rate	1976–93[d]	1976–81 May and 1983–94 Outgoing Rotations of the Current Population Surveys. Conducted by the Bureau of the Census for the Bureau of Labor Statistics. Washington: Bureau of the Census [producer and distributor]. Santa Monica, CA: Unicon Research Corporation [producer and distributor of CPS Utilities], 2001
Rate of unemployment	1976–93	Bureau of Labor Statistics

Notes
a The sample includes individuals aged 18–64 who worked full-time in the civilian sector in the year prior to the survey. A "full-time" worker is defined as one who worked at least 30 hours in their usual workweek and worked more than 48 weeks in the previous year. Self-employed individuals and individuals working without pay are excluded from the analysis. The wage data refers to real weekly earnings. Wages are deflated by the Consumer Price Index. Workers earning less than $67 in weekly wages in 1982 dollars are excluded from the analysis, and the wages of workers whose earnings are top coded are multiplied by 1.45. These data refinements are similar to those of Katz and Murphy (1992), Borjas and Ramey (1994), and same with those of Black and Brainerd (2004).
b The four-digit SIC coded industry-level trade data are aggregated at the three-digit (CIC) level based on the 1980 Census definition.
c Real investment per labor is calculated as follows: The four-digit SIC coded industry-level investment data are aggregated at the three-digit (CIC) level based on the 1980 Census definition, deflated by the Consumer Price Index, and then divided by the number of workers in industry i at year t.
d Missing values for the years 1982–3, 1985–9, and 1993 are computed by linear interpolation.

Notes

1 Similar to Borjas and Ramey (1994), Black and Brainerd (2004) also hypothesize that, in competitive industries, increased import competition will have less of an impact on both male and female wages since wages (and the gender wage gap) in these industries are already at the competitive level.
2 The residual gender wage gap is the portion of the gender wage gap that remains unexplained by differences in men's and women's productivity-related characteristics such as education and experience.
3 Author's calculations from Bureau of Labor Statistics data.
4 Due to changes in the definitions of occupations between 1976 and 1993, in the March CPS data, the two-digit blue- and white-collar occupations were categorized into more aggregated categories of high-wage blue-collar, low-wage blue-collar, high-wage white-collar, and low-wage white-collar occupations.
5 While the lingering stereotype of a blue-collar (production) worker is a male, a closer examination into the gender composition of the US manufacturing workforce in 1976 reveals that women were underrepresented not in production occupations but rather in high-wage occupations (Table 11.2).
6 Between 1976 and 1993, the ratio of women's to men's median weekly earnings increased from 65 to 71 percent in the US, and from 54 to 63 percent in manufacturing. Within manufacturing, when gender differences in productivity-related characteristics are taken into account, the ratio increases in both years to 55 and 72 percent, respectively.

7 Industries in the sample are listed in Appendix 11.A.

8 Focusing on the residual gender wage gap allows the results presented in this chapter to be comparable to Black and Brainerd's (2004) findings. Controlling for education and experience differentials by gender also allows us to isolate trade from the well-documented improvements in women's relative education and experience over the same period (O'Neill 1985; Levy and Murnane 1992; O'Neill and Polachek 1993; Blau and Kahn 1995, 1996, 1997).

9 Black and Brainerd's model utilizes the concentrated versus nonconcentrated distinction to capture the noncompetitive versus competitive industries. In one specification' they utilize "price-cost margin" which is defined as "value added – labor costs/total sales" as an alternative measure of market power. In this study, this alternative measure is utilized since being able to put a markup on the final price is a better measure of market power that would enable the industries to finance discrimination.

10 Following Katz and Murphy (1992), Greene and Hoffnar (1995), and Black and Brainerd (2004), four education categories are: less than high school, high school, some college, and college or more. The March CPS data do not report actual labor market experience. Therefore, following Katz and Murphy (1992) potential experience is defined as either "age-years of schooling-7" or "age – 17," whichever is minimum. This residual wage calculation controls for a greater number of variables than does the calculation of Black and Brainerd (2004), which did not control for marital status, regional, or city or suburb residence.

11 See Appendix 11.B for the data refinements and sources.

12 Studies that investigate the impact of technological advances on labor demand do so utilizing various proxies for technological advances. The most commonly utilized variables are research and development (R&D), the share of capital in value added (Mincer 1993; Berman, Bound and Griliches 1994; Sachs and Shatz 1994), investment in computers (Berman, Bound and Griliches 1994), and sectoral productivity growth (Mincer 1993). In this chapter, real investment per labor is used as a proxy for technological change, since the variables mentioned earlier are either not available in a more detailed format beyond the two-digit level for all manufacturing industries (R&D expenditure), and/or lose their precision when they are aggregated into three-digit level (total factor productivity growth).

13 The list of industries in Appendix 11.A indicates those that outsource by italics. Outsourcing is inferred from increasing export as well as import shares.

14 Production processes were also outsourced in apparel, leather goods, and footwear industries leading to a decline in the female share in low-wage production employment in these industries. This decline, however, seems to have been offset by the trends in other competitive industries that were exposed to increased import competition. This is likely because apparel, leather goods, and footwear industries employed less than half (42 percent) of the workers in competitive industries that were exposed to international competition. Job losses in these industries further reduced the significance of these industries in the industry mix to 34 percent. Trends in other competitive industries that were exposed to import competition, therefore, were able to offset the declines in female share in production due to outsourcing and drive the results.

15 In 1976, 40 percent of workers in noncompetitive industries and 30 percent of workers in competitive industries were unionized. In both concentrated and competitive industries, unionization rates were higher for men. In concentrated industries, 43 percent of men and 31 percent of women were unionized. These numbers were 33 and 22 percent in competitive industries (author's calculations from March CPS data files).

16 Between 1976 and 1993, in concentrated industries, total, male, and female unionization rates declined to 24, 26, and 16 percent, respectively. In competitive industries, these numbers were 15, 16, and 11 percent (author's calculations from March CPS data files).

17 The inclusion of this variable does not necessarily help isolate the impact of deunionization from that of increased import competition since they are likely to be closely linked.

There is evidence to suggest that, over the past few decades, employers reacted to increased international competition by relocating in the nonunionized Southern states, and also outsourcing their operations to Third World countries. Both of these would have led to declines in the unionization rates. Moreover, especially, after the passage of NAFTA, the threat of locating offshore alone was enough to reduce the bargaining power of unions (Bronfenbrenner 2000).

18 Black and Brainerd (2004) test whether increased import competition led to an increase in the female share in employment among managers, rather than high-wage white-collar workers. They find a positive and statistically positive coefficient on the interaction term between the concentrated industry dummy variable and the trade variable (p. 554). For comparison purposes, equation 11.3 was also estimated for the managerial sample. Contrary to Black and Brainerd, we found no support for a trade-related increase in the share of women among managers in concentrated industries. Different sample sizes may account for the contradictory results.

19 A decline in gender discrimination must reflect either an increase in the female share in employment in traditionally male dominated high-wage occupations or a decline in the gender wage gap among at least one of the four occupational categories (high-wage production, low-wage production, high-wage nonproduction, and low-wage nonproduction). There is no support for the former. Estimating equation 1 separately for four occupational categories shows no support for a decline in the residual gender wage differentials among any of the four groups of workers. It should be mentioned that given the previous finding that there is no evidence to suggest that increased import competition did not help women enter traditionally male occupations, a decline in the gender wage gap among workers in these occupations would be a rather weak support. Whether import expansion had a significant impact on female share in low-wage nonproduction occupations was also tested. The results were insignificant. These results are not reported here for brevity and are available from the author.

20 The Federal Trade Act of 1974 established the "Trade Adjustment Assistance" (TAA) program to assist individuals who have become unemployed as a result of increased imports. With the passage of NAFTA, "The North American Free Trade Agreement Implementation Act of 1993," established the NAFTA Transitional Adjustment Assistance Program (NAFTA-TAA) to provide adjustment assistance to workers who have become unemployed as a result of imports specifically from Canada and/or Mexico, or as a result of a shift of production to Canada and/or Mexico. The adjustment assistance programs provide benefits to trade-displaced workers in the form of training, job placement, and wage insurance.

References

Acevedo, L. (1990) "Industrialization and employment: changes in the patterns of women's work in Puerto Rico," *World Development*, 18 (2): 231–55.

Bartel, A. and Sicherman, N. (1999) "Technological change and wages: an interindustry analysis," *Journal of Political Economy*, 107 (2): 285–325.

Becker, G. (1971) *The Economics of Discrimination*, Chicago, IL: University of Chicago Press.

Berik, G. (2000) "Mature export-led growth and gender wage inequality in Taiwan," *Feminist Economics*, 6 (3): 1–26.

Berik, G., Van der Meulen Rodgers, Y., and Zveglich, J. (2004) "International trade and gender wage discrimination: evidence from East Asia," *Review of Development Economics*, 8 (2): 237–54.

Berman, E., Bound, J., and Griliches, Z. (1994) "Changes in the demand for skilled labor within U.S. manufacturing: evidence from the Annual Survey of Manufactures," *The Quarterly Journal of Economics*, 2 (May): 367–97.

Bertola, G. and Ichino, A. (1995) "Wage inequality and unemployment: United States vs. Europe," *NBER Macroeconomics Annual 1995*, Cambridge, MA: MIT.

Bhagwati, J. (2004) *In Defense of Globalization*, New York: Oxford University Press.

Black, S. and Brainerd, E. (2004) "Importing equality? The impact of globalization on gender discrimination," *Industrial and Labor Relations Review*, 57 (4): 540–59.

Blau, F. and Kahn, L. (1995) "The gender earnings gap: some international evidence," in R. Freeman and L. Katz (eds), *Differences and Changes in Wage Structures*, Chicago, IL: University of Chicago Press.

—— (1996) "Wage structure and gender earnings differentials: and international comparison," *Economica*, 63 (250): 29–62.

—— (1997) "Swimming upstream: trends in the gender wage differential in the 1980s," *Journal of Labor Economics*, 15 (1): 1–42.

Bluestone, B. and Harrison, B. (1988) *The Great U-Turn: corporate restructuring and the polarizing of America*, New York: Basic Books.

Borjas, G. and Ramey, V. (1994) "The relationship between wage inequality and international trade," in J. Bergstrand, T. Cosimano, J. Houck, and R. Sheehan (eds), *The Changing Distribution of Income in an Open U.S. Economy*, New York: North Holland.

—— (1995) "Foreign competition, market power, and wage inequality," *The Quarterly Journal of Economics*, November: 1075–110.

Borjas, G., Freeman, R., and Katz, L. (1991) "On the labor market effects of immigration and trade," in G. Borjas and R. Freeman (eds), *Immigration and the Work Force: economic consequences for the U.S. and source areas*, Chicago and London: University of Chicago Press.

Bound, J. and Johnson, G. (1992) "Changes in the structure of wages in the 1980's: an evaluation of alternative explanations," *The American Economic Review*, 82 (3): 371–92.

Bronfenbrenner, K. (2000) "Uneasy terrain: the impact of capital mobility on workers, wages, and union organizing," report submitted to the U.S. Trade Deficit Review Commission, Washington, DC, September 6, 2000.

Burke, J., Epstein, G., and Choi, M. (2004) "Rising foreign outsourcing and employment losses in U.S. manufacturing, 1987–2002," Political Economy Research Institute, Working Paper No. 89, Amherst: University of Masachusetts.

Çağatay, N. (1996) "Trade and gender in issues of concern," Asian and Pacific Developing Economies and the first WTO Ministerial Conference, ESCAP Studies in Trade and Investment No. 22, Jakarta: UNDP.

Çağatay, N. and Berik, G. (1990) "Transition to export-led growth in Turkey: is there feminization of employment?" *Review of Radical Political Economics*, 22 (1): 115–34.

—— (1994) "What has export-oriented manufacturing meant for Turkish women?" in P. Sparr (ed.), *Mortgaging Women's Lives: feminist critiques of structural adjustment*, London and New Jersey: Zed Books Ltd.

Çağatay, N. and Özler, S. (1995) "Feminization of the labor force: the effects of long-term development and structural adjustment," *World Development*, 23 (11): 1883–94.

Cockburn, C. (1985) *Machinery of Dominance: women, men and technological know-how*, London: Pluto Press.

Feenstra, R.C. (1996) "U.S. Imports, 1972–1994: data and condordances," NBER Working Paper No. 5515. Cambridge: National Bureau of Economic Research.

Galbraith, J.K. and Calmon, P. (1994) "Industries, trade and wages," in M. Bernstein and D. Adler (eds), *Understanding American Economic Decline*, Cambridge: Cambridge University Press.

Greene, M. and Hoffnar, E. (1995) "Gender earnings inequality in the service and manufacturing industries in the U.S.," *Feminist Economics*, 1 (3): 82–95.

Hartmann, H., Spalter-Roth, R., and Collins, N. (1994) "What do unions do for women?" *Challenge*, 37: 11–18.

Joekes, S. (1995) "Trade-related employment for women in industry and services in developing countries," Occasional Paper No. 5, Geneva: UNRISD.

Joekes, S. and Weston, A. (1994) *Women and the New Trade Agenda*, New York: UNIFEM.

Katz, L. and Murphy, K. (1992) "Changes in relative wages 1963–1987: supply and demand factors," *Quarterly Journal of Economics*, (107) 1: 35–78.

Kongar, E. (2005) "Is deindustrialization good for women?" paper presented at the Eastern Economic Association Annual Conference, New York City, March 4–6, 2005.

Kucera, D. (2001) "Foreign trade of manufactures and men and women's employment and earnings in Germany and Japan," *International Review of Applied Economics*, 15 (2): 129–49.

Kucera, D. and Milberg, W. (2000) "Gender segregation and gender bias in manufacturing trade expansion: revisiting the 'Wood Asymmetry'," *World Development*, 28 (7): 191–210.

Levy, F. and Murnane, J. (1992) "U.S. earnings levels and earnings inequality: a review of recent trends and proposed explanations," *Journal of Economic Literature*, 30 (3): 1333–81.

Maurer-Fazio, M. and Hughes, J. (2002) "The effects of market liberalization on the relative earnings of Chinese women," William Davidson Working Paper No. 460, Ann Arbor, MI: William Davidson Institute.

Mehra, R. and Gammage, S. (1999) "Trends, counterparts, and gaps in women's employment," *World Development*, 27 (3): 533–50.

Mincer, J. (1993) *Studies in Human Capital: collected essays of Jacob Mincer*, Brookfield, VT: Edward Elgar Publishing Company.

Murphy, K. and Welch, F. (1992) "The structure of wages," *Quarterly Journal of Economics*, 107 (1): 285–326.

O'Neill, J. (1985) "The trend in the male-female wage gap in the United States," *Journal of Labor Economics*, 3 (1): 91–116.

O'Neill, J. and Polachek, S. (1993) "Why the gender gap in wages narrowed in the 1980s," *Journal of Labour Economics*, 11 (1): 205–28.

Özler, S. (2000) "Export orientation and female share of employment: evidence from Turkey," *World Development*, 28 (7): 1239–48.

Packard, L. (2004) "Gender dimensions of Vietnam's comprehensive macroeconomic and structural reform policies," background paper for *UNRISD Report on Gender Equality: striving for justice in an unequal world*, Geneva: United Nations Research Institute for Social Development (UNRISD).

Pearson, R. (1995) "Male bias and women's work in Mexico's border industries," in D. Elson (ed.), *Male Bias in the Development Process*, Manchester: Manchester University Press.

Sachs, J. and Shatz, H. (1994) "Trade and jobs in U.S. manufacturing," *Brookings Papers on Economic Activity*, 1: 1–84.

Schumacher, D. (1984) "North–South trade and shifts in employment: a comparative analysis of six European countries," *International Labour Review*, 123 (3): 333–48.

Seguino, S. (1997) "Export-led growth and the persistence of gender inequality in the newly industrialized countries," in J. Rives and M. Yousefi (eds), *Economic Dimensions of Gender Inequality: a global perspective*, Westport, CT: Greenwood Press.

Seguino, S. (2000) "Gender inequality and economic growth: a cross-country analysis," *World Development*, 28 (7): 1211–30.

—— (2005) "Gender inequality in a globalizing world," background paper for UNRISD *Report on Gender Equality: striving for justice in an unequal world*, Geneva: UNRISD.

Shulman, S. (1987) "Discrimination, human capital, and black-white unemployment: evidence from cities," *Journal of Human Resources*, 22 (3): 361–76.

Standing, G. (1989) "Global feminization through flexible labor," *World Development*, 17 (7): 1895–911.

—— (1999) "Global feminization through flexible labor: a theme revisited," *World Development*, 27 (3): 583–602.

Tzannatos, Z. (1999) "Women and labor market changes in the global economy: growth helps, inequalities hurt and public policy matters," *World Development*, 27 (3): 551–69.

United Nations (1999) *World Survey on the Role of Women in Development: globalization, gender and work*, New York: United Nations.

US International Trade Commission (USITC) (1999) *Production Sharing: use of U.S. components and materials in foreign assembly operations, 1995–1998*, Washington, DC: USITC.

Wood, A. (1991) "North–south trade and female labour in manufacturing: an asymmetry," *The Journal of Development Studies*, 27 (2): 168–89.

—— (1994) *North–South Trade, Employment, and Inequality*, Oxford: Oxford University Press.

Part IV

Feminist approaches to trade policy

12 Gender, codes of conduct, and labor standards in global production systems

Stephanie Barrientos

Introduction

Trade liberalization combined with labor market deregulation have witnessed both an increased feminization of employment and also a perceived "downward spiral" in employment conditions in many sectors producing for global exports. Much of the employment generated by export production is flexible and insecure, with women workers particularly affected by low levels of employment security, poor employment conditions, and lack of employment rights. The ILO is the pivotal organization that has laid down internationally agreed Conventions on workers rights. But in a global economy government implementation of ILO Conventions has been constrained or in some cases avoided. A number of civil society actors (particularly, northern NGOs, and trade unions) have engaged in campaigns for improved employment conditions in export production. Pressure for compliance with international labor standards in trade has taken place at different levels – through social clauses in WTO or bilateral trade agreements, and through company implementation of voluntary codes of labor practice and multi-stakeholder initiatives around ethical trade. The call for inclusion of international labor standards in trade agreements has fuelled a sometimes heated debate within the WTO as well as feminist and wider civil society movements. The adoption of codes of labor practice by companies has proved less controversial and they are now widespread, but questions have been raised as to the effectiveness of such voluntary initiatives. Following the World Commission on the Social Dimensions of Globalization, the ILO is focusing on a strategy of promoting decent work in global production systems, which provides a wider basis for promoting social dialogue on employment and the rights and protection of workers. From a gender perspective, there are serious questions to be asked of all these approaches, and whether they can address embedded discrimination that underlies the poor employment conditions of women workers in a global economy.

Globalization has seen both the liberalization and expansion of trade, and also significant changes in the commercial relationships that underpin the international flow of goods and services. Trade between different commercial actors is determined not only through market relationships based on supply and demand at international market prices, but increasingly through the establishment of commercial linkages between firms at every stage of the production and distribution process.

Global production system analysis provides a framework to examine the production and exchange of goods, based on complex networks of producers and agents, dominated by large corporate buyers and retailers that operate across international boundaries. These networks operate in a commercial environment with strong competitive pressures (facilitated by trade liberalization), but feed into global value chains dominated by regional and global buyers. These buyers are focused on meeting consumer trends that allow them to extract economic rents and retain value at the top of the chain. They transfer risk and costs down to agents and suppliers, who further offset risks onto lower tier subcontractors within the wider production network. Workers are ultimately at the interface of this process – providing high quality goods at low prices with fast turn around. Meeting these commercial dynamics requires a highly mobile workforce that combines skill, flexibility, and low cost. In many sectors this involves a feminized workforce that is often employed on an informal basis with lack of employment security. The gendered economy within which employment takes place provides the social and institutional context that feeds global production. This provides the context that needs to be better understood if international labor standards are to enhance the rights of women workers in a global economy.

This chapter examines the debate over enhancing labor standards for women workers in export production. It develops a global production systems framework to analyze the changing nature of employment and associated employment conditions for women workers, and extends it to incorporate a gendered economy approach. It argues that the embedding of global production systems in a gender economy has both helped to transform women's role in paid work and recast their subordination through the intensification of work insecurity and mobility. This undermines the ability to address labor standards within global production systems, reinforced by the commercial dynamics of buyers' purchasing practices.[1] It weighs up the ability of social clauses in trade agreements and codes of labor practice to address labor standards in global production systems. Finally, it considers the more recent emergence of the ILO strategy of decent work within global production systems, and considers the potential challenges such a strategy faces from a gender perspective. It concludes that only an integrated approach that incorporates a range of actors and policy instruments has the potential to address the challenges of improving the rights of women workers in the contemporary commercial context.

Gender and work in global production systems

The conventional approach to international trade was built on assumptions of exchange between independent buyers and sellers exchanging goods in competitive international markets. Whilst these assumptions have been modified to take account of factors such as intra-firm trade through the rise of multinational corporations (MNCs), trade models still remain largely abstracted from the commercial realities underpinning much contemporary trade. Globalization has transformed the international flow of goods as MNCs have increasingly outsourced production. Large global and regional buyers or retailers have emerged that own no production, but rely solely on global and regional networks of independent suppliers and agents. This involves the export of goods through these integrated global production networks where commercial relations are formally independent, but in reality dominated by the control of MNCs, global and regional buyers or retailers. The changing contemporary commercial reality underpinning trade has had important consequences for changing levels of employment, employment relationships, and the ability to address labor standards in export production.

Global production systems

A number of related analytical perspectives have evolved to better conceptualize this changing dimension of global production and trade. Global value chain (GVC) has provided an important entry point by tracing the linkages between the different stages of production, distribution, and consumption of products (Gereffi 1994; Kaplinsky 2000). These linkages are globally interconnected and embody a network of activities and actors. Gereffi (1994) helped to identify a shift from producer-driven towards buyer-driven value chains. In the latter global buyers do not own, but coordinate a supply network that focuses on market positioning and developing sophisticated responses to consumer requirements. The analysis focuses on key aspects of the functioning of global value chains. A key feature is the governance of chains by global buyers. This relates to the power relations that determine how financial, material, and human resources are distributed within the chain. Global buyers are able to accrue economic rents at the upper end of chains through their dominance of value-added activities such as design and branding, and their control of lower value-added activities at lower ends of the chain. Economic upgrading involves the process of engaging in those activities that facilitate access to higher economic rents or moving to a more dominant position within the chain. GVC analysis has been extended and further developed through the global production systems approach. It incorporates a more flexible notion of global production networks, which shifts the focus from a linear to a more complex analysis of relations between a wide range of agents, producers, subcontractors, intermediary and primary suppliers that feed into large regional and global MNCs, buyers and retailers (Dicken *et al.* 2001).

A global production systems approach puts more emphasis on understanding the institutional context in which production networks function, and on viewing them as socially embedded in local economic and social institutions that facilitate their operation. A GPS is seen as "the interaction of not only various [production] networks but also different levels and domains of policy, institutions and their social actors that impact upon the functioning of the system. Defined as such, a global production system entails a social as well as an economic dimension" (Efendioglu *et al.* 2005). Within global production systems, buyers, MNCs, and retailers are both able to exercise high levels of indirect commercial power. But they also distance themselves from the networks that feed them through ostensibly open market activity, and engage in fierce competition as they strive for market share. This commercial dynamic has contributed to a number of different forms of linkages between firms. These have been characterized as ranging between arms length, modular or hierarchical relations, and forms of governance (Gereffi *et al.* 2005).

The commercial dynamic of global production systems also contributes to a number of tensions. On the one hand there is a drive for product innovation and quality enhancement, but on the other there is a drive to pass costs, risks, and uncertainty onto the agents, suppliers, and subcontractors within the global production networks (Barrientos and Kritzinger 2004). The tension between quality innovation and risk is played out through global buyers and retailers insisting on increasingly stringent quality standards from suppliers (contributing to a concentration of sourcing amongst larger first-tier suppliers). At the same time, it generates a search for new sourcing opportunities, the provision of weak supply contracts, short lead times, lower prices, and less favorable payment terms. Suppliers wanting to access regional and global markets have to be ready to meet demands on them, but find innovative strategies that help them to withstand the commercial pressures. The consequence has been increasing concern over the "purchasing practices" of large global buyers and retailers, and their implications for both suppliers, and ultimately workers engaged in global production networks (Acona 2004; Barrientos and Kritzinger 2004; Oxfam 2004).

Analysis of global value chains and production networks has tended to focus on commercial and industrial linkages between firms, but to date have been fairly limited on the inclusion of labor (Barrientos 2001). Where employment is included labor tends to be treated as an economic asset that can be numerically aggregated, with little consideration of its social dimension. The dichotomy is that workers both sell labor that provides a factor of production and are people with rights situated in different social and economic contexts. Workers are at the interface between productive employment that is driven by the dynamics of global capital and its operation in diverse social and economic contexts where the sites of production are located. Expanding the analysis from a narrow value chain to a global production systems approach widens the scope to include both the industrial linkages and the institutional context in which global production takes place. Labor markets are central institutional pillars that are both the purveyors of labor as an economic asset and socially embedded in communities from which labor is drawn. They mediate the complexities of labor demand and supply based on the dynamics of commercial power, and the social norms and regulations that condition the complexities of work. This is an avenue now being pursued by the ILO in its search to address decent work in the context of contemporary global production (Efendioglu *et al.* 2005).

This provides an opening for a gender economy approach that facilitates a better understanding of labor markets as gendered institutions that underpin the operation of global production systems. A gender economy approach focuses on the interrelation between the reproductive and productive spheres, and their combined. This includes not only market-oriented productive activity, but also reproductive activity (unpaid domestic work and child care undertaken largely by women) that underpins the functioning of markets and trade (Folbre 1994; Çağatay *et al.* 1995;

Elson 1999; Grown 2000; Whitehead 2001). Labor markets are embedded in a social division of labor where the reproductive role of women has been deemed subordinate, and women largely relegated to the private sphere away from formal productive activity. But global production itself is challenging the norms on which the social division of labor is based, particularly where it generates female employment in societies where women have not traditionally taken up paid work. Whilst it is generating new openings for female employment within formal production processes, much of it is not on the basis of formal employment relations (Barrientos *et al.* 2003). It is intensifying types of employment where it is difficult for workers to access their rights, employment benefits, or labor protection. Women are largely concentrated in these categories of work, and are thus experiencing new forms of subordination *within* the formal productive sphere.

Gendered labor markets and global production

The expansion of female employment in export manufacturing, agriculture, and business services has been significant. The exact numbers are difficult to estimate. Many workers are employed by suppliers and subcontractors, and it is not possible to differentiate from sectoral labor force data what percentage are engaged in supplying global buyers as opposed to domestic buyers or local markets, where there are no specified inter-firm linkages. In addition, many women workers are employed on an informal basis, and do not necessarily appear in official labor force surveys. It is estimated that there are 40 million garment workers globally, approximately 75 percent female (Hale and Wills 2005). In agriculture, it is estimated that there are 450 million waged workers, approximately 40 percent female (Hurst *et al.* 2005). These figures do not differentiate export-oriented employment, but both sectors are an important source of exports. It is also estimated that approximately 50 million workers are employed in Export processing zones (Efendioglu *et al.* 2005), but many export suppliers are not based in EPZs. These figures can thus only give us an indication of the potential magnitude of employment in global production.

However, the type of employment created has not been homogeneous. On the one hand suppliers have to assure quality of production and meet new demands for innovation to access global markets. This requires at least a core of semi-skilled or experienced workers that can maintain consistency of output. On the other hand, mobility of global sourcing, insecurity of orders, falling lead times, and falling prices require a highly flexible labor force and put pressure to minimize labor costs. This has driven the use of temporary, casual, and migrant labor, often hired through third-party labor contractors, that can be called on as and when production peaks require (Barrientos and Kritzinger 2004; Oxfam 2004). This tension has helped to intensify the gendering of employment. The socialization of women's skills facilitates low cost but high quality labor-intensive production, meeting the demanding requirements of global buyers (Collins 2003). It is also deemed socially "acceptable" that women move flexibly between paid and unpaid work, hence they are used as an integral part of the labor force that provides the buffer needed to accommodate just-in-time ordering and retailing systems (Barrientos 2001). Hence much female employment is low paid and insecure. Global production systems thus draw on and transform women's reproductive role, recasting their subordinate position within the realm of paid productive work.

Employment in global production systems is characterized by a range of workers (often working in the same enterprise), from permanent and regular through to casual and contract. These different categories of work have been classified by a number of writers using a "gendered employment pyramid" (Barrientos *et al.* 2003; Kabeer 2003; Chen *et al.* 2004; Hale and Wills 2005). Figure 12.1 provides a simplified example At the tip of the pyramid workers are in permanent employment with better benefits and ability to organize. Moving down the pyramid, temporary and casual workers are likely to have poorer working conditions, less access to benefits, and less ability to organize. Home workers, migrant labor and workers hired through third-party labor providers at the base of the pyramid are normally in the worst position. The gender composition of these categories can vary by sector and country, but evidence suggests that women are less likely to be found in permanent work, and more likely to be found in the insecure categories where conditions are poorest. These different categories of workers are found at all tiers of supply within global production systems. Case studies in agriculture and manufacturing across a range of countries have found that even first level suppliers, with direct linkages to internationally recognized brands and retailers, often use casual, migrant, and contract labor to meet seasonal fluctuations in demand or sudden changes in orders (Smith *et al.* 2004; Hale and Wills 2005; Barrientos and Smith 2006; Mahmud and Kabeer 2006). But flexible, mobile, and insecure workers of all types can be found throughout the lower tiers of subcontractors and primary suppliers that feed into global production.

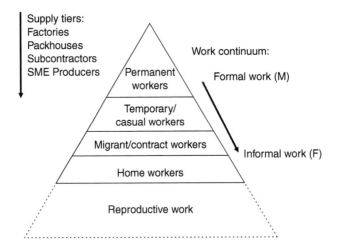

Figure 12.1 Gender employment pyramid.

Source: Adapted from Barrientos, S., Dolan, C., and Tallontire, A. (2003) "A gendered value chain approach to codes of conduct in African horticulture," *World Development*, 31 (9): 1511–26.

The categories of work described by the employment pyramid also reflect the position of workers in relation to formal and informal work. The ILO definition of formal/informal sectors used to be based on the size of enterprise, with the informal sector characterized as small enterprises with less than five employees (street traders, etc.). But the ILO (2002) redefined this to capture the informal economy, in which an increasing number of workers are employed (whether for small or large firms) without a formal contract of employment, legal benefits, or social protection. This redefinition provides recognition of the changing nature of employment in the context of globalization. The relation between formal and informal work is now being described as a "continuum" (Lund 2000; Chen *et al.* 2004). At the formal end, workers have a permanent employment contract, enjoy full employment benefits and social protection. At the informal end they receive none of these. On the right side of Figure 12.1 the work continuum indicates that permanent workers are more likely to be in formal work, and migrant, third-party contract, and home workers are more likely to be found in informal work.[2] The ILO has estimated that women constitute a majority of the informal economy, and women are more concentrated at the informal end of the continuum (Chen *et al.* 2004). Estimates of the number of informal workers engaged in export industries are unreliable, but case studies suggest this can be significant.

Many workers found in global production systems are informal according to this new definition. They are likely to be located in between the two ends of the continuum, receiving some benefits and protection but not others. It is not simply that employers are being unscrupulous. Global production systems have generated a commercial dynamic that generates a flexible and highly mobile labor force. These workers often have high job turnover and low employer attachment. Many are migrant (either internal or from other countries), from different ethnic, religious, or caste backgrounds, often with limited language ability in the host enterprise. Increasingly, third-party labor contractors (or networks of agents) are used to manage the rapid movement of workers between enterprises and sectors, or across borders (Theron and Godfrey 2000; Barrientos and Kritzinger 2004). Both men and women are employed on this basis, but women face multiple challenges of discrimination based on gender as well as employment status. A key challenge for international labor standards is to address the rights of these workers, and particularly the gender needs of women who form a significant proportion of this workforce.

Social clauses and voluntary codes in export production

International labor standards have been established through ILO Conventions based on tripartite negotiation between employers, trade unions, and government. The ILO itself has no formal teeth, but member countries that have ratified individual Conventions are meant to implement them through legislation, ensuring the rights of all workers, male and female, are met. In 1998 the most important of these were identified in the ILO's Declaration on Fundamental Principles and Rights at Work. All ILO members are meant to enforce the core labor standards, irrespective of whether they have formally ratified them. These cover freedom of association and collective bargaining, no discrimination, no child labor, and no forced labor.[3] However, it has been argued that trade liberalization and the globalization of production have undermined the ability and resolve of governments to ensure workers' rights (Çağatay 2001; Sengenberger 2002).

Many governments compete in international markets for foreign direct investment and export orders on the basis of low labor costs. Export processing zones, in which trade union and other rights are banned, are the most concrete expression of this. The ability of governments to ensure workers' rights in global production systems is also undermined where large corporate buyers *influence* production and consequently labor conditions, but bear no formal responsibility for employment and are beyond the legal reach of the countries from which they source. These trends stimulated growing campaigns by a number of global union federations and international NGOs against what is perceived as a "race to the bottom" in terms of deteriorating employment conditions in the value chains of global corporations. This civil society movement has led to diverse pressures for international labor standards to be enforced through other means (Luce 2005). Prominent amongst these are social clauses in international trade agreements and corporate codes of labor practice. More recently, following the World Commission on the Social Dimensions of Globalization, the ILO has focused on a strategy of decent work in global production systems.

An examination of these approaches requires consideration of gendered labor markets that provide the context in which labor standards evolved. ILO Conventions and much labor regulation are premised on an implicit assumption of permanent full time employment, where the worker (usually male) is separated from reproductive activity (usually female) (Elson and Gideon 1999). The rights and protection of paid workers are normally channeled primarily through their employers. Trade union organization and collective bargaining, employment insurance and benefits effectively require strong employer attachment. In countries with independent trade unions, labor regulation is also premised on employees being free to unionize and be represented in collective bargaining agreements (Ladbury and Gibbons 2000). This reflects a gender economy based on a social division of labor between full-time male workers dominating paid productive work and women in unpaid reproductive work. As we have seen, this model has been challenged within global production systems through the expansion of female employment based on increased flexibility, informality, and mobility of work. A key challenge for implementing international labor standards is thus the predominance of women workers who are not in permanent or regular employment, and do not fit the employment "norm." The gap between labor standards and the reality of employment is essentially a gender gap, with women workers one of the groups least able to improve their employment conditions. We will consider each of the approaches to labor standards – social clauses, voluntary codes, and decent work in global production systems – from the perspective of this gender lens.

Social clauses in trade agreements

In the 1990s, pressure mounted to include social clauses based on core ILO conventions into WTO negotiations and bilateral trade agreements. The aim was to enforce core labor standards through trade agreements, and provide a means of giving teeth to Core ILO Conventions. However, motives for advocating social clauses were mixed, as were divisions between those who supported and opposed their implementation. This issue stimulated a heated debate between some feminists and civil society actors as to whether trade agreements are a viable instrument for addressing workers' rights (Joekes and Weston 1994; Luce 2005). Those arguing for social clauses in trade agreements believe that they establish internationally agreed universal rights, which should apply to all workers irrelevant of country (Çağatay 2001; Polaski 2003; Luce 2005). Those arguing against have argued that they represent a new form of protectionism to keep southern imports at bay, and protect northern jobs at the expense of southern workers (Singh and Zammit 2000). Feminist critics believe the demand for social clauses has come about largely through misplaced understanding of the benefits export employment has bought women which could have potential detrimental effects on women workers (Kabeer 2004). The clear protectionist stance by some players (particularly in the US) undermined the argument for social clauses as a means of ensuring workers' rights as a universal principle, and enforced the defensive position of many southern governments. Debate over a social clause within the WTO itself was stalled by division between northern and southern members. The issue was formally referred to the ILO, which set up the World Commission on the Social Dimensions of Globalization. However, a number of bilateral trade agreements have included reference to international labor standards, but these have been with the consent of the relevant southern country, and have formed part of a package that promoted greater market access.[4]

This debate helped to raise the principle that where workers are integrated into modern export production, they should have access to international labor standards that encompass internationally agreed rights of workers. It became polarized around an inconclusive debate over whether the introduction of labor standards through trade agreements would help or hinder developing countries entering global export markets.[5] However, it took insufficient account of the commercial realities of global production systems, where trade is increasingly dominated by large corporate buyers and their agents. Global production generates high levels of earnings for export producers and agents, and even higher economic rents to corporate buyers and retailers, with labor accounting for only a small percentage of the final retail price (Oxfam 2004). From this perspective, there are strong arguments that workers contributing to the production of high value goods should reap benefits through an improvement in labor standards, and share in the fruits of globalization. Trade agreements, however, provide a blunt tool to achieve this. They put the onus on supplying countries, and not the pressures exerted on suppliers by regional and global buyers. They more easily relate to workers in formal employment, and are less likely to help the many hidden workers bought into production on an informal basis at most tiers of the production system (where female employment is often located). They cover final traded goods, and take little account of the complex production networks that underlie exports where the poorest conditions of employment are often found. It is here that gender subordination is most embedded through informal employment relations that labor standards through trade agreements are less likely to reach. Hence whilst there are strong ethical grounds for social clauses in principle, the commercial reality of global production is likely to limit their effectiveness in reality.

Corporate codes of labor practice

Corporate codes of labor practice enshrine a different approach to addressing poor labor standards in global production systems. They have arisen as a paradox of the linkages within global production. NGOs and trade unions have been able to target global buyers and retailers because of the increasingly integrated nature of their value chains. Whilst large brand name companies did not own production, they could be directly linked to specific suppliers and poor working conditions, putting their brand reputation at risk of adverse publicity and campaigns. In response many global buyers developed their own company codes of labor practice, on the assumption that these could resolve labor issues in their supply base.[6] However, company codes had on their own little legitimacy without any form of external validation or accountability. Multi-stakeholder initiatives involving companies, trade unions, and NGOs established an independent approach to codes based in defending workers' rights. The Ethical Trading Initiative (ETI) and Social Accountability International (SAI) are examples of multi-stakeholder initiatives involving companies, trade unions, and NGOs. The ETI and SA 8000 codes are based on Core ILO Conventions.[7] They also include other ILO and Human Rights Conventions covering workers' rights and protection. These and other multi-stakeholder initiatives have provided a new leverage point for global unions and international NGOs to address issues around workers' rights in the context of global production.

Evidence on the impact of codes on women workers is only now beginning to emerge and provide mixed findings.[8] An impact assessment of the ETI Base Code included five comparative case studies across agriculture, garments, and footwear in five countries. It included interviews with a wide range of trade and civil society actors, agents, and suppliers, and 400 workers (Barrientos and Smith 2006). This study indicated that codes of labor practice are normally only applied in the upper tiers of a buyer's value chain, where production can be more easily linked to the buying company. Where improvement has taken place, it is more likely in relation to "visible" issues such as health and safety, but less likely in relation to "nonvisible" issues such as discrimination and freedom of association. Workers in permanent and/or formal employment are more likely to have seen improvements and enjoy better pay and conditions as a result of codes. Workers in more insecure employment (casual, migrant, contract labor, and home workers) often endure much worse conditions, but codes appear to have had less impact on workers in lower tiers of global value chains, especially casual, migrant, contract, or home workers (Barrientos and Smith 2006). Given large numbers of women workers are employed on a casual or informal basis, often at lower tiers of global value chains, the impact on their employment conditions appears to have been ineffective to date.

Some companies that have operated codes for a long time, and been subject to vigorous civil society campaigns, are beginning to recognize the complexity of code implementation. The most notable (and public) have been GAP and Nike. The GAP Corporate Social Responsibility Report acknowledged the challenges it faced in implementing its code (Gap 2004). It started working actively with NGOs and trade unions to address key employment issues in its value chains (particularly relating to women workers). Nike has had a code since 1992. Twelve years on it has published a Corporate Responsibility Report documenting code noncompliance across its global value chain (Nike 2005).[9] This highlighted the challenges Nike faces in relation to issues such as discrimination and abuse of a largely female labor force. Nike's supply base covers 650,000 workers in contract factories globally, the majority of whom are women of between 19 and 25 years of age. Table 12.1 provides selected instances of noncompliance reported in Nike audits carried out in 2003–4 that covered 33 percent of workers in their supply base.

As with social clauses, a key limitation of codes of labor practice is the onus they place on suppliers to implement workers' rights, with little focus on the commercial pressures that reinforce poor employment practices within global production systems. In terms of practical issues, suppliers in a number of studies have reported the difficulty of complying with codes when buyers from the same companies are making commercial demands that promote contravention of the same code (Barrientos and Kritzinger 2004; Oxfam 2004; Hale and Wills 2005; Barrientos and Smith 2006; Mahmud and Kabeer 2006). One example is in relation to falling lead times, where buyers are placing orders at increasingly short notice, requiring overtime in excess of code limitations to fulfill. Overtime is a particularly important gender issue, where women have difficulties in making

Table 12.1 Code compliance by NIKE suppliers

Code issue	Audits with one or more instance of noncompliance
Freedom of association not provided where legal	1–10%
Workers report abusive treatment (verbal, physical, psychological, sexual)	25–50%
Confidential grievance procedure not provided	25–50%
Work hours exceed legal limit	25–50%
Wage below legal minimum	25–50%
Overtime refusal results in penalty	10–25%
Overtime rate is less than legal or calculation inaccurate	10–25%

Source: http://www.nike.com/nikebiz/gc/r/fy04/docs/FY04_Nike_CR_report_full.pdf.

arrangements for child care at short notice and have to juggle work and domestic responsibilities (Oxfam 2004; Smith *et al.* 2004).

The benefit of codes is that they help to promote the principle of adherence to labor standards not just at the point of export of final goods, but also further down within complex production networks. The limitation of codes is that they have tended to operate in a top-down manner driven by the goal of limiting brand risk. They mainly reflect a paternalist approach to improving labor conditions implemented by buyers. Many suppliers view them simply as a tool of compliance to obtain orders, and do not recognize them as embodying workers' rights. Many workers are unaware of the existence of codes, even on sites that have been audited. Social auditors are meant to uncover areas of noncompliance within sites. But they often fail to reveal more fundamental issues such as discrimination and can easily overlook the employment conditions of less visible workers, such as those employed on a casual basis or through third-party contractors (CCC 2005; Barrientos and Dolan 2006). Women workers in particular face gender specific issues, such as job discrimination, sexual harassment by supervisors, and lack of access to maternity or child care, that codes often fail to address (Smith *et al.* 2004; Hale and Wills 2005; Barrientos and Smith 2006). Thus in reality the reach of codes tends to be limited to higher tiers of suppliers, and more formal and regular workers who are more often male. They may extend further than labor standards applied through trade agreements, but their reach or ability to address gender discrimination still remains limited within global production systems.

At a more fundamental level, commercial pressures operating in global production systems are generating an intensification in the mobility and insecurity of work that is undermining the ability of workers to access their rights. Insecurity of employment and low employer attachment reduces the likelihood of workers receiving their employment entitlements and undermines their ability to organize or join trade unions. This is most prevalent in the case of third-party labor contractors, who constantly move between sites, have high labor turn over, and over whom there is little means of enforcement of labor regulation. Women are particularly affected given their concentration in more insecure and casual forms of work. Household and child care responsibilities also place constraints on their participation in worker organization. Hence, poor labor standards are rooted in global production systems that have replicated the subordination of women within paid work. Voluntary codes have opened up new spaces for trade unions and NGOs to engage in action to address poor labor standards globally. They have created the basis for new alliances between trade unions, NGOs, and companies, and provided an entry point for women's NGOs to raise specific gender issues. But originating from within the commercial sector, they have done little to address systemic gender discrimination that underpins poor employment practices.

Decent work in global production systems

A more recent approach to addressing labor standards has come through the ILO's strategy of decent work in global production systems. This approach was given impetus by the Global Commission on the Social Dimensions of Globalization which aimed to examine the wider implications of globalization and export production for workers and poor groups. It highlighted the impasse in public policy debate on globalization, and called for the strengthening of core labor standards and fairer trade rules, but avoided a direct linkage between the two. It called for a shift in the policies of international organizations "away from external conditionality to national ownership of policies" and support for countries that do not have the same capabilities as those that developed earlier (ILO 2004).

There are four pillars to the decent work agenda. These cover employment, workers' rights, social protection, and social dialogue (Efendioglu *et al.* 2005). Employment includes the security of work, and thus opens up wider issues of the type or categories of work generated in global production systems, rather than just aggregate numbers of workers. Rights based on the Fundamental Principles and Rights at Work include discrimination and equal pay. Linking these to the nature of employment is critical, where these rights are being undermined through the intensification of work insecurity in global production. Social dialogue can include interaction between all actors able to address the rights of workers, including women's organizations and NGOs that have largely been excluded from formal engagement in mechanisms for addressing workers' rights. This is not that women's organizations constitute independent representative organizations of workers, but that their voice can raise issues traditionally overlooked through a gender blind lens. Finally, a decent work agenda links all these issues to a strategy of social protection for workers. In a context of trade liberalization where government regulation and provision for workers has been undermined, this provides the basis for a renewal of the linkages between government and other interventions that help to ensure the well-being and rights of workers (Lund and Nicholson 2003). A social protection strategy can cross the divide between support for workers in both their productive and reproductive capacity, and thus open the way for a more holistic gender approach

Linking the different strands of decent work provides the basis for a more holistic approach to enhancing workers' rights in global production. However, there are a number of challenges addressing embedded gender discrimination in the context of global production systems. At the root is the challenge of generating employment that promotes the capabilities of workers, and allows them to earn a decent livelihood. The issue here is not simply the numerical generation of jobs, but enhancing the security of that employment where the subordination of women is recast within global production through their concentration in less secure forms of employment. The challenge of addressing the rights of workers is inextricably linked to this. Freedom of association and the right of workers to independent union organization is essential to counter the power imbalances between workers and employers. But traditionally that organization is premised on strong worker affiliation to one employer or sector. Where workers are mobile between employers, sectors, and even countries, the ability to organize or join a union is constrained. This constraint is compounded for women workers who have little time to organize, who often view unions skeptically if they fail to promote gender issues.

Some unions are beginning to introduce more innovative approaches to support and organize women workers who are not in secure employment (ICFTU 2004), but these need to be extended.

Linked to this, there are significant challenges in promoting social dialogue that incorporates the voice of women workers. Employers tend to take a paternalist perspective, which fails to recognize the rights of workers, particularly those who are not in regular employment such as women. Many trade unions have traditionally been weak in their recruitment of women workers, and led by predominantly male leaderships. A key challenge is how to integrate the voice of women into the process of social dialogue, when there are few genuinely independent representative women's organizations recognized as trade unions. Finally, social protection has traditionally been divided between work-based entitlements and insurance (that assume strong employer attachment), and nonwork-based safety nets for those without employment. Providing social protection for women workers who are mobile between jobs and regularly move in and out of employment requires a shift beyond this division, and recognition of the greater interface between paid work and unpaid reproductive work.

The ILO strategy of decent work in global production systems is still at an early stage of implementation. But it widens the scope of policy from the narrow focus of trade agreements and voluntary codes to a wider and more integrated perspective on addressing workers rights. It provides greater potential for taking into account the changing nature of global production, where employment conditions are embedded in a gender economy that reinforces poor labor standards at multiple tiers of production across complex production networks. It provides openings for a range of actors to work more collaboratively, ranging from high level engagement between global union federations, international NGOs, brands, and donors through to local level engagement between civil society groups and suppliers in different sectors. This includes women's organizations and NGOs that have traditionally been excluded from the table of social dialogue. Finally, it provides an entry point for more integrated linkages between labor regulation and wider interventions that help support the rights and well-being of workers.

Conclusion

In this chapter we have explored some of the challenges of addressing labor standards for workers in the context of contemporary global production. These challenges are complex, and reflect the embedding of global production systems in gender economies across different socioeconomic contexts and circumstances. It strongly supports the principle that the rights of all workers linked to global production should be upheld. But it explores the way in which workers' rights have been restricted differently across multiple tiers of suppliers and subcontractor, and across different categories of worker. A crucial factor for women is their concentration in insecure and casual work, with low employer attachment. This type of work is being intensified through the purchasing practices of large corporate buyers.

This paper has examined different policy tools that have been used to address the challenge of enhancing the rights of women workers in this context. It has argued that social clauses in trade agreements have limitations because of their bluntness in focusing on final traded goods and formal employment, not the complex networks of producers underpinning these and more hidden categories of informal employment, plus their onus on suppliers not commercial buyers. Company codes of labor practice provide a different entry point. Nominally they extend further down the value chains that generate export goods, but rarely extend into the more complex tiers of subcontractors and informal workers that underlie the gender subordination prevalent in global production. In reality codes are driven by a compliance approach that favors buyers' risk avoidance over workers' rights, and have failed to address the commercial dynamics that are intensifying employment insecurity helping to undermine those rights. The advantage of codes is that they have catalyzed new forms of collaboration between private sector and gender aware civil society organizations, and opened up spaces for new actors, particularly women's organizations and NGOs to play a role in addressing these issues. The ILO strategy of decent work in global production systems is more recent. It provides a more holistic approach to improving the rights of workers within export sectors by linking employment, rights, social dialogue, and social protection. But it still faces strong challenges if it is to address the underlying constraints on improving the rights of women workers linked to global production systems. Ultimately, there is no single solution, but this chapter highlights part of an unfolding process that involves greater interaction between multiple actors – commercial and civil society – where gender inequity remains embedded, but is beginning to have a higher profile in strategies to address the rights of workers globally.

Notes

1 This chapter draws on a number of case studies in agriculture and manufacturing on gender and labor standards in global production, but considers the wider issues rather than providing detailed empirical information. For the latter see, for example: Smith *et al.* 2004; Barrientos and Smith 2005; Collins 2003; Hale and Wills 2005; Jenkins *et al.* 2002; Mahmud and Kabeer 2006.
2 Note that being a permanent worker does not automatically mean you are formal, or temporary worker informal; this depends on whether you have a contract, etc. But research indicates that the further down the pyramid a worker is located the more likely they are to be informal.
3 The key ILO Conventions for women are: C111 Discrimination (Employment and Occupation) Convention and C100 Equal Remuneration Convention.
4 For a discussion of the integration of labor standards into different bilateral trade agreements see, for example, Luce 2005; Polaski 2003.
5 In a review of the evidence on whether labor market regulations would undermine economic development, Freeman (1993) does not find conclusive evidence for either side of the argument.
6 Codes of labor practice will not be reviewed in depth here. For further information see Jenkins *et al.* 2002; Barrientos and Dolan 2006; Hale and Wills 2005. This paper is addressing codes based on Core ILO conventions – ETI Base code, SA 8000 and company codes that adopt the same principles. Many individual company codes do not uphold these standards.

7 In a study of 258 codes of conduct that address labor practices, Urminsky (undated) found that: 72 percent contained reference to health and safety; 70 percent referred to discrimination based mainly on self-definition (though very few to equal remuneration); 47 percent referred to child labor; 42 percent prohibited forced labor; 33 percent covered freedom of association and/or collective bargaining.
8 The Ethical Trading Initiative undertook an Impact Assessment, coordinated by the Institute of Development Studies, which reported in 2006. Clean Clothes Campaign (CCC) and SAI are also advancing along this route.
9 Nike went one step further than GAP by naming companies in its supply base, although it did not identify individual supplier noncompliance.

References

Acona (2004) *Buying Your Way into Trouble? The challenge of responsible supply chain management*, London: Insight Investment Management Ltd.

Barrientos, S. (2001) "Gender, Flexibility and Global Value Chains," *IDS Bulletin*, 32(3): 83–93.

Barrientos, S. and Dolan, C. (eds) (2006) *Ethical Sourcing in the Global Food System*, London: Earthscan.

Barrientos, S. and Kritzinger, A. (2004) "Squaring the circle – global production and the informalisation of work in South African fruit exports," *Journal of International Development*, 16: 81–92.

Barrientos, S. and Smith, S. (2006) *ETI Impact Assessment*, London: Ethical Trading Initiative, available online at www.ethicaltrade.org/d/impactreport

Barrientos, S., Dolan, C., and Tallontire, A. (2003) "A gendered value chain approach to codes of conduct in African horticulture," *World Development*, 31 (9): 1511–26.

Çağatay, N. (2001) *Trade, Gender and Poverty*, New York: UNDP: 1–42.

Çağatay, N., Elson, D., and Grown, C. (1995) "Special issue: gender and macroeconomics," *World Development*, 23 (11): 1827.

CCC (2005) *Looking for a Quick Fix: how weak social auditing is keeping workers in sweatshops*, Amsterdam: Clean Clothes Campaign.

Chen, M., Vanek, J., and Carr, M. (2004) *Mainstreaming Informal Employment and Gender in Poverty Reduction*, London: Common wealth secretariat.

Collins, J. (2003) *Threads: gender, labor and power in the global apparel industry*, Chicago, IL: University of Chicago Press.

Dicken, P., Kelly, K.O., and Wai-Cheung Yeung, H. (2001) "Chains and networks, territories and scales: towards a relation ional framework for analyzing the global economy," *Global Networks*, 1 (2): 89–112.

Efendioglu, U., Posthuma, A., and Rossi, A. (2005) "Decent work in global production systems: an integrated approach to economic and social upgrading," Executive summary of an ILO Working Paper in progress, Geneva: ILO.

Elson, D. (1999) "Labor markets as gendered institutions: equality, efficiency and empowerment issues," *World Development*, 27 (3): 611–27.

Elson, D. and Gideon, J. (1999) *The International Covenant on Economic, Social and Cultural Rights and the Empowerment of Women*, New York: UNIFEM.

Folbre, N. (1994) *Who Pays for the Kids? Gender and the Structures of Constraint*, London: Routledge.

Freeman, R. (1993) *Labor Market Institutions and Policies: help or hindrance to economic development*, Proceedings of the World Bank Annual Conference on Development Economics, Washington, DC: World Bank.

Gap (2004) *Social Responsibility Report*, available online at www.gapinc.com/public/documents/CSR_Report_03.pdf (accessed December 2005).

Gereffi, G. (1994) "Capitalism, development and global commodity chains," in L. Sklair (ed.), *Capitalism and Development*, London: Routledge.

Gereffi, G., Humphrey, J., Kaplinski, R., and Sturgeon, T. (2005) "The governance of global value chains," *Review of International Political Economy*, 12 (1): 78–104.

Grown, C., Elson, D., and Çağatay, N. (2000) "Introduction to special issue on gender, macroeconomics, trade and finance," *World Development*, 28 (7): 1145–56.

Hale, A. and Wills, J. (eds) (2005) *Threads of Labor: garment industry supply chains from the workers' perspective*, Oxford: Blackwell Publishing.

Hurst, P., with Termine, P. and Karl, M. (2005) *Agricultural Workers and the Contribution to Sustainable Agriculture and Rural Development*, Rome: FAO/ILO/IUF.

ICFTU (2004) "The informal economy: women on the front line," Trade Union World Briefing No. 4, Brussels.

ILO (2002) *Decent Work and the Informal Economy*, Geneva: International Labor Conference, 90th Session.

—— (2004) *Decent Work*, Geneva: International Labor Organization.

Jenkins, R., Pearson, R., and Seyfang, G. (2002) *Corporate Responsibility and Labor Rights: codes of conduct in the global economy*, London: Earthscan.

Joekes, S. and Weston, A. (1994) *Women and the New Trade Agenda*, New York: UNIFEM.

Kabeer, N. (2003) *Gender Mainstreaming in Poverty Eradication and the Millennium Development Goals*, London: Commonwealth Secretariat.

—— (2004) "Globalization, labor standards and women's rights: dilemmas of collective (in)action in an interdependent world," *Feminist Economics*, 10 (1): 3–35.

Kaplinsky, R. (2000) "Spreading the gains from globalization: what can be learned from value chain analysis?" IDS Working Paper No. 110, Brighton: Institute of Development Studies.

Ladbury, S. and Gibbons, S. (2000) *Core Labor Standards. Key issues and a proposal for a strategy*, London: Department for International Development.

Luce, S. (2005) "The case for international labor standards: a 'Northern' perspective," IDS Working Paper No. 250, Brighton: Institute of Development Studies.

Lund, F. and Nicholson, J. (eds) (2003) *Chains of Production, Ladders of Protection: social protection for workers in the informal economy*, Durban: University of Natal.

Lund, F. and Srinivas, S. (2000) *Learning from Experience: a gendered approach to social protection for workers in the informal economy*, Geneva: ILO.

Mahmud, S. and Kabeer, N. (2006) "Compliance versus accountability: struggles for dignity and daily bread in the Bangladesh garment industry," in P. Newell and J. Wheeler (eds), *Rights, Resources and the Politics of Accountability*, London: Zed Books.

Nike (2005) *Corporate Responsibility Report*, available online at www. nike.com/nikebiz/gc/r/fy04/docs/FY04_Nike_CR_report_full.pdf (accessed October 15, 2006).

Oxfam (2004) *Trading Away Our Rights: women working in global supply chains*, Oxford: Oxfam International.

Polaski (2003) *Trade and Labor Standards*, US: Carnegie Endowment for International Peace.

Sengenberger, W. (2002) *Globalization and Social Progress: the role and impact of international labor standards*, Bonn: Fredrick Ebert Stiftung.

Singh, A. and Zammit, A. (2000) *The Global Labor Standards Controversy: critical issues for developing countries*, Geneva: The South Centre.

Smith, S., Auret, D., Barrientos, S., Dolan, S., Kleinbooi, K., Njobvu, C., Opondo, M., and Tallontire, A. (2004) "Ethical trade in African horticulture: gender, rights and participation," IDS Working Paper No. 223, Brighton: Institute of Development Studies.

Theron, J. and Godfrey, S. (2000) *Protecting Workers on the Periphery*, Cape Town: Institute of Development and Labor Law Monograph 1.

Urminsky, M. (ed.) (Undated) "Self regulation in the workplace: codes of conduct, social labeling and socially responsible investment," MCC Working Paper No. 1, Geneva: ILO.

Whitehead, A. (2001) "Trade, trade liberalization and rural poverty in low-income Africa: a gendered account" (Background Paper for the UNCTAD 2001 Least Developed Countries Report), Brighton: University of Sussex.

13 Gender indicators for monitoring trade agreements

Irene van Staveren

Introduction

Although concerns have been raised about the negative impacts of trade liberalization, there is little attention to, and research on, the differentiated impact of trade agreements on women and men, and even less on the two-way relationship between gender and trade. As has been argued in this volume, the pattern of gender relations *is* importantly related to trade, while at the same time gender relations do influence trade outcomes.

Most governments, in the South as well as in the North, have adopted policies on gender equality over the past decade. Since the UN Women's conference that was held in Beijing in 1995, a gender perspective is being integrated in a wide variety of policy areas. Gender equality and women's empowerment are no longer regarded as a separate policy area, independent of sectoral policies. This so-called *mainstreaming* of gender into a variety of policy areas reflects the acknowledgement that gender equality cannot be achieved without changes in a wide variety of policies, including, for example, labor market, fiscal, and financial policies. Why then should we assume it could be achieved in isolation from trade policy? The Beijing Platform for Action explicitly refers to trade policies as an area of concern for gender mainstreaming. One paragraph urges governments to ensure that trade agreements will not have negative impacts on women, while another paragraph advises governments to closely monitor trade and other policies, in order to prevent negative impacts that might arise (UN 1996). In these two paragraphs, governments are advised to:

> Para 165 k: "Seek to ensure that national policies related to international and regional trade agreements do not have an adverse impact on women's new and traditional economic activities."

> Para 165 p: "Use gender-impact analyses in the development of macro and micro-economic and social policies in order to monitor such impact and restructure policies in cases where harmful impact occurs."

But UN recommendations need to be turned into concrete policy measures in order to have an impact. NGOs have been lobbying the WTO, UN organizations, the EC, and individual governments to take gender issues into account in the design, implementation, and monitoring of trade agreements.[1] However, the response has been limited. The European Commission, for example, adopted a Regulation on gender equality in development cooperation in 1998, which was followed up by a more elaborate Regulation in 2004, emphasizing gender mainstreaming in all EU policies and activities.[2] In practice, however, only a few policy areas are mentioned; trade is not mentioned in the 2004 Regulation, and mentioned only as a potential area for mainstreaming in a report on equal opportunities in the EU (European Commission 2000: 26). At the same time, the EC Directorate General of Trade has developed an initiative for "sustainability impact analyses" of trade, which provides a clear opportunity for the European Union to mainstream gender concerns in its trade reviews, along with social and environmental concerns.

The objective of this chapter is to develop a tool for policy makers to mainstream gender equality goals in trade agreements. The proposed tool consists of a set of gender and trade indicators. The chapter discusses the methodology chosen for the development of the indicators, presents 11 indicators, and illustrates their use in relation to the bilateral trade agreement between the European Union (EU) and the four Southern American countries, Argentina, Brazil, Uruguay, and Paraguay, associated in Mercosur.

Methodology and methodological limitations

A policy tool, even for a complex task such as the monitoring of impacts of trade agreements, should be clear in its formulation and user-friendly in its application if it is to be of any use for policy makers, or for others who may be interested in the monitoring of trade impacts, such as NGOs. Indicators for monitoring policy should have the following characteristics:

- *simple*, to facilitate their use;
- *comparable*, to allow comparisons over different trading partners;
- *dynamic*, to enable the monitoring of gender impacts of trade over time;
- *feasible*, that is, constructed of variables for which information is available in national or international databases.

Elasticity indicators are likely to meet these criteria. An elasticity compares the percentage change in one variable, with the accompanying percentage change in another variable. An elasticity may be positive, indicating that the change in both variables is in the same direction; or negative, indicating that the change in one variable is in the opposite direction to the other variable. The relationship is "inelastic" when the value of the elasticity is between plus one and minus one and "elastic" when the value of the elasticity is greater than plus or minus one.

Here we construct a series of trade elasticities of gender equality, in which the denominator measures changes in trade, whereas the numerator measures changes in gender equality. An example is the trade elasticity of the gender wage ratio, which measures how women's wages as a share of men's wages has changed as trade has changed. Applying this to a case when trade has expanded following a new trade agreement, if the value of the ratio is positive this shows that trade expansion has been accompanied by an improvement in the gender wage ratio; if negative, it shows that trade expansion has been accompanied by a deterioration of the gender wage ratio. If the elasticity is between plus and minus one that suggests that changes in the gender wage ratio have not been very sensitive to changes in trade, and conversely values outside this range suggest that changes in the gender wage ratio have been sensitive to changes in trade. Trade elasticities of gender equality may provide initial guidance on where trade expansion has been helpful for women's empowerment, or signal where additional policy measures are required in order to prevent possible negative impacts of trade on gender equality.

Elasticity indicators have some attractions because they are relatively simple to calculate and to apply. But they suffer from serious limitations as well. In particular, elasticities by themselves do not imply any causal relationship between the two variables in the numerator and denominator. They have to be formulated and interpreted in the light of theory and of other empirical evidence. Moreover, they abstract from a wide range of other factors that may influence changes in the numerator and the denominator. This is a drawback because it is difficult to distinguish between effects of trade on gender equality and effects originating from other factors.[3] Changes in the degree of gender equality in the labor market, for instance, may arise from a variety of factors, such as labor supply trends, labor market policies, macroeconomic reform, technological change, investment choices, or fluctuations in aggregate demand.

In addressing this problem, I share the position taken by Burda and Dluhosch (1999), as well as by Gregory (2000), who argue that trade and technology factors are not mutually exclusive explanations for labor market changes, but are interrelated phenomena whose impact may be mutually reinforcing. A further problem is to distinguish between the impacts of a trade agreement between two trading partners on the one hand and impacts of trade agreements with third parties on the other hand. This problem can be addressed, at least partially, by only calculating the elasticities for trade between major trading partners, focusing on relatively high volumes of trade. In this context, it is important to check whether a trade agreement between two partners has resulted in a net expansion of trade or merely trade diversion, away from other trading partners (this point will be further explained later).

A final problem in using trade elasticities of gender equality is lack of appropriate data disaggregated by sex. Even if data is disaggregated by sex, it can be misleading due to difference in the coverage of males and females. For instance, labor market data undercounts informal employment, and because women are more concentrated in informal employment than men, their employment and incomes are more subject to undercounting than those of men (Standing 1999). Moreover, the measurement of gender equality requires data on variables that have traditionally not been included in most statistical surveys; for instance, time spent on unpaid work caring for families and communities.

Taking these methodological limitations into account, the gender and trade indicators to be presented in this chapter should be treated with considerable caution. Their advantage is their simplicity, but the disadvantages mean that they should be treated as diagnostic tools which reveal symptoms not causes. If the symptoms suggest cause for concern, then the elasticity indicators need to be complemented by more in-depth analysis, using tools such as multiple regression analysis that would investigate the roles of factors other than trade, and historical case studies that can investigate transmission mechanisms between trade and gender equality.

Now, we turn to specification of the elasticities. Let us first consider the possibilities for the denominator, that is, the trade variables. The denominator can be calculated in at least four different ways for trade in any given period between two countries, blocks, or regions (in which subscript i refers to the country for which the elasticities are to be calculated, and subscript j refers to a trading partner, or to all trading partners, so that EX_{ij} stands for the exports from country i to country j or all other countries). The formulations all include the delta sign, which means change in a variable over a period of time. The four options are listed here:[4]

- total value of trade of a country or a region ($dEX_{ij} + dIM_{ij}$) or separate values for exports and imports (dEX_{ij}) and (dIM_{ij});
- total value of trade as a share of GDP of a country or a region ($dEX_{ij} + dIM_{ij})/dGDP_i$ or separate values for exports and imports ($dEX_{ij}/dGDP_i$) and ($dIM_{ij}/dGDP_i$);
- bilateral or regional value of total trade as a share of total trade of a country or region ($dEX_{ij} + dIM_{ij})/(dEX_i + dIM_i$) or separate values for exports and imports (dEX_{ij}/dEX_i) and (dIM_{ij}/dIM_i);
- openness measured as tariff reductions of $\times$ percent, hence *dTariff*.

The choice between the four options for the denominator of trade elasticities follows from the type of relationship one is interested in, bearing in mind a number of technical caveats (for an overview of such caveats, see Rodriguez and Rodrik 2001). The first trade variable measures the absolute value of trade, without separating the impact of trade agreements on trade values from the impact of other causes. The second variable is share of trade in GDP, which indicates the relative importance of trade in an economy. Hence, this measure is best used when trade policy leads to substantial shifts in the relative importance of trade, compared to the value of consumption of domestically produced goods, government expenditures, and investment. The third variable highlights trade with a particular trading partner, relative to trade with all other trading partners. This variable is relevant in cases of shifts in relative importance of trading partners or possible cases of trade diversion. Finally, the fourth trade variable is a direct measure of the change in trade policy. This is most closely related to the objective of monitoring policy, but does not throw any light on how changes in trade policy have affected trade values.

For the numerator, a wide variety of gender equality measures can in principle be identified, but data limitations mean there are only a small number of feasible measures. Moreover, it is important to choose dimensions of gender equality which existing research suggests may be sensitive to trade. Feasibility and relevance suggest the use of measures of gender equality in income, employment, wages, and in unpaid domestic work. The next section brings together the trade and gender variables to create a number of trade and gender equality elasticities. It uses the change in the share of trade in GDP as the denominator, for illustrative purposes.

Trade and gender equality elasticities

In arguing for the relevance of the particular measures identified here, I will rely in particular on Çağatay *et al.* (1995) and Grown *et al.* (2000), two special issues of *World Development* dealing with relationships between gender and macro-economic policies, including trade policies, and upon other chapters in this volume. The indicators will all be formulated in such a way that a positive elasticity refers to the case in which an increase in trade is accompanied by an increase in gender equality, whereas a negative elasticity implies gender equality is negatively associated with trade expansion.

Income

In the literature, there are only very few analyses of the relationship between trade and household or personal income. The dominant position, advanced by main-stream economics and international organizations like the WTO, World Bank, and IMF, is that trade liberalization has a positive effect on the personal incomes of poor people, through the intermediate variable of economic growth. Critics of the dominant position on the relationship between trade and income question the presumption of a trickle-down effect, and point out, that in any case, trade does not always lead to economic growth. Rodrik (2001) demonstrates with cross-country multiple regression analysis that there is no systematic positive relationship between trade liberalization and economic growth. The regressions actually indicate that the reverse may be true. "The only systematic relationship is that countries dismantle trade restrictions as they get richer" (Rodrik 2001: 22). He argues that only after countries have experienced economic growth are they able to benefit from opening up their markets. Even if trade liberalization is associated with economic growth, it may also be associated with widening income inequality (Cornia 2004; Wade 2004).

We now turn to the gender dimension of the relationship between trade and income. While most countries do not provide data on personal income disaggregated by sex, there is a wealth of evidence that women's personal incomes are less than those of men. Women, for instance, have fewer assets than men, on average their wages are lower, and they benefit as individuals less than do men from social insurance.[5] Personal income is often not a good measure of personal consumption because of intra-household income transfers. But it does signal personal command over resources, and is a measure of economic power. If an expansion of trade is associated with a rise in the personal incomes of the less well-off, this can be expected to contribute to an increase in gender equality in personal incomes.

The ratio of female income to male (Y^f/Y^m) measures women's personal income compared to that of men. A proxy for this is regularly published in the UNDP Human Development Report, which uses the ratio of female to male earned income as one of the components of the Gender Empowerment Measure. However, this is extrapolated from female labor force participation rates and the ratio of female to male nonagricultural wages, rather than being calculated from household survey data. The income data from the latter are rarely made available in sex-disaggregated form. Trade elasticity of gender equality in personal income:

$$d(Y^f/Y^m)/d(EX_{ij} + IM_{ij})/(GDP_i) \tag{13.1}$$

Employment

Çağatay and Özler (1995) have shown, based on cross-country regression analysis, that with increasing ratios of exports to GNP, the share of women in the labor force increases. Their model includes a variable measuring feminization of the labor force and controls for the well-known U-shaped relationship between women's labor force participation and GDP per capita.[6] This suggests the following gender and trade indicator, with the female share of the labor force as the numerator. Trade elasticity of gender equality in labor force shares:

$$d(L^f/L)/d(EX_{ij} + IM_{ij})/(GDP_i) \tag{13.2}$$

However, this measure aggregates the behavior of different sectors of the economy and masks differences in sector-specific behavior with respect to trade expansion. Employment effects are likely to differ between agriculture, manufacturing and services, and for export sectors and import-competing sectors. It also masks the difference between employed and unemployed members of the labor force. Thus additional employment-related indicators are required. First we consider sector-specific indicators, beginning with a review of some relevant evidence.

Joekes and Weston (1994) found that export expansion in developing countries is frequently accompanied by increases in female employment shares in manufacturing and services. Moreover, they argue that "manufacturing export employment generally provides women in developing countries with better opportunities than alternative employment even if the conditions are poor compared to those available for men in the same country, or for women in manufacturing industries in developed countries" (Joekes and Weston 1994: 82). However, women in developing countries may also experience trade-related employment loss, as has happened, for example, in Mexico since NAFTA (Benería and Mendoza 1995; Oxfam International 2002).

There has been some debate about the impact of expansion of manufacturing exports from developing countries on women's employment in developed countries. Wood (1991) found that while female manufacturing employment in developing countries has increased in absolute terms, and as a share of manufacturing employment in those countries, the share of female manufacturing employment in total manufacturing employment in developed countries has not fallen. Wood attributes this asymmetry, at least in part, to competition from developing countries, suggesting that developed countries might have replaced male labor with cheaper female labor in import-competing industries. Others, however, have challenged Wood's research findings on empirical grounds, arguing that the female share of manufacturing employment did go down in OECD countries, as predicted by trade theory. Kucera and Milberg (2000 and in this volume) have applied factor content analysis showing that trade-related employment losses have disproportionately affected women workers in OECD countries. The explanation they provide for this gender bias in employment losses is that the industries that suffer particularly from import penetration from developing countries, such as textiles, apparel, leather, and leather goods, are all female-labor-intensive industries.

A study of the labor market position of the low-skilled in Europe (Gregory 2000) found that on average labor market policies and social policies in the EU have helped to protect disadvantaged workers, but in doing so, they benefited women less than men. Despite women's increased educational attainments, in many European countries now equal with that of men, women earn lower wages, are more likely to be employed in low-skilled jobs, and experience higher unemployment rates. This makes women in Europe more vulnerable to trade-related employment-loss than men.

Armah (1994) studied trade effects on women's employment in the services sector in the USA. He found that women are more often employed in trade-sensitive services sectors than men, even more so for black and hispanic women. Moreover, women appeared to be more vulnerable to employment losses due to international trade than men, with minority women being most vulnerable. In a follow-up article, Armah (1995) found that male workers in the USA benefited more from trade-related employment gains in the services sector than female workers, even though men in this sector were less-educated and less-skilled compared to female employees. He argued that over time, employment gains from trade in the services sector are decreasing, and women's gains, particularly minority women's gains, are decreasing at the fastest rate.

To take account of sectoral differences in trade-related employment changes, two further elasticities are proposed. Indicator (13.3) focuses on the export sectors. It is the trade elasticity of gender equality in shares of export employment:

$$d(L^f_{ex}/L_{ex})/d(EX_{ij})/(GDP_i) \qquad (13.3)$$

This indicator uses the female employment share in the export sector (L^f_{ex}/L_{ex}) as the gender equality measure, but may just as well, if data permits, use more detailed sectoral measures such as female employment shares in agricultural, manufacturing, or services export production. The rationale for this is that an increase in the female share in export employment may be regarded as an increase in gender equality (even though the conditions of employment may fall short of ILO standards), because it is an increasing share of an expanding sector.

Indicator 13.4 focuses on the import-competing sectors. It is the trade elasticity of gender equality in shares of employment in import-competing sectors:

$$d(L^m_{imc}/L_{imc})/d(IM_{ij})/(GDP_i) \tag{13.4}$$

The gender variable for this elasticity (L^m_{imc}/L_{imc}) measures male share of employment in import-competing sectors. Again, this variable could be further disaggregated by sector. The reason why this indicator includes the male share, rather than the female share, of employment is that in the context of trade liberalization, the import-competing sector is a shrinking sector. An increase in the female share in employment in this sector points to an increase in the vulnerability of women's jobs, relative to those of men, that is, an increase in inequality rather than equality.

The review of some relevant sector-specific evidence shows that women can lose, as well as gain, jobs from trade expansion. Trade expansion may be accompanied by a rise in female unemployment rates, as Ghosh (1996) shows for Asia over the 1980s and early 1990s. Indicator (13.5) brings unemployment into the frame. It is the trade elasticity of the gender gap in unemployment rates:

$$d(U^m/U^f)/d(EX_{ij} + IM_{ij})/(GDP_i) \tag{13.5}$$

The gender variable in this elasticity measures the ratio of the male unemployment rate to the female unemployment rate (U^m/U^f), and may also be disaggregated over export or import-competing sectors. However, in many developing countries unemployment data is a poor indicator of lack of an adequate means of making a living, because in the absence of welfare support, people will try to make a living in the informal economy, as low-paid temporary, part-time, or seasonal workers. This may be regarded as a form of underemployment, either because the worker is not able to work as many hours as they would wish, or because the worker is unable to achieve the level of productivity that they are capable of. Indicator (13.6) focuses on underemployment (denoted by L_x, in which x may refer to a variety of proxies for underemployment, such as temporary work, part-time work, and seasonal work). Trade elasticity of the gender gap in underemployment:

$$d(L^m_x/L^f_x)/d(EX_{ij} + IM_{ij})/(GDP_i) \tag{13.6}$$

The indicators considered so far are indicators of employment quantity. They do not indicate whether trade expansion challenges occupational sex-segregation or intensifies the crowding of women into a few highly "female" occupations. To examine this we need an indicator that includes a measure of occupational sex-segregation. Indicator (13.7) incorporates a well-known measure of the latter, that is, the Dissimilarity Index, or Duncan Index, (DI).[7] An increase in the inverse of this index signals a decrease in job segregation, and thus an increase in gender equality. Indicator (13.7) could be measured for the economy as a whole (13.7a) or by sector (13.7b and 13.7c).

Trade elasticity of gendered job segregation:

$$d(1/DI)/d(EX_{ij} + IM_{ij})/(GDP_i) \tag{13.7a}$$

Trade elasticity of gendered job segregation in the export sector:

$$d(1/DI_{ex})/d(EX_{ij})/(GDP_i) \tag{13.7b}$$

Trade elasticity of gendered job segregation in the import-competing sector:

$$d(1/ID_{imc})/d(IM_{ij})/(GDP_i) \tag{13.7c}$$

Wages

There is a considerable literature on the relationship between trade and the gender wage gap. Some contributions investigate the impact of the gender wage gap on trade; others investigate the impact of trade on the gender wage gap. An example of the first type of contribution is provided by Seguino (2000a,b), who analyzes how the gender wage gap affects exports, investment, and growth, in a group of semi-industrialized countries. Using cross-country regression analysis, she shows that wage inequality and GDP growth are strongly positively correlated. She finds that the link works through the positive effect of the gender wage gap on the growth of exports and investment.

Some of the investigations of the impact of trade expansion on the gender wage gap find a positive impact, and some a negative impact. An example of positive impact is provided by Black and Brainerd (2003) who argue, on the basis of US data, that import competition reduces the ability of firms to discriminate against women, and hence, that trade expansion reduces the gender wage gap through this mechanism. This conclusion is disputed by Kongar (this volume) who provides an alternative explanation for the reduction in the gender wage gap in the USA. A cross-country analysis of 62 developed and developing countries by Weichselbaumer and Winter-Ebmer (2003) finds that national equal treatment laws are significant, as well as international competition, in reducing the gender wage gap. Oostendorp (2004) confirms this finding in a study covering more than 80 developed and developing countries. He also found evidence that the impact of trade is different on the gender gap in low-skilled and high-skilled work: the expansion of trade narrows the gender wage gap for low-skilled labor in developing countries but not for high-skilled labor in these countries.

In a study on effects of import competition on the gender wage gap in Taiwan and Korea, Berik and van der Meulen Rodgers (2004) have challenged the hypothesis that more competition reduces gender discrimination in wages. They found that increased competition was positively correlated with wage discrimination against women, probably due to a reduction in women's bargaining power.

This brief literature review on the relationships between trade and the gender wage gap suggests that the relationship may be different for different countries and groups of workers. So, whatever the relationship may be, it seems plausible to expect some effect of trade expansion on the gender wage gap. This is reflected in the following indicators.

Trade elasticity of the gender wage gap in the export sector:[8]

$$d(W^f/W^m)/d(EX_{ij})/(GDP_i) \qquad (13.8a)$$

Trade elasticity of the gender wage gap in the import-competing sector:

$$d(W^f/W^m)/d(IM_{ij})/(GDP_i) \qquad (13.8b)$$

Export expansion may also raise women's wages in the export sector, relative to women's wages in other sectors. This can be captured by the trade elasticity of women's wages in the export sector, relative to women's wages in other sectors (W^f):

$$d(W^f_{ex}/W^f)/d(EX_{ij} + IM_{ij})/(GDP_i) \qquad (13.9)$$

Unpaid domestic work

The expansion of trade may have impacts on unpaid domestic work as well as on paid work. Unpaid domestic work is primarily done by women and girls, and includes tasks such as housework, child care, care for sick and infirm household members, production of food for the family, and collecting water and fuel. Floro (1995) analyzed a variety of case studies on combined effects of macroeconomic reform and export orientation on women's unpaid domestic work in developing countries. She concludes that women bear most of the burden of adjustments, increasing both their paid and their unpaid labor time and increasing the intensity of their work. Export expansion may provide more paid work to women while trade liberalization will likely have indirect effects on women's unpaid work through its effects on public finance. Tax revenue from trade taxes has fallen in many developing countries (Khattry and Rao 2002). This has led to reductions in public expenditure (measured as share of GDP) on infrastructure, education, and health (Khattry 2003). In turn, this is likely to increase women's unpaid work burden, as they will try to produce substitutes for public services.

A key aspect of women's unpaid domestic work is providing meals for their families, either from food they have grown themselves, and/or from food they have purchased. The literature suggests that trade may affect food security in several ways. When the volume of food exports increases, domestic food prices may rise (Pinstrup-Andersen 2003; and for Argentina, see Gerchunoff and Llach 2003). When, however, the volume of food imports increasess, food prices tend to fall. A rise in food prices will not be gender neutral. It will tend to increase the time spent on providing meals by women who purchase most of their families' food, as they try to offset the price rises by spending more time in shopping for bargains, and in buying food which is less processed and takes more time to prepare. For women farmers who produce food for their families and sell surpluses on local markets, a rise in food prices will tend to increase their incomes. However, it may also lead to pressure from their husbands to divert their time from production of food for the family to produce food crops for export, the proceeds from which are controlled by their husbands. (For a discussion of these complex possible effects on farming women, see Darity, this volume, and Warner and Campbell 2000.)

In order to capture the effects of trade on gender equality on unpaid domestic work, the following indicator can be formulated, where $UNPT^m/UNPT^f$ is the ratio of time that males spend in unpaid domestic work to the time spent by females. Trade elasticity of the gender gap in unpaid labor time:

$$d(UNPT^m/UNPT^f)/d(EX_{ij} + IM_{ij})/(GDP_i) \qquad (13.10)$$

However, time series data on time spent on unpaid work is only available for a few countries. It is easier to obtain data on food prices, and use changes in food prices as a proxy for changes in time spent in purchasing food and preparing meals for families. The change in the inverse of the food price index (100/FPI) is an indicator of the affordability of food. An improvement in food affordability is likely to reduce the time that women who buy food have to spend in providing meals for their families, and thus to reduce the gender gap in time spent in unpaid work. Trade elasticity of food affordability in relation to exports:

$$d(100/FPI)/d(EX_{ij})/(GDP_i) \qquad (13.11a)$$

Trade elasticity of food affordability in relation to imports:

$$d(100/FPI)/d(IM_{ij})/(GDP_i) \qquad (13.11b)$$

Positive values for indicators (13.10), (13.11a), and (13.11b) would imply that trade expansion would improve gender equality in time spent in unpaid domestic work.

An example: EU–Mercosur trade relations

In this section, I will illustrate how the gender indicators may be applied to a particular trade relation. A trade agreement between the European Union and Mercosur was initiated in 1995 and ratified in 2000, hence, it came gradually into being since 1995. Trade between the partner regions has increased since 1995, and is expected to increase further when the trade agreement is followed by a more wide-ranging association agreement, including a free trade area, as is currently being negotiated between the two blocks.[9] Trade between the two partners follows a traditional North–South pattern of specialization (see Table 13.1).

Table 13.1 Composition of Mercosur trade with EU (2002)[a]

Sector	Mercosur exports to EU (%)	Mercosur imports from EU (%)
Agriculture	70	7
Manufacturing	30	90

Source: EUROSTAT, 2006.

Note

a The import data do not add up to 100 percent because of other relevant categories not included in the table.

The Mercosur economies have experienced falls in their GDP in various years since 1995, particularly for Argentina (10.8 percent decline in GDP) and Uruguay (12.7 percent decline in GDP).[10] Since 2002, Mercosur GDP growth rates have been positive. The data will be taken for a 10-year period 1995–2004, but it must be noted that this period includes a serious economic crisis, especially for Argentina. At the same time Mercosur members have had currency devaluations, boosting their exports and discouraging their imports, which is reflected in the trade data. The combination of falling GDP and rising trade has dramatically increased trade as a share of GDP in the Mercosur, but this is primarily due to the economic crisis and the monetary and fiscal polices used to address this, rather than the trade agreement with the EU. Hence, the denominator of the elasticities to be presented in this section will measure percentage changes in trade values between Mercosur and the EU, not in the trade share in GDP.

As recommended in the discussion of methodology, it is important to check that trade between the two trading partners is substantial, vis-à-vis other trading partners, and to consider the possibility that an expansion of trade between the chosen trading partners is simply the result of diversion away from trade with other partners. Table 13.2 shows that the EU was the most important trading partner for Mercosur, both in 1995 and in 2004. The changes in trade shares in the table suggest that the EU–Mercosur agreement has not implied trade diversion away from other regions, since it shows that the EU's share of the total trade of the Mercosur declined slightly from almost 27 percent to just over 24 percent. However, the EU's share of Mercosur exports has increased. For the EU, however, Mercosur is only a minor trading partner, representing about 2 percent of EU trade (Eurostat 2006). Because of this marginal importance, only gender and trade indicators for the Mercosur trading partner will be presented in this chapter, not for the EU.

From these data, we can now calculate the denominator values for the gender trade elasticities between Mercosur and the EU, for the period 1995–2004 as follows:

Increase in value of total Mercosur–EU trade: $d(EX_{ij} + IM_{ij})$ of 41.9 percent
Increase in value of Mercosur exports to EU: dEX_{ij} of 77.3 percent
Increase in Mercosur imports from EU: dIM_{ij} of 12.6 percent

For the numerator values, available data for relevant gender variables and changes in them over time in the Mercosur are presented in Table 13.3.[11]

Table 13.2 Values and shares of Mercosur trade with major trading partners (million USD)[a]

	1995				2004			
	EU	USA and Canada	Mercosur[b]	World	EU	USA and Canada	Mercosur[b]	World
Imports	22,055	17,354	14,495	79,528	24,835	20,926	17,910	98,276
	(27.7)	(21.8)	(18.2)	(100)	(25.3)	(21.3)	(18.2)	(100)
Exports	18,217	11,026	14,199	70,008	32,299	27,135	16,721	138,892
	(26.0)	(15.7)	(20.3)	(100)	(32.9)	(19.5)	(12.0)	(100)
Total	40,272	28,380	28,694	149,536	57,134	48,061	34,631	237,168
trade	(26.9)	(19.0)	(19.2)	(100)	(24.1)	(20.3)	(14.6)	(100)

Source: UNCTAD *Handbook of Trade Statistics*, 2006.

Notes
a Shares (%) are shown in brackets below values. The major regional trade shares do not add up to the world share because other regions are not included in this table.
b The differences between the import and export totals for intra-Mercosur trade are due to measurement errors.

Table 13.3 Gender equality indicators, Mercosur 1995–2004

	1995	2004	Change (%)
Food affordability index (100/food price index, 2000 = 1)	1.15	0.67	−42.0
Gender gap in unemployment (male unemployment rate as % of female)[a]	72.4	71.1	−1.8
Female share of agricultural employment (%)[b]	31.6	29.8	−5.7
Male share of manufacturing employment (%)[b]	62.2	44.5	−28.5
Agricultural gender wage ratio (female as % of male)[c]	101.5	87.2	−14.1
Manufacturing gender wage ratio (female as % of male)[c]	56.9	61.3	7.7

Source: *Human Development Report* 2004, New York: UNDP; LABORSTA, ILO, 2006; ECLAC Gender Indicators, 2006. All values are calculated with weighted for share of population size for each country in Mercosur.

Notes
a 2003 data.
b No data available for Paraguay; all data for 2003.
c There is no annual data for the gender wage gap, hence, for Argentina 1997 was used, for Brazil 2001, for Uruguay 1994, and for Paraguay 1996 and 2001.

In combination with the denominator values presented earlier, the gender data result in the following gender and trade elasticities, presented in Table 13.4.

As noted in the discussion earlier about methodological limitations, the indicators are tools for diagnosis. If they show that an expansion of trade has been accompanied by a decline in gender equality (i.e. the elasticity is negative), then

Table 13.4 Gender and trade indicators for Mercosur trade with EU 1995–2004

Trade elasticity of:	Value	Elastic?
Food affordability	−1	Yes, negative
Gender gap in unemployment	0	No
Gender equality in export employment (i.e. in agriculture)	−0.1	No
Gender equality in import competing employment (i.e. in manufacturing)	−2.3	Yes, negative
Gender wage gap in export sector (i.e. in agriculture)	−0.2	No
Gender wage gap in import competing sector (i.e.in manufacturing)	0.6	No

Source: Author's calculations from ILO data base (LABORSTA) and UNCTAD Trade Statistics, both online 2006.

there is a need for further research, either quantitative (multiple regression analysis including other factors than trade influencing gender inequalities) and/or qualitative (case studies on the trade agreement and its institutional context, and the transmission mechanisms through which trade expansion impacts on gender equality). So, the values of the elasticities in Table 13.4 should be regarded as providing a preliminary assessment that may signal areas of concern in future negotiations between the Mercosur and the EU.

The trade elasticity for food affordability is unity and negative ($-42/41.9 = -1$). Mercosur exports mainly food items, the same that are consumed domestically. This may have led to a crowding out of domestic food supply by foreign demand, following the currency devaluations. The indicator suggests that it has become more difficult for women to perform their assigned roles in households as food providers, because women in Mercosur are net food buyers, not growers (over 80 percent of the population lives in urban areas). This is even more so the case, because absolute female (and male) income levels have declined over the period.

Table 13.3 shows that the ratio of male unemployment to female unemployment has declined slightly. Since there has been a substantial increase in trade, the indicator is inelastic. It appears that trade expansion has not helped much in reducing the gender gap in unemployment rates.

For changes in the female employment share, it is important to distinguish between the two main trade sectors with the EU: agriculture and manufacturing. As Table 13.1 has already indicated, the exports to EU largely consist of agricultural products, whereas the imports from the EU are mainly manufactured products. The elasticities, therefore, need to distinguish between these two sectors. The indicator for the female employment share in the major export sector, agriculture, is negative and inelastic ($-5.7/77.3 = -0.1$). So, the enormous increase in agricultural exports has not helped to increase the female employment share in this stable and expanding export sector in Mercosur.

At the same time, we find that the trade indicator for the male employment share in the major import sector, manufacturing, is negative and elastic ($-28.5/12.6 = -2.3$).

Thus there has been an increase in women's share of jobs in the sector that faces import competition. Further research needs to be done in order to find out whether this process is paralleled by increasing flexibility and vulnerability of these jobs, and pressure on labor standards. Also, there may be different gender impacts for subsectors in manufacturing, for example, depending on the capital intensity of a subsector. Such detailed analysis within a sector may reveal whether the position of women is improving vis-à-vis men because the position of both improves while women are catching up, or, alternatively, whether, the positions of both are deteriorating but men's position is deteriorating faster than women's. But, whereas in many other developing countries, a move of women from agriculture to manufacturing is generally an improvement of their employment condition since manufacturing is an expanding factor, in Mercosur it implies a shift away from an expanding stable export sector towards an import-competing sector.

Table 13.3 shows that the aggregate gender wage gap in Mercosur has improved by 8.3 percent, but the indicators for the responsiveness of the gender wage gap to trade in both export and import sectors are inelastic. It is interesting to note that the gender wage gap has worsened for agriculture and improved for manufacturing. This may reflect shifts in relative labor scarcity along gender lines, because, as we have seen, the female employment share in agriculture has declined, while it has increased in the manufacturing sector. Again, further analysis, preferably at industry level, is required in order to find underlying mechanisms. Most of the values for the gender equality indicators of Mercosur–EU trade over the 1995–2004 period are inelastic. This suggests that trade expansion with the EU does not do a great deal to help to improve gender equality in the Mercosur region, at least, not in terms of women's relative unemployment rates, women's employment share in the expanding export sector, and the gender wage gap. The indicators for food affordability and for gender equality in employment in the import-competing sector are elastic and negative. This suggests that the expanded trade with EU may actually have contributed to worsening food affordability, and hence made women's task of providing food for the household more difficult. Moreover, the negative elasticity for the male share of employment in the import-competing sector (manufacturing) indicates that women's share of jobs had increased in the sector that is most vulnerable to imports from the EU, and hence most vulnerable to job losses and informalization of work.

The value of these indicators for policy makers and other stakeholders (including NGOs and trade unions) is that they signal possible negative gender impacts of the Mercosur–EU trade agreement. It should be emphasized that the indicators presented here need to be complemented with further analysis. Moreover, the indicators, aided by further analysis, can provide an information basis for policy measures that could become part of the trade agreement in the future, or can function as complementary measures to the trade agreement. Examples of such policy measures would be training in gender analysis for members of the trade delegations, effective legislation on equal pay for jobs of equal worth, food assistance for poor households, and skills training programs for unemployed women for jobs in export growth sectors.

Finally, combining the information from all four tables, the case study also suggests that there may be impacts from persistent gender inequalities in Mercosur, such as in the labor market, on its trade relationship with the EU. In particular, the data seem to suggest that the 'lock-in' situation of Mercosur in a traditional trade pattern with EU (exports of primary products and imports of manufactures) may actually be reinforced by the gender inequalities in the labor markets of the four countries in South America. Whereas women's average level of education is higher than that of men, they are paid less and find themselves increasingly employed in a sector which is threatened by imported manufactured goods from the EU. This does not seem to be the most efficient allocation of human resources and is not very likely to help Mercosur to move into higher value-added exports, because that would require a better use of human resources, partly through higher returns to female human capital (which is higher than male human capital in Mercosur), which in turn would help to stimulate labor productivity. Trade with other external partners, as well as intra-Mercosur trade, appears to be less traditional. Catão and Falcetti (2002), for example, have shown the importance of the Brazilian market for the expansion of Argentinean manufacturing exports, at least during the first seven years of Mercosur (1991–7). A recent Mercosur report shows that currently, exports to the rest of the world have an increasing share of higher technology (IDB 2004). Hence, it is not unlikely that these other trading partners provide more opportunities for higher value-added exports than the trade relationship with the EU. In short, a possible two-way relationship between trade and gender should be taken into account in any follow-up research for the monitoring and evaluation of the Mercosur–EU trade agreement.

Conclusions

The literature reviewed in this chapter for the development of gender and trade indicators shows that mainstreaming gender into trade policies is not an unimportant matter: trade does appear to be capable of impacting upon gender relations in a variety of ways. The set of 11 gender and trade indicators presented earlier is constructed in such a way that the indicators are likely to reflect at least a part of such impacts. However, the indicators need to be complemented by detailed research, at regional level, country level, and subsector level, taking into account the peculiarities of each trade relation and institutional setting in which trade takes place. As the literature indicates, gender impacts may be positive or negative, depending on the pattern of trade, the values of imports and exports, the sectoral distribution of exports and import competition, the skill level of male and female employment, labor market policies and institutions, laws and the enforcement of antidiscrimination laws, the gender division of labor in households, and the cultural pattern of male and female roles in the economy at large, including the unpaid economy.

If the indicators proposed here are to be used as a tool for gender mainstreaming in trade policy, more efforts will be needed in the collection of data.

Sex-disaggregated employment and wage data need to be collected allowing for a distinction between export sectors and import-competing sectors. Data on time spent on unpaid work should be collected by regular national surveys and included in standard socioeconomic statistical databases.

Policy makers, NGOs, trade unions, and other stakeholders may use these indicators at various stages of a trade agreement. Before an agreement is negotiated, the indicators may serve to provide a base line, showing how trade and gender variables have moved in the past between the trading partners. During negotiations (which may take several years) and various stages of the implementation of an agreement, policy makers may use the indicators in order to signal possible gender impacts of the trade agreement. When the agreement has been implemented for some time, the indicators may serve as a monitoring tool for policy makers as well as for civil society organizations, and possible negative indicator values may be used for the demand for and development of changes in trade policy measures or complementary policies. Overall, the indicators would serve to help in bringing consistency between trading partners' trade policies and gender policies, that is, in mainstreaming gender in trade agreements. Policy responses should include both direct and indirect measures. Direct policy measures would be needed to prevent or to redress negative gender impacts, and would include actions that are directly related to trade and the trade policy context, such as the inclusion of gender expertise in trade delegations, stimulation of foreign investment into particular sectors of the economy, technical support in the enforcement of labor laws in export processing zones, and stricter social accountability requirements for subsidiaries of companies that have their headquarters in the trading partner's country. Indirect policy measures are not part of trade policies but address the wider institutional setting in which trade takes place. They include labor market policies, in particular those addressing the problems of gendered job segregation and the gender wage gap; fiscal policies including expenditure in services such as child care; and policies in the area of human resource development.

The set of gender and trade indicators presented in this chapter is only one way to address possible linkages between trade and gender. They need to be integrated into a wider set of tools, such as a broader trade impact analysis, and used to inform trade negotiations and evaluations; agenda setting for WTO ministerial meetings; and civil society discussions about actual and desirable relationships between trade, on the one hand, and social issues on the other hand.

Notes

1 It is mainly women's networks of activists and researchers that have pointed to the gender dimension of trade impacts. For example, the International Gender and Trade Network (IGTN) and the Informal Working Group on Gender and Trade (IWGGT) with members in Africa, Asia, Latin America, Europe, and North America have lobbied the WTO on gender issues since it was set up (WIDE 1996, 1997; IWGGT 1998; WIDE and other NGOs 1999; Hale and Hurley 2001; IGTN 2001; IWGGT 2001). In addition, the UN has expressed concerns about gender inequality in trade liberalization: for example,

the UN Economic and Social Council noted in 2000 that women were largely excluded from the WTO decision-making structures, and that the rules evolved by WTO are largely gender-insensitive.

2 Council Regulation No. 2836/98 and Council Regulation No. 806/2004. The progress of gender equality in the EU is well documented, for example, in European Commission (2000).

3 Some authors hold that they are able to separate trade and other factors. For example, Baldwin (1995) argues that shifts in employment and wages depend less on international trade than on technology, labor supply, and the demand for goods and services. Also Lawrence (1996) notes that it is not so much trade which is responsible for the loss in employment for low-skilled labor in developed countries, but technological developments that reduce the ratio of blue collar to white collar labor everywhere, in OECD countries as well as in developing countries. Others argue that trade factors and other factors cannot be separated in the models used so far. For example, Leamer (1999) admits that models based on the Heckscher–Ohlin theory as well as the Stolper–Samuelson theorem are simply not able to disentangle trade and technological change as underlying causes of changes in relative wages for low-skilled labor between developed and developing countries.

4 For a careful discussion about the choice of trade variable for impact analysis of trade liberalization, see Rodriguez and Rodrik (2001).

5 See, for example, UNIFEM (2002), which provides an overview with quantitative and qualitative data on the economic status of the world's women.

6 The U-shaped relationship between female labor force participation and economic growth reflects a global trend, that female labor force participation decreases as a country makes the transition from a least developed country to a middle-income country, but then starts to increase again when countries further increase their GDP per capita. For literature on this phenomenon, see, for example, Mehra and Gammage (1999).

7 *DI* values range between 0 (no segregation) and 1 (total segregation). *DI* is calculated in its most simple version as the female share in occupation X over the female share in the labor force minus the male share in occupation X over the male share in the labor force. See Anker (1998) for a comprehensive analysis of gendered job segregation.

8 In the literature W^f/W^m is often referred to as the gender wage gap, but is in formal terms the ratio of female to male average wages. Strictly speaking, the gender wage gap is $(1 - W^f/W^m)$. In this chapter we follow the literature in measuring the gender wage gap as a ratio rather than a difference.

9 It is important to note that in the ten-year period for which data will be used, the EU increased from 15 to 25 member states in the last year. For 2004 the EU25 data will be used, whereas for 1995 EU15 data will be used. The difference is small, though, as the EU15 is the most important trading group in the EU25. In 2004 the EU15 export share was 93 percent of EU25 exports, while for imports the share was 92 percent.

10 Average data for the four Mercosur countries is weighted for population share, with Argentina 16 percent, Brazil 79 percent, Uruguay 2 percent, and Paraguay 3 percent of the total Mercosur population of 235 million.

11 For reasons of clarity and consistency, all indicators have been formulated in such a way that a positive elasticity implies an improvement of gender equality with the expansion of trade. This has led, in some cases, to nonstandard formulations for numerator variables, such as male/female ratios instead of female/male ratios.

References

Anker, R. (1998) *Gender and Jobs: sex segregation of occupations in the world*, Geneva: ILO.

Armah, B. (1994) "Impact of trade on service sector employment: implications for women and minorities," *Contemporary Economic Policy*, 12: 67–78.

—— (1995) "Trade-affected workers in the service sector: 1987 and 1990," *American Journal of Economics and Sociology*, 54: 163–77.

Baldwin, R. (1995) "The effect of trade and foreign direct investment on employment and relative wages," NBER Working Paper No. 5037, Cambridge, MA: National Bureau of Economic Research.

Benería, L. and Mendoza, B. (1995) "Structural adjustment and social investment funds: the case of Honduras, Mexico and Nicaragua," *European Journal of Development Research*, 7 (1): 53–76.

Berik, G. and van der Meulen Rodgers, Y. (2004) "International trade and gender wage discrimination: evidence from East Asia," *Review of Development Economics*, 8: 237–54.

Black, S. and Brainerd, E. (2003) "Importing equality? The impact of globalization on gender discrimination," *Industrial and Labor Relations Review*, 57: 540–59.

Burda, M. and Dluhosch, B. (1999) "Globalisation and European labor markets," in H. Siebert (ed.), *Globalisation and Labor*, Tübingen: Mohr Siebeck:181–207.

Çağatay, N. and Özler, S. (1995) "Feminisation of the labor force: the effects of long-term development and structural adjustment," *World Development*, 23: 1883–94.

Çağatay, N., Elson, D., and Grown, C. (1995) "Introduction," *World Development*, 23: 1827–36.

Catão, L. and Falcetti, E. (2002) "Determinants of Argentina's external trade," *Journal of Applied Economics*, V (1): 19–57.

Cornia, G.A. (ed.) (2004) *Inequality, Growth and Poverty in an Era of Liberalization and Globalization*, Oxford: Oxford University Press.

European Commission (2000) "Report on equal opportunities for women and men in the European Union 1999," Brussels, COM (2000) 123 final, 08-03-2000.

Eurostat (2006) Internet resource to be found at http://ec.europa.eu/comm/external_ relations/mercosur/intro/05

Floro, M. (1995) "Economic restructuring, gender and the allocation of time," *World Development*, 23: 1913–29.

Gerchunoff, P. and Llach, L. (2003) "Ved en Trono a la Noble Igualdad. Crecimiento, Equidad y Política Económia en Argentina, 1880–2003," Working Paper 003, Buenos Aires: Fundación Pent.

Ghosh, J. (1996) "Gender, trade and the WTO: issues and evidence from developing Asia," paper for UN Economic and Social Commission for Asia and the Pacific, in preparation of First WTO Ministerial Conference, September 4–6, 1996, Jakarta.

Gregory, M. (2000) "Employment and labor markets: some issues for the new millennium," *International Journal of Manpower*, 21: 160–76.

Grown, C., Elson, D., and Çağatay, N. (2000) "Introduction," *World Development*, 28: 1145–56.

Hale, A. and Hurley, J. (2001) "What does the phase out of the MFA quota system mean for garmentworkers?" paper available at http://www.poptel.org.uk/women-ww/free_sheet_ mfa_phaseout.htm (accessed May 29, 2006).

IDB (2004) *Mercosur Report 2003–2004*, Buenos Aires: IDB-INTAL.

IGTN Bulletin (2001) Paper available at http://www.igtn.org/page/bulletins/ (accessed May 29, 2006).

IWGGT (1998) "Gender and trade: some conceptual and policy links," briefing statement of the Informal Working Group on Gender and Trade (IWGGT) for the Second Ministerial Meeting of the WTO, Geneva, May 18–20, 1998.

—— (2001) Paper available at http://www.coc.org/pdfs/coc/IGTNdoha.pdf (accessed May 29, 2006).

Joekes, S. and Weston, A. (1994) *Women and the New Trade Agenda*, New York: UNIFEM.

Khattry, B. (2003) "Trade liberalization and the fiscal squeeze: implications for public investment," *Development and Change*, 34 (3): 401–24.

Khattry, B. and Rao, M. (2002) "Fiscal faux pas? An analysis of the revenue implications of trade liberalization," *World Development*, 30: 1431–44.

Kucera, D. and Milberg, W. (2000) "Gender segregation and gender bias in manufacturing trade expansion: revisiting the 'Wood Asymmetry'," *World Development*, 28: 1191–210.

Lawrence, R. (1996) *Single World Divided Nations? International Trade and OECD Labor Markets*, Paris: OECD Development Centre.

Leamer, E. (1999) "Competition in tradables as a driving force of rising income inequality," in H. Siebert (ed.), *Globalization and Labor*, Tübingen: Mohr Siebeck: 119–52.

Mehra, R. and Gammage, S. (1999) "Trends, countertrends, and gaps in women's employment," *World Development*, 27: 533–50.

Oostendorp, R. (2004) "Globalization and the gender wage gap," Policy Research Working Paper Series No. 3256, Washington, DC: World Bank.

Oxfam International (2002) *Rigged Rules and Double Standards*, Oxford: Oxfam.

Pinstrup-Andersen, P. (2003) "Agricultural development, food security, and trade: the challenges ahead," paper presented at the conference on Agricultural Policy Reform and the WTO: where are we heading? Capri, June, 23–26.

Rodriguez, F. and Rodrik, D. (2001) "Trade policy and economic growth: a skeptic's guide to the cross-national evidence," revised May 2000, Ben Bernanke and Kenneth Rogoff (eds), *Macroeconomics Annual 2000*, Cambridge, MA: MIT Press for NBER.

Rodrik, D. (2001) "The global governance of trade as if development really mattered," background paper for the Trade and Sustainable Human Development Project, New York: UNDP.

Seguino, S. (2000a) "Gender inequality and economic growth: a cross-country analysis," *World Development*, 28: 1211–30.

—— (2000b) "Accounting for gender in Asian economic growth," *Feminist Economics*, 6: 27–58.

Standing, G. (1999) "Global feminisation: through flexible labor: a theme revisited," *World Development*, 27: 583–602.

UN (1996) *The United Nations and the Advancement of Women 1945–1996*, New York: United Nations.

UNIFEM (2002) *Progress of the World's Women 2002: gender equality and the millennium development goals*, New York: UNIFEM.

Wade, R.H. (2004) "Is globalization reducing poverty and inequality?" *World Development*, 32 (4): 567–89.

Warner, J. and Campbell, D.A. (2000) "Supply response in an agrarian economy with non-symmetric gender relations," *World Development*, 28 (7): 1327–40.

Weichselbaumer, D. and Winter-Ebmer, R. (2003) "The effects of competition and equal treatment laws on the gender wage differential," Economics Series No. 138, Vienna: Institute for Advanced Studies.

WIDE (1996) "Briefing paper for the first WTO ministerial meeting," Singapore, December 9–13, 1996.

—— (1997) "Trade traps and gender gaps: women unveiling the market," Brussels: WIDE.

WIDE and other NGOs (1999) *Open letter to WTO member states, to heads of delegations of the WTO member states, and EU commissioner for trade, Mr. Lamy*, Brussels: WIDE.

Wood, A. (1991) "North–South trade and female labor in manufacturing: an asymmetry," *Journal of Development Studies*, 27: 168–89.

14 Gender issues in the multilateral trading system

Mariama Williams

Introduction

The World Trade Organization (WTO) sits at the pinnacle of the contemporary multilateral trading system.[1] The WTO came into force in 1994 and began its oversight of the implementation of the Uruguay Round Agreements.[2] Six ministerial meetings have been held (Singapore 1996; Geneva 1998; Seattle 1999; Doha 2001; Cancun 2003; and Hong Kong 2005). There are stark differences between the WTO system, which seems to be premised on more aggressive and rapid multilateral liberalization of trade, and the previous more flexible GATT system, with its many allowances for multiple forms of Special and Differential Treatment (S&DT) for developing countries. Increasingly, these differences are generating tensions between the trade agenda and the development agenda.

The multilateral trading system is based on what is claimed to be a principle of "nondiscrimination." This means that a country cannot normally differentiate between its trading partners in WTO agreements. A tariff reduction granted on imports from one country must normally be extended to imports from all other countries (the so-called Most Favored Nation principle). It also means that a country cannot normally differentiate between the treatment accorded to domestic and foreign producers (with the exception of levying tariffs). This is the principle of National Treatment. According to the WTO, these principles promote "open, fair and undistorted competition" (WTO 2006). There is still some allowance for S&DT for developing countries, in recognition of the disadvantage they face in competing with developed countries, but the scope has been much reduced (Williams 2005).

In many developing countries trade liberalization has led to faster import growth than export growth. The UNCTAD *Trade and Development Report 1999* provides evidence that rapid trade liberalization led to trade deficits in the South, as exports stayed flat or did not keep pace with rising imports. At the end of the 1990s, the average trade deficit of the South was higher by 3 percent than the 1970s and the average economic growth rate was lower by 2 percent (UNCTAD 1999: vi). Furthermore, the implementation of multilateral trade agreements on intellectual property rights and on services (such as water and health care) have been implicated in raising the cost of medicines and health care in the South and increasing the vulnerability of the South to food insecurity (FAO 1999, 2000; Oxfam 2002).

Small, poor countries have been particularly disadvantaged by the WTO system since multilateral trade liberalization erodes the preferential access that they have enjoyed to the markets of industrial countries. At the same time they do not have large enough domestic markets to give them sufficient bargaining power in the reciprocal bargaining that is at the center of the WTO system (Mattoo and Subramanian 2004).

These problems were supposed to have been addressed by the Doha Development Agenda proclaimed by the Fourth Ministerial Meeting of the WTO at Doha in 2001. The Doha Development Agenda attempted to make development the centerpiece of the subsequent Doha Round of trade negotiations. It further promised that nontrade concerns such as animal welfare, biodiversity protection, employment, environment and food security would be taken into account for the first time in the negotiations on trade in agriculture. However, the Doha Round was suspended in July 2006 because of failure to reach agreement on key issues.

There has been increasing concern about how global trade negotiations impact on governments' commitments to gender equality (inscribed in the Convention on the Elimination of All Forms of Discrimination Against Women, the 1995 Beijing Platform of Action and the Beijing Plus Five Outcome Document). Such concerns have been voiced by a number of intergovernmental organizations, including the International Labor Organization, the United Nations Conference on Trade and Development (UNCTAD), and the Commonwealth Secretariat,[3] and by international nongovernmental organizations, including the International Gender and Trade Network, Oxfam and Development Alternatives with Women for a New Era.

This chapter examines the contemporary multilateral trading system through a gender and development lens, with a particular focus on agricultural liberalization under the Agreement on Agriculture (AOA); liberalization of trade in services with a specific focus on the General Agreement on Trade in Services (GATS); and the Trade Related Intellectual Property Rights (TRIPs) agreement. The chapter concludes with a brief discussion of the possibilities of incorporating gender into some of the measures which may be used to mitigate the adverse effects of trade agreements in poor countries, and into the mechanism to monitor compliance with WTO agreements.

Some gender implications of the multilateral trading system

Trade agreements are the set of modalities, rules, and procedures governing the setting of tariff, nontariff measures, and other restrictions, and the bounds of reciprocity and nonreciprocity on the cross-border flow of goods. This also includes limited provisions for safeguards for domestic producers, as well as procedures for settling disputes between trade partners.

Traditionally, the multilateral trading system focused primarily on measures affecting the international trade of goods. Today, however, WTO trade agreements extend to trade in services. They cover issues which are seen as trade-related, such as intellectual property rights. In the name of creating a "level playing field" for local and foreign businesses, WTO trade agreements increasingly have implications for many domestic policies, such as environmental regulations, patent protection, and government procurement, so-called "behind the border" issues. Domestic policies which seem to constrain the profit-making opportunities of big business are labeled "trade-distorting."

A key focus of WTO trade negotiations is reduction of tariffs, and other barriers to international trade. In the short run tariff reductions tend to make basic household goods cheaper, benefiting poor women who buy these items for their families. But they also may have a negative impact on the livelihoods of women who produce these items for consumption by their families, and sell their surpluses in domestic markets (FAO 2000). In the longer run, they may have costs for both groups of women, if export earnings become inadequate to continue to fund imports, and/or domestic capacity to produce has been seriously weakened (FAO 2003). Import liberalization makes women's responsibilities for the day-to-day provisioning of their households, whether through purchasing or producing, more vulnerable to the vagaries of international markets.

Import liberalization can also result in the loss of tariff revenue. Khattry and Rao (2002) found that trade liberalization has resulted in declining government revenue in developing countries. A study of the impact of this on public expenditure (Khattry 2003) found that the loss of revenue from trade taxes led to reduced spending on infrastructure, education, and health, in relation to the level of GDP. The IMF suggests that revenue losses can be avoided by increasing other indirect taxes (IMF 2003), but ignores the regressive nature of many indirect taxes. If loss in trade taxes is compensated for by the imposition of regressive value added taxes this will also be felt more acutely by poor women.

Trade liberalization does increase market access for exporters. In countries which export labor-intensive manufactures, this tends to increase women's employment. Much more attention has been paid to gender impacts in these countries than to gender impacts in countries that export primary products. Improved access for agricultural exports from the South should help women farmers, but the cost and availability of information, credit, inputs, and technical assistance may still present barriers for women, who have less access to these services than do men. Moreover, a shift from production of food for local markets to production of export crops may actually deprive women of land, and jeopardize the food security of rural families. The gender implications of the Agreement on Agriculture are explored in the next section.

Gender and the liberalization of agricultural trade

The Agreement on Agriculture (AOA)[4] was made during the Uruguay Round of trade negotiations that ended in 1994. The WTO presides over its implementation. The AOA focuses on reducing barriers to market access, reducing export subsidies, and reducing support to domestic production.[5] The AOA is lopsided, in that the rich countries were able, through a variety of mechanisms, to continue to subsidize their agriculture while the developing countries' agricultural sectors were left relatively unprotected.[6]

Food is being exported to many poor developing countries at prices well below cost,[7] a practice known as "dumping," that jeopardizes the livelihoods of small farmers, and may jeopardize food security in poor countries which are now much more dependent on imported food. Thus far, the primary effect of trade liberalization in agriculture seems to have been to generate increasing food insecurity. In a recent 14-country FAO study (FAO 2000), the total cost of food imports in all 14 of the developing countries rose significantly (ranging from 30 to 168 percent) following implementation of the AOA. The increase in the cost of food imports outweighed the benefits of increased export sales, leaving 11 of the 14 countries worse off from a food security (and balance of payments) perspective. The AOA lacks adequate Special & Differential Treatment measures (S&DTs) to ensure food self-sufficiency, as well as insufficient Special Safeguard Mechanisms (SSM) to protect production of local food staples.[8]

In the early years of the Doha Round, there appeared to be the prospect of an agreement to exempt certain agricultural and food-related measures undertaken by developing countries from the full provisions of the AOA. In the later stages of the negotiations this was replaced by an argument for introducing a "Special Products" (SPs) category in the Agreement on Agriculture which would allow developing countries to designate certain crops, based on the principles of food security, livelihood, and rural development. Developing countries would be able to protect these crops using appropriate tariffs.[9]

Agricultural liberalization raises a number of critical issues for gender equality, women's empowerment, and poverty eradication stemming from gender divisions in agricultural production, and food procurement, preparation, and consumption. Women are the invisible producers in the agricultural sector as small farmers in their own right, unpaid family labor on farms of male relatives, and as wage workers in agribusinesses. According to FAO, women are responsible for half the world's food production and produce between 60 and 80 percent of food in most developing countries (www.fao.org/Gender/ en/agri-e.htm). Women provide about 90 percent of the work of processing food crops, fetching water and securing fuel and wood and about 80 percent of the work of harvesting and marketing in Africa, while in Asia women account for between 10 and 50 percent of labor for various crops (World Bank 1996). Nearly 50 percent of the world's economically active women work in agriculture. In the least developed countries the vast majority of economically active women (79 percent) work in agriculture (UNCTAD 2004: 82).

Trade liberalization is leading to the commercialization of small farms. An FAO survey of the gender impacts of small farm commercialization projects in 14 developing countries found that the increased income made possible by commercialization generally entailed an increase in household workload. The extra demands on time were onerous for women, as they continued to be fully responsible for the unpaid domestic work of maintaining and caring for families and communities. In about half the projects, there was believed to be a positive impact on women's participation in household decision-making and status in the community, but in the other half there was no improvement, and in some cases there was a negative impact (UNCTAD 2004: 109–10).

With commercialization, women farmers are exposed to new risks. Women farmers are particularly vulnerable to surges of agricultural imports following trade liberalization. For instance, in Senegal women farmers had switched from growing subsistence crops to growing tomatoes. They had also taken out micro-credit loans to start tomato paste businesses. However, when the government lowered tariffs on food imports, cheap foreign tomatoes flooded the market. The women could not pay back the loans and did not have their traditional food to feed their families. They thus ended up in a worse economic position than when they had started out (Sparr 2002).

All small farmers in developing countries are finding it difficult to compete with the better-resourced farmers from developed countries (UNCTAD 2004: 78, 107–8). Women, compared to men, are particularly disadvantaged by lack of access to credit, agricultural extension services, tools, and ownership of land (World Bank 2001; FAO 2002; Grown *et al.* 2005).

AOA provisions on reducing domestic support to agriculture therefore present particular problems for women farmers, who need assistance from government if they are to overcome the gender-based constraints they face. Traditionally, some developing countries' governments have provided subsidies for credit, fertilizers, and water. But with the implementation of trade liberalization under structural adjustment programs, many governments have eliminated many forms of input subsidies on fertilizers, credit, and irrigation. As a result, prices for inputs such as fertilizers rose in the 1990s in Africa.[10] Gladwin (1991) demonstrated the adverse implications of these policies for women farmers in Cameroon and Malawi, who lacked sufficient cash and credit to buy at the higher prices.

Increases in nontraditional agricultural exports (NTAEs), such as flowers, fruit, and vegetables, have generated employment for women in many countries in Latin America and sub-Saharan Africa (Bifani-Richard 1999; UNCTAD 2004: 111–13). Much of this employment is as temporary seasonal employees in large commercial farms, often exposing women to health hazards through use of pesticides. Permanent jobs tend to go to men. Some women small-holders do produce NTAEs for export but this may jeopardize their ability to produce crops to feed their families and lead to threats to their food security, as is argued to be the case in Uganda (Kasente *et al.* 2002). In some countries, such as the Philippines, the production of NTAEs has diverted land and water from small-holders to large-scale farmers (UNCTAD 2004: 93–4).

The round of WTO negotiations following the trade ministers meeting in Doha in 2001 was supposed to address the inequalities inherent in the AOA, both those between rich and poor countries and those between different types of farmers. However, these negotiations collapsed in July 2006, because the developed countries, especially the USA, were not willing to make steeper cuts in the subsidies they provide for their farmers (Bernardino 2006).

In any case, a reduction in export subsidies in developed countries would by now have a negative impact on poor food-purchasing households in the many poor countries which have become net food importers. This would happen because a reduction in export subsidies in developed countries would raise world food prices by between 4 and 5 percent (Mattoo and Subramanian 2004: 15).

Gender and liberalization of trade in services

Services as varied as water, health care, education, and accounting are being liberalized under the General Agreement on Trade in Services (GATS), which came into force in January 1995. The GATS distinguishes between how a service is provided (mode of service provision) and sets rules on how countries should treat foreign service providers. For example, foreign telephone companies and foreign universities, providing international telephone calls and distance learning, are covered by Cross Border Services (Mode I); tourism and travel for health care are covered by Consumption Abroad (Mode II); subsidiaries of foreign banks and foreign fast-food providers are covered by Commercial Presence (Mode III); foreign nurses, doctors, and management consultants are covered by Temporary Movement of Natural Persons (Mode IV).

Ultimately, GATS seeks to liberalize all measures affecting trade in services (including government laws, policy, and regulatory and administrative rules such as grants, subsidies, licensing standards, and qualifications; limitation on market access, food safety rules, nationality requirements, residency requirements, technology transfer requirements, restriction on ownership of property or land; and tax measures which affect the foreign provision of services).

GATS also provides a framework for progressively higher levels of liberalization of all services (Sinclair 2000). Article XIX mandates negotiations to increase trade liberalization in services by entering into more or deeper specific commitments in market access and national treatment, starting in 2000. In addition, other GATS provisions mandate the start of negotiations to develop disciplines on domestic regulation (Article VI.4) as well as new GATS rules, including those on trade-distorting subsidies (Article XV), government procurement (Article XIII), and restrictions (such as the development of an emergency safeguard mechanism (Article X). The GATS does recognize the sovereign right of a country to regulate services for legitimate purposes. Its preamble also allows for the introduction of new regulations on the supply of services in order to meet national policy objectives (see also Article VI on domestic regulations). GATS commitments apply to all levels of government, as well as to NGOs when they are acting on the basis of authority delegated to them by the state (Sinclair 2000).

To date the GATS negotiations have been concerned with the process of submitting "requests" relating to services that countries desire their trading partners to liberalize, while in return making "offers" of additional liberalization of their own services. Though defenders of the GATS argue that governments can protect their basic services by excluding them from their "offers," critics of GATS are concerned that poor developing countries will be pressured to include basic services by organizations such as the IMF and World Bank.

The rest of the discussion in this section will focus on the GATS and health (health insurance is classified in the GATS as a financial service but will also be discussed). About 60 WTO members have scheduled commitments to liberalize trade in health services, including not only cross-border movements of individual health professionals, but also of foreign providers of hospitals, laboratories, ambulances, and residential care. Several countries have also scheduled commitments to liberalize the provision of health insurance. There is concern that government regulations designed to ensure equal access to good quality health care may be seen as a trade barrier by a foreign service supplier, and thus lead to challenges to the regulations, through the framework provided by the WTO.

The impact of GATS on health services is particularly important for gender equality, as it can change the quality, geographic coverage, and cost of different types of services, procedures, and technologies, as well as access of different population groups to them (Grown 2006). There may also be effects on women's unpaid work providing health care to family members, and women's paid employment in the services sector as both domestic and migrant workers.

Each GATS Mode potentially has implications for health-related activities, although research on specific impacts is still limited (Grown 2006; Lipson 2006). Mode I concerning cross-border supply may have limited affect on certain types of services that are critical to women's health, especially reproductive health. For instance, the highly personal nature of reproductive health services means they are unlikely to be delivered through telemedicine on a cross-border basis, except perhaps for highly specialized diagnostic services (Lipson 2006). Mode I may also have gendered employment impacts. To the extent that trade increases, it may create employment for women, for instance, through the outsourcing of medical transcription services.

Mode II of the GATS, involving consumption abroad, could have a positive benefit for health care in low- and middle-income countries if they invest in the education and training of medical and nursing personnel, medical technology, and equipment at public health centers, and if they raise wages and make other improvements that make them desirable medical care destinations. However, there is concern that consumption abroad can create a dual market system consisting of a high quality expensive structure catering to wealthy nationals and foreigners, and a lower quality and resource-constrained system for the poor (Grown 2006). In practice, the lack of public funds and insurance portability for care obtained in other countries means that GATS commitments in Mode II have little or no benefit for the majority of low- and middle-income people who cannot afford to travel abroad, and cannot afford to pay for health services out-of-pocket (Lipson 2006). Mode II may also create additional jobs for women in low-income countries to meet the demand created by people who travel from higher-income countries to lower-income countries for medical care.

Mode III, concerning commercial presence, opens up the provision of health services within a country to foreign firms. This may increase employment for women health service employees, and increase the provision of services to women. But it may also have the effect of diverting health service staff from the provision of public health services to low-income people, to the provision of private health services to high-income people. It is likely that women's access to health services will be reduced and their burdens of unpaid health care intensified if there is no system for cross-subsidy of services and no system for poor people to obtain free or subsidized treatment. Future negotiations on the GATS must safeguard such provisions.

Overall, Mode IV, concerning the temporary movement of natural persons, may be welfare-enhancing for many women health care professionals in poor countries, as it permits them to migrate and provides them with opportunities for higher wages, wider knowledge, and skills and experience working with superior health care facilities. However, its impact on the society from which they migrate can potentially be disastrous, as it may lead to a shortage of health care professionals, and thus less access to health care, a reduced range of services, and lower quality of health care. At present, few countries use GATS Mode IV as a tool for facilitating cross-border migration of health personnel, instead relying on national immigration or health workforce training and recruitment policies (Lipson 2006).

As noted earlier, GATS classifies health insurance as a financial service. More than 100 WTO members have made a commitment in the financial services insurance subsector, which covers health insurance unless a country explicitly excludes it; few, however, have done so (Lipson 2006). Both developed and developing countries that have made GATS commitments in the sector scheduled numerous restrictions or limitations, for example, on the form of commercial presence (subsidiary, joint venture, and level of equity participation) or the number of foreign service suppliers. Although there may be some benefit to foreign participation in health insurance if it results in a greater choice of options, in reality, for-profit firms often market such policies to the best "risks" – higher-income people in good health. This underscores the importance of having an adequate regulatory system to guard against insurance companies engaging in consumer fraud, and to set rules so they contribute to social policy objectives (Lipson 2006).

Essential public services that are critical for gender equality should be protected. A possible model is in the proposals for Special Safeguard Mechanisms in the Agreement on Agriculture.

Gender and trade-related intellectual property rights

Intellectual property rights (IPRs) are ownership rights and legal protection granted to ideas, inventions, artistic creations, and so on. The TRIPs agreement, which came into force in 1995, obliges all WTO members to apply uniform standards to IPR. This means developing countries must introduce IPR legislation similar to that in developed countries.

The TRIPs agreement makes all inventions patentable, including living organisms and products based on traditional knowledge, as well as the industrial products. While plants and animals may be exempted from patenting by member states, micro-organisms, bacteria, and fungi are patentable, and new varieties of plants are also included. The patenting of micro-organisms, biotechnology techniques, food-related biological sources, and essential drugs raise numerous ethical, legal, and developmental problems.

The TRIPs agreement has important implications for women as farmers, and as managers of natural resources and family health. Patenting biological materials effectively privatizes genetic materials and imposes user fees on material that was once abundantly available, especially to poor households. Such patents can deprive poor people of the fruits of years of inter-generationally acquired knowledge. This has an important gender dimension in many countries where women have a special role in the preservation of seeds.

Patents (or other extensions of plant breeders' IPRs) on seed and micro-organisms (such as algae, bacteria, and fungi) increase the cost of seed and fertilizers. Increasingly, many of the inputs needed for farming must be obtained in the market. Patents encourage restriction on the exchange, use, or sale of seeds by farmers. This puts resource-poor farmers, many of whom are women, at a severe disadvantage. Given the existing disparities between women's and men's access to cash and credit, which are necessary to purchase fertilizer and seed, the rising expenses of farming induced by the TRIPs agreement are likely to exacerbate existing gender inequalities.

The TRIPs agreement also has important implications for health. The most important relates to the way it strengthens the effective monopoly of patent-holders over medicines, thus keeping their prices high. There is scope in the agreement for compulsory licensing, by which governments can authorize the production of generic versions of a patented product without the permission of the patent holder, under certain conditions. This is allowed when the patented medicine is essential, but unavailable due to lack of supply or an unreasonably high price or for public noncommercial use or to remedy anticompetitive practices. But compulsory licensing only extends to production for domestic use, and thus limits availability in countries that have no production capability.[11] This issue is particularly pertinent to antiretroviral treatments for controlling HIV. Although the cost of antiretroviral medicines has fallen dramatically, they are still prohibitively expensive in many developing countries (see Maharaj and Roberts 2006 for a case study of TRIPs in South Africa).

Towards trade agreements for gender equitable development

The negotiation of trade agreements that are gender-equitable means that gender has to be "mainstreamed" into the ways that trade policy is framed. This requires a shift from framing issues in terms of gender-blind notions of "people," "farmers," "business owners," and "workers" to a framework that is explicitly gender-aware and gender-sensitive. Information on women's and men's location in the economy, their relative access to productive resources, and their relative contributions to economic and social development need to be factored into the formulation of trade policy and trade regulations. However, as noted by Durano (2005), it is important to recognize that a gender perspective goes beyond counting the numbers of men and women in a given location or sector in the economy. It must also recognize the importance of the interaction between paid work and the unpaid work of caring for families and communities.

Here we discuss the use of gender analysis to inform discussion on a range of measures which may be used to mitigate adverse effects of trade liberalization, such as Special Products and Special Safeguard Mechanisms, Special and Differential Treatment, Trade-Related Capacity Building and Aid for Trade, and also how gender analysis might be integrated into the Trade Policy Review Mechanism.

The International Gender and Trade Network has begun work on specifying gender-based criteria and indicators for the choice of Special Products (SPs). Hernandez (2005) argues that in "the process of specifying SPs two main questions should be asked: (a) who are the key socioeconomic groups to protect? and (b) what kinds of products are to be protected?" The socioeconomic groups that most need protection are small farmers, landless peasants, and other rural poor people. Hernandez points out that "within these groups, women are crucial stakeholders due to their significant participation in the agricultural sector...and their responsibilities as the major food providers for their families and communities" (Hernandez 2005: 7). She suggests that an important indicator is the ratio of females to males in specific groups of agricultural producers, and the ratio of females to males in the production of specific domestically produced and consumed crops that are important for household food security.

A similar exercise is possible with regard to Special Safeguard Mechanisms (SSMs), the designation of which permits developing countries to "increase tariffs temporarily on key products and those able to protect their domestic farmers from short-term fluctuations in prices and/or from import surges" (Hernandez 2005: 8). It is not yet clear whether the designation of SSM would be limited to SPs or available to all agricultural products, whenever there exists periods of extremely depressed international prices and/or import surges (the latter is the preference of developing countries advocating for SPs and SSMs).

Trade-related capacity building (TRCB) aims to improve the capacities of developing countries in the negotiation and implementation of trade agreements, and in adjusting production (WTO/OECD 2005). CIDA has developed a framework for engendering TRCB, which includes improving the participation of women in trade negotiations and improving the access of women entrepreneurs to trade-related training, marketing information, communications technology, and finance (CIDA 2003).

Trade-related capacity building is central to the discussion on Aid for Trade (AfT). An Aid for Trade Task Force was established in February 2006 with a mandate to discuss how AfT "might contribute most effectively to the development dimension of the Doha Development agenda" and tabled its recommendations to the WTO General Council July 27–28, 2006. The report was endorsed by the General Council in its October 10, 2006 meeting. The importance of gender in AfT was flagged in the report (under section F); however, the treatment was rather superficial. Francisco (2006) cautions that if gender comes into play simply in terms of trade impact assessment exercises, which are often hampered by lack of sex-disaggregated data, then there is a danger of lack of attention to the policy changes required to deal with system-wide gender inequality.

Gender analysis should be integral to the Trade Policy Review Mechanism (TRPM).[12] Currently the scope of the TRPM is narrow and excludes questions of gender bias and gender inequality. However, there are possible entry points for gender analysis at different stages of the preparation of the WTO report that forms part of the TRPM. For example, as part of their technical work, the WTO staff collect information from economic databases, and national and international sources such as academic institutions and libraries, the IMF and World Bank, the Internet and local newspapers. Women's groups and researchers on gender equality can provide case studies, research papers, briefings, and policy papers through sector ministries and women's ministries. The TRPM includes a fact-finding mission by a WTO team. Teams spend anywhere from a week to 10 days in a country's capital, visiting government agencies and meeting with business and other stakeholders. This provides a possible entry point for women's ministries to present studies and policy briefs. WTO mission staff also meet with university academics and independent research institutions. Gender-aware researchers could be included in these consultations.

It is not, however, sufficient to mainstream gender analysis within the current multilateral trading system. A gender perspective calls into question the whole basis on which the system is constructed. Removing barriers to international trade does not make competition "fair." Those with few resources will not be able to compete on the same basis as those with many resources, even if aid is given to improve trade performance. Moreover, a calculus of costs and benefits that focuses only on paid work and marketed outputs will always disadvantage those who have been assigned special responsibilities for unpaid work and the production of the nonmarketed outputs that are critical for the well-being of families and communities. A gender-equitable unilateral trading system would require a different set of core principles, replacing formal rules for "nondiscrimination" (such as MFN) with substantive international and national action to secure equitable outcomes, both between countries and within countries (Williams 2005).

Notes

1 There is also a network of bilateral, regional, and quasi-regional arrangements on aid, development, and trade cooperation assistance. These include the Lomé Convention (now the Cotonou Agreement) between the European Union and African, Caribbean and Pacific states (EU–ACP); the African Growth Opportunity Agreement: and the Caribbean Basin Initiative (now the Caribbean Basin Trade Partnership Act – CBTPA). They also include an increasingly complex array of preferential trade agreements, including the North American Free Trade Agreement (NAFTA), between the US, Canada and Mexico, to the more comprehensive agreements of the European Union, which in 2006 included 26 countries.

2 The Uruguay Round Agreement has three main components: the updated multilateral trade agreements (GATT 1994); the General Agreement on Trade in Services (GATS); and the agreement on Trade-Related Aspects of Intellectual Property Rights (TRIPs). GATS and TRIPs are very important because they extended multilateral trade agreements (MTAs) into areas never before considered. GATS extended the MTAs into services (and in a limited way to investment); in addition, the TRIPs agreement, and some

provisions within GATS, extended it into the areas of domestic regulatory standards, as distinct from trade policy. The Marrakech Declaration (1994) established the WTO to oversee implementation of the Uruguay Round Agreement as well as to enforce the dispute settlement process regarding members' rights and obligations.

3 UNCTAD, which was one of the first intergovernmental organizations to host an expert group meeting on the subject of Gender and Trade in 1999, is now the focal point of the UN Inter-Agency Task Force on Gender and Trade. The Commonwealth Secretariat has organized three international seminars with policy makers, women's machinery, and trade negotiators on the subject of gender and trade. In addition, the Commonwealth Secretariat has produced a handbook on gender mainstreaming in the multilateral trading system (Williams 2003).

4 The AOA excludes fish, fish products, and forest products (i.e. timber). Other agricultural-related WTO agreements such as Sanitary and Phytosanitary Agreements (SPS) cover all agricultural products.

5 "Domestic support" is finance given by governments to farmers to subsidize production of specific products or to subsidize expenditure on infrastructure and research. "Export subsidies" are payments made by governments to producers or exporters to enable them to sell goods abroad at lower prices than they could otherwise afford. The export subsidies of the EU and the US also include export credits and are compatible with 1995 WTO agreements but are subject to commitment to agreed reductions. Within the AOA, some categories of support are generally argued to be "non-trade distorting" while others are identified as being "minimally trade-distorting." *Green box* items are minimally trade-distorting support and are not subject to reduction commitments. These may include research, extension, food security stocks, disaster payment, and antinarcotic incentives. However, they may be challenged by countries that can prove injury to their domestic economy after the Due Restraint Provision (Peace Clause) of the agreement lapsed in 2003. *Blue box* items have tended to be dominated by EU and US systems of augmenting farmer's income in return for reducing production or only maintaining levels of production at an agreed level. It also includes the EU's "set aside" programs and the US deficiency payments. These are not subject to reduction commitments. *Amber box* items include support payments made directly to farmers for each unit of output. These are seen as trade-distorting and are subject to reduction commitments. The *De minims clause* allows a country to maintain a certain minimum level of support to farmers. At the end of the Uruguay Round for the rich countries this was up to 5 percent of the value of production for individual products and 5 percent of total agricultural production, while for the developing countries it was up to 10 percent of the value of total agricultural production. Special & Differential Treatment provisions in the AOA include some allowances for developing countries to provide input and investment subsidies, but these are widely regarded as inadequate.

6 The Green and Blue boxes (see footnote 5) cover much of the US Farm Subsidies as well as the EU Common Agricultural Program.

7 Levels of dumping hover around 40 percent for wheat, between 25 percent and 30 percent for corn (maize) and levels have risen steadily for soybeans, to nearly 30 percent. This means that wheat, for example, is selling for 40 percent less than it costs to produce. For cotton the level of dumping for 2001 rose to a remarkable 57 percent and for rice it has stabilized at around 20 percent (IATP 2004: 2, cited in Hernandez 2005).

8 S&DT refers to provisions and measures in trade agreements that attempt to take account of and adjust for economic disparities between states. These measures are meant to establish equity and fair competition where structural conditions are different and to avoid distortions due to differences in negotiating power. Under the old GATT framework, the approach to S&DT was very comprehensively embedded in a wide system of preferential access for developing countries (nonreciprocal concessions). There was wide scope for policy discretion, and flexibility was granted to developing

countries to maintain trade barriers to deal with balance of payment issues, protect infant industries, and to support domestic industries. However, under the WTO framework, S&DT has been reduced to a longer transitional period (five years for middle-income and 10 years for least developing countries) to implement WTO agreements. After this it will be phased out. SSM refers to an exception to the general rule of not exceeding the agreed tariff rate and not applying quantitative restrictions on imports. These exceptions apply when there has been a sudden increase in imports and the increase is threatening injury to domestic production. In such cases, a member of the WTO may take import restraint measures. The designation of an SSM in the AOA would permit developing countries to increase tariffs temporarily on key products to be able to protect their domestic farmers from short-term fluctuations in prices and/or from import surges (Hernandez 2005).

9 Paragraph 41 of Annex A of the WTO General Council Decision states, "Developing country members will have the flexibility to designate an appropriate number of products as Special Products, based on criteria of food security, livelihood security and rural development needs. These products will be eligible for more flexible treatment. The criteria and treatment of these products will be further specified during the negotiation phase and will recognize the fundamental importance of Special Products to developing countries."

10 Currency devaluation may also contribute to the rise in input prices. For example, in Malawi the final removal of all fertilizer subsidies in 1995/96 coupled with a 100 percent devaluation of the kwacha in 1994, meant 200 percent to 300 percent increase in the price of fertilizer without corresponding increases in maize price in 1995/96 and 1996/97 (Benson 1997).

11 In 2001, the Doha Declaration on TRIPS and Public Health reaffirmed the right of government to regulate IPRs to meet public health concerns. Paragraph 6 of the Declaration "recognized that these countries face difficulties in making effective use of compulsory licensing" and mandated the TRIPS Council to find a solution to this problem and report to the General Council (TWN 2005). This problem of compulsory licensing arises due to Article 31(f) of the TRIPS Agreement, wherein production of generic drugs under compulsory license has to be predominantly for the supply of the domestic market, thus limiting exports and constraining the supply of medicines to countries that are unable to produce such drugs (TWN 2005). On August 30, 2003, the WTO General Council took a decision to enable the producing countries to waive the condition that production under compulsory license must be predominantly for the domestic market. However, this was seen as only a temporary solution and not a permanent amendment of the TRIPs agreement. In December 2005 the WTO General Council finally adopted the August 30th Decision as a permanent amendment to the TRIPs Agreement. However, health advocates such as Médecins Sans Frontières question whether this drug-by-drug and country-by-country approach, which is to be ratified by December 2007, will really resolve the problem of access to affordable medicines by countries without capacity to produce generic drugs.

12 The mandate of the Trade Policy Review Mechanism (TRPM) is to review the trade policies and practices of member countries. The four members with the largest shares of world trade (the QUAD) are reviewed every two years, the next 16 are reviewed every four years, and others are reviewed every six years. A longer period may be fixed for least developed countries. The TRPM generally looks at the direction of trade policies rather than impacts. The WTO insists that its main focus is macroeconomics analysis, not welfare analysis. However, it does look at impact in some sectors. Two reports are usually generated: a policy statement from the country and a report prepared by economists in the WTO Secretariat's Trade Policy Review Division. These are discussed in a review process with the Trade Policy Review Body (actually the General Counsel of the WTO operating under special rules and procedures).

References

Benson, T. (1997) "The 1995/96 fertilizer verification trial – Malawi," report by Action Group I. Maize Productivity Task Force, Ministry of Agriculture and Livestock Development, Lilongwe: Government of Malawi.

Bernardino, N. (2006) "Notes on the WTO General Council Meeting," *International Gender and Trade Network Monthly Bulletin*, 6 (4): 3–5.

Bifani-Richard, P. (1999) "Notes on trade, sustainable development and gender," in UNCTAD (ed.), *Trade, Sustainable Development and Gender*, Geneva: UNCTAD.

Canadian International Development Agency (CIDA) (2003) *Gender Equality and Trade Related Capacity Building: a resource tool for practitioners*, Quebec: CIDA.

Durano, M. (2005) "Women in international trade and migration: examining the globalized provision of care services," Gender and Development Discussion Paper Series No.16, Bangkok: UN Economic and Social Commission for Asia and the Pacific.

FAO (1999) "Issues at stake relating to agricultural development and food security," FAO Symposium on Agriculture, Trade and Food Security, Geneva, September 23–24. Online. Available http://www.fao.org/doccrep/meeting/X2998E.htm (accessed April 2006).

—— (2000) "Synthesis of the country case studies," *Agriculture, Trade and Food Security*, vol. II. Country Case Studies, Rome: FAO.

—— (2002) "Gendered access to land," *FAO Land Tenure Studies*, vol. 4, Rome: FAO.

—— (2003) "Some trade policy issues relating to trends in agricultural imports in the context of food security," Committee on Commodity Problems, 64th Session, Rome, March 18–21.

Francisco, G. (2006) "Comments on aid for trade and gender," IGTN Panel on Aid for Trade and Gender, WTO Annual Public Symposium, October 2006.

Gladwin, C. (1991) "Fertilizer subsidy removal programs and their potential impacts on women farmers in Malawi and Cameroon," in C.H. Gladwin (ed.), *Structural Adjustment and African Women Farmers*, Gainesville: University of Florida Press.

Grown, C. (2006) "Trade liberalization and reproductive health: a framework for understanding the linkages," in C. Grown, E. Braunstein, and A. Malhotra (eds), *Trading Women's Health and Rights*, London and New York: Zed Books.

Grown, C., Rao Gupta, G., and Kes, A. (2005) *Taking Action: achieving gender equality and empowering women*, London: Earthscan.

Hernandez, M. (2005) *Incorporating Gender Considerations for the Designation of Special Products in the WTO Agricultural Negotiations*, Geneva: International Gender and Trade Network.

IMF (2003) *Development of the Doha Round and Selected Activities of Interest to the Fund*, Washington, DC: IMF.

Institute for Agriculture and Trade Policy (IATP) (2004) "United States dumping on world agricultural markets," WTO Cancun Series Paper No.1, Minneapolis, MN: Institute for Agriculture and Trade Policy.

Kasente, D., Lockwood, M., Vivian, J., and Whitehead, A. (2002) "Gender and the expansion of non-traditional agricultural exports in Uganda," in S. Razavi (ed.), *Shifting Burdens: gender and agrarian change under neoliberalism*, Geneva: UNRISD.

Khattry, B. (2003) "Trade liberalisation and the fiscal squeeze: implications for public investment," *Development and Change*, 34 (3): 401–24.

Khattry, B. and Rao, J.M. (2002) "Fiscal faux pas? An analysis of the revenue implications of trade liberalization," *World Development*, 30 (8): 1431–44.

Lipson, D. (2006) "Implications of the general agreement on trade in services for reproductive health services," in C. Grown, E. Braunstein, and A. Malhotra (eds), *Trading Women's Health and Rights*, London and New York: Zed Books.

Maharaj, P. and Roberts, B. (2006) "Tripping up: AIDS, pharmaceuticals and intellectual property in South Africa," in C. Grown, E. Braunstein, and A. Malhotra (eds), *Trading Women's Health and Rights*, London and New York: Zed Books.

Mattoo, A. and Subramanian, A. (2004) "The WTO and the poorest countries: the stark reality," IMF Working Paper WP/04/81, Washington, DC: International Monetary Fund.

Oxfam (2002) "Generic competition, price and access to medicines: the case of antiretrovirals in Uganda," Oxfam Briefing Paper No.26, Oxfam International. Online. Available http://www.Oxfam.org/en/files/pp020710_no26_generic_competition_briefing_paper.pdf/download (accessed April 2006).

Sinclair, S. (2000) *GATS: how the WTO's new "Services" negotiations threaten democracy*, Ottawa: Canadian Centre for Policy Alternatives.

Sparr, P. (2002) "A gender primer of trade and investment policies," North America Gender and Trade Network (NAGT-US) Economic Literacy Series #2. Online. Available http://www.igtn.org/EconoLit/primer.pdf (accessed April 2006).

UNCTAD (1999) *Trade and Development Report*, Geneva: UNCTAD.

—— (2004) *Trade and Gender: opportunities and challenges for developing countries*, UN Inter-Agency Network on Women and Gender Equality, Task Force on Gender and Trade, UNCTAD/eDM/2004/2, Geneva: UNCTAD.

Williams, M. (2003) *Gender Issues in the Multilateral Trading System*, London: Commonwealth Secretariat.

—— (2005) "Tensions between the role of trade, development and gender equality," presentation for WTO Public Symposium, April 20–22, Geneva.

World Bank (1996) "Women key to global food production," paper for World Food Summit, Rome, November 13–17.

—— (2001) *Engendering Development: through gender equality in rights, resources and voice*, World Bank Policy Research Report, Oxford: Oxford University Press.

World Trade Organization (2006) "Understanding the WTO principles of the trading system," Online. Available http://www.wto.org/English/thewto_e/whatis_e/tif_e/ fact2_e.htm (accessed May 2006).

WTO/OECD (2005) Joint WTO/OECD Report on Trade Related Technical Assistance and Capacity Building. Online. Available http://tcbdb.wto.org (accessed May 2006).

15 Gender equity and globalization

Macroeconomic policy for developing countries

Stephanie Seguino and Caren Grown

Introduction[1]

Over the last two decades, a number of development economists have critically assessed mainstream trade and growth strategies, propelled by a concern with persistent gender inequality. That body of work explores the linkages between macro-level policies and the gender distribution of resources and responsibilities at the micro-level. Research underscores that macro-level policies can hinder or help achieve gender equity, and that gender inequities, in turn, can promote or hamper the attainment of macroeconomic objectives. There is thus a two-way causality between macroeconomic variables and gender equity.

This chapter reviews the gender and macroeconomics research, drawing attention to insights that can inform strategies for shaping macro policy in a way that enables gender equity. This is followed by an effort to outline the broad contours of gender-equitable macroeconomic policy. This is a difficult task, given wide variations in types of economies, institutional mechanisms, and cultural forces that reinforce gender inequalities. Nonetheless, there are some generalizable approaches alongside more specific policy proposals for countries at different levels of development. Achieving the combined goals of improving women's relative well-being and promoting economic growth requires policies that can shift a profit-led export-oriented economy to one that is wage-led – that is, an economy in which equity in incomes is compatible with growth. This chapter outlines several international and national strategies to achieve that goal, based on an analysis of the structural constraints to gender equity.

The chapter is organized as follows. The next section explores the goal of gender equity and provides a feminist–Kaleckian perspective on desirable macroeconomic outcomes that will facilitate attainment of that goal. The subsequent section examines the evidence on gender outcomes in employment, wages, and job quality as well as macroeconomic conditions in the recent period of globalization. Based on that analysis, a set of feminist–Kaleckian macro-level policies to promote greater gender equity is advanced. The final section concludes.

Gender equity as a macroeconomic goal

The unequal distribution of income and resources, and in particular, gender inequality, is a central concern in the quest to improve well-being. This is because economic inequality can contribute to or perpetuate various forms of unfreedoms – such as discrimination, social intolerance, and lack of political power – that inhibit the acquisition of individual capabilities (Sen 1999). Freedoms are inter twined and any feminist agenda for gender-equitable macro policies would benefit from a move for simultaneous change in other arenas as well, especially the political.[2]

A gender equitable economy requires policies to achieve several important goals. First, equitable access to jobs is required through elimination of discriminatory employment barriers. Second, equity in earnings is needed, with both women and men able to earn living wages – wages sufficiently high to permit adults to adequately provision for their families.[3] Provisioning for families requires relatively secure income sources. This is particularly necessary for women who are sole breadwinners in their households, but is also a prerequisite for women who are part of two-adult households. This is because secure earnings are an important means to improve women's power to negotiate for an equitable distribution of household resources and unpaid labor. A further requirement is equitable distribution of state resources that can contribute to a closure of gender gaps in economic and social well-being, such as access to health, education, basic infrastructure, and other public goods, and to redress market and social gender inequalities.

With these goals in mind, we explore the evidence on the gender effects of globalization in order to uncover the "pressure points" that inhibit movement toward greater gender equity. From that analysis, we delineate a set of macro-level policies capable of producing high-quality growth and development, where quality is defined as the capacity for policies to close gender gaps without lowering men's average well-being. This approach differs from the mainstream, which sees the goal of macroeconomic and trade policies as price stability, the elimination of barriers to trade, sustainable debt, and for the more Keynesian, full employment. That is, both mainstream and Keynesian goals are defined without a view to addressing the problem of gender inequality in well-being. Rather, policies that might promote gender equality are most often an afterthought. Further, some mainstream and Keynesian policies that promote growth actually preclude or make gender equity more difficult to achieve. Thus, it is necessary to start with the explicit goal of promoting gender equity in well-being, and then proceed to an examination of the policy options consistent with that goal in the context of a particular economic structure and set of international institutions.[4]

The context: gendered effects of globalization as market liberalization

An examination of the gender effects of globalization and neoliberal policies that have led to trade and financial market liberalization is a starting point for assessing the policies for promoting gender equity. In this section, we consider the gendered employment effects of liberalization, the impact of globalization on macroeconomic performance, and shifts in the state's economic role in provision of a social safety net and social spending on health and education.

Gendered employment and earnings effects

Much has been made of women's increased participation in paid labor activities over the last 40 years. These trends, though not universally observed (Antecol 2000), underscore the increased opportunities that globalization has provided for women. In many instances, women's increased participation is voluntary, but there are many other cases of distress sales of labor – the so-called "added worker effect" – whereby falling household incomes and male wages push women to seek waged work. There can and often is, however, a gap between women's willingness to do paid work and the availability of such employment. The question of whether women have benefited from increased access to work in this era of globalization requires a consideration of a broader set of labor market outcomes, including the jobs that women can get as well as the conditions and pay of those jobs.

Gender and job access

Globalization has propelled women into labor markets in economies of varying structures. Semi-industrialized economies that emphasize export manufacturing have experienced a rise in the female share of employment, especially in the early phases of industrialization. Women have been largely "crowded" into labor-intensive export manufacturing, facing both explicit and implicit restrictions on their access to more skill-intensive jobs in nontradable fix-price industries[5] (Standing 1989, 1999; Nam 1991; Hsiung 1996; Mehra and Gammage 1999; Özler 2000).[6] Women provide a cost advantage to firms facing severe price competition from other export-oriented economies. The attractiveness of female workers is also related to the ease of shedding these workers, based in part on gender norms that relegate women's paid work to secondary importance after their reproductive responsibilities.

Over time, as semi-industrialized economies mature, the process of feminization of export employment may decline or even reverse.[7] In Taiwan, Hong Kong, South Korea, and Singapore – that is, among the East Asian "tigers" – as well as in Mexico's maquiladoras, women's share of manufacturing employment has fallen in recent years. Defeminization appears attributable to the dual process of tight female labor markets that lead to upward pressure on female wages and the emergence of lower wage sites in Asia and Latin America (Brown and Cunningham 2002; Ghosh 2002; Berik 2004; Jomo 2004). This cost squeeze has led to industrial restructuring in mature semi-industrialized economies (SIEs) with manufacturing production shifting to a greater emphasis on skill-intensive goods. It is not clear why women should be impeded from entering skill-intensive industries, as educational gaps are narrowing in many countries. One possibility is that firms prefer to invest in training for male workers, consistent with the view that men deserve the more secure employment and are less likely to leave paid work to fulfill domestic responsibilities. Women displaced from manufacturing have found employment in service jobs, which have expanded as a share of total output, such that female shares of employment have in fact declined only in the manufacturing sector (Mehra and Gammage 2000).

An exception to the trend of feminization of employment has been in those developing economies with less competitive manufacturing sectors, particularly in Africa. Trade liberalization forced these economies to reduce tariffs on imports of labor-intensive manufactures such as clothing, resulting in job losses for women who outnumbered male workers in the garment industry. Many laid-off workers have been pushed into informal employment (Fontana 2003). The evidence is not clear on whether women are disproportionately hurt by this shift from formal to informal work since male-dominated industries have also been affected. It is clear though that women as well as men have experienced income declines and increased job insecurity in the shift to informal employment, a topic that is discussed later (Benería 2003).

In agriculturally-oriented developing economies that have emphasized exports of cash crops as part of their liberalization strategy, women have increased job opportunities as seasonal or contract workers or as laborers on husbands' or relatives' land in the production of export cash crops.[8] In some cases, such as Latin America, economic restructuring, crisis, and globalization have led to the feminization of agriculture as women seek remunerative employment to supplement declining family income (Deere 2004). Some women have become producers of nontraditional agricultural exports (NTAEs). In Latin America and South Africa, NTAEs are often produced on large-scale enterprises, with women forming up to 80 percent of the workforce (Carr *et al.* 2000).

Finally, in developing economies that rely heavily on service exports to propel growth (such as informatics and tourism), women constitute a large share of export workers (Davison and Sanchez-Taylor 1999; UNDP 1999; Freeman 2000). An additional form of service sector export labor is that of workers who emigrate to work as nurses and domestics, remitting income to family members at home, and thus generating foreign exchange for the home economy.[9] The large majority of these workers are female (UNDP 1999).

Paradoxically, a number of countries also have very high relative rates of female unemployment. Unemployment data are of questionable use due to measurement problems.[10] However, the case of Caribbean economies is one where the data provide a more accurate picture of women's and men's job access, due to the way unemployment is measured.[11] Women's unemployment rates there remain almost double men's already very high rates.[12] Similarly, in transition economies, women have experienced declines in access to jobs relative to men (Bridger *et al.* 1996; Fodor 2004).

In sum, the clustering of women in export industries suggests the "feminization of foreign exchange earnings,"[13] as countries increasingly rely on export earnings to purchase needed imports and to service external debts. While women are preferred workers in price-elastic export industries (where there is a greater probability that higher wages will result in employment losses), they continue to face difficulties in gaining access to jobs that are more secure in nontradables industries. Further, when there are job shortages, women are sent to the back of the job queue.

Gender and conditions of employment

Employment has become increasingly flexible in the recent process of globalization as employers attempt to reduce costs (Standing 1989, 1999). A notable trend is the expanded use of women as subcontracted or home workers in manufacturing.[14] Ghosh (2002) provides evidence for India that the trend toward casualization, in the form of subcontracting and home production, was evident before the Asian financial crisis, highlighting the competitive pressures amongst firms to lower costs in the context of an increasing number of suppliers (e.g. China and post-NAFTA Mexico) vying for access to developed country markets. The trend extends to the agricultural sector where trade liberalization has created seasonal employment in the area of agricultural exports (UNDP 1999; Deere 2004; UNRISD 2005). In the case of Chilean and South African export grape industries, women are the preferred source of temporary workers and hold a small share of permanent jobs (Barrientos 2001).

This trend is due in part to the continued adherence to a "male breadwinner" bias, which slots women for insecure jobs or home work.[15] Men are affected by these trends as well, as the jobs they hold take on the character of women's jobs (temporary or casual status, limited job mobility, few or no benefits), but the percentage of women in "flexible" jobs greatly exceeds that of men (UNDP 1999). For that reason, women's increased incorporation into the paid economy is under conditions inferior to those necessary to provide them with secure income. The types of jobs they have access to constrain their ability to raise their incomes and improve their working conditions, and come at a high cost.[16] The seasonality of agricultural jobs, for example, implies there are no sustained improvements in women's employment status.

Gender, wages, and income

Gender wage inequality persists despite the feminization of labor which was predicted to portend well for women's relative wages – rising demand for female labor should drive up their wages relative to men's. In some countries, evidence suggests a narrowing of gender wage gaps (Tzannatos 1999; World Bank 2001; Oostendorp 2004),[17] although in others, gaps have widened (Standing 1989, 1999; Mehra and Gammage 1999; Artecona and Cunningham 2002; UNRISD 2005). The case of the East Asian "tigers" is instructive. Despite rapid growth in exports that relied on female labor, gender wage gaps remain large and have worsened in some cases (Jomo 2004). As the data in Table 15.1 show, during the 1990s the ratio of female to male wages in manufacturing fell in a number of countries. Declines are also evident in Chile and Hong Kong (not shown here).

To understand the effect of globalization on gender wage gaps, it is necessary to disentangle the wage effects of increased educational attainment for women,

Table 15.1 Female to male manufacturing ratios (%), selected countries

	1990	*1995*	*1998*	*1999*
Africa				
Egypt	67.9	73.6	68.8	75.2
Kenya	73.3	92.8		
Swaziland	87.7	86.6		
Latin America				
Brazil	53.6	56.9	60.9	61.7
Costa Rica	74.3	70.9	79.9	73.1
El Salvador	94.1	96.6	70.1	62.0
Mexico		68.7	71.0	69.7
Panama			95.5	93.2
Paraguay	66.5	79.5	81.1	54.6
Asia				
Bahrain			45.3	43.6
Cyprus	57.6	60.1	57.9	54.2
Korea	50.3	54.1		55.6
Malaysia	50.1	57.9		
Philippines		74.3	78.2	79.9
Taiwan		61.6	63.9	64.8

Source: International Labor Organization, *Yearbook of Labor Statistics* 2004. For Taiwan, DGBAS (2002).

as compared to the effects of indicators of globalization. Several studies have controlled for alternative factors that might raise female wages in order to isolate the effects of trade and foreign direct investment (FDI) liberalization. A negative effect of export-orientation on female relative wages has been found in both developing and developed economies (Gupta 2002; Oostendorp 2004).

In Taiwan and South Korea, for example, competition from foreign trade in concentrated industries is positively associated with wage discrimination against women (Berik *et al.* 2004). There has been no tendency for the gap between male and female wages to decline in China, with data indicating instead expanding inequality between men's and women's earnings (Maurer-Fazio *et al.* 1999; Maurer-Fazio and Hughes 2002). Indeed, the proportion of the gender wage gap that is unexplained by individual productivity characteristics is larger in the most liberalized sectors of the economy and the smallest in the least liberalized – the state sector (Maurer-Fazio and Hughes 2002). The portion of the gender wage gap in China that is unexplained by productivity differentials (and thus is attributed to gender discrimination) rose from 52.5 percent in 1988 to 63.2 percent in 1995 (Gustaffson and Li 2000).

In contrast, in Brazil, there is evidence of a decline in the discriminatory component of the gender wage gap in the 1990s, although in part this was the result of a decline in male wages, resulting from stringent austerity policies (Arabsheibani *et al.* 2003). The extent to which the narrowing of the wage gap in

Brazil can be attributed to liberalization of trade and investment remains a question. Given the small share of exports and imports in GDP in Brazil, this may not have been a causal factor in reducing gender wage gaps.

In agricultural work, female earnings lag men's substantially. The distribution of benefits in the Chilean grape industry underscores the disadvantaged position of female workers. For seedless grapes produced in 1993–4, producers accounted for 11 percent of costs (of which 5 percent went to workers), while exporters received 28 percent, importers 26 percent, and distributors 35 percent (Barrientos *et al.* 1999). The greater bargaining power of capital over labor highlights the difficulty of raising women's relative wages in this industry.

There are some exceptions to the negative picture we have drawn of the effect of globalization on women's relative earnings in the agricultural sector. Women's earnings have improved in some cases of NTAE production where they have access to or control over land. One such case is Uganda (Fontana *et al.* 1998) although this enlarged area of economic activity for women does not appear to have disturbed the wide gender gap in earnings in other sectors of the economy where women's wages are roughly 40 percent below those of men (Appleton *et al.* 1996).[18]

Several forces militate against closure of the gender earnings gap. Women in semi-industrialized economies are "crowded" into labor-intensive export industries – precisely the ones with the lowest sunk costs and which thus tend to be more mobile. Firm mobility produces a "threat effect" that makes it difficult for women to obtain higher wages. Firm mobility also makes it easier for firms to appropriate the gains of productivity growth. In the case of Bangladesh's female-dominated garment industry, Bhattacharya and Rahman (1999) found, for example, that profit margins increased from 13 to 24 percent in the early 1990s as productivity rose, with the wage share of value-added falling.

Rodrik (1997) describes this phenomenon in terms of a flattened labor demand curve, made more elastic by the emergence of alternative labor supplies beyond the domestic economy. Workers bear the costs of increased capital mobility in the form of lower wages (Seguino 2007). Seguino (2000a) finds evidence of this effect in the case of Taiwan where the gender wage gap widened in the period 1982–90. The increase in total FDI (the absolute value of the sum of inward and outward FDI), which reflects greater firm mobility, appears to have weakened women's relative bargaining power.[19]

A second phenomenon that inhibits closure of the gender wage gap is the informalization of labor contracts through the process of subcontracting and outsourcing. Workers in these arrangements, as noted, are largely women. Because of their unstable work arrangements and isolation, they face greater difficulties in bargaining for higher wages than formal sector workers. There is evidence that wages in this type of employment are significantly lower than for workers similarly employed in the formal sector (Roh 1990; Kabeer 2000; Balakrishnan 2002). The gender wage gap is thus probably even wider than the official figures imply, because wages of home workers often go unrecorded in official surveys.

Further, low wages in this sector are likely to hold down wage gains for women employed in the formal sector.

There is some evidence that gender wage inequality is functional to growth with gender gaps in earnings positively related to growth rates of GDP in SIEs where women are segregated in export manufacturing industries (Seguino 2000b).[20] Under those conditions, efforts to close the wage gap without counter-measures to offset the negative effect on export demand will slow growth, putting gender equity and economic growth at odds. In light of all these factors, evidence of rising profit shares of income in numerous economies is not surprising (Epstein and Power 2002; Harrison 2002). Thus an important effect of globalization is a redistribution from labor to capital as economies become more profit-led.

Effects on gender inequality in leisure and caring labor

Theoretically, job access for women can improve their level of well-being and that of the children they care for – if this provides more income, and if women can find a way to juggle their care responsibilities (or if men take on more unpaid care work). Time use data are sparse, and in particular, trend data are lacking. What little evidence is available suggests that women's time burdens have increased with globalization. Further, studies such as Floro (1995) indicate that the time intensity of women's labor has increased. Men's performance of unpaid labor does not appear to have increased enough to compensate, suggesting a decline in female leisure.

To date, there is little research that examines the long-term effects on women's well-being and empowerment of their increased employment access. Are there measurable effects that show up in measures of well-being or household bargaining power? We need to answer this question in order to determine whether economic and trade liberalization provide the conditions for women to achieve equitable standards of living and power with men over time, even if women's incorporation into the labor force in the short term is under unfavorable – and indeed exploitative – conditions.

Some studies find that as women's access to outside income rises, they are better able to renegotiate the distribution of resources within the household to the benefit of themselves and their children. The source and stability of that income appears to play a role in influencing women's bargaining power. For example, Kabeer's (2000) study of Bangladeshi garment workers found that women employed as home workers with insecure and intermittent earnings were less able to renegotiate their position in patriarchal households than women with higher and more stable earnings.

One study considers these questions for Asian economies where rapid growth was fueled by low-cost female labor in a period of otherwise global economic stagnation (Seguino 2002). A variety of well-being indicators suggest there has been some closure of gender gaps in well-being, but those countries that have improved the most were the slowest growing in the region and the least successful as "open" economies. In the case of South Korea, China, and India, a disturbing trend has been the declining ratio of females to males in the population (Klasen and Wink 2003). In these economies, deemed to be performing well macroeconomically, women's life chances relative to men's have diminished – a trend linked to sex selective abortion. Population ratios can be viewed as a measure of society's valuation of women. Their access to paid employment in these countries has apparently not resulted in sufficient leverage to alter gender perceptions that devalue women.

Macroeconomic effects of globalization

The macroeconomic effects of globalization on gender equality can be subdivided into two categories: (1) demand-side effects and (2) the shifting role of the state. These are discussed in turn.

Demand-side effects

In the context of globalization, external factors increasingly determine the level of output and employment, while the importance of domestic demand is lessened. Trade liberalization raises the share of exports and imports in demand. Further, investment liberalization that facilitates inward and outward FDI requires domestic economies to compete with conditions, including labor costs, in other countries.

These changes alter the relationship between income distribution and growth. In particular, as external factors have a larger effect on aggregate demand, economies are more likely to become profit-led – redistribution to profits raises output and employment (You 1989; Bhaduri and Marglin 1990). This is because higher wages, once a benefit in the form of a demand-side stimulus in more closed economies (assuming spending out of wage income exceeds spending out of profit income), now have a potentially negative demand-side effect on exports and investment demand. This negative effect is based on an assumption that wage increases do not affect labor productivity.

Thus, while liberalization may result in a demand-side stimulus if exports and investment rise, this can only occur if wage growth is constrained, particularly the wages of those employed in "mobile" export industries. Women are more adversely affected as they tend to be disproportionately concentrated in industries where vertical FDI dominates. Vertical FDI, as compared to horizontal FDI, implies production for export rather than sale to the domestic economy. Vertical FDI also means that firms take advantage of differences in factor costs among countries, concentrating labor-intensive activities in those countries with lower labor costs (Kucera 2001).[21]

Financial market liberalization can also produce negative demand-side effects. Four effects are especially important for gender relations: (1) balance of payments difficulties, (2) constraints on use of monetary policy, leading to slower rates of growth, (3) increased economic volatility, and (4) reduced latitude for use of fiscal policy as a stabilization tool. Regarding the first, the inflow of financial capital raises the demand for imports. If inflows are too rapid, inflation and exchange rate appreciation may result, leading to balance of payments difficulties, particularly if inflows are directed toward nonproductive expenditures such as luxury goods and real estate speculation. The result may be a contraction of aggregate demand. Beyond the short-run effect of balance of payments difficulties and tendencies toward stagnation, in the longer run, sustaining a trade deficit causes external debt to build up, leading to capital flight and a financial crisis if it becomes seen as unsustainable (Bhaduri 1999).

Second, financial liberalization can contribute to a decline in growth rates. Liberalization permits investors to cross borders to seek out the highest rate of return on financial instruments, leading monetary authorities to raise interest rates in an effort to establish credibility with financial markets. The cumulative effect is that globally, interest rates have been ratcheted upward and are historically high (Eatwell 1996; Felix 1998).[22] High interest rates, it is argued, have contributed to a slowdown in economic growth and employment generation. A further effect of financial liberalization is economic volatility, as seen in the 1990s. Financial panics, more common in the age of elimination of capital controls, can lead to rapid capital outflows, sharp declines in asset prices, bankruptcies, and recession as evidenced by events in Mexico in 1994 and Asia in 1997.

Finally, because financial markets interpret fiscal deficits as inflationary, governments are constrained in available policy instruments for stimulating output and employment. Deficit spending increasingly becomes difficult to manage without precipitating a capital outflow, to which countries respond by raising interest rates. The pressure to reduce state spending is increased as footloose capital gains increased leverage to bargain for lower tax rates as a condition of investment (Tanzi 1995; Poterba 1997).[23] If spending levels are to be maintained, taxes must be borne by the immobile factor, labor, while taxes on the mobile factor fall. Thus, there is a tendency toward reduction of government spending, and a redistribution of the burden of that spending from capital to labor (Wallerstein and Przeworski 1995).

The net effect of these processes has been a slowdown in economic growth globally (Maddison 1995). Because women are more likely than men to be unemployed, the difficulties of stimulating growth and employment in open economies weigh more heavily on them. It thus appears that a major vehicle for improving gender equity – improving women's relative access to jobs – is increasingly unobtainable in the era of globalization.

The shifting role of the state

Economic and trade liberalization have contributed to restrictions on state intervention in the economy in two important arenas (in addition to demand management policies discussed earlier) – the provision of a social safety net and the reduction in tools required for states to promote development and productivity growth.

Reduction in the provision of social services is related to the pressure on states to eliminate budget deficits. This pressure, as noted earlier, is due to financial market liberalization, stabilization, structural adjustment policies, and declining corporate tax contributions. Of course, even prior to the current period of liberalization, entitlement programs to a greater or lesser degree differentially benefited full-time workers – mainly males. Temporary or part-time workers, and those who spend time in unpaid labor – largely women – have had less coverage.

This problem has been exacerbated by cuts in social expenditures on health care, education, food, and housing subsidies, and the imposition of user charges for public services on which low-income women have relied.[24] As a result, women, who act as the economic "shock absorbers," face increasing demands on their time with labor effort rising to maintain family well-being in order to accommodate the decline in public services.

The ability of states to intervene in the development process to promote higher value-added production activities has also narrowed. Countries have been under pressure to privatize domestic industries and to relinquish the tools of industrial/ agricultural policy. This trend has been accompanied by trade and investment agreements (institutionalized in the WTO) which require governments to liberalize trade, drop preferential treatment of domestic firms, and allow unrestricted foreign direct investment. These conditions make it increasingly difficult to pursue policies that would provide domestic producers with the resources needed to move up the industrial ladder to more skill-intensive goods production where prices are more inelastic and terms of trade are not declining.[25] Further, a number of countries have made central banks independent of government, limiting their ability to use preferential lending as a means to support the growth of strategic manufacturing, service, or agricultural industries.

In agriculturally-based economies, such as in Africa, investment is public-sector-led. Public sector spending on infrastructure can "crowd in" private sector spending, acting as a stimulus to productivity growth, due in part to market failures where farmers lack access to resources, such as credit and training. Constraints on public investment have gendered effects in a number of African economies, where women comprise the bulk of farmers. Cuts in infrastructure investments and restrictions on the use of formerly public resources owing to privatization have led to an increase in women's unpaid labor burden.[26] Further, agriculturally-based economies, wedded to the production of export commodities with falling terms of trade, require government investment to improve the productive capacity of small, largely female farmers in order to raise income.

Feminist macroeconomic policies to promote gender equity

Given the context described earlier, what macro-level policies should feminists advocate to promote equity in the medium- to long-run? First, such a policy framework should include promotion of the type of development consistent with full employment and in which economies are wage-led with rising productivity. By full employment, we refer to the absence of involuntary unemployment, part-time, and informal employment. By wage-led growth, we refer to the set of structural, policy, and institutional conditions in which a redistribution to wages from profits is a stimulus to growth.

Our usage of the term full employment differs from the standard usage, which often ignores unpaid labor, as well as the level of pay.[27] It would not be ideal to promote full employment (i.e. the eradication of involuntary unemployment and underemployment) without a concomitant increased sharing of unpaid labor by men, so that women's access to paid work could be offset by a reduction in unpaid labor. Full employment that produces labor shortages can make it easier for women to access employment in male-dominated industries that pay higher wages, facilitating job integration and narrower wage gaps. The movement toward full-employment also helps to put upward pressure on women's wages by tightening labor markets. For this strategy to work, however, economies must be wage-led – that is, redistribution to wages must be a stimulus to output and growth, thus ratifying higher relative female wages.

Income distribution and growth

The promotion of full-employment wage-led growth in open economies is in essence a problem of the relationship between income distribution and macroeconomic outcomes, explored in recent years by neo-Kaleckian economists.[28] In these models, some components of aggregate demand are a function of the distribution of income and the models explore the macroeconomic conditions necessary for redistribution from profits to wages (through, for example, a higher minimum wage or increased worker bargaining power) to stimulate output and growth.

While most neo-Kaleckian models are not gendered, it is possible to engender these models by incorporating gendered patterns of labor supply and demand. One approach is to model labor supply to economic sectors as segregated along gender lines, reflecting women's greater responsibility for care activities as well as the tendency to segregate women in labor-intensive export activities in the productive sector.

Macro models that recognize gendered job allocation give some insight into the conditions required to make higher wages compatible with growth. Blecker and Seguino (2002), for example, model output and growth in an export-oriented semi-industrialized economy. In this two-sector model, female labor is used to produce export goods and male workers are concentrated in the nontradables sector (the model does not consider the care economy). Higher relative female wages could stimulate aggregate consumption (assuming female workers have a higher propensity to consume than capitalists), thereby producing a demand-side stimulus. But those higher wages will also cause export prices to rise, in which case export demand declines. Alternatively, higher wages will squeeze profits in that sector, resulting in a decline in sectoral investment. This is especially likely in labor-intensive industries in which "footloose" firms find it easier to relocate to lower-wage sites. The negative demand-side effect of higher female wages on exports and investment is likely to be larger than the potential consumption stimulus, especially if exports are price elastic. As a result, higher female wages in such an economy are deflationary.

State-level development strategies

Given these constraints, state-level policy can be used to attenuate the deflationary impact of higher female wages. This can be partially achieved by incentives to firms to shift the production mix in female-dominated labor-intensive industries to produce exports with a low price elasticity of demand (e.g. where quality matters). Higher female wages in that case reduce the negative effect on export demand. Further, in economies that are articulated, that is, where export goods are also domestically consumed, higher female wages may stimulate consumption demand, offsetting the decline in export demand. Both of these possibilities imply the need for an industrial/agricultural development strategy to promote both articulation and an export product mix that permits female wages to rise without a (large) negative effect on exports.

To make gender equity compatible with growth in an open economy also requires boundaries on the behavior of firms, and in particular, limits on physical capital mobility (inward and outward FDI). Policies to slow the speed at which firms "run" from higher wages allow for the possibility that wage hikes can stimulate productivity growth, either because firms make greater efforts to achieve efficiency by investing in technological improvements, or because workers are induced to be more productive as a result.

In the first case, incentive structures that force firms to respond to higher wages by investing in technological improvements cause investment to *rise* rather than fall as wages rise, thus producing a demand-side stimulus.[29] There may be limits on the effectiveness of this type of policy in labor-intensive industries in which women are employed, given that technological frontiers will eventually be reached, thus prohibiting firms from further overcoming higher wage costs with technological improvements. Nevertheless, evidence from a number of semi-industrialized economies suggests that there can be a positive wage-investment-productivity nexus over some range of wages and technological level.

Absent a positive effect of wages on investment, efficiency wage effects of higher wages may emerge when FDI is less mobile. This implies that unit labor costs stay constant and may even fall when wages rise.[30] In this case, competitiveness is not hampered by higher wages, and export and aggregate demand do not fall. Inward FDI might also be restricted to strategic industries and excluded from others for some period of time, giving domestic firms the opportunity to gain competitiveness, with the state using its leverage to assist firms to raise productivity in response to higher wages.

Managing FDI is possible, even in a globalized economic environment. As Chang (1998) notes, multinational corporations are willing to accommodate restrictive policies so long as changes are predictable and announced in advance. Moreover, FDI tends to be influenced by the political and economic climate, the quality of the government bureaucracy that implements policy, and financial and exchange rate policies. Policies that stabilize the economy, including capital controls that act as speed bumps, can reduce volatility and may attract FDI.

Portions of the strategy outlined here have been effectively implemented in several countries. South Korea, for example, has successfully moved up the industrial ladder, relying heavily on state intervention. It used a variety of tools to discipline and support "immobile" domestic firms to increase their productivity as they moved into targeted strategic industries (FDI was greatly restricted). Firms that wanted access to government subsidies and other benefits were required to increase exports. With rising wages and limited mobility, the only alternative to escape the profit squeeze was for firms to raise productivity, even in labor-intensive industries where the potential for productivity gains was thought to be limited. The result was a rise in wages that stimulated investment and productivity growth (Seguino 1999–2000). As a result, employment expanded even as wages rose.

South Korea's strategy was built on the premise that state intervention is required to stimulate productivity and to move the economy into higher value-added industries.[31] This strategy is time-consuming for private firms to underwrite without government support, and thus is otherwise unlikely to be undertaken. These policies were accompanied by state investment in education, technology, and support of research and development – public sector spending that "crowded in" private investment, raising profitability by increasing productivity. Restrictions on FDI made it easier for the state to discipline as well as reward firms, and to nurture domestic capital, with pressure on these firms to share their gains with workers in the form of higher wages.

None of these conditions implies the need to close the economy to trade and investment, but they do highlight the importance of managing these, a policy approach that we could label "industrial policy under conditions of strategic openness" – openness that is managed to achieve specific development and growth goals that serve the broader goal of achieving gender equity.

Industrial and agricultural development policies would have to be accompanied by compatible monetary policies. Because low wages for women substitute for currency devaluation, a crawling peg that adjusts for rising female wages can offset the negative effect on aggregate demand in cases where devaluations are not contractionary. Devaluations also close the gender wage gap in that real male wages fall (since some consumption goods are imported and are now more costly).[32] This topic has been relatively unexplored, but here we point to the importance of incorporating gender equity goals in the formulation of monetary policy.

Collective action at the international level

There are a number of external constraints that would need to be overcome in order to achieve higher rates of growth induced by rising wages and productivity. The poorest countries have the weakest power vis-à-vis multinationals because their enticement is primarily low wages. Bargaining strength of these countries may be enhanced by regionally coordinated industrial policies. For example, the Caribbean has a locational advantage as a tourism destination, but many of the benefits of this type of activity flow to multinational tourism firms. A coordinated Caribbean tourism policy would allow countries to collectively bargain for higher regional wages and greater backward linkages to local economies, for example, in local sourcing for food purchases. Without a locational advantage with which to bargain, it may be that poor countries are constrained to permit inward FDI that capitalizes on low wages.

Second, a change in policies and rules emanating from the World Trade Organization (WTO) and trade agreements is needed to permit special and differential treatment for developing countries that allow the use of national-level tools to influence the direction and rate of economic growth. These include support for strategic industries, protection of infant industries, and implementation of rules on foreign direct investment beneficial to domestic firms and productivity growth.[33]

The achievement of gender equality also depends on demand expansion in industrialized economies, which, however, has slowed appreciably since the 1970s. Further, income inequality has risen in those economies, suggesting an additional demand-side constraint on the growth of developing economies. While open economies are more likely to be profit-led, the global economy can be viewed as a closed wage-led economic system. The declining income of those at the bottom of the distribution in industrialized economies has reduced demand for manufactured or primary commodity exports from developing economies – goods that higher income groups are less likely to consume. To rectify this, redistributive policies in the north coupled with coordination of expansionary macroeconomic policies could stimulate northern demand for southern goods, thus permitting greater growth of (female) wages in the south.

Summary and conclusions

How do we raise women's well-being in export industries while at the same time promoting economic growth? This chapter answers that question by arguing for a heightened role for the state in managing the economy in controlling physical and financial capital flows, and setting industrial or agricultural policy. Country-specific development policies will differ depending on the structure of the economy, the nature of gender employment segregation, and human capital differences. Nevertheless, the basic goal is to provide a policy framework that: (1) allows productivity to rise in female-dominated industries; (2) promotes strategic industries which can afford to pay high wages to workers; and (3) allows pursuit of full employment through demand-side management policies.

In this context, macroeconomic policies could include restrictions on physical capital mobility in a way that constrains firms to upgrade rather than run from higher wages. A nonexhaustive list of corollary policies include state-level investments in education and health, expenditures that permit women and men to combine paid and unpaid work, capital controls, and gender-sensitive monetary policy.

Proposing increased state intervention in the economy at a time when political pressures are in the opposite direction may seem fanciful. It seems even more unlikely that individual countries, especially small, poor countries, will be able to effectively challenge the winds of economic and trade liberalization. That said, those concerned with economic and social equity can still find entry points for action. Engaging in national debates on gender equitable proposals is the first step in stimulating discussion beyond domestic borders. This may eventually lead to broad consensus at the international level, be it within international bodies or in regional organizations.

These proposals, if they achieve the desired results, would fundamentally alter power relations. They stand in opposition to current trends that limit the possibility for increasing women's bargaining power. Nevertheless, the improvement in women's status – now an internationally recognized Millennium Development Goal adopted by 170 governments – has the potential to alter unequal gender relations and may be met with resistance. That conflict can be lessened if the economic pie is expanding so that women's access to resources does not come solely from a reduction in the material resources going to men. We can also hope that gender norms and stereotypes change along the way such that economic goals include a greater emphasis on the achievement of well-being for women and the families they care for.

Notes

1 We are grateful to a number of people who have given us insightful comments and raised challenging questions about earlier versions of this chapter. In particular, we thank Ajit Singh, Korküt Erturk, Maria Floro, Will Milberg, Marianne Ferber, Elissa Braunstein, and participants in the symposium "New Directions in Research on Gender-Aware Macroeconomics and International Economics" in April 2002 at the Levy Economics Institute.
2 This chapter does not deal directly with change in other arenas, especially the political. On the role of greater equity in the distribution of material resources to promote gender equity, see Blumberg (1988). For further discussion of the notion of people-centered development, as this approach is frequently called, see UNDP (1997) and Elson and Çağatay (2000).
3 In the case of self-employment, including on-farm employment, we imply the need for gender equity in access to and control over income.
4 Elson and Çağatay (2000) label this the "transformatory" approach insofar as the goal of policy is to alter a given set of gender relations and distribution of resources to promote greater equity.
5 It is useful to think of the nontradables as fix-price industries where goods are priced with a fixed markup over unit costs due to oligopolistic structure and chronic excess capacity. The tradables sector is analogous to a flex-price market, where prices are set with a flexible markup that responds to changes in the real exchange rate. An important gender difference is that goods produced in the nontradables sector also have lower price elasticity of demand than export goods, due to relatively fewer substitutes. As a result, wages in these industries can rise without substantial negative effects on product demand or employment.
6 The feminization of labor in the manufacturing sector may be a developing country phenomenon. Kucera and Milberg (2000), for example, find evidence of declines in the

female share of manufacturing employment in a number of industrialized economies in response to increased north–south trade. That is, women employed in the formal manufacturing sector in the north have been displaced in response to increased trade with southern countries that are more intensively using women in labor-intensive industries.

7 It would be interesting to explore the process of defeminization and whether its rate has been slower in some countries (i.e. South Korea) than in others. This has implications for trends in the gender wage gap.

8 Countries that export unprocessed primary products (e.g. ores) do not fit the stylized facts that we present here. First, exports have not expanded as a share of GDP to the extent they have in other developing economies. Also, these industries tend to be male-dominated, such that any expansion of output is likely to benefit male workers in employment and wages (Fontana 2002). Liberalization has, however, had negative effects on women's employment and income in these economies, in part through loss of manufacturing jobs, but also due to pressures on the state to reduce expenditures, resulting in a disproportionately large loss of female jobs.

9 The sex trade is also one of the fastest growing and most profitable service industries; see Williams (1999).

10 Moreover, unemployment data are of limited significance in low-income economies where the majority of the population engages in forms of economic activity that tend not to be counted – usually informal employment or self-employment.

11 For a description of unemployment measurement in several Caribbean economies, see Seguino (2004).

12 This occurs, despite the reliance on service exports to fuel growth in the region. Evidence indicates that during economic upturns the gender gap in unemployment rates widens as men are hired first, suggesting that capital's preference for cheap labor is mitigated by patriarchal norms that give men first access to jobs (Seguino 2004).

13 This phrase is from Samarasinghe (1998) in reference to trends in Sri Lanka. It is clearly, however, a process that extends beyond Sri Lanka to many developing economies.

14 On this topic, see Fernandez-Kelly and Sassen (1993), Carr *et al.* (2000), Sayeed and Balakrishnan (2002), and Balakrishnan (2002).

15 This bias results in women being treated as though their earnings are supplementary while men are assumed to have the right to jobs whose pay is regular and where there is upward mobility.

16 In agriculture, health hazards associated with working with chemical pesticides further dampen the positive employment effects (Thrupp *et al.* 1995; Dolan *et al.* 1999). Some recent studies note that some progress has been made on labor conditions and on women's empowerment (Newman 2000; Stephen 2000). Nevertheless, work conditions are relatively harsh and prospects for advancement are limited.

17 Oostendorp (2004) finds evidence of declining gaps in wages within occupational categories in tradable industries, but not in nontradables, based on data from the ILO October survey, noting, however, the extensive problems with this data set that make it "one of the least-used sources of cross country data in the world" (2004: 5). These data weaknesses and the standardization procedure used to convert earnings to monthly wages raise questions about the reliability of the results.

18 A second case of women's increased earnings from NTAEs is Vietnam. Trade liberalization and a reduction in government subsidies for modern health care (Sowerine 1999) led to increased demand for medicinal plants. This has had a positive effect on women's income since they are dominant along the chain of production of medicinal plants. Again, however, this partial equilibrium perspective is overshadowed by broader evidence suggesting that gender inequality has increased in Vietnam (Long *et al.* 2000).

19 This result differs from industrialized economies such as the US where men have been concentrated in import-competing industries, such as autos and steel, and have also faced "threat effects" of corporate relocation. Since men were disproportionately employed in these industries, the result has been a narrowing of the gender wage gap but in a gender conflictive sense, whereby men's wages have fallen significantly and women's have risen slightly (Mishel and Bernstein 1999). Black and Brainerd (2002) attribute this to increased trade competition which forces firms to give up their discriminatory hiring practices to employ female labor, thus driving up women's relative wages. Kongar (this volume) contradicts this explanation, instead attributing the narrowing gender wage gap in concentrated US industries to firms' ability to extract wage concessions from male workers, at the same time laying off female workers in low productivity occupations, thus raising the average wage of remaining female workers. Import competition and the decline of job opportunities for males thus resulted in a greater supply of males willing to work for lower wages, thereby decreasing the cost of discrimination. These results imply a relative decline in female manufacturing employment, a finding consistent with Kucera and Milberg (2000).

20 Some recent studies show, however, that when gender equality is measured in terms of education, equity stimulates growth (Hill and King 1995; Dollar and Gatti 1999; Klasen 2002). The causal mechanisms are several. Gender inequalities in education and access to other productive resources create inefficiencies. Further, women's greater education enhances household bargaining power that can improve children's access to resources, thus enhancing the quality of the future labor supply and economy-wide productivity. These results are not necessarily inconsistent with Seguino (2000b) whose empirical analysis is focused on the short- and medium-run. Increase in female education relative to men can raise women's relative productivity. But if women lack the bargaining power to translate that productivity into higher wages, unit labor costs and thus export prices fall and/or firm profits rise. Employers and foreign buyers thus appropriate the gains from increases in women's education.

21 Conversely, horizontal FDI is motivated by the desire to gain access to a domestic market to avoid import restrictions or local content requirements, or reduce transport costs. In such a case, labor costs have a smaller negative effect on inward FDI.

22 Proponents of liberalization argue that efficiency is promoted as investment funds flow from surplus economies, where marginal rates of return are low to economies with higher marginal productivity of investment, thereby stimulating investment and growth worldwide. Felix (1998) challenges this view, arguing that higher interest rates dampen investment and slow economic growth, and economic inefficiency.

23 This occurs between countries and within countries, such as the US where individual states compete for investment by lowering corporate tax burdens.

24 Elson and Çağatay (2000) note also the trend to commodify state-based entitlements, with health, retirement, and education pushed into the market realm, available primarily to those whose incomes are sufficient to cover the costs.

25 While agricultural and semi-industrialized economies differ structurally, there are some commonalities related to their susceptibility to external factors, according to Ertürk (2001). Semi-industrialized economies are attempting "immiserizing growth" which results from overreliance on low-tech manufacturing goods that have taken on the pricing characteristics of primary commodities – that is, with declining terms of trade. The emergence of new producers of these homogenous goods had led to a crisis of overproduction, causing export prices to fall. This has led to competitive devaluations and pressured firms to lower costs or relocate to lower wage sites.

26 These unpaid labor burdens are costly in terms of foregone income. For example, in Tanzania, a reduction of women's time burdens in providing basic commodities to their households was found to raise cash incomes 10 percent, labor productivity 15 percent, and capital efficiency 44 percent on smallholder farms (Blackden and Bhanu 1999).

27 We are grateful to Nilüfer Çağatay for this point.

28 See Blecker (2002) and Setterfield (2003) for excellent reviews of research in this area.
29 Evidence of a positive relationship between wages and investment can be found in a variety of contexts. See, for example, Seguino (1999–2000) on South Korea, and Marquetti (2004) for a variety of industrialized countries.
30 If unit labor costs stay the same, of course, then this is not a case of wage-led growth in the classic demand-driven sense. But it is wage-led in the supply-side sense, whereby higher wages stimulate productivity improvements, attenuating any negative demand-side effects that might result from a decline in profits.
31 For further discussion of this strategy and the theory behind it, see Amsden (1998).
32 There are constraints on the effectiveness of exchange rates to lead to a closure of the gender wage gap, however. Currency devaluations can be inflationary in economies in which imports are rigid and are a large share of GDP. This can dampen export demand, and will lower women's real wages. Further, financial markets may respond negatively to anticipated inflation in response to a currency devaluation, leading to rising interest rates, bankruptcy, and deflation. Thus women may gain in terms of higher wages relative to men, but they may also suffer employment losses so that the female share of the wage bill falls. Also, unless supply schedules are elastic, it may be difficult to shift resources to the export sector. For more on the limits of devaluation to promote output growth, see, for example, Panic (1998).
33 Many would agree that a shift in the IMF policy framework is also required to permit developing countries to manage financial capital flows, thus allowing domestic interest rates to fall. In addition, an end to the IMF's push for contractionary policies in response to balance of payments crises as a way to slow imports is needed. Further, the emergence of an international lender of last resort in times of balance of payments crises would reduce pressures on domestic economies to maintain high levels of reserves and interest rates that slow growth. These stances have been broadly discussed, but the engine of change in this case seems to rest more on political power than economic analysis.

References

Amsden, A. (1998) "A theory of government intervention in late industrialization," in L. Putterman and D. Rueschemeyer (eds), *State and Market in Development: synergy or rivalry?* Boulder, CO: Lynne Rienner Publishers.

Antecol, H. (2000) "An examination of cross-country differences in the gender gap in labor force participation rates," *Labour Economics*, 7: 409–26.

Appleton, S., Hoddinott, J., and Krishnan, P. (1996) "The gender wage gap in three African countries," Centre for the Study of the African Economies Working Paper No. 96–7, Oxford: University of Oxford.

Arabsheibani, G.R., Carneiro, F., and Henley, A. (2003) "Gender wage differentials in Brazil: trends over a turbulent era," World Bank Policy Research Working Paper No. 3148, Washington, DC: World Bank.

Artecona, R. and Cunningham, W. (2002) "Effects of trade liberalization on the gender wage gap in Mexico," Policy Research Report Working Paper No. 21, Washington, DC: World Bank.

Balakrishnan, R. (ed.) (2002) *The Hidden Assembly Line: gender dynamics of subcontracted work in a global economy*, Bloomfield, CT: Kumarian Press.

Barrientos, S. (2001) "Gender, flexibility, and global value chains," *IDS Bulletin*, 32 (3): 83–93.

Barrientos, S., Bee, A., Matear, A., Vogel, I., and Kay, C. (1999) *Women and Agribusiness: working miracles in the Chilean fruit export sector*, London: MacMillan.

Bénería, L. (2003) *Gender, Development, and Globalization: economics as if people mattered*, New York and London: Routledge.

Berik, G. (2004) "Growth and gender equity in East Asia," background paper for the UNRISD Report *Gender Equality: Striving for Justice in an Unequal World*, Geneva: United Nations Research Institute for Social Development (UNRISD).

Berik, G., Rodgers, Y., and Zveglich, J. (2004) "International trade and gender wage discrimination: evidence from East Asia," *Review of Development Economics*, 8 (2): 237–54.

Bhaduri, A. (1999) "Macroeconomic theory and policy in developing countries," in D. Baker, G. Epstein, and R. Pollin (eds), *Globalization and Progressive Economic Policy*, Cambridge: Cambridge University Press.

Bhaduri, A. and Marglin, S. (1990) "Unemployment and the real wage: the economic basis for contesting political ideologies," *Cambridge Journal of Economics*, 14 (4): 375–93.

Bhattacharya, D. and Rahman, M. (1999) "Female employment under export propelled industrialization: prospects for internalizing global opportunities in the apparel sector in Bangladesh," Occasional Paper No. 10, Geneva: UNRISD.

Black, S. and Brainerd, E. (2002) "Importing inequality? The effects of increased competition on the gender wage gap," NBER Working Paper No. W9110, Cambridge, MA: National Bureau of Economic Research (NBER).

Blackden, C.M. and Bhanu, C. (1999) "Gender, growth, and poverty reduction," World Bank Technical Paper No. 428, Washington, DC: World Bank.

Blecker, R. (2002) "Distribution, demand and growth in Neo-Kaleckian macro models," in M. Setterfield (ed.), *The Economics of Demand-led Growth: challenging the supply-side vision of the long run*, Cheltenham: Edward Elgar.

Blecker, R. and Seguino, S. (2002) "Macroeconomic effects of reducing gender wage inequality in an export-oriented semi-industrialized economy," *Review of Development Economics*, 6 (1): 103–19.

Blumberg, R.L. (1988). "Income under female vs. male control: hypotheses from a theory and data from the Third World," *Journal of Family Issues*, 9 (1): 51–84.

Bridger, S., Kay, R., and Pinnick, K. (1996) *No More Heroines? Russia, women and the market*, New York and London: Routledge.

Brown, C. and Cunningham, W. (2002) "Gender in Mexico's maquiladora industry," Working Paper No. 2002–8, Edinburg, PA: Center of Border Economic Studies, University of Texas-Pan American.

Carr, M., Chen, M., and Tate, J. (2000) "Globalization and home-based workers," *Feminist Economics*, 6 (3): 123–42.

Chang, H.J. (1998) "Transnational corporations and strategic industrial policy," in R. Kozul-Wright and R. Rowthorn (eds), *Transnational Corporations and the Global Economy*, London: MacMillan Press Ltd. for WIDER.

Davison, J.O. and Sanchez-Taylor, J. (1999) *Sun, Sex and Gold: sex tourism in the Caribbean*, Lanham, MD: Rowman and Littlefield.

Deere, C.D. (2004) "The feminization of agriculture? Economic restructuring in rural Latin America," background paper, Geneva: UNRISD.

Directorate General of Budget, Accounting and Statistics (DGBAS) (2002) *Yearbook of Earnings and Productivity Statistics*, Taipei City, Taiwan: DGBAS.

Dolan, C., Humphrey, J., and Harris-Pascal, C. (1999) "Horticulture commodity chains: the impact of the UK market on the African fresh vegetable industry," IDS Working Paper No. 96, Brighton: Institute of Development Studies.

Dollar, D. and Gatti, R. (1999) "Gender inequality, income, and growth: are good times good for women?" Policy Research Report on Gender and Development, Working Paper Series No. 1, Washington, DC: World Bank.

Eatwell, J. (1996) "International financial liberalization: the impact on world development," Discussion Paper Series, New York: UNDP, Office of Development Studies.

Elson, D. and Çağatay, N. (2000) "The social content of macroeconomic policies," *World Development*, 28 (67): 1347–64.

Epstein, G. and Power, D. (2002) "The return of finance and finance's returns: recent trends in rentier incomes in OECD countries, 1960–2000," Research Brief 2002–2, Amherst, MA: Political Economy Research Institute.

Erturk, K. (2001) "Overcapacity and the East Asian crisis," *Journal of Post-Keynesian Economics*, 24 (2): 253–75.

Felix, D. (1998). "Asia and the crisis of financial globalization," in D. Baker, G. Epstein, and P. Pollin (eds), *Globalization and Progressive Economic Policy*, Cambridge: Cambridge University Press.

Fernandez-Kelly, P. and Sassen, S. (1993) "Recasting women in the global economy: internationalization and changing definitions of gender," Russell Sage Foundation Working Paper No. 36, New York: Russell Sage Foundation.

Floro, M. (1995) "Economic restructuring, gender and the allocation of time," *World Development*, 23 (11): 1913–29.

Fodor, E. (2004) "Women at work: the status of women in the labour markets of the Czech Republic, Hungary, and Poland," background paper for UNRISD Report on *Gender Equality: striving for justice in an unequal world*, Geneva: UNRISD.

Fontana, M. (2002) "Modeling the effects of trade on women at work and at home: a comparative perspective," Mimeo, Washington, DC: International Food Policy Research Institute (IFPRI).

—— (2003) "The gender effects of trade liberalisation in developing countries: a review of the literature," Discussion Paper in Economics No. 101, Brighton: University of Sussex.

Fontana, M., Joekes, S., and Masika, R. (1998) "Trade liberalisation: gender issues and impacts," London: Department for International Development (DFID).

Freeman, C. (2000) *High Tech and High Heels in the Global Economy: women, work, and pink collar identities in the Caribbean*, Durham, NC: Duke University Press.

Ghosh, J. (2002) "Globalisation, export-oriented employment for women, and social policy: a case study of India," Geneva: UNRISD.

Gupta, N.D. (2002) "Gender, pay, and development: a cross-country analysis," *Labour and Management in Development Journal*, 3 (2): 1–19.

Gustaffson, B. and Li, S. (2000) "Economic transformation and the gender earnings gap in urban China," *Journal of Population Economics*, 13: 305–29.

Harrison, A. (2002) "Has globalization eroded labor's share? Some cross-country evidence," Mimeo, Berkeley: University of California.

Hill, M.A. and King, E. (1995) "Women's education and economic well-being," *Feminist Economics*, 1 (2): 21–46.

Hsiung, P.C. (1996) *Living Rooms as Factories: class, gender, and the satellite factory system in Taiwan*, Philadelphia, PA: Temple University Press.

International Labor Organization (ILO) (2004) *Yearbook of Labour Statistics*, Geneva: ILO.

Jomo, K.S. (2004) "Globalization, export-oriented industrialization, and female employment in East Asia," paper prepared for UNRISD project on Globalization, Export Oriented Employment for Women and Social Policy, Geneva: UNRISD.

Kabeer, N. (2000) *The Power to Choose: Bangladeshi women and labour market decisions in London and Dhaka*, London: Verso.

Klasen, S. (2002) "Low schooling for girls, slower growth for all? Cross-country evidence on the effect of gender inequality in education on economic development," *World Bank Economic Review*, 16 (3): 345–73.

Klasen, S. and Wink, C. (2003) "Missing women: revisiting the debate," *Feminist Economics*, 9 (2–3): 263–99.

Kucera, D. (2001) "The effect of core worker rights on labour costs and foreign direct investment: evaluating the 'conventional wisdom'," Mimeo, Geneva: International Institute of Labor Studies.

Kucera, D. and Milberg, W. (2000) "Gender segregation and gender bias in manufacturing trade expansion: revisiting the 'Wood Asymmetry'," *World Development*, 28 (7): 1191–210.

Long, L., Hung, L., Truitt, A., Phuong, M.L., and Nguyen, A.D. (2000) "Changing gender relations in Vietnam's post *Doi Moi* era," World Bank Policy Research Report Working Paper No. 14, Washington, DC: World Bank.

Maddison, A. (1995) *Monitoring the World Economy 1890–92*, Paris: OECD.

Marquetti, A. (2004) "Do rising real wages increase the rate of labor-saving technical change? Some econometric evidence," *Metroeconomica*, 55 (4): 432–41.

Maurer-Fazio, M. and Hughes, J. (2002) "The effects of market liberalization on the relative earnings of Chinese women," *Journal of Comparative Economics*, 30 (4): 709–31.

Maurer-Fazio, M., Rawski, T.G., and Zhang, W. (1999) "Inequality in the rewards for holding up half the sky: gender wage gaps in China's urban labor markets, 1988–1994," *The China Journal*, 41: 55–88.

Mehra, R. and Gammage, S. (1999) "Trends, countertrends, and gaps in women's employment," *World Development*, 27 (30): 533–50.

Mishel, L. and Bernstein, J. (1999) *The State of Working America 1997–98*, Armonk, NY: M.E. Sharpe, Inc.

Nam, J.L. (1991) *Income Inequality between the Sexes and the Role of the State: South Korea 1960–1990*, unpublished PhD dissertation, Bloomington, IN: Department of Sociology, Indiana University.

Newman, C. (2000) "Worker and firm determinants of piece rate variation in agricultural labor markets," *Economic Development and Cultural Change*, 49 (1): 137–69.

Oostendorp, R. (2004) "Globalization and the gender wage gap," World Bank Policy Research Working Paper No. 3256, Washington, DC: World Bank.

Özler, S. (2000) "Export orientation and female share of employment: evidence from Turkey," *World Development*, 28 (7): 1239–48.

Panic, M. (1998) "Transnational corporations and the nation state," in R. Kozul-Wright and R. Rowthorn (eds), *Transnational Corporations and the Global Economy*, London: MacMillan Press Ltd for WIDER.

Poterba, J. (1997) "The rate of return to corporate capital and factor shares: new estimates using revised national income accounts and capital stock data," Working Paper No. 6263, Cambridge, MA: National Bureau of Economic Research.

Rodrik, D. (1997) *Has Globalization Gone Too Far?* Washington, DC: Institute for International Economics.

Roh, M. (1990) "A study on home-based work in South Korea," *Women's Studies Forum*, Seoul, Korea: Korean Women's Development Institute.

Samarasinghe, V. (1998) "The feminization of foreign currency earnings: women's labor in Sri Lanka," *Journal of Developing Areas*, 32: 303–26.

Sayeed, A. and Balakrishnan, R. (2002) "Why do firms disintegrate? Towards an understanding of the firm level decision to sub-contract and its impact on labor," in W. Milberg (ed.), *Labor and the Globalization of Production: causes and consequences of industrial upgrading*, New York: Palgrave MacMillan.

Seguino, S. (1999–2000) "The investment function revisited: disciplining capital in Korea," *Journal of Post-Keynesian Economics*, 22 (2): 313–38.

—— (2000a) "The effects of structural change and economic liberalization on gender wage differentials in South Korea and Taiwan," *Cambridge Journal of Economics*, 24 (4): 437–59.

—— (2000b) "Gender inequality and economic growth: a cross-country analysis," *World Development*, 28 (7): 1211–30.

—— (2002) "Gender, quality of life, and growth in Asia 1970 to 1990," *The Pacific Review*, 15 (2): 245–77.

—— (2004) "Why are women in the Caribbean so much more likely than men to be unemployed?" *Social and Economics Studies*, 52 (4): 83–120.

—— (2007) "Is more mobility good? Mobile capital and the low wage–low productivity trap," *Structural Change and Economic Dynamics*, 18 (1): 27–51.

Sen, A. (1999) *Development as Freedom*, New York: Anchor Books.

Setterfield, M. (2003) "Neo-Kaleckian growth dynamics and the state of long-run expectations: wage- versus profit-led growth," in N. Salvadori (ed.), *Old and New Growth Theory*, Cheltenham: Edward Elgar.

Sowerine, J. (1999) "New land rights and women's access to medicinal plants in northern Vietnam," in I. Tinker and G. Summerfield (eds), *Women's Rights to House and Land: China, Laos, and Vietnam*, Boulder, CO: Lynne Rienner Publishers.

Standing, G. (1989) "Global feminization through flexible labor," *World Development*, 17 (7): 1077–95.

—— (1999) "Global feminization revisited," *World Development*, 27 (7): 583–602.

Stephen, L. (2000) "Sweet and sour grapes: the struggles of seasonal women workers in Chile," in A. Spring (ed.), *Women Farmers and Commercial Ventures: increasing food security in developing countries*, Boulder, CO: Lynne Rienner Publishers.

Tanzi, V. (1995) *Taxation in an Integrating World*, Washington, DC: Brookings Institution.

Thrupp, L., Bergeron, G., and Waters, W. (1995) *Bittersweet Harvests for Global Supermarkets: challenges in Latin America's agricultural export boom*, Washington, DC: World Resources Institute.

Tzannatos, Z. (1999) "Women and labor market changes in the global economy: growth helps, inequalities hurt and public policy matters," *World Development*, 27 (3): 551–69.

United Nations Development Programme (UNDP) (1997) *Human Development Report 1997*, New York: Oxford University Press.

—— (1999) *World Survey on the Role of Women in Development: globalization, gender, and work*, New York: UNDP.

United Nations Research Institute for Social Development (UNRISD) (2005) *Gender Equality: struggling for justice in an unequal world*, Geneva: UNRISD.

Wallerstein, M. and Przeworski, A. (1995) "Capital taxation with open borders," *Review of International Political Economy*, 2 (3): 425–45.

Williams, P. (1999) "Trafficking in women and children: a market perspective," in P. Williams (ed.), *Illegal Immigration and Commercial Sex: the new slave trade*, London: Frank Cass.

World Bank (2001) *Engendering Development Through Gender Equality in Rights, Resources, and Voice*, New York: Oxford University Press.

You, J.I. (1989) "Capital-labor relations and economic development," unpublished PhD dissertation, Boston, MA: Harvard University.

Index

Note: Page numbers in bold type denote charts/figures/tables.

For Product Safety Concerns and Information please contact our EU
representative GPSR@taylorandfrancis.com
Taylor & Francis Verlag GmbH, Kaufingerstraße 24, 80331 München, Germany

www.ingramcontent.com/pod-product-compliance
Ingram Content Group UK Ltd.
Pitfield, Milton Keynes, MK11 3LW, UK
UKHW021851240425
457818UK00020B/806